LOVE, SEX,
AND AGING

LOVE, SEX, AND AGING

A Consumers Union Report

Edward M. Brecher
and The Editors of
Consumer Reports Books

Little, Brown and Company
Boston   Toronto

FIRST EDITION

Consumers Union gratefully acknowledges the following for permission to reprint previously copyrighted material:

Brunner/Mazel, Inc., for excerpts from *Disorders of Sexual Desire* by Helen Singer Kaplan, M.D., Ph.D. (1979).

The Kinsey Institute for Sex Research, for excerpts from *Sexual Behavior in the Human Male* and *Sexual Behavior in the Human Female*, both by Alfred C. Kinsey et al.

Harold Matson Company, Inc., for excerpts from *Every Woman's Book of Health* by Maxine Davis. Copyright © 1961 by Maxine Davis.

Medical World News, for excerpts from the January 21, 1980, issue.

Times Books/The New York Times Book Company, for excerpts from *The Illustrated Manual of Sex Therapy* by Helen Singer Kaplan, M.D., Ph.D. Copyright © 1975 by Helen Singer Kaplan.

Library of Congress Cataloging in Publication Data

Brecher, Edward M.
　　Love, sex, and aging.
　　　1. Aged—United States—Sexual behavior.
　　2. Aged—United States—Attitudes.　I. Consumers
　　Union of United States.　II. Consumer reports.
　　III. Title.　[DNLM: 1. Love—In old age.　2. Sex
　　behavior—In old age.　3. Aging.　HQ 30 B829L]
　　HQ30.B73　1983　　306.7'0880565　　83-14910
　　ISBN 0-316-10718-2

M

Designed by Patricia Girvin Dunbar

Published simultaneously in Canada
by Little, Brown & Company (Canada) Limited

PRINTED IN THE UNITED STATES OF AMERICA

Contents

5

Introduction

DURING THE WINTER OF 1978–79, 4,246 WOMEN AND MEN AGED 50 to 93 supplied Consumers Union with information on a variety of topics including love and sex. They told us not only about their experiences through the decades but also about their attitudes, opinions, hopes, and concerns. Here is our account of what they told us.

This report demonstrates that older people, like younger people, differ from one another in many ways and to a remarkable extent. It should therefore help readers appreciate what a wide range of alternatives may lie ahead for those who are approaching their fiftieth year — and for those who have already passed it.

We announced this study in the November 1977 issue of Consumers Union's monthly magazine, *Consumer Reports:*

IF YOU WERE BORN BEFORE 1928, CU REQUESTS YOUR HELP
Consumers Union is planning a book on a sensitive subject of great importance for our time: enhancing the quality of personal relationships — family, social, and sexual — during the later years of life. The preliminary research is under the direction of Edward M. Brecher, award-winning science writer and social historian, and author of numerous CU studies over the years.

To obtain data for this study, detailed questionnaires — to be answered anonymously — are being prepared for women and men born

---

before 1928, especially those born before 1913. The questionnaires will include a number of highly personal questions about how things are with you now, and about how you might like things to be. Your questionnaire responses can contribute to a better understanding of family and social relationships and human sexuality in middle and old age. Answering the questions may also prove a rewarding experience for you: an opportunity to review how you really feel about these intimate matters. *Questionnaires need not be signed.*

You can help CU begin this study by requesting questionnaires for yourself and for one or two others also 50 and over. We are especially eager to hear from persons 65 and over. Use the form below, or drop us a note or card. Questionnaires will be mailed to participants early next year.

Consumers Union, Box JL, Mount Vernon, N.Y. 10550
Please send me the following copies of CU's anonymous questionnaires on personal relationships during the later years.

	Male	Female	Age
One questionnaire for	□	□	___
Second questionnaire for	□	□	___
Third questionnaire for	□	□	___

Name_____

Address_____

City_____State_____Zip_____

The response was highly encouraging: More than five thousand women and men requested more than ten thousand questionnaires.

The questionnaire we drafted sought detailed information about many aspects of our respondents' lives — their education, health, and income level, degree of religious commitment, close friendships, periods of loneliness, attitudes toward retirement among those approaching retirement, and impact of retirement on the quality of life among retirees. We wanted to know about love relationships and falling-in-love experiences, and about sexual experiences, beliefs, feelings, and fantasies.

The sexual questions proved the most difficult to draft. Members of the over-50 generation were widely reputed to be conservative about sexual matters. How far dared we go in probing the most intimate aspects of their sexuality?

After prolonged discussions, we opted for total candor. We asked not only about sex within marriage but also about sex in nonmarital, extramarital, and postmarital relationships, homosexual as well as heterosexual — including a wide range of behaviors presently or formerly considered taboo.

We asked what respondents would *like* to do as well as what they are currently doing. Under friendship, for example, we asked not only whether a respondent currently has close friends but also whether he or she would like more opportunities to meet a woman or a man who might become a close friend — and whether such opportunities were restricted by lack of money, poor health, lack of privacy, inadequate transportation, lack of social activities, not enough time, shyness, or other factors. With respect to twenty specific sexual activities we asked not only, "Have you done this since [age] 50?" but also "If you have done this, did you like it?" and "If you have not done this, would you like to try it?" We hoped that out of so broad a range of questions, the data emerging would prove of benefit to others living through, or approaching, the years after 50.

The complete questionnaire and its covering letter appear in the Appendix.

Relatively few of our respondents, it turned out, wanted to write about religion in the later years, or about transportation problems after age 50. What interested them most — and what they wrote about most eloquently and at greatest length — was, quite simply, love and sexuality.

Some of our respondents are deeply conservative in their sexual opinions; some are outspokenly liberal. Many in their seventies and eighties are still happily and monogamously married to, and in love with, their first sweethearts; many are not. Some respondents skipped questions, and a few left whole sections blank. But the vast majority were enthusiastic and candid in telling us and the world what their lives have been like since age 50.

In this as in other respects, our report inevitably follows the lead of our respondents. While we shall present some data on education, health, economic problems, friendship, loneliness, retirement, and other matters of general interest, this is primarily a report on love and sexuality in the later years because that is what we have learned the most about.

In designing our questionnaire, we combined two quite different approaches. Some of our questions can be answered with an X, a yes or no, a date, or in some other manner amenable to computerization. The advantage is that vast quantities of data can be succinctly, objectively, and understandably synthesized. In our case, computerization has made it possible to analyze and summarize in this report more than a million answers supplied by our 4,246 respondents.

The shortcoming of this approach is that it can handle *only* "bits" of information. The rich flow of life as it is lived in the real world escapes through the holes in the punch cards. We accordingly supplemented our computerizable objective questions with open-ended questions designed to elicit feelings and beliefs in each respondent's own words. Here is an example:

"Some older people regret some of the sexual things they did in their younger days. Some regret not having done certain sexual things. If you had your life to live over, what would you change or do differently with respect to love and sexual relationships?"

More than 2,500 of our respondents wrote out or typed out on the questionnaire's "Comment Pages" their answer to that question — some only a sentence or two, others a page or more.

We also invited respondents to comment in their own words, at any length, on *any* question contained in the questionnaire; thousands did. In retrospect, we can now see that the richness of the data we received arose out of our combining all of these features in a single questionnaire: total frankness and intimate detail on love and on sexual matters; the exploration of preferences, desires, and opinions as well as current and past behavior; and the securing of both objective, computerizable replies and extended essay-type replies.

It is one thing to draft so comprehensive a questionnaire; it is another to get people to answer it. Our questionnaire is so long that it takes roughly an hour and a half to answer the computerizable questions — plus whatever time may be devoted to writing out personal comments. To determine whether our questionnaire was feasible despite its frank sexual content and its length, we first mailed out 400 copies as a pretest.

We received just over 200 replies. Half a dozen or so were unusable; a few people sent back blank questionnaires and a few denounced our project. But a much larger proportion contributed comments such as this from an 83-year-old woman:

> I know younger readers will thank you for the book because it gives them hope for their old age. Older readers will thank you for bringing their feelings and actions out of the closet of inhibition and perhaps help them to have joy in their old age.

Encouraged by the 50-percent pretest response rate and by the quality and enthusiasm of the replies, we made a few revisions in the questionnaire based on the pretest returns and mailed more than 9,800 copies in the fall of 1978. More than 4,000 were filled out and returned, for a total (including the pretest) of 4,246 in usable form.

Our sample is not only large but variegated. Here are some of its subgroups whose responses we are able to compare and contrast in subsequent chapters:

1,844 women
2,402 men

801 women in their 50s
719 women in their 60s
324 women aged 70 or older

823 men in their 50s
981 men in their 60s
598 men aged 70 or older

1,245 wives
1,895 husbands

512 formerly married and never-married women
413 formerly married and never-married men

Similarly, our sample is large and variegated enough so that we can review separately the 524 wives and husbands who have had sex outside their marriage since age 50, the 111 women and men who have engaged in homosexual activities since age 50, the 317 women and men who have had heart attacks, the 635 women who have had a hysterectomy, the 408 postmenopausal women who are taking estrogen, the 302 men who have had prostate surgery, and many other subcategories.

By dividing up our data in such ways, we are able to draw comparative generalizations about our respondents, such as the following:

• The sexual aspect of marriage is more important for the husbands than for the wives.

• Unmarried women and men who remain sexually active after 50 (either with a partner or through masturbation) report higher levels of life enjoyment than those who do not engage in sex.

• More husbands than wives have engaged in extramarital sex since age 50.

• More men than women have engaged in homosexual activities since age 50. More women than men, however, have felt sexually attracted to a person of their own gender since age 50.

• Most of our men and women who are still working look forward to retirement with negative feelings — or with mixed feelings at best. After retirement, however, there is a marked change. Most of our men and women who have already retired have only positive feelings toward retirement.

• Fewer women and men in their eighties are sexually active than are our younger women and men; but some women and men in their eighties continue to engage in and enjoy a wide range of sexual activities.

• Relatively few men engage in sex with prostitutes after 50. Some of those who do, however, report that their encounters with prostitutes contribute substantially to their enjoyment of life.

• Postmenopausal women taking estrogen are more active sexually than postmenopausal women not taking estrogen.

Some of these generalizations, and others like them throughout this book, can be interpreted in more than one way. The last in the series above, for example, may mean that postmenopausal estrogen enhances sexual function — or it may mean that women who are very active sexually are the ones more likely to be taking estrogen. In some but not all of these ambiguous cases, we are able to determine which interpretation is the right one, or the more probable one. In chapter 7, for example, we cite our reasons for concluding that for some women postmenopausal estrogen does in fact enhance sexual function.

The limitations of this report are for the most part inherent in the responses we received (and did not receive):

First, our respondents do not comprise a random or representative sample of the United States population. (This is also true of all previous surveys of human sexuality.) Our sample is limited to readers of *Consumer Reports* and their relatives and friends.

Moreover, our sample is self-selected. (This, too, is true of all other human sexuality surveys.) It is limited to those particular readers of *Consumer Reports* who filled out and returned the November 1977 coupon — and to their relatives and friends. It is also limited to those who, having received the questionnaire in the fall of 1978, answered the questions and mailed back their answers during the next few months. It is probable that sexually inactive women and men were less likely than the sexually active to mail back their questionnaires — though some did. No doubt those with little interest in sex, or with a dislike of sex, were also less likely to mail back the questionnaires — though some did.

This self-selection makes it impossible to extrapolate our findings to the total U.S. population over 50. Note, however, that this does not necessarily limit the significance of our findings solely to our 4,246 respondents. The findings may also apply to other groups that resemble ours — those with higher-than-average income and education, better-than-average health, greater interest in sex, and so on. We are confident, indeed, that many or most of our findings apply to a very broad segment of Americans over 50. Readers of this book, to cite a convenient example, are quite likely to vary from the national average in much the same ways our respondents vary.

One characteristic of our sample is clearly visible throughout this report: the clarity, frankness, wit, and wisdom with which respondents comment on their lives and on the joys and sorrows of aging. Each respondent represents no one but herself or himself — yet, as readers will soon see, these women and men collectively present a strikingly detailed picture of how richly rewarding life can be after 50.

Medical students learn the science of medicine only in part from textbooks; they also learn much from the case histories of individual patients and from making bedside rounds. Law students similarly study individual cases as well as general law. We have tried in this study to present our data in both ways: statistical tables and charts to illustrate patterns within the sample, and individual life stories to demonstrate how those patterns look, feel, and operate in individuals' lives.

Many earlier discussions of aging have been quite properly concerned with the impoverished, the chronically ill, and the socially isolated. Such groups constitute important segments of the older population. But the attention focused on them has led far too many people to conclude, we believe mistakenly, that almost all older people suffer such handicaps — and that almost all younger people are headed toward a similar fate. Much of the anxiety that younger people feel about growing old may stem from knowing too little about the life-enjoying segment of the older population that this report brings into view.

The best-known of all human sexuality surveys is the one launched in 1938 by Dr. Alfred C. Kinsey and his associates at Indiana University's Institute for Sex Research.* Kinsey had far

---

* *Sexual Behavior in the Human Male* (1948) and *Sexual Behavior in the Human Female* (1953).

more respondents overall than we have; but despite his best efforts, few women and men over 60 volunteered for his study. As shown in the table below, we have far more respondents in the older age groups than Kinsey had:

Kinsey Sample versus CU Sample

Age	Kinsey sample*	CU sample
50 through 60	813	1,781
61 through 70	213	1,697
71 through 80	46	689
Over 80	8	79†
Totals	1,080	4,246

Our sample no doubt differs from the Kinsey sample, to a greater or lesser extent, in terms of income, education, degree of religious commitment, proportion of white and non-white respondents, and other factors. In one respect, however, our sample resembles his: date of birth. Most of our respondents (73 percent) were born between 1905 and 1924, as were the majority of Kinsey's respondents (61 percent). Thus, from the point of view of age our report can be seen as an account of what "the Kinsey generation" is like today.

The panorama of love, sex, and aging here presented is far richer and more diverse than the stereotype of life after 50, or than the view presented by earlier studies of aging. Both the quality and the quantity of sexual activity reported can properly be described as astonishing. Hence the question arises: If life after 50 is in fact so sexually rich and diverse for so many, why has this been kept a secret? Why haven't older people said so before?

One reason is that few have ever been asked. Most prior stud-

* From *The Kinsey Data, 1938–1963*, published in 1979 by Paul H. Gebhard and Alan B. Johnson, Tables 1, 2, 432, 433, 570, and 571.
† Three of our respondents are in their nineties—two women aged 90 and a man of 93.

ies of sex and aging were either small* or else failed to ask frank sexual questions.

Until quite recently, moreover, few older people were *ready* to speak out about sex. The Victorian taboo against even mentioning sexual matters, which they had learned at their mother's knee, kept them silent.

By the time they were three or four years old, children of the generation born before 1928 had learned not to touch themselves "down there" — or, if they did, not to let anyone find out. By seven or eight, they knew they weren't supposed to engage in mutual explorations or physical intimacies with other boys and girls — and certainly not to let their sex play be discovered. During adolescence, activities then called necking and petting, more recently known as "making out," were kept a closely guarded secret.

Engagements, marriages, and pregnancies were, of course, matters of common knowledge. But with the arrival of their children a new need for secrecy arose: *Their sexuality had at all costs to be kept hidden from their children.* In some families the children did not even see their parents kiss. Above all, the children must be given no possible clue to the fact that their parents ever engaged in sexual intercourse.

Quite a few of our respondents confirm this account, and describe in their returned questionnaire the great relief they felt when their last child left home and they could at long last have sex in their own bed without restraint or fear that the children might "hear noises."

"I'm sorry I was too worried about the children (three daughters) 'coming upon us' when we were having sex," a 60-year-old Chicago wife and mother recalls decades later. "Since college (and their marriages) and we have the house to ourselves, I'm less inhibited and feel I can respond to my husband's (and my) needs for sex more readily."

One New York State wife, aged 60, and husband, aged 63,

---

* The largest survey of geriatric sexuality prior to ours was *The Starr-Weiner Report on Sex and Sexuality in the Later Years,* by Bernard D. Starr and Marcella Bakur Weiner (Stein and Day, N.Y., 1981). That report was based on 800 respondents aged 60 to 91 — 518 women and 282 men.

married for thirty years, still keep their sexuality a secret from their two children. Those children, now aged 26 and 29, live at home and "interfere with our lives in many ways — especially in our freedom to talk [about sex] and to have sex anytime we feel the desire."

Unlike most secrets, moreover, the secret of parental sexuality was in many families *successfully* kept. Many adults today still recall their shudder of dismay when they realized, as late as age twelve or fourteen, that their own parents *must* have engaged in the awful act of sex at least a few times or no children would have been born.

The late philosopher-humorist Sam Levinson recalled: "When I first found out how babies were born, I couldn't believe it! To think that my mother and father would do such a thing! . . . My father, maybe; but my mother — never!"*

It is thus hardly surprising that today's young people, taught to think of their parents as nonsexual even when those parents were in their twenties and thirties, continue to think of their parents in their fifties and beyond (and of other older people) as *still* nonsexual.

We asked our respondents whether they agree or disagree with the statement:

"Society thinks of older people as nonsexual."

The vote was overwhelming: More than 3,000 of our respondents agreed; fewer than 500 disagreed. Lifelong secrecy, in short, has had its effect. The world really is convinced that people over 50 or 60 have few sexual interests, needs, wants, or activities.

Some see this misconception as a serious handicap for older people today. A 67-year-old consultant to this study writes:

Having successfully pretended for decades that we are nonsexual, my generation is now having second thoughts. We are increasingly realizing that denying our sexuality means denying an essential aspect of our common humanity. It cuts

---

* Quoted by A. C. Claman in the *Canadian Medical Association Journal* 94 (1966):207.

us off from communication with our children, our grandchildren, and our peers on a subject of great interest to us all — sexuality. The rejection of the aging and aged by some younger people has many roots; but surely the belief that we are no longer sexual beings, and therefore no longer fully human, is one of the roots of that rejection.

A 58-year-old husband and father writes: "It has been my experience that children in the 15-to-25-year range are horrified if not disgusted at the thought of their 45-to-60-year-old parents having intercourse." Then he recalls that he too was disgusted, decades ago, when he first realized that *his* parents were having sex — and that his wife had reacted similarly when she first realized this about *her* parents. "Something should be done — and I can't suggest what," he continues, "to convince [young people] that a married couple having intercourse in their 50s, 60s, and later is normal, natural, even beautiful but definitely not dirty or weird or odd."

Many older people have devoted themselves to keeping the secret not only from their children and from other young people but from one another as well. The result is that they themselves are seriously misled about the nature and extent of sexuality in their own generation. Many of them know, of course, that their own personal sexual interests, needs, wants, and activities continue unabated; but looking about at their peers, they think of themselves as exceptions to the general rule. Some of them even wonder whether their continuing sexuality is "abnormal" or "perverted." "I must be an animal to [still] desire sex," writes a troubled 71-year-old widower.

How can such common misconceptions about love and sex after 50 be corrected? Clearly, older people themselves must supply the data, demonstrating that their sexuality is no longer something to hide or be ashamed of. Our 67-year-old consultant quoted above makes this point with fervor:

The common view that the aging and aged are nonsexual, I believe, can only be corrected by a dramatic and courageous process — the *coming-out-of-the-closet* of sexually active older women and men, so that people can see for themselves what the later years are really like.

That, in fact, is what happens in this book. Our respondents by the thousands have embraced the opportunity to come out, to set the record straight — many with enthusiasm and even with delight.

"I am grateful for the opportunity to express these thoughts," writes a 59-year-old husband. "I have never put my sexual experiences, thoughts, and fantasies on paper and feel better for it."

"Please, not just a factual report on how it *is* with us," writes a 66-year-old widow, "but some definite shoves in the right direction to make it better, more fulfilling and more rewarding and worthwhile."

"Let us silver-haired sirens out of the closet!" writes a 54-year-old divorcée. "We have a lot to 'show and tell' the world."

Two of our respondents came out of the closet years ago. One is a 65-year-old widow from the Southwest with a 50-year-old lover. She writes:

Each semester I talk to pre-med students at the university here on aging and retirement. The professor (M.D., psychiatrist) is a friend. We always leave 20–25 minutes for a no-holds-barred question-and-answer period. I share my life with them and answer all questions frankly. To me, sharing my life is on the same order as my [late] husband and me giving our bodies to science.

The other is an 83-year-old widow who also lectures annually at a medical school (where she is known as "Ms. X"), and who frankly answers questions about her own sexuality — including her numerous lovers since age 50 and her masturbation with and without a vibrator.

We all know that young people today are much different from young people half a century ago. Our questionnaire returns bear eloquent testimony to the similar changes that have occurred among older people. Today's grandmothers and grandfathers are notably different from *their* grandmothers and grandfathers. They are also different from what they themselves were like in their own youth; for example, they are now sexually much freer. Evidence for this freeing-up process will be found throughout this report.

The freeing-up process, moreover, is a continuing one. As readers will see in many of the chapters that follow, what is often called "the sexual revolution" is going on among older people right now. By the 1990s, when young people now in their thirties reach fifty and people now in their fifties reach seventy, the resemblance between older and younger people will no doubt be even closer than it is today.

We hope that this report will challenge popular stereotypes in another important respect. We all know how different we ourselves are from many of our friends and neighbors our own age. When we look at those much younger or much older than we are, however, we tend to see only the uniform forest rather than the strikingly variegated individual trees. In particular, we may think of all teenagers as exhibiting one uniform set of characteristics and of all "old people" as exhibiting a quite different set. In this report, we have been diligent in tracing the common themes that emerge from our data; but we have been equally diligent in presenting our respondents as a diverse assortment of individual women and individual men with widely differing activities, opinions, goals, customs, and fantasies. Thus "what it's like to be 50" or "what it's like to be 80" should be viewed, and is here presented, not as a single image but as a broad panorama of alternatives. Both the general themes and the individual life stories reveal the decades after 50 to be far more exciting and far more fulfilling than is commonly supposed.

What lies ahead for each of us depends in part on factors beyond our control — but it also depends in part on factors *within* our control. The panorama here presented should help readers to review their personal preferences, to clarify their own thinking and feelings, and to head in the direction they choose from among the alternatives open to them.

Readers who think of Consumers Union as primarily concerned with brand-name ratings of automobiles, washing machines, insurance policies, and other consumer products and services may wonder why CU has sponsored a study of *this* kind. The answer is simple. This study grew quite naturally out of a variety of other Consumers Union activities on behalf of consumers of all ages.

To meet the concerns of many hundreds of thousands of *Consumer Reports* readers aged 50 or over, we published during the 1960s a four-part series of articles on nursing homes,* later reprinted in pamphlet form, and other articles of special interest to older readers and their families. During the past few years, we published a guide to low-cost nutrition for older people,† and a Consumers Union edition of a book about some of the emotional, physical, and financial needs of older people.‡ The response to those publications was sufficiently enthusiastic to show we were meeting important needs of our readers, and to encourage our going further — but in what direction?

Reports on the economics of aging, on health and aging, and on housing and transportation for the aging were obvious possibilities. We decided against them primarily because these urgent needs have already been competently documented. Clearly, the greatest need on these issues now is for action rather than further reports.§ Our next study, we decided, should continue our consideration of the emotional and physical needs of older people, and explore an area insufficiently documented: the interpersonal aspects of aging. We envisioned a study that would approach older people as individuals whose needs and wants go far beyond material things — encompassing companionship, intimate friendships,

---

* *Consumer Reports*, January, February, March, and April 1964.
† *Eating Right for Less* by the Editors of Consumer Reports, Consumers Union, 1975, updated 1977.
‡ *You and Your Aging Parent* by Barbara Silverstone and Helen Kandel Hyman, Pantheon Books, 1976, revised edition 1982.
§ This is even truer in the 1980s, after cutbacks in government services for the aging, than it was when we reached our decision in 1977.

love, and sexual enjoyment and fulfillment. The findings of such a study, we anticipated, could have profound implications for improving the lives of many older Americans.

As director of the proposed study, and as senior author of the report emerging from it, we selected Edward M. Brecher, who has been associated with Consumers Union from time to time since 1938 in a variety of roles, including writer, editor, and consultant. His largest single CU undertaking was the book *Licit and Illicit Drugs* (1972), which has sold almost 350,000 copies. For many years, Brecher's main area of concern and expertise has been human sexuality. He was co-author with his late wife Ruth E. Brecher (also at one time a CU writer and editor) of *An Analysis of Human Sexual Response* (1966). The Brechers were joint recipients of the Albert Lasker Medical Journalism Award for 1963, and of the American Psychiatric Association's Robert T. Morse Writers Award for 1971 "in recognition and appreciation of their distinguished contributions to the public understanding of psychiatry." (The Brechers also researched and wrote CU's four-part series on nursing homes, referred to above.) Following Ruth Brecher's death, Brecher wrote *The Sex Researchers* (1969; expanded edition 1979). He is a fellow and a former board member of the Society for the Scientific Study of Sex, and formerly book review editor of its *Journal of Sex Research*. (He has also been Justice of the Peace, Town of Cornwall, Connecticut, since 1966.) Brecher was 65 years old in the spring of 1977, when he first became associated with this CU study of love, sex, and aging.

CU and Brecher recruited a broad range of consultants specially qualified to advise us on numerous aspects of our project, as well as reviewers to read and comment on the series of drafts we prepared. While those named below are not responsible for any of our conclusions, they have contributed notably both to our thinking and to the form in which our data have been presented.

Sharon G. Nathan, Ph.D., and Jane M. Traupmann, Ph.D., were concerned with the entire manuscript. James R. Allen, David T. Burhans, Jr., Ph.D., and particularly John J. Kochevar, Ph.D., were concerned with computerization and statistical aspects of the study. Others with whom we consulted on a variety of issues included Consumers Union's Medical Adviser, Marvin M. Lipman, M.D., and Sally K. Binford, Ph.D., Nan Corby, Ph.D., Morris Notelovitz, M.D., Kenneth J. Ryan, M.D., Isaac Schiff, M.D., Judith E. Steinhart, Ed.D., Felicia H. Stewart, M.D., and Wulf H. Utian, M.D.

Jonathan Leff, Director of Consumer Reports Books, directed the Consumers Union survey researchers, statisticians, editors, and other CU staff members who contributed to the project.

Numerous life stories and quotations appear throughout this book. They are derived from our respondents' questionnaires — sometimes from specific answers to objective questions, sometimes from written comments, sometimes from both. In preparing these life stories and quotations for publication, we were obligated to preserve the factual and emotional essence of each story without disclosing the identity of the respondent. That obligation was specified in the covering letter we sent with each questionnaire: "Because your responses cannot be identified with you in any way, you may feel free to answer even the most sensitive questions with complete assurance that your confidences will be respected."

In reliance on that pledge, many respondents entrusted us with very intimate accounts of their lives. Where we make use of these accounts, we have made appropriate changes designed to preserve anonymity.

These camouflaging changes, we are confident, are sufficient to ensure that each respondent's identity remains inviolate. We can also assure readers that the changes made to mask the identities of respondents do not alter or impair the essential significance of what our respondents have told us.

A few respondents requested that we withhold certain information from publication; we have, of course, honored these requests.

Our procedure does have one drawback: Many respondents are no doubt proud of their contributions to this study and may therefore be disappointed to find that they *cannot* be identified by others. To them we apologize.

None of the camouflaging alterations designed to safeguard privacy has been made within a quotation. In some quotations, spelling, punctuation, or grammar has been corrected. As is customary, deletion of words is indicated by ellipses (. . .) and words added or substituted are enclosed in square brackets [   ]. No other changes have been made within a quotation. Each exclamation point was placed there by the respondent, and words in italics were underlined by the respondent.

All information provided by our respondents is presented as of the fall and early winter of 1978-79, when our questionnaires were filled out and returned to us. Such terms as "now" and "the present time" refer to that time period, and the dollar amounts are for that time as well.

"Since age 50" refers to the time since a respondent's fiftieth birthday, including the year during which he or she was 50 years old.

"Married" refers to respondents who report they are married and living with their spouse. The 73 respondents who are legally married but separated from their spouse are included within the "divorced or separated" category.

Many spouses of respondents to our questionnaire did not participate in our study. Our data therefore do not reflect numbers of marriages but rather numbers of wives and of husbands, many — but by no means all — of whom are married to each other.

Sometimes our statistical data appear within the body of the text, sometimes in tables or graphs. In a few cases, we have data from all of our 4,246 respondents; but usually the total is smaller, either because the question was addressed only to a subgroup of respondents, or because some who should have answered failed to do so, or for other reasons. The number (N) of respondents on whom a table or portion of a table is based is usually shown in the table. Where a substantial proportion of those who should have answered a question failed to do so we sometimes note that fact in the text.

Most tables present the data for women and for men separately. The two are combined only where the differences are negligible.

We have rounded percentages to the nearest whole number. This sometimes results in a total of 101 percent or 99 percent, instead of 100 percent.

We have used statistical tables and statistical statements in our text to succinctly summarize large volumes of data, to support our generalizations, and to demonstrate that some of the individual respondents we quote sometimes speak for others as well as themselves. Inevitably, some readers will find our reliance on numbers and percentages a distraction or a burden, while others will find our approach too casual or oversimplified.

In this study of love, sex, and aging, we report many differences — and some similarities — among various groups in our sample, involving many, many opinions and activities reported by our respondents. With statistical methodology, one can test mathematically for what researchers call the "statistical significance" of differences found among groups — that is, whether differences found in random samples are likely to reflect real differences in the population from which the sample was drawn, or result merely from the chance effects of sampling. Passing a test for statistical significance, however, does not necessarily endow data with importance or even interest. And, conversely, failure to pass a test for statistical significance does not necessarily mean that data are unimportant or unworthy of interest.

As explained earlier, our respondents do not comprise a random sample, and such tests for statistical significance are therefore not strictly appropriate for this study. Yet, most of our group comparisons pass the mathematical tests for statistical significance. This could be, at least in part, the result of our having such a large sample; with large groups, differences — even those of a few percentage points — can achieve statistical significance by the very size of their numbers.

In sum, in deciding which of our voluminous data should be included in this book, we used as the principal criterion not the passing of statistical significance tests but rather our best judgment of what would be of importance and interest to our readers.

PART I

❧ ❧

THE MARRIED—
AND THE UNMARRIED—
AFTER 50

≷ 1 ≷

Panorama

I have been in love with the same woman for 53 years, and we have never cheated or been untrue to each other. We have complete trust in each other. The only trouble with a relationship like this is, when one of us passes on, it is going to be catastrophic for the one left behind.

So writes an 80-year-old husband of his 75-year-old wife. They live in their own home in New England on an income of between $10,000 and $15,000 a year. Neither graduated from high school; the husband retired ten years ago. Their health is good except that both have high blood pressure.

Among the questions we asked our respondents were the following:

"Please characterize your overall enjoyment of life at the present time. Your feelings may match the phrase at the left-hand side, or the phrase at the right-hand side, or they may fall somewhere in between. Check the box that best expresses your feelings."

| Life is very enjoyable for me | ☐ 1 | ☐ 2 | ☐ 3 | ☐ 4 | ☐ 5 | ☐ 6 | ☐ 7 | Life is not at all enjoyable for me |

"Check the box that best represents how happy your marriage or relationship is."

| Very happy | ☐ 1 | ☐ 2 | ☐ 3 | ☐ 4 | ☐ 5 | ☐ 6 | ☐ 7 | Very unhappy |

"Check the box that best represents how enjoyable for you sex with your [spouse]/partner is at the present time."

| Very enjoyable | ☐ 1 | ☐ 2 | ☐ 3 | ☐ 4 | ☐ 5 | ☐ 6 | ☐ 7 | Not at all enjoyable |

The answers given by this wife and husband are identical—all "1" at the far left of our 1-to-7 scales — with only one small exception: the husband indicates a "2" for life enjoyment.

Asked what he regrets in his life, he reaches back sixty years to recall his one and only encounter with a prostitute. "It was the most disgusting sexual experience I ever had." He adds, however, that if he hadn't had that experience, "I wouldn't know how disgusting it could be."

Both husband and wife report that they have no intimate friends and no desire to make new friends; they are too busy and hardly ever lonely. Both say that they are currently in love — with one another, of course.

"Participating in sex interests me only with my wife," the husband states. They have sex about once a week, and both are satisfied with this frequency. Both agree that this is less frequent than at age 40, and that they can now go for two or three weeks without release of sexual tension before they begin to feel uncomfortable or restless. Both reach orgasm almost always — more than 90 percent of the time — during their sexual encounters. Both say that the sexual side of their relationship is very important to them both.

He reports that it now takes him longer to get an erection, that when fully erect his penis is not as stiff, that it takes more stimulation to reach orgasm, and that his refractory period — the time it takes to be able to have another erection after orgasm — is longer now; but he regards none of these changes as "a serious problem." She confirms these symptoms, and adds that he more frequently loses his erection during sex, but she does not consider these to be serious problems, either.

Both wife and husband report that they enjoy stimulating one another's breasts or nipples and having their own breasts or nipples stimulated. Both enjoy stimulating one another's genitals manually and having their own genitals stimulated manually. The husband enjoys stimulating his wife's clitoris with his fingers during intercourse; the wife also enjoys stimulating her clitoris with her own fingers during intercourse. Both enjoy oral sex — both active and passive. Neither reports having engaged in any sexual activity he or she didn't enjoy; and neither reports any activity they have not engaged in but would like to try — except that the husband would like sometime to watch other people having sex. The husband sums up:

> My wife and I both believe that keeping active sexually delays the aging process. Neither of us is troubled with false modesty; and if we are troubled with an erection or lubrication, we turn to oral methods or masturbation of each other. We keep our interest alive by a great deal of caressing and fondling of each other's genitals. We feel it is much better to wear out than to rust out.

In this chapter, we present the life stories of six women and four men. One is in her fifties, two are in their sixties, five in their seventies, and two in their early eighties. Four are married, five are widowed, and one is divorced. Seven are still having sex with a partner; the other three remain sexually active through masturbation. Nine are exclusively heterosexual.

We did not select these ten men and women as "typical" of our respondents. No respondent is typical. Rather, they were selected to illustrate the astonishingly broad panorama of life patterns that older people can and do develop for themselves. Like younger people, older people vary widely among themselves — and it is this variability that provides a key to understanding the experience of aging. Indeed, these ten life stories were also selected to demonstrate that underlying the statistical data in this book are individual human beings — each with a unique past, present, and future, and each with unique needs, wants, beliefs, and hopes.

Sixty-four percent of our respondents describe their health as excellent or very good and 26 percent say good. What of the remaining 11 percent whose health is only fair or poor? Some of them, too, appear to be enjoying life — and enjoying love and sexual fulfillment as well, as the following life story illustrates.

The husband is 76 and the wife 74. They recently celebrated their golden wedding anniversary. He is retired on an income of between $20,000 and $25,000 a year; they live in a condominium on the West Coast. Despite high blood pressure (for which he takes anti-hypertensive medication), he describes his own health as good, better than average for his age. His wife, however, suffers from a chronic degenerative disease — a serious problem for them both.

This husband reports that communications between his wife and himself are very good and that they are very comfortable in discussing sex together. Having sexual intercourse together, however, is impossible. Because his wife has a spastic paralysis, she cannot spread her legs.

"So," he explains, "we've had to devise an alternative to the usual frontal coitus. But it works! And when, occasionally, we achieve coincidental orgasms, it's as satisfactory as when we were in our 20s. It's a cooperative effort — a kind of mutually contrived double masturbation."

The two have sex together in this way several times a month. He and she initiate the activities leading to sex about equally often. She reaches orgasm about 75 percent of the time; he, about half of the time. They usually have sex in the morning because both of them are more readily arousable then. In addition to sex with his wife, he masturbates once a month or so, as an additional form of sexual satisfaction.

Like many of our other respondents, female and male, this

husband makes use of sexual fantasies for self-arousal both during sex with his wife and during masturbation. He explains:

> I find that fantasies help, and sometimes, while preparing for
> coitus, deliberately try to reconstruct some of the best and
> unusually pleasurable sexual experiences we've had together.
> Or, rarely, take myself back to my casual relationships with
> other females — in fantasy assuming we'd embraced the op-
> portunities that could have arisen. That sometimes works,
> too.

He has enjoyed a variety of sexual activities with his wife since
age 50: undressing her, having her undress him, mutual oral sex,
mutual masturbation, manually stimulating her clitoris during sex.
They have enjoyed reading sexually explicit materials together —
but do not enjoy viewing hard-core pornographic films or photos.
He enjoys it when she stimulates his breasts or nipples but he
does not stimulate her breasts or nipples, because she "had double
mastectomy. (I discovered the lumps while fingering her breasts.)
So this activity is one we both regret we can't perform."

Love as well as sex have survived this husband's erectile problems and his wife's spastic paralysis and double mastectomy.
After more than fifty years of marriage, he is still in love with his
wife; and in a reminiscent mood he adds:

> Spouse and I fell in love in high school; and except for brief
> infatuations during college, never seriously considered any
> other eventual marriage partners. Love and dependence on
> each other have increased, year by year. (Maybe we're
> headed for trouble when one of us dies first.) But the "love
> curve" is still upward!

In later chapters we shall recount a number of other marriages
in which sex is engaged in and greatly enjoyed despite health ob-
stacles that to others might seem insuperable.

But what of our aging women and men who are not married?
One of them, a 74-year-old New Hampshire widow, lives

alone in her own home on an income of between $25,000 and $35,000 a year. She describes herself as in good health, better than average for her age, and moderately religious. She has close friends, both women and men, but fewer now than at age 40. She sometimes finds herself feeling lonely, and would like to have more men friends; but "many in my age group have died," she notes sadly. "Friendships of long standing become increasingly precious as time goes on. Later friendships are good, but require more nurturing."

She has been married twice; but she tells us nothing about either of her husbands. Instead, she writes of a love affair that began back in 1926, when she and her lover were both 22 — and that still continues.

"My present relationship (sexual)," she writes, "has continued for 52 years — through two marriages on my part, one on his, and long, long separations in distance and time. It is still the source of my joy of living, and my only real interest in sex."

She and her lover cannot marry, she explains, because he is still married to someone else. The only problem in her relationship with him is that "distance renders frequent meetings difficult." She says sex is still "very important" for both herself and her lover. When they are together, they have sex daily. He always reaches orgasm and she almost always does. When they are not together, she masturbates once a month or so.

"Young people should know," she concludes, "that love grows stronger if it is good in the beginning — and sexual relationships can be rewarding."

For the respondents whose life stories have been reviewed so far, sex was important before the age of 50, and — perhaps in part for that reason — remains important and fulfilling in the later decades. But for some older men and women sex has ceased to be important. Can sexual interests revive?

One respondent, aged 68, was unhappily married for thirty-nine years and is now a widower. He states that his youth was spent on a farm and that, since graduating from high school, he has been employed "in heavy basic industry at arduous labor under unhealthy working conditions and at piecework rates." He has long been politically active; his late wife was not. She was religious; he is not. He says that he and his wife had religious problems, health problems, sex problems, disagreements about how to spend their leisure time, and general incompatibility; communications between them were poor and they were uncomfortable discussing sex.

He describes the 1950s as a time of great stress for him; "those were years of McCarthyite harassment and my livelihood precarious. My wife was loyal but never understanding and supportive during those years — and to the end we remained ideologically alienated and hence mismated."

This respondent checks all six of the symptoms of declining sexual potency listed in our questionnaire: it takes him longer to get an erection, his penis when fully erect is not as stiff as before, he more frequently loses his erection during sex, it takes more stimulation to reach orgasm, he more often fails to reach orgasm, and his refractory period is longer nowadays. He considers loss of erection and longer refractory period to be "serious problems." During intercourse he reaches orgasm only about half the time. He has consulted both a physician and a psychiatrist about his sexual problems — but neither was helpful. He does not masturbate, and he does not dream about sex or wake up with an erection. Trapped for years in an unhappy marriage and now faced with declining potency, he appears to be a very likely candidate for a loveless, sexless old age. *However —*

Two years ago, at age 66, he fell in love and launched "my only . . . love affair . . . the first of a lifetime. I enjoyed the company of an understanding and kindred soul [who] shared my interest in helping build a classless society."

He and his beloved now have sex — but only a few times a month. "To sum up succinctly," he writes, "I indulge less and enjoy it more with a receptive partner of similar tastes and interests."

This respondent now states that sex is "very important" to him, and he believes that "sexual relationships are an essential ingredient for the aging." Of twenty sexual activities listed in our questionnaire, he has engaged in only six since age 50 — but he would like to try all fourteen of the others. He concludes: "The overall quality of life of the aged would be improved if more knowledge of the sexuality of those in their twilight years were disseminated."

A somewhat similar story of a late-flowering romance is told by an 81-year-old widow. She has survived a wretched marriage, enjoys good health, has a moderate income (under $15,000 a year), lives alone in her own home in the Midwest, and describes herself as "slightly religious."

She was married back in 1922, at the age of 25. "My husband became an alcoholic by the time he was 35," she recalls. "His whole life AND MINE were deeply affected by his uncontrolled drinking — loss of jobs, etc. This surely affected our sex life together. He became impotent at an early age — 35 or so. He was never highly sexed; I was more so, and was resentful over his condition. I just had to accept it and that was that." Her husband lived on, still alcoholic and still impotent, until 1973 — when she was 76.

Despite this sad history, our respondent rates her enjoyment of life as 1, "very enjoyable" — until a few months ago. She explains why. Following World War I, and before she met the man who became her husband, she received a proposal of marriage. She turned it down. In 1967, when she was 70, and shortly after she had a hysterectomy, her youthful suitor (now aged 71 and a widower) reentered her life. They launched an affair that filled her next eleven years — the last six years of her husband's life plus her first five years of widowhood.

During the first part of the current year, she notes, she and her lover, aged 81 and 82, had sex about once a week. They couldn't get together more often because he lived in a different state and neither wanted to give up the independence of a separate home. She reached orgasm every time she had sex with her partner; he usually reached orgasm, but required more stimulation of his penis than he did in earlier years. His diminished sexual potency does not seem to have impaired her enjoyment of their sex together, which she rates as 1. She felt that sex once a week was not frequent enough, so she masturbated a few times a month in addition, usually reaching orgasm. When asked how easily she becomes sexually aroused at the present time, she replies, "very easily." She sometimes dreams about sex, but has not had an orgasm in her sleep or while waking up since she was 70.

This life story, alas, does not have a happy ending. She and her lover "had a beautiful relationship until his recent death," which occurred a few months before she filled out our questionnaire.

All of our other respondents so far in this chapter were able sooner or later to find an appropriate spouse or continuing partner with whom they could be happy. This is true of most respondents in our study — but there are exceptions. One 62-year-old widow came close on one or two occasions, and she continues to try — but she has not reached more than briefly the state of marital or extramarital contentment described in the life stories above.

She is moderately religious and lives alone in her own home in a southern city on an income of less than $10,000 a year. "I was early conditioned by Victorian parents against sex," she writes, "but, thank God, nature was stronger than conditioning. My mother told me as I left home for college, 'Never kiss a man until he has proposed marriage' — but she added, 'If you get into trouble, *come home!*' "

This respondent's older sister "was so thoroughly conditioned to feel sex was 'dirty' and one should not enjoy it that she has never experienced an orgasm in her life." Now at long last, at the age of 67, this sister has begun taking an interest in sex and "has been doing some reading — but 'now' is fairly late in the day," our respondent notes sadly.

She is one of several respondents who filled all four of our Comment Pages and then added extra sheets for additional comments. She tells us in particular about each of the half-dozen men in her life. The first was a "strange man" with whom she fell in love when she was 19, back in 1935. He "always got satisfaction from his or my handling of his genitals" during their sexual encounters; but "we never had intercourse nor did he ever even try to bring *me* to orgasm. . . . I was technically a virgin until I was 25. . . . It's a marvel to me I survived as well as I did. . . . I think if I could do it over, I would not have chosen those barren years until 25."

At 25, she launched her first sexually consummated relationship, but broke it off almost immediately when she learned that her lover was living with another woman. She felt betrayed, and she still feels betrayed when she thinks about him or when she happens to meet him and his current wife on the street.

She married for the first time in 1943, at the age of 27. Sexual activity in this marriage "was lacking the glorious emotional component. We were really not suited to each other. . . . He was basically inhibited; he had a sex drive (quite normal!) but was totally impersonal in bed. Mechanically, matters succeeded. I had orgasms." But that, for this woman, was not enough.

Reflecting on this first marriage, she comments:

> The trend today is better; my two married children both lived with their spouses before marriage. If I had done so, I would never have married Husband #1. But I can't *regret* it because of our four children and the other good experiences. I am in favor of the openness about sex that is now taking place.

At the age of 41, she had a hysterectomy with removal of both ovaries (surgical menopause). After the surgery, her husband "wanted nothing but oral sex. . . . I felt 'used.' " On rare occasions, her husband also had intercourse with her by entering her vagina from the rear; but she found this unsatisfactory. During their thirteen years of marriage after her hysterectomy, she recalls only two orgasms with her husband. "I felt by this time his lack of affection for me," she writes, "and may have turned *myself* off."

At 51, she met "a former suitor" whom she had known when she was 18, "and we fell in love. We were both most unhappily married. But it was a fantasy — at least on my side. I was in love in that adolescent first-love style with the man I *thought* he was. We made love three times — then he broke it off. We have not communicated with each other for over 13 years; I am sure we never will. My husband never knew of this affair." This was her only extramarital venture.

Eight years ago, after twenty-seven years of marriage, she divorced her husband. Three years ago, when she was 59 years old, she met a man of 72, and after a brief courtship, they married. Her second husband's sex drive, she notes, "was not strong — but it really didn't matter; we were both affectionate and demonstrative, enjoying the many 'touching' pleasures *this* side of orgasm. *He* did have orgasms; I did not. We were happy."

Her second husband, she continues, died suddenly of a stroke seven months after they were married. "It is now a year since his death. In January of this year I met an 81-year-old man. In April we fell in love and in that month and May we made love four times." This latest lover of hers "had had no woman in his life" since his divorce thirty-four years earlier. Now, aged 81, "he is still virile."

She reports that in this relationship, sex is very important to her lover and moderately important to herself. She terminated sex with him, however, because "when I perceived that he and I could never temperamentally *live* together or *marry*, my ardor disappeared — much to his sorrow. After some weeks of not seeing each other, we have resumed friendship — tender and caring without sex. His age *per se* was not the cause of our dissolution as lovers. I realize my loneliness from having lost my husband of seven months has made me quite vulnerable."

Today, at 62, this respondent has abandoned in several respects what she describes as her puritanical upbringing. During her recent relationships, she has enjoyed both active and passive oral sex, stimulating her partner's genitals manually and having him stimulate hers manually, stimulating her clitoris with her fingers during sex, having her partner stimulate her clitoris with his fingers during sex, and masturbating with a vibrator. She enjoys reading sexually explicit materials and strongly disagrees with the statement that "communities should have the right to ban all pornographic materials." She has never had a homosexual experience but she writes: "I am in favor of defending rights of homosexuals (one of my [children] is gay)."

Our respondent reports that she can now go comfortably without orgasm for two or three weeks; then she masturbates, to release sexual tension and because she enjoys masturbating. "I think masturbation for older people is a good outlet if they need it," she writes. "No embarrassment. I find my single women friends take it for granted."

Upon reflection, she wonders why so many men in her generation "knew nothing much and cared nothing much about what happens to the woman making love. I married two men, neither of whom knew what to do. . . . I tried to help them help me, but both of them were prudish. . . . Why shouldn't [our culture] instruct both sexes about love-making? Of course, the many magazines and books now do that!"

What lies ahead for her?

"As long as I live," she writes confidently, "I shall have people I love. . . . My current libido is less than it was ten years ago — but my longing to love and be loved is as strong as ever or maybe more. Capacity grows with the years. I feel I could have a marriage now and be happy with virtually no intercourse."

Most of our respondents are in at least moderately comfortable financial circumstances. One exception is a 77-year-old man whose wife died twenty-five years ago and who lives alone in a small town in the Far West. He writes:

> I retired at age 63 because I was a widower and my children were grown and self-supporting. Except for missing my wife's companionship, I am much happier in retirement. I enjoy the companionship of grandchildren . . . and am soon to have a great-grandchild. I keep busy reading, writing, listening to music, watching the better TV programs including news, sports, and documentaries, writing and hearing from old friends, doing some gardening, etc. . . .
>
> I am able to live on a modest income [less than $5,000 a year] because I am in good health and my small home is paid for.

He describes himself as moderately religious. He has both women and men friends, but he is sometimes lonely. "My close friends are members of my family," he explains, "plus a few I correspond with. . . . I have no need of more friends at this time of life, but I would like to be able to visit with those at a distance."

He describes his health as very good, better than average for his age — and he attributes this in part to masturbation:

> I get relief about once a week by masturbation while reading or looking at pornographic material. Possibly as a result, I have no prostate difficulties and appear much younger than my age of 77. A doctor recently said he would have guessed I was 65. Certainly it would be more pleasant to have sexual intercourse with an attractive, warmly receptive and companionable woman, but I know of none available.

He describes his present interest in sex as "strong" and says that he is sexually aroused "moderately easily" — both about the same as at age 40. He becomes uncomfortable if he goes without sexual release for more than a week or so. He reaches orgasm every time during masturbation.

Why has he not remarried? He replies:

> Since my wife's death, I have had warm friendships with attractive women my own age who have also lost spouses, but . . . memory of my wife remains so vivid and endearing, I don't feel I would be happy with another woman. Four of the women I believe I could have married have considerably more money than I. Each is a fine, intelligent, attractive person and we remain friends.

This respondent "moderately agrees" with the statement, "It's okay for older couples who are not married to have sexual relations." He adds: "I would have welcomed sexual relations with an attractive, companionable woman in recent years, but have not found a convenient opportunity and have not tried to find one. Women I've . . . known and liked live in other states or something might have developed." When he was near them, however, he did

not propose sex — "probably due to my own shyness in that regard." His only sexual experiences during his twenty-five years as
a widower were five encounters with prostitutes during the first
year.

Most of our respondents in sexual relationships report that
they are having sex with only one partner. Some however, have
two current sexual partners (usually a spouse and a lover); and a
few report multiple partners. One of these is a 58-year-old Illinois
divorcée (whose filled-in questionnaire reached us too late to be
included in our statistical study) who lives alone, on an annual income of between $10,000 and $15,000.

Since her divorce, she has enjoyed what she calls "a network
of Intimate Friendships" — a term she adopted from the title of a
book, *Intimate Friendships*, by James Ramey. She explains: "I deeply
love three men. . . . I have a sexual relationship with one of
them — and have had with the other two in the past. I also love
very much three other men with whom I currently have an active
sexual relationship." Of these six men, "three are long-term relationships in which we share our lives fully on all or many
levels. . . . Where the man is married or living with someone else, I
am also [in most cases] a close friend of that woman."

She reports having had sex with "about 20" partners in all
since age 50; and with "about 15" during the past year. Some of
these were in group-sex situations, but she writes: "I am not a
swinger; that is, I rarely have a casual sexual relationship, and
never go to a party for the purpose of engaging in sexual activity."
She refers to "the spirituality of deep and loving sexual *relating*" as
being far preferable to casual sex. She adds, however, that she
enjoys group sex, and she comments: "Group sex is alien to most
people. It is thought of as an ugly 'orgy' or 'gang bang.' It can,
however, be very different."

Asked what she regrets in her life, she replies:

I feel very fortunate in saying I have no regrets. If I could
add one thing, it would be a live-in sexual partner where my
activity was steady and consistent. But I would not trade that

for the rich sexual life I have had and am having. Ideally, a relationship like that would be "open" for both of us.

Concerning marriage, she writes: "I don't want to get married just now. Maybe never."

In 1981 this respondent wrote us to bring her questionnaire up to date. She reports that, at 61, she has just entered her second marriage — an open marriage — with a 49-year-old husband.

Not all of our 4,246 men and women wrote as fully or as frankly about themselves as those whose life stories we have just reviewed. But a surprising number of our respondents proved willing and able to describe, at length and in depth, many intimate aspects of their lives. We believe that the insights that emerge from their accounts — many of which appear in subsequent chapters — make a unique contribution both to the study of aging and to the study of love and sex without regard to age.

❧ 2 ❦

Married Women and
Married Men

• What keeps a marriage happy after wife and husband pass age 50?

• Does affluence assure a happy marriage in the later years? Does poverty undermine marital happiness?

• Are wives and husbands in their seventies and eighties more or less happily married than those in their fifties and sixties?

• How do high school dropouts, after they pass 50, compare with respondents with graduate degrees? The devoutly religious with the not-at-all religious? The remarried with the married-only-once?

• How does poor health affect marital happiness?

• Are wives more or less happy with their marriage than husbands?

• What of marriages in which the wife is much younger or much older than her husband?

• Is good sex essential to a happy marriage? Can unhappily married wives and husbands still enjoy sex together?

• How is adultery related to marital happiness? Do many happily married spouses engage in outside sex? Can a marriage remain a happy one even though one spouse knows that the other is having an affair?

Questions such as these have long been debated; but they have never before been explored in depth in a population aged 50 and over.

We have voluminous data supplied by more than three thousand happily and unhappily married wives and husbands. By comparing the happily with the unhappily married, and the wives with the husbands, we are able to illuminate the above questions and others like them.

HOW MARITAL HAPPINESS WAS MEASURED

We classified 3,040 of our wives and husbands as happily or unhappily married in accordance with their replies to the following question:

"Check the box that best represents how happy your marriage or relationship is."

Here are the replies we received from the wives and husbands:

Very happy	(46%) □ 1	(29%) □ 2	(12%) □ 3	(7%) □ 4	(3%) □ 5	(2%) □ 6	(1%) □ 7	Very unhappy

To facilitate comparisons, we combined those who checked 1, 2, and 3 as the "happily married," and those who checked 4, 5, 6, and 7 as the "unhappily married." The result: 2,645 happily married wives and husbands and 395 unhappily married — 87 percent versus 13 percent. If we had chosen to combine the data from our seven-point scale in some other way, of course, the percentages would have been different.

It is possible that some of our 2,645 respondents who *say* they are happily married are just following a social convention, giving the answer that is expected of them in our culture. After reading thousands of their detailed comments, however, we are confident that this is not an adequate explanation for the preponderance of happy marriages in our sample. Too many of the descriptions of marital happiness "ring true." Consider, for example, the wife, married for thirty-eight years, who writes: "Sometimes I'm so happy I get scared it will cease too soon."

And consider this statement from a husband married for forty-five years:

> Love in the mature years is much more a sharing operation with a learned process of giving on both sides — a little less exciting but surer and deeper. It's a wonderful warm coat on an awfully cold day.

Consider the 62-year-old husband, married for thirty-seven years, who describes "that catch in the heart when [my wife] walks into a room, the anticipation of seeing her after being separated for several hours."

Finally, consider this statement from a wife married for thirty-eight years:

> Love in the later years is just as great as love in the earlier years. I still get a thrill when I see my husband on the street or hear his voice on the telephone. And when he touches me, oh my!

These comments, and countless others like them, persuade us that for many of our aging and aged couples, avowals of "marital happiness" are not just socially conventional statements; they are deeply experienced facts of life.

How does it *feel* to be happily (or unhappily) married? Three marriages in our sample, two happy and one unhappy, are so vividly described by respondents that their feelings are almost palpable.

PORTRAITS OF TWO HAPPY MARRIAGES

A 68-year-old wife and her 75-year-old husband live in their own home in the Southwest on an income of less than $10,000 a year. The wife reports:

My husband and I are still very much in love. We celebrated our 50th wedding anniversay [this year] with over 300 guests — and still a glance from my man across the room and a wink give me a thrill.

I don't regret a thing. We married when I was 18. He was 25. Our sex life was wonderful — still is, no changes needed.

She continues:

Older people have earned the right to dress as they please and to act as they wish. I ride a motor bike on trails, ride a horse — and have no problem getting along with young people. Our [home] is always full of people of every age from 80 to three months.

This wife and husband have sex together about once a week. He says he reaches orgasm "almost always." She confirms this and adds that she reaches orgasm every time. Both agree that each of them initiates the activities leading to sex about equally often, and both like it that way.

Unlike many couples of their generation, this wife and husband did not try to keep sex a secret from their children. "They grew up watching us kiss and hug and pinch — and they do the same in front of their children." All three of the children, she adds parenthetically, are still married to their first spouses. "No divorces. We have grand times together" — and with their grandchildren, several of whom are already grown up.

She continues:

Love in the later years is an enduring love — not the great passionate love of the teens but a greater love. [You enjoy] the knowledge that you are loved and wanted, that you are still beautiful to your husband. You have shared happiness, sorrow, death — watching your sons leave for the wars, seeing your friends grow old and feeble, then dying. You hold out your hand and your husband clasps it, then draws you near. Sleeping close together. Having sex whenever you want. We talk together sometimes for hours. . . .

We are just happy to be together. This is a far greater love than the one we started with — although it is the same in some ways. . . .

Sometimes we just want to lie together to touch. Sex is not always needed to show our love. Just being close at night is wonderful.

Even her sexual dreams, this wife notes, are about her husband: "Sometimes I and my husband are in a jungle or on a cloud. In the jungle he chases me and I run; on the cloud we are floating over the ocean."

As might be expected, both wife and husband rate the happiness of their marriage as 1, "very happy." At 75, he rates his enjoyment of sex with his wife as 1 — and she at 68 rates her enjoyment of sex with him as 2.

Our second prototype happy marriage is different in a number of respects. This wife and husband were married fifty-six years ago, when they were both 25; they are now 81. The husband has been retired for a decade, and they live in their own home in New England. He writes:

The Christian missionary society with which I was associated did not have a fixed retirement age; but the board of directors (mostly businessmen) felt that 65 was the proper age for retirement so they replaced me. I accepted a little reluctantly — and kept on working as a missionary in an unofficial capacity, with pay, for six more years. Today I would like to go back to my work; but I realize that I would not do it as well as I would like to.

This ex-missionary husband and wife both describe themselves as "very religious," and they are quite conservative in their sexual opinions. They believe, for example, that masturbation is never proper and feel strongly that it is *not* right for unmarried older people to have sexual relations. They strongly believe that sex without love is *not* better than no sex at all. They take a strongly conservative position on laws against pornography and homosexuality as well.

The husband checks all six of the major symptoms of declining sexual potency, and considers three of them serious problems: it takes him longer to get an erection, his erect penis is not as stiff as before, and it takes more stimulation to reach orgasm. Nevertheless, he and his wife continue to have sex a few times a month. Both report that they seldom reach orgasm nowadays.

Asked about various sexual activities since 50, the husband indicates that he has enjoyed stimulating his wife's breasts or nipples, stimulating her genitals manually and having her stimulate his genitals manually. He writes "no, no, no," quite emphatically, concerning both active and passive oral sex. He checks five other sexual activities he has not tried since 50 but would like to try: being undressed by his wife, undressing his wife, viewing hardcore pornographic films or photos, reading sexually explicit material, and watching other people have sex. He rates his enjoyment of sex with her as 5 and she rates her enjoyment of sex with him as 6.

At 81, this husband rates his overall enjoyment of life as 1; his wife rates hers as 3. Both rate the present happiness of their marriage, after fifty-six years, as 1.

The husband sums up:

> Love today is fervent but less passionate than in earlier years. It has an enduring quality. . . . Please emphasize the long-term value and enjoyment of true love and the importance of self-discipline, temperance, and restraint — not only in personal conduct but also in the exploitation of sex.

His wife sums up in her own more personal way:

> Love and appreciation of my husband deepens with the years. He improves with age — and I hope I do, too. We are more thoughtful and considerate. We appreciate loyalty and commitment. . . . Expressing affection by word and touch has increased in recent years. Children and grandchildren bind us together.

Portrait of an Unhappy Marriage

"This questionnaire is being filled out on my 25th wedding anniversary and you'll excuse me if I get a little cynical," writes a 52-year-old wife and mother in a New York City suburb:

> Have been married 25 years to a person [of the same age] who shares none of my interests. . . .
>
> My husband is a hyper-active loud-mouth. Can't tell him anything. Although he has been a good provider, and faithful (I think), he is terribly short-tempered and [has] an irritability that flares into rage at the least little thing.
>
> He loves me — tells me he does — but I do not love him — never have, and how desperately I wish I knew what love is.

Her husband is not employed, and "is in a deep depression which hangs over our heads like a black cloud and envelops all of us." Their daughter and three sons, however, "are a source of pride and the only good thing about our marriage."

How does a couple get into such a trap?

"[I] was raised in a very strict Catholic background," this wife explains. "[I] was pushed into a loveless marriage. . . . I was a virgin when I got married and have never known anyone else."

Asked about the problems in her marriage, she checks five categories: financial problems (the family income for four people is between $15,000 and $20,000 a year); job problems (she is employed full-time, her husband is not); conflicts with children; how to spend leisure time; and sex problems. She characterizes communications between her husband and herself as "poor."

Despite her religious upbringing and conventional life-style, she now feels strongly that children should be reassured there's nothing wrong with masturbation, and that it's proper for older people to masturbate too. She feels strongly that it's all right for older people who are not married to have sexual relations — but she also feels strongly that sex without love is *not* better than no sex at all. (Here, presumably, she is thinking of sex with a husband she does not love.) She feels strongly that communities should *not* have the right to ban pornography, that the anti-homosexual laws should *not* be enforced, and that homosexual relations between older people are nobody else's business. She describes herself as "not at all religious" these days, but her husband has retained a religious approach to sex. She writes: "I'm all for the [sexual] revolution. We were raised with too many guilt feelings which we carry over into marriage and later life."

But while her opinions have changed, her personal feelings and response patterns have not. "I wish I could enjoy sex," she notes sadly, "and not feel it's 'what dogs do.'"

She and her husband have sex once a week, always on his initiative; she considers this too often. Her enjoyment of sex with her husband she rates as 7, "not at all enjoyable." He always reaches orgasm during intercourse; she seldom does. But when she masturbates — once a month or less frequently — she always reaches orgasm.

"At our house," she tells us, "sex is as perfunctory as brushing your teeth!!! . . . His idea of sex is a quick 'let's get at it' thing. . . . I would sometimes like a little tenderness that does not end in intercourse. The thought never enters his mind."

Of the twenty types of sexual activity listed in our questionnaire, she has engaged in seven — but would like to try twelve of the others. The only activity she would *not* like to try is having sex with someone she doesn't know very well.

She wishes there were a way "to liberate us from our guilt feelings or the 'we've-always-done-it-this-way' syndrome. [I] am sure there are a lot of good things that we could do — but we don't."

Asked what she'd like to have done differently in the past, she replies:

If I had it to do over, I would marry for love or not at all. Would not want my [children] to follow my mistake and I often warn them not to allow themselves to be pushed into a corner where there is no way out except marriage. I envy the freedom that today's young people enjoy.

Many women in this situation would long ago have escaped through divorce, but that road seems closed to this respondent. She writes:

> We are in our early fifties and it scares me to think that this is the way it will be the rest of my life. We have two children still at home. . . . I don't know what we will do when they are gone, too.
>
> Being Catholic (he is — I quit years ago over the birth-control issue), I suppose there is no way out — or at least I am not brave enough to take it. . . . I [don't want to] hurt him; he says he loves me and I guess he does. I don't know what love is — and that's sad.

She concludes:

> Thanks for the opportunity to get this out of my system. These are things I have never said aloud to anyone!!!

NONSEXUAL FACTORS AND MARITAL HAPPINESS

The question is often asked whether sexual or nonsexual factors are more important as determinants of marital happiness. We cannot answer that question, for sexual and nonsexual factors are intimately interwoven, and interact with one another in subtle and sometimes covert ways. We can, however, explore the relationships between marital happiness and a variety of specific factors, sexual and nonsexual alike.

About one-third of our questionnaire is devoted to nonsexual factors, including demographic information. We particularly wanted to know the relationships of fifteen of these factors with marital happiness. For example, are wives and husbands with dependent children living at home more or less likely to be happily married than those with "empty nests"? Does retirement increase or decrease the proportion of happily married husbands and wives?

Of the nonsexual factors we selected for study, we found only one that is in fact very closely associated with marital happiness. Six others show some small or modest relationship. The remainder show inconsistent or negligible relationships, or none at all.

Gender

It is often said that marriage as it is structured in the United States today favors the needs and wants of husbands rather than wives. The women's movement has publicized the existence of financially exploited wives, overworked wives, wives tied to their homes for long hours, emotionally and sexually frustrated wives, and even physically battered wives. The wife who works a 40-hour week and whose husband expects her in addition to tend the children, do the housework, cook the meals — and do it all with charm and grace — has become the paradigm of the sexist inequity inherent in traditional marital customs.

Against this background, we might expect a much smaller proportion of happy wives than of happy husbands among our respondents — and, conversely, a greater proportion of unhappy wives than of unhappy husbands. That, however, is not the case. When rating their own marital happiness, our wives and husbands show negligible differences:

	Wives	*Husbands*
	(N = 1,201)	(N = 1,839)
Happily married	86%	87%
Unhappily married	14	13
	100%	100%

Age

The wives in our sample (as is true of wives generally) are somewhat younger (median age 60) than are the husbands (median age

64). The older our respondents are, the more likely they are to report happy marriages — but the differences from decade to decade are small:

	In their 50s	In their 60s	Aged 70 and over
Wives and husbands*	(N = 1,196)	(N = 1,268)	(N = 576)
Happily married	84%	88%	91%
Unhappily married	16	12	9
	100%	100%	100%

What appears to be a rising frequency of happy marriages as couples age is in part the result of divorce, which progressively culls unhappily married respondents from our married sample. It is possible that happily married people live longer and are therefore more often found in the later years. These are not, however, the only explanations. Quite a few of our respondents assure us that good marriages, like good wines, really do improve with age. One wife, aged 54 and married for thirty years, writes:

> My husband and I have become even more companionable and close since his retirement. . . . Love gets better and sex slows down just a little bit. . . . Love becomes comfortable and secure and the individuals make it as exciting as love in the early years.

A husband, aged 51 and married for thirty-two years, writes that he and his wife

> are aware of being far deeper in love now. The physical relationship is far better and more diverse. Our deep respect for each other is an increased thrill and we want to touch and

---

* The same proportions are visible when wives and husbands are considered separately.

show affection and love more than ever. It is better now than ever.

Even troubled and threatened marriages *sometimes* improve with age. A 51-year-old wife, married at age 17, writes from Iowa:

I married a clergyman when we were both young and immature. There were times when our marriage was held together by a thread — the thread being our commitment to God. [We had problems but] we had made some promises to each other before God and witnesses. Thank Heavens, ours were the type of problems that could be worked out and our marriage became a good one. . . . A good marriage that has weathered the storms of immaturity, child-rearing, financial crises, etc., adds a new dimension with age — respect and true caring, and time for each other's interests.

A happily married Philadelphia husband, aged 69 and married for forty-three years, writes:

Teach the young and not-so-old the five stages of marriage:
1. Infatuation
2. Disenchantment
3. Misery — most divorces occur at this stage
4. Enlightenment
5. Love (it may take years).

There are also examples, of course, of the opposite process: initially happy and successful marriages that sour and wither with age. Most of these, however, do not appear in our marital statistics, the couples having already separated or secured divorces. Some have remarried, and others are found among the formerly married whose lives will be reviewed in chapter 3.

The "empty nest syndrome"

It has often been alleged that wives become unhappy when their children leave home and they find themselves without a significant role to play in life. This has been labeled the "empty nest syndrome." Over the years it has been invoked by a variety of observers — ranging from mental health professionals to writers in popular magazines to stand-up comedians — to explain various "female problems." We find little trace of the empty nest syndrome, however. More empty nests than full nests are reported to be happy by our wives:

Wives	With dependent children living at home	Without dependent children living at home
	(N = 334)	(N = 2,706)
Happily married	80%	87%
Unhappily married	20	13
	100%	100%

The proportions for husbands with empty nests are quite similar.

Instead of an "empty nest syndrome," quite a few of our respondents describe what might be called their "empty nest honeymoon." Here are three examples, the first provided by a 56-year-old Oklahoma wife married for thirty-four years:

Now that the children are grown and gone, we are delighted to be a 'single couple' once again and have been on a honeymoon ever since we have been alone. We find that our shared experiences have made us closer, wiser, and funnier. Our little understandings, communicated by a lifted eyebrow during some cocktail party; the little words that are a private joke within the family and the ability to sit down and talk about feelings have all come with age. We like being able to make love in the afternoon, if we wish, or to wait a few days longer than usual if one or another of us is not in the mood. It is a LOVELY time of life.

A 54-year-old wife, married for twenty-seven years, writes:

Love in the earlier years was too mixed with feelings about family affairs — *i.e.,* children's problems, housing, and installment payments, etc.; but now it's love because there are only two of us to enjoy each other and to feel free with each other.

Our third example is supplied by a 66-year-old Indiana husband married for thirty-three years:

After children are reared and educated and have struck out on their own, the love between a husband and wife becomes more concentrated on each other. This is particularly true after retirement, when the tensions of job and commutation no longer exist.

Place of residence

Our respondents are drawn from all parts of the United States, plus at least 81 from Canada. East or west, Sun Belt or Frost Belt — region of residence makes no difference in the proportion of our respondents who report happy marriages.

Four percent (115) of our wives and husbands live in retirement communities. When we compare our wives in retirement communities with our other wives, we find little difference (88 percent versus 86 percent) among those who report being happily married. Among our husbands, a higher proportion of those in retirement communities (92 percent versus 87 percent) report marital happiness.

One wife gives a strong endorsement of life in that setting:

The news media make . . . fun of retirement places. . . . I think just the opposite is true. When we go back to our home towns, all our old friends are still working and very busy. They have no time for fun. When one is retired and lives in his home town, everyone treats him like an old, old person.

This wife is 66 and her husband 67, and both are married for the second time. They have lived in their retirement community in Florida, on an income of more than $50,000 a year, for the past seven years of their eight-year marriage. Both rate their marital happiness, enjoyment of life, and enjoyment of sex with each other as 1.

Living in a retirement community, this wife writes, contributes much to their life enjoyment:

> We have many close, intimate friends who live in our com-
> munity — wonderful people and friends, so that we are
> never lonely. We all play golf, have hobbies, play cards and
> have fun together. I never dreamed that life at my age could
> be so good.
> We also travel a lot, all over the world. We have more
> income than many in this community; but even the ones on
> small fixed incomes have a wonderful life here.

Indeed, marital happiness in a retirement community is not only for the wealthy. For example, another couple reports from a retirement community in the Southwest — but on a family income of less than $10,000 a year. They are both 85 years old. The husband is in good health but has had a prostatectomy. After fifty-five years of marriage, both of them rate their enjoyment of life, marital happiness, and enjoyment of weekly sex with each other as 1.

Family income

Of our 2,926 wives and husbands who report both their family income and their marital happiness or unhappiness, 7 percent have an annual income of less than $10,000 a year — and of these, 85 percent are happily married. This appears to contradict a common saying: "Love flies out the window when poverty comes in the door."

Our data, however, tend to confirm another common saying: "Money cannot buy happiness." Among our husbands, marital happiness varies only slightly with family income — and there is no consistent pattern. Unhappily married men are found in equal proportions among those with a family income under $10,000 a year and those with a family income of $35,000 to $50,000 a year:

Husbands	Under $10,000 (N = 118)	$10,000– 20,000 (N = 423)	$20,000– 35,000 (N = 678)	$35,000– 50,000 (N = 323)	$50,000 and over (N = 255)
Happily married	84%	89%	88%	84%	90%
Unhappily married	16	11	12	16	10
	100%	100%	100%	100%	100%

Among our wives, too, the variation with family income is small and shows no consistent pattern. The proportion of unhappy wives with a family income under $10,000 a year is little different from the proportion with a family income of $50,000 a year or over:

Wives	Under $10,000 (N = 83)	$10,000– 20,000 (N = 313)	$20,000– 35,000 (N = 402)	$35,000– 50,000 (N = 184)	$50,000 and over (N = 147)
Happily married	86%	82%	88%	91%	84%
Unhappily married	14	18	12	9	16
	100%	100%	100%	100%	100%

These figures prompt us to offer one generality, but not much more: Family income has neither a major nor a consistent effect on marital happiness among our husbands and wives.

In particular cases, of course, too low (or perhaps too high) an income may have a marked effect on marital happiness. An inadequate income can indeed be the most important and most distressing element in the life of some of our respondents, especially some of our unmarried women. One widow in particular, as we shall see in chapter 3, reports a life of grinding work and poverty. And she makes a searing comment on marriage and sex:

> If I ever marry again, it will be to better my circumstances — material, financial, etc. I've had it with this passionate stuff. Quiet companionship and a good friendship and comfortable support is what I want now.

Education

Almost all of our respondents completed their formal education three decades or more ago, and some left school half a century or more ago. Nevertheless, the amount of education that they received is associated with their current marital happiness. Both wives and husbands with more education are slightly more likely to report that they are happily married:

	High school graduate or less	Education beyond high school
Wives and husbands	(N = 650)	(N = 2,375)
Happily married	84%	88%
Unhappily married	16	12
	100%	100%

Retirement

We asked employed respondents whether they view retirement with positive, negative, or mixed feelings — and we similarly asked those who have already retired how they feel about retirement. We found that retirement is for many husbands and wives a mere bugaboo — distressing in anticipation but enjoyable after it occurs. Note in the table below that, for both husbands and wives, the proportion reporting positive feelings toward retirement rises sharply following retirement — while the proportions reporting mixed or negative feelings drop very substantially:

	Employed	Retired
Husbands	(N = 826)	(N = 803)
Positive feelings toward retirement	44%	78%
Mixed feelings	42	19
Negative feelings	14	2
	100%	100%
	Employed	Retired
Wives	(N = 348)	(N = 386)
Positive feelings toward retirement	38%	75%
Mixed feelings	49	22
Negative feelings	14	3
	101%	100%

Retirement has little effect on marital happiness for either wives or husbands:

	Employed	Retired
Wives	(N = 418)	(N = 386)
Happily married	86%	88%
Unhappily married	14	12
	100%	100%
	Employed	Retired
Husbands	(N = 1,040)	(N = 775)
Happily married	86%	89%
Unhappily married	14%	11%
	100%	100%

Only 24 wives and 33 husbands were unemployed and looking for work when they filled out our questionnaires back in 1978; they are excluded from the tables above.

We found one additional fact of interest about wives and employment. Several employed wives mention in their comments that they would like to work part-time. Our data confirm the wisdom of this; 90 percent of our 157 wives employed part-time as compared with 83 percent of our 261 wives employed full-time report that they are happily married. Among our husbands, the differences are negligible.

Religion

Our wives and husbands who consider themselves religious are somewhat more likely to report happy marriages:

	Very or moderately religious	Slightly or not at all religious
Wives and husbands	(N = 1,574)	(N = 1,418)
Happily married	89%	85%
Unhappily married	11	15
	100%	100%

Health

We had expected that health would be associated with marital happiness — and it is, to a modest extent:

	Excellent or very good health	Good, fair, or poor health
Wives and husbands	(N = 1,929)	(N = 1,095)
Happily married	89%	84%
Unhappily married	11	16
	100%	100%

We also asked our respondents whether they consider their health better than average, about average, or worse than average as compared with others of their own age. The responses reflect a pattern similar to that in the table above — except that the 50 wives who consider their health worse than average are much more likely (26 percent) to report an unhappy marriage.

One New York City wife, married for 37 years, reports a state of health that is far worse than average. She is 79 and her husband 75. She experienced menopause at 42, accompanied by a marked decrease in interest in sex. She has had a mastectomy. She has had surgery for brain cancer, followed by partial paralysis and several subsequent operations. She takes medication for epilepsy and for anemia, plus two types of tranquilizer. Both wife and husband say that her poor health is the only problem in their marriage.

They have had no sex, either inside or outside of their marriage, for the past seventeen years; both say that stopping sex was a mutual decision — because of the wife's ill health.

The husband rates his enjoyment of life as 1; the wife rates hers as 7. Yet both rate the happiness of their marriage as 2. The wife explains:

> The earlier stage of sex love is replaced with diminishing desire but with increasing respect — without which later marriage is a failure. . . . Sex love is not the be-all and end-all.

The husband's view is similar:

> The lessening of sexual desire is inevitable and does not indicate loss of love. . . . Sexual love . . . in the later years of one's life fades, and the sex side becomes less imperative. This does not create much apprehension, but is accepted as part of the aging process.

Duration of marriage

Many of the marriages reported by our respondents are remarkably durable. Nearly three-quarters of our wives and two-thirds of our husbands have been married to their present partners for

thirty years or more. Fifty-two wives and 98 husbands have celebrated their golden wedding anniversary.

One of those wives, a Virginian, married at 17 a man then 19.
Many very early marriages of this kind come apart — but not this
one. After fifty-two years of marriage, the 69-year-old wife gives a
rating of 2 to her overall enjoyment of life, the happiness of her
marriage, and her enjoyment of sex with her husband. She says
that he, at 71, experiences all six signs of declining sexual potency
and seldom reaches orgasm — but they still have sex together two
or three times a week, and she usually reaches orgasm. She writes:

> I have dreamed my husband was having sex with me, [then
> I] wake up and find he is peacefully asleep. [I] used to wake
> him up, but leave him sleeping now. There is a lot of affec-
> tion mixed up with love, and if one can't laugh at some
> of the sex problems that crop up, things could get pretty
> bad. We have been married 52 years and still enjoy each
> other.

Duration of marriage has a complex relationship to marital
happiness among our respondents. Wives and husbands aged 50
and over who have been married for less than five years enjoy a
"honeymoon effect"; the proportion of happy marriages in this
group is among the highest in our entire study. This honeymoon
effect tends to wear off after five years, but there is a rise again
after thirty years. After fifty years of marriage, the proportion
happily married is as high as during the five "honeymoon" years.

	Less than 5 years	5 to 29 years	30 to 39 years	40 to 49 years	50 years or more
Wives and husbands	(N=126)	(N=779)	(N=1,301)	(N=674)	(N=148)
Happily married	93%	83%	86%	91%	93%
Unhappily married	7	17	14	9	7
	100%	100%	100%	100%	100%

As noted earlier, the rising proportion of happy marriages as the decades roll by is due in part to the fact that, decade after decade, more and more unhappy marriages are terminated by divorce.

Remarriage

The great majority of our wives and husbands are still married to their first spouse:

	Wives (N=1,206)	*Husbands* (N=1,815)
Married once	80%	72%
Married twice	16	22
Married three times	3	5
Married four or more times	1	1
	100%	100%

A higher proportion of first marriages than of remarriages are happy, but the difference is small:

Wives and husbands	*Married once* (N=2,206)	*Remarried* (N=721)
Happily married	88%	85%
Unhappily married	12	15
	100%	100%

It is sometimes said that happiness is a *personal* characteristic, which some people possess and others lack, regardless of the circumstances — including the marriage — in which they happen to find themselves. It is also sometimes said that a man or woman who makes a mistake and marries the wrong partner the first time is prone to make the same mistake the second time round — and the third. These generalizations may (or may not) be true of some respondents; but the comments supplied by many of our remarried wives and husbands demonstrate that a miserably unhappy first marriage may in fact be followed by an ecstatically happy second marriage. One 52-year-old woman writes from Hawaii:

This is my second marriage. I was previously married for 28 years; the first half was not really satisfactory — the last half hell. My first husband and I simply did not belong together. It took me much too long to accept that. I just kept trying.

My second husband and I met [and] fell in love — Zap! [After five years], I have never been happier. This marriage was the "made in Heaven" variety — corny, but true. Love the second time round is more giving, kind, loving. . . . I am a happy, lucky woman. This man and I belong together.

A twice-married Chicago husband writes similarly:

My [present] wife and I met and fell in love when I was 50 and she 46. [After five years], we are more in love and loving every day — not bothered with the disruptive selfishness and over-sensitive hurts or need to show superiority that we felt in our younger years. We communicate!

A remarried 56-year-old woman writes from Georgia:

My first husband had too much sex drive to suit me, which caused a lot of unhappiness in our time together. In this marriage I find we are much more attuned to each other's needs.

A 64-year-old husband remarks that his first marriage was happy but "sexually restricted." He continues;

With my second love . . . , I experienced all the excitement, thrill and unabashed kittenishness of my first true love. But it was tempered with feelings of assurance and determination to succeed in the relationship and unfettered with the restrictions of a rather Puritan upbringing.

His second wife is 54 and they have been married for two years. She had a mastectomy shortly after the wedding.

"Among the satisfactions of my present union," this husband continues, "is the capacity — thanks to my wife's freedom from inhibitions — to discuss intimate features of [our] sexual relationship . . . with her. [Our] new sexual activities have satisfied the fantasies that arose during and after my . . . first marriage. The greater knowledge of and freedom to explore sexual activity have been most satisfying to me."

His present wife, he notes, no longer experiences "the intensity of orgasmic climax that she did before," and it takes him longer to reach orgasm. He adds, however, that "the longer period before climax is perhaps due to more deliberate techniques, learned through recent reading. No problem — on the contrary, a good change."

One of our Gulf Coast respondents recently married her fifth husband. She is 50, he 35. She writes:

I used to have a guilty feeling about my many marriages, but not any more. Every one of them was like a stepping stone to something better. I feel sorry for my ex-husbands because they are incapable of ever achieving [either] the ultra in sex satisfaction or the peace and contentment of a straight-speaking and feeling marriage.

She says that the love she and her present husband feel for each other "is more stable and meaningful than my other marriages." Communications in this marriage are excellent and she is very comfortable discussing sexual matters with her husband. "I was not as open [about] sex with my previous husbands," she explains, "because they were not."

Of her new husband, she writes:

I could not find a man my age or older that had my feelings about life — but I did find a man fifteen years younger than I (35–50) who is very companionable and sexy for me. I am enjoying my voluntary retirement. Now I can do things I want to do for me — and benefit for my husband also.

Autumnal marriage

Late marriages are often frowned upon in our culture. Sometimes the children of an elderly widow or widower seek to prevent a late remarriage — perhaps because they think it unseemly, or perhaps because they fear to lose an inheritance. "Why on earth do you want to remarry at *your* age?" is a comment sometimes heard. Yet 5 percent of our wives and 10 percent of our husbands have in fact entered into marriage after 50.

It used to be said that women who marry late do so for companionship, or for affection, or for financial or other practical reasons — but certainly not for sex.* We did not ask our respondents why they married, but we did ask them how important they consider the sexual side of their marriage. Of our wives who married after 50, 42 percent consider the sexual side of their marriage "very important," as compared with only 28 percent of our wives who married before 50.

Among our husbands, whether married before or after 50, nearly half consider the sexual side of their marriage "very important."

A bride of 73 describes in detail her autumnal marriage. She married her second husband, 74, shortly before filling out our questionnaire. The two live together in Nevada on an income of less than $10,000 a year.

Of her first husband she writes:

---

* A celebrated Victorian authority on sex explained: "As a general rule, a modest woman seldom desires any sexual gratification for herself. She submits to her husband, but only to please him; and, but for the desire for maternity, would far rather be relieved of his attentions." (Dr. William Acton [1813–1875], in *The Functions and Disorders of the Reproductive Organs, in Childhood, Youth, Adult Age, and Advanced Life, Considered in Their Physiological, Social, and Moral Relations.*)

I was married 45 years to a fine man, had lovely children. We enjoyed sex over the years; and since he had some trouble getting a hard penis, we turned to oral sex and enjoyed that. As he aged, he [became] impotent, due partly to diabetes. . . . For three years before his death, very suddenly, we had no sex at all.

Over the years I had been disturbed by the fact that if we touched each other at all, he thought it meant bed and intercourse. Why couldn't we touch and enjoy just that? Somehow, I thought, before I die I'll solve this to my satisfaction. Since I am quite a sexual being, I was utterly miserable for [the] three years before he died.

I believe in prayer and used it, asking for relief. Couldn't I have a few years of real intercourse and real loving touching?

For two years before the death of her husband, she "had been writing to an old boyfriend of college days and [we] decided to meet after 50 years. It was a real love affair from the beginning."

She told her college friend of her husband's impotence and of her need for physical loving. He confessed that he, too, was impotent. How about oral sex? she asked. He had never done it "but was ready to try."

Shortly after her husband died, she married her "boyfriend of college days." They now have oral sex together, she reports, four to six times a week. She reaches orgasm on every such occasion, and often has multiple orgasms. He reaches orgasm occasionally. She says that she is having sex more often now, at 73, than she did at age 40 with her first husband. She rates the happiness of her new marriage, her enjoyment of life, and her enjoyment of sex with her new 74-year-old husband as 1.

She comments that the oral sex is

delightful and the touching is perfect. We switched to a king-size bed after both of us had used twin beds all our married lives. . . . We sleep nude, often wrapped around each other. We may wake in the night and have sex. Sometimes now his penis is hardening. We are very much in love and know marriage is the right thing.

[My] children have been all for it since I announced what I was going to do. They are all established in their lives, and delighted that I have someone to be with and share my life. . . .

One further comment on intercourse versus oral sex. My [new] husband said in this way he [can] pleasure me and so get pleasure himself; and this is surely happening. I find that men who have real strong intercourse with orgasm turn right over in bed and go to sleep, thus forgetting the wife. So, this other way prolongs the fun.

A twice-married California woman, 68, is very conservative in her views. She strongly believes, for example, that communities should have the right to ban all pornographic materials and that laws against homosexuality should be enforced. She strongly disagrees with the statement that "it's okay for older people who are not married to have sexual relations," and she explains: "This stems from my strict upbringing by a widowed mother." (She did, however, become pregnant before her first marriage, and had an abortion.) She disapproves of masturbation, reporting that she herself has never masturbated. She describes herself as moderately religious, and she adds: "Prayers *have* helped me, and I firmly believe in spiritually healing prayers." She continues:

My first marriage was a mistake — a man who was kind and considerate prior to marriage turned into a beast and drunk who was unfaithful constantly. I felt the marriage vows tied me to him forever; but if I could do it all over again, I would have left him.

Forty years ago, when she was 28 years old, our respondent fell in love with a man also 28, and her love was reciprocated. The two neither married nor launched an affair, however, and the relationship lapsed. Then, ten years ago, when they were both 58, the two came together again. "The same *old* love remained — only perhaps even stronger." The two became lovers, and married "after my first husband died and his first wife died," the wife reports. That was not quite two years before she filled out our questionnaire.

"The feeling [that sex without marriage is wrong] stays with me," she explains, "although I did have relations with my present (second) husband before we were married. I did [but felt] guilty about it!"

This recently wedded wife, at age 68, rates her marital happiness, enjoyment of life, and enjoyment of sex with her new husband as 1.

Another participant in an autumnal marriage is a twice-married 81-year-old husband, retired in South Carolina on an income of between $15,000 and $20,000 a year. He has had a heart attack and takes medication to prevent a recurrence; he describes his health as fair — about average for his age. His first wife died three years ago, when he was 78. He promptly fell in love again — with a widow of 61. A year later they married.

Now, after two years of marriage, he and his wife have sex together a few times a month: Both think this is about right. Both consider the sexual side of their marriage "moderately important." He always initiates the activities leading to sex; both say they are satisfied with this arrangement. They are also satisfied with the variety of sexual activities in which they engage. He reports no problems in their marriage; she cites one problem, "health."

At 81, he reports two symptoms of diminishing potency, neither of which he views as serious: When fully erect, his penis is not as stiff as before, and it takes him longer to be able to have another erection after orgasm. His wife adds two others: It takes him longer to get an erection, and he more frequently loses his erection during sex.

Two major discrepancies emerge from this couple's reports. He says they both reach orgasm "almost every time"; she says that he *always* does and she *never* does. He rates his enjoyment of sex with her as 1; she rates her enjoyment of sex with him as 4. Nevertheless, both wife and husband rate the overall happiness of their marriage and their enjoyment of life as 1.

Another autumnal marriage is reported by a wife who married for the second time at 59. After eight years with her second husband, she writes as if they were still on their honeymoon.

"It is important to feel wanted and needed," she begins. "I have been fortunate to have remarried a very wonderful person. There were some [doubts at first] as to the sexual side of this step — however, it has been a rebirth of emotions, wonderful experiences, and . . . I am having a very full life."

She and her husband, now aged 67 and 68, have sex together two or three times a week — more often than she did at age 40 with her first husband. They both reach orgasm almost every time. She does not masturbate, explaining: "Fortunately, I have all the sex I need."

She rates her marital happiness, enjoyment of life, and enjoyment of sex with her husband as 1, and adds:

> Love continues to soar and soar and sexual relationships become intensified. Younger people should understand that there should be no concern over possible loss of sex feelings; they do *not* deteriorate.

To other older women contemplating an autumnal marriage, she gives this advice: "There will always be those who disapprove, but they will be overbalanced by the contentment, the sharing of sorrows and joys, and the many new friends you will meet."

Not all autumnal marriages, of course, are as happy as these. About seven years ago, one respondent, aged 55 and recently widowed, married a man then 65. She is his fourth wife. They live in an apartment in a New England town. She writes sardonically:

> After four wives, he *should* know something. He was less informed when we married than my son at age 14. He feels (as *most* men do) that he is a lover; I feel he knew as much when we married as a lone hermit in Alaska.

I *was* married to a *Lover;* now I'm married to a black-
smith.

On balance, however, such unhappy autumnal marriages are
few. Indeed, there appears to be little difference in the proportion
of happy marriages between wives and husbands married after 50
and those married earlier:

	Married before 50	Married after 50
Wives and husbands	(N=2,767)	(N=252)
Happily married	87%	90%
Unhappily married	13	10
	100%	100%

First marriage after 50

Most autumnal marriages are remarriages, of course, but a few respondents — too few to warrant tabulation — married for the first
time after 50. One woman, indeed, first married at age 69. Another
late-marrying wife reports:

My situation is different from most, since I preferred a
career to marriage. . . . Had single women been as accepted
in society then as now, I might have remained single.

At 48, however, she decided to get married, and "actively
sought ways to meet men." At 50 she had sex with a partner for
the first time in her life, and a few months later married a divorced
man of the same age.

That was twenty-two years ago. Now 73 and retired in the
Southwest, this woman rates her marital happiness as 2, her enjoyment of life as 4, and her enjoyment of sex with her husband
as 6.

She and her husband have sex together three times a week, but she seldom reaches orgasm; she doesn't know how often her husband reaches orgasm. "We prefer to have intercourse on schedule," she writes, "the same three nights [each] week."

Asked what she would do differently, she replies: "Considering everything as it happened, I would not change. My only regret is that I am not a very good wife, or housewife. My husband deserve a woman better prepared for marriage after [his] very unhappy [first] marriage."

Wife-much-younger or much-older marriages

As noted earlier, the median age for our wives is 60 and for our husbands 64. Such wife-younger marriages are customary in our culture, but there are exceptions.

There has traditionally been a prejudice against marriages with wide age differences. To gauge the extent of disapproval among our respondents, we asked whether they agree or disagree with these two statements:

"I think it's a mistake for an older man to marry a much younger woman."

"I think it's a mistake for an older woman to marry a much younger man."

Of those giving an opinion on an older man marrying a much younger woman, more than one-third of our women and more than one-quarter of our men declare themselves neutral. Among those who take a stand, the men are split virtually down the middle, half agreeing that such a marriage is a mistake and half disagreeing. A similar proportion of the women agrees that such a marriage is a mistake, but somewhat fewer women disagree.

Of those giving an opinion on an older woman marrying a much younger man, almost 30 percent of both our women and our men declare themselves neutral. Among those who take a stand, both the women and — to a somewhat lesser degree — the men who agree that such a marriage is a mistake greatly outnumber those who disagree.

"I think it's a mistake for an older man to marry a much younger woman."

	Women (N=1,792)		Men (N=2,374)	
Strongly agree	13%	} 35%	14%	} 36%
Moderately agree	22		22	
Neutral	36		28	
Moderately disagree	17	} 29%	22	} 37%
Strongly disagree	12		15	
	100%		101%	

"I think it's a mistake for an older woman to marry a much younger man."

	Women (N=1,793)		Men (N=2,372)	
Strongly agree	21%	} 45%	16%	} 41%
Moderately agree	24		25	
Neutral	29		28	
Moderately disagree	15	} 26%	19	} 31%
Strongly disagree	11		12	
	100%		100%	

Note that among our women as well as our men, a larger proportion believes a wife-much-older marriage is a mistake than believes that about a wife-much-younger marriage.

Our questionnaire returns make it possible to determine how 452 wife-much-younger or much-older marriages are actually faring. For statistical purposes, we chose to define a wife-much-younger marriage as one in which the wife is ten or more years younger than her husband and a wife-much-older marriage as one in which a wife is five or more years older than her husband.

For both kinds of marriage, the answer is the same: The older spouse is more likely to report being happily married and the younger spouse is less likely to report being happily married than is true for marriages where the spouses are approximately the same age:

	Relative age of spouses		
	Wife 10 or more years younger	Wife about the same age	Wife 5 or more years older
Wives	(N=90)	(N=1,062)	(N=48)
Happily married	83%	86%	90%
Unhappily married	17	14	10
	100%	100%	100%
Husbands	(N=257)	(N=1,525)	(N=52)
Happily married	91%	87%	81%
Unhappily married	9	13	19
	100%	100%	100%

In sum, a substantial age difference in either direction is not a barrier to marital happiness — though it does appear to reduce the marital happiness odds for the younger spouse.

The San Francisco wife in one wife-older marriage might be described as a "late bloomer." She did not even fall in love until she was 32 or 33. Then, at 44, "I married . . . a man who is 15 years my junior." Age 44 was also the year she reached menopause.

Today, at 65, she describes her 50-year-old husband as "handsome, talented, and very good and devoted to me. There was no one that I loved or thought I loved in my earlier years that could measure up to him so I would have to say that love in the later years of my life is infinitely better."

She says life is much better for her today than when she was 40 and single. She does complain of inadequate vaginal lubrication, and notes that her husband shows three of the six signs of declining potency — but they still have sex together a few times a month. She rates the happiness of her marriage as 1 and her enjoyment of sex with her husband as 2.

Meanwhile, what of her fifteen-year-younger husband? He confirms many of her statements — but reports five rather than three signs of declining potency. Like his wife, he rates his marital happiness as 1 and his enjoyment of marital sex as 2. Asked what he would do differently, he replies: "I would do nothing differently."

The wife in one wife-younger marriage was born in 1924. She writes:

> I was part of the first wave — the young adults of the 1940s who helped bring in the sexual revolution. I'm not sure it was all for the good. I had a very active sex life as a young woman; I would imagine I felt as free about sex as young women today. Yet strangely (or perhaps not), the first really deep sexual enjoyment came after I was married to my present husband and began to establish a close personal relationship — trust, affection, mutual dependency.

Her earlier experiences included four marriages, all of them short-lived, plus an unstated number of affairs. She entered into her current marriage when she was 27 and her new husband 46. She is now 54 and he 73. They live in a small Midwestern city. How is her fifth marriage faring?

After twenty-seven years with a husband nineteen years older, this wife rates her marital happiness, enjoyment of life, and enjoyment of sex with her husband as 1. They now have sex together about once a week; she reports she would like to have it more often. She reaches orgasm almost every time; her husband, usually. He reports all six signs of diminishing sexual potency — but she has noticed only four of them, and considers only one of them a "serious problem": that he more often loses his erection during sex nowadays.

This wife, despite her many earlier affairs, reports no extramarital sex in her present marriage, and comments:

> For me, anyway, casual sex is all right — better than nothing — but deep married love has it beat by a mile! How would I say this to my children? I suspect they know it by watching their parents live together happily. One son is marrying soon — to an exceptional girl. It should be a fine marriage; so maybe, without preaching, the message gets across.

A 70-year-old wife, married to a husband now 83, explains: "I was widowed at 32, and my energy and attention were of necessity directed to earning a living and rearing two children." Then, "having had no sexual activity for 16 years," she married a man thirteen years her senior. They live on the East Coast.

"Falling in love and marrying at age 48," she recalls, "was practically on a par with the thrill and excitement of my first marriage. In many ways, the added maturity was a distinct advantage. It has been a very happy marriage [for twenty-two years], and the fact that my husband [at 83] is very interested in and capable of having intercourse has contributed to our happiness."

A 51-year-old wife has been married for twenty-six years to a husband now 67. They live in their own home in the Southeast. She reports that during the early years of their marriage, sex was unsatisfactory; she was brought up with too many sexual hangups. "Trying to shift from holding back all the time before marriage — and then turning into a hot tomato all of a sudden after marriage — is hard to do," she comments.

She used to worry about too frequent pregnancies: "[I] enjoyed sex more after my husband had a vasectomy. I had five children first. I could relax more once the fear of pregnancy was taken away.

"Also, he started stimulating my genitals with his mouth, which brought me to more multiple orgasms." Asked what she would do differently, she replies, "I . . . wish I had let my husband stimulate my genitals orally early in our marriage."

In another wife-much-younger marriage, the husband is now 52. Four years ago his first wife died, and the following year he married his present wife, who is now 26. They live in their own home in upstate New York. He describes a problem that may be faced by other older men who marry a very young woman soon after a first wife's death:

> All the friends who had been associated with me and my first wife disassociated [themselves from] me and my second wife. . . . I feel that our age difference is a deterrent to making close friends. We do count as friends . . . people who were friends of my [present] wife before we married — but we see them infrequently.

"We are . . . very happy together," he continues, and he adds, "My second marriage is at least as fulfilling as my first."

A 50-year-old respondent writes of her grandfather who lived to a ripe old age:

> Marrying, at age 72, a woman half his age was one of the best things my grandfather ever did — for both of them. They had 18 good years together; and I know she feels it was well worth the two bad years at the end.

Quality of communications

The last of the nonsexual factors considered here — quality of communications between husband and wife — turns out to be the most important one.

We asked:

"In general, how would you characterize communications between you and your [spouse]?"

Wives and husbands who rate the quality of communications in their marriage as excellent or very good enjoy an astonishingly high proportion of happy marriages — the highest for any group in this study. Wives and husbands who report good, fair, or poor communications are much less likely to be happily married:

Wives and husbands	Excellent or very good communications (N=1,807)	Good, fair, or poor communications (N=1,216)
Happily married	98%	71%
Unhappily married	2	29
	100%	100%

Open communications between wife and husband thus provide an almost iron-clad guarantee of a happy marriage for our respondents. It is almost impossible for a couple to be unhappily married if communications between them are excellent or very good.

Note, however, that less-than-very-good communications do not inevitably condemn a couple to marital unhappiness. More than 850 of our respondents with good, fair, or poor communications are nevertheless happily married.

That open, constructive communications become increasingly important during the later years of a marriage is noted by several respondents — including a 55-year-old husband, married for thirty-five years, who writes:

When you are young, love is predominantly influenced by sexual activities. In later life, you still relate love to sex — but other things become more important. These things are companionship, doing things together, communicating [with] and relating to your wife.

A 70-year-old wife married for forty-three years, writes:

> [Nowadays] we travel together more, spend more evenings
> together at home reading, and we feel less need to entertain
> friends or relatives. . . . When we were young we bought
> fewer books, read less and discussed what we did read with
> more heat and less mature judgment, it seems to me. . . . We
> are more honest with each other [now] on likes and dislikes
> . . . and yet we are more considerate of each other's feelings.
> We really know each other better.

Communications need not always be verbal, of course — as
one husband points out: "Problems of all kinds are seen through
together. You have this background, and you communicate with
each other by a look, a touch, a feeling."

But for some wives and husbands, nonverbal communication,
however tender, is not enough. They need the communion of
verbal sharing, and love withers in its absence. Let us quote again
from the wife whose unhappy marriage is presented early in this
chapter:

> I find myself at a total loss for want of anything to talk
> about [with my husband]. We can spend the entire evening
> together — he staring at the boob-tube . . . I reading or
> needlepointing — and I can't think of one word to say to
> him even if you paid me a dollar a word.

Our review of these fifteen nonsexual factors has thus un-
earthed only one that is closely associated with marital happiness:
quality of communications between wife and husband. Six other
factors appear to show a slight or small association: education;
being employed or retired; degree of religious commitment;
health; first marriage versus remarriage; and marriage before versus after 50. The remaining factors show inconsistent patterns or
no differences worth noting.

Sexual factors and marital happiness

We asked our wives and husbands:

"How important is the sexual side of your [marriage] to you?"

More husbands than wives consider the sexual side of their marriage important; conversely, more wives consider the sexual side of little importance:

	Wives		*Husbands*	
	(N=1,177)		*(N=1,822)*	
Marital sex very important	30%		48%	
Moderately important	45	75%	39	87%
Of little importance	25		12	
	100%		99%	

Our questionnaire returns contain eloquent testimonials to the importance of marital sex during the later years. For example, a 74-year-old husband writes, "It's amazing how much sex satisfaction can be had with a very understanding mate, *especially* after age 60."

A wife, aged 60, writes: "When I look back on the sexual aspects of my own 36-year-marriage, I see a picture of gradual growth in sexual pleasures — beginning with a warm husband and a somewhat frigid wife! And, at the age of 60, I feel there may still be new wonders to discover with my spouse."

A husband, aged 65 and married for thirty-nine years, comments: "I was surprised that our sex life kept on being enjoyable. I thought when I was younger that by my age (65) it would all be over. [Sex is] less intense and less frequent [now], but very enjoyable and satisfying."

A 56-year-old wife, married for thirty-four years, reports: "In our later years my husband and I are having a much more exciting love and sex relationship than when we were younger. I expect a good part of that is due to the absence of responsibility for children, having more time to spend together doing things only we enjoy — plus we take great pleasure in each other's company and conversation."

A husband of 55, married thirty-six years, writes: "Younger people should know that love and sexual relationships change as they grow older. Not necessarily do they become less enjoyable, because I believe they become more enjoyable ... deeper, warmer, more considerate, and the sexual relationship becomes less wild and animal-like but becomes more tender and has deeper feeling."

Another 56-year-old wife, married thirty-seven years, writes: "Love is more stable in later years. You have learned each other's shortcomings and don't worry about each other's love; even if one doesn't show it, you know it's there.... Sex is love and is enhanced by kindness and tenderness throughout the day. I don't feel that sex should be used to end an argument but rather to prevent an argument."

A 59-year-old husband, married for thirty-five years, writes:

The mass-media Youth Cult is so dominant that retirement-age couples often feel that normal sex lives are unseemly and improper. America's best-kept secret: that the "bangs" are just as powerful in the [fifties] (I can't speak of later decades) as in the twenties. This unexpected discovery is a tremendous morale-booster, helping to keep a retired man from seeing himself as a piece of partial human wreckage — an object of pity who is dragging himself through years of unrelieved deprivation and depression.

In marked contrast, one wife reports: "Sex was never a big deal anyway, but I enjoyed it once things were started. Now I want to get it over with as quickly as possible."

This wife is 59 years old and has been married for thirty-six years. She rates both her enjoyment of life and her enjoyment of sex as 7, "not at all enjoyable." She and her husband have sex, she says, a few times a month; she considers this "too often." She says her husband reaches orgasm every time and she never does. If she were starting over, "I would try to find a husband who did not have sex on his mind so much of the time. . . . He is ready any time of the day or night." Asked about masturbation, she replies: "OK for those who want to. I would feel foolish."

Asked what younger people should know about sex in the later years, she answers: "They should know that sex doesn't 'turn off' after the 50th birthday — as far as the men are concerned."

Of the scores of sexual factors explored by our questionnaire, we have selected ten to determine their relationship with marital happiness. Most of the ten, as we shall see, are more closely associated with marital happiness than any of the nonsexual factors reviewed above — except for quality of marital communications.

Having sexual intercourse with spouse

Eighty percent of our wives and 77 percent of our husbands report that they are currently having marital intercourse. These wives and husbands are far more likely to report happy marriages than the wives and husbands who are *not* having sexual intercourse with their spouse.

	Having intercourse with spouse	Not having intercourse with spouse
Wives	(N = 986)	(N = 198)
Happily married	90%	67%
Unhappily married	10	33
	100%	100%
Husbands	(N = 1,443)	(N = 377)
Happily married	92%	71%
Unhappily married	8	29
	100%	100%

Enjoyment of sex with spouse

We asked our respondents to indicate the number on our 1-to-7 scale "that best represents how enjoyable for you sex with your [spouse] is at the present time."

One thousand twenty-six wives and 1,544 husbands responded. We condensed their responses in the same way we measured marital happiness at the beginning of the chapter: 1, 2, and 3 indicating a high degree of enjoyment, and 4, 5, 6, and 7 a low degree of enjoyment. When thus grouped, 76 percent of the wives and 87 percent of the husbands rate their enjoyment of sex with their spouse as high. Conversely, 24 percent of the wives and 13 percent of the husbands rate their enjoyment as low.

Both wives and husbands who report high enjoyment of sex with spouse also report a very high proportion of happy marriages. Conversely, low enjoyment of sex with spouse turns out to be an extremely important predicter of marital unhappiness:

	High enjoyment of sex with spouse	*Low enjoyment of sex with spouse*
Wives	*(N = 767)*	*(N = 247)*
Happily married	95%	68%
Unhappily married	5	32
	100%	100%
Husbands	*(N = 1,326)*	*(N = 207)*
Happily married	95%	62%
Unhappily married	5	38
	100%	100%

Is it possible for wives and husbands to enjoy sex together even though they consider themselves unhappily married? The answer is yes — and it is surprisingly common: Of the 116 unhappily married wives and 145 unhappily married husbands who provide data, 32 percent of the wives and 46 percent of the husbands report high enjoyment of sex with their spouse.

Frequency of sex with spouse

We asked both wives and husbands who are having sex with their spouse how frequently they have sex. Here is what they told us:

	Wives	*Husbands*
	(N = 1,016)	(N = 1,515)
Sex with spouse more than once a week	28%	25%
Once a week or less frequently	72	75
	100%	100%

While marital happiness, as we have seen, is closely linked to "having sex with spouse" and "enjoying sex with spouse," it is less closely linked to "frequency of sex with spouse":

	Sex with spouse more than once a week	*Sex with spouse once a week or less*
Wives and husbands	(N = 662)	(N = 1,869)
Happily married	94%	89%
Unhappily married	6	11
	100%	100%

Satisfaction with frequency of sex

We asked our respondents if they are satisfied with the frequency of sex with their spouse. Of the 1,034 wives who responded, 77 percent report it's about right, 18 percent say it's not frequent enough, and 5 percent say it's too frequent. The proportion of un-happily married wives is exceedingly high among wives who want less sex:

Wives	It's about right (N=780)	It's not frequent enough (N=188)	It's too frequent (N=50)
Happily married	93%	84%	58%
Unhappily married	7	16	42
	100%	100%	100%

Of our 1,533 husbands who responded to the same question, 59 percent report that the frequency of sex with their wife is about right, while 41 percent want sex more often. Only eight husbands feel that sex with their wives is too frequent.

The relationship of marital happiness to frequency of marital sex for our husbands is similar to the relationship for our wives, shown in the table above — except for the dearth of husbands who want less sex:

Husbands	It's about right (N=896)	It's not frequent enough (N=619)	It's too frequent (N=8)
Happily married	95%	84%	7 husbands
Unhappily married	5	16	1 husband
	100%	100%	

Difficulties may arise, of course, when one partner wants sex more frequently while the other partner thinks they already are having sex too frequently. A 62-year-old wife and her 69-year-old husband provide an example. They have been married for forty-one years, and live in an apartment in Boston. The wife says they have sex about once a week and this is too frequent for her. The husband says they have sex two or three times a week — and this is not frequent enough for him. Both agree that he reaches orgasm almost every time, and that she never does. The wife says that since age 50 she has engaged in seven of the twenty sexual activities listed in our questionnaire and has enjoyed none of them; the husband says he has enjoyed the activities they have engaged in and would like to try all of the others. Both agree that the husband always initiates the activities leading to sex. The husband writes:

> My wife has no interest whatever in sexual activity; however, she permits me to have intercourse — with no participation on her part. If she participated and would initiate sexual activities, even infrequently, things would be much better and I would be completely happy.

In addition to sex with his wife, this husband masturbates once a month or less frequently to relieve sexual tension; he sometimes has fantasies during sex with his wife and often has fantasies during masturbation. Asked about the content of his fantasies, he replies:

> One time when we were both much younger, my wife was lying on me with my penis in her mouth and her vagina over my mouth. We both had an orgasm at the same time. This was my most satisfying and enjoyable sexual experience. I dream about or fantasize about this experience quite often — but not, of course, with any comparable enjoyment.

His wife leaves her Comment Pages blank.

Frequency of orgasm

It was often alleged in past decades that having orgasms may be important for the marital happiness of husbands, but not for the marital happiness of wives.* Our data offer no support whatever

---

* See, for example, "I'm Sorry, Dear," by the late Dr. Leslie H. Farber, a psychoanalyst, in *An Analysis of Human Sexual Response*, Ruth and Edward Brecher, eds. (Boston: Little, Brown, 1966).

for this hypothesis. Wives as well as husbands who always, almost always, or usually experience orgasm during sex with their spouse are more likely to report happy marriages than those who reach orgasm less often:

	Orgasm every time, almost every time, or usually	*Orgasm half the time, seldom, or never*
Wives	(N=631)	(N=373)
Happily married	93%	83%
Unhappily married	7	17
	100%	100%
Husbands	(N=1,423)	(N=104)
Happily married	91%	84%
Unhappily married	9	16
	100%	100%

Communications about sex

As noted earlier, the quality of communications between wife and husband is a very powerful predicter of marital happiness. So, more specifically, is the quality of communications about sexual matters.

We asked:

"How comfortable are you discussing sexual matters with your [spouse]?"

Husbands and wives who are uncomfortable discussing sex with their spouse are much more likely to be unhappily married than are those who are comfortable.

Discussing sex with spouse

	Very comfortable or comfortable	Uncomfortable or very uncomfortable
Wives	(N=928)	(N=253)
Happily married	93%	64%
Unhappily married	7	36
	100%	100%
Husbands	(N=1,451)	(N=371)
Happily married	92%	70%
Unhappily married	8	30
	100%	100%

Quite a few of our married respondents comment on the importance of open sexual discussions. A 56-year-old husband in Washington State, married for thirty-six years, says it all in a single, eloquent sentence:

"With my wife, the strong-growing love and increasing openness about everything, especially sex, has made my life increasingly worthwhile."

A 63-year-old wife stresses the adverse impact on a marriage when sexual discussion is blocked. Married for thirty-seven years, she reports that for many of those years she was unable to reach orgasm during intercourse with her husband. Now that she has learned how, she reaches orgasm almost every time. Asked what she would do differently, she replies: "I would have discussed sex more openly with my husband. I would have started genital manipulation sooner."

A 68-year-old wife, married for forty-two years, writes similarly from New Hampshire: "I refrained from obtaining adequate knowledge regarding sex. Therefore, I lacked the proper information to really enjoy sex in my younger years." Her husband tried to initiate discussions of sex but she resisted. Then, she continues,

"I finally took time to read a book and discovered what my husband *tried* to tell me was true." She is now comfortable talking about sex with her husband — and he is very comfortable talking about sex with her.

Let us recall the comment of the 64-year-old husband quoted earlier in our discussion of remarriage: "Among the satisfactions of my present union is the capacity — thanks to my wife's freedom from inhibitions — to discuss intimate features of [our] sexual relationship with her."

A New York City couple had a sexual problem through the first nineteen years of their twenty-nine-year marriage. The wife explains:

"I have to admit it wasn't until the last ten years — through great efforts on my husband's part — [that] he has been able to get me to discuss . . . the things I like him to do with my body in our sexual relations. It was a hang-up of mine [which did not allow me] to speak out and tell him what aroused me the most in our love-making." She adds that "there are times even now when I can't blurt it out" — but she has apparently blurted out enough to improve their sexual encounters: both she and her husband now rate their enjoyment of sex together as 1.

Asked what he would do differently, her husband thinks back on those years before the two learned to communicate about sex, and writes: "I would attempt experimentation at an earlier stage of marriage. Male sexual education would be of enormous help. My ignorance prevented the pleasure not experienced until later in life."

In contrast, some respondents still cannot discuss sex comfortably with their spouse but want to — and wish they knew how. One is a 66-year-old California wife who, like a number of our other wives, can always reach orgasm through masturbation but never through sexual intercourse. She writes:

I wish I could bring myself to tell my husband I masturbate, but I can't. His efforts to stimulate my clitoris fail. Perhaps I could do it myself [during sex with him] and reach an orgasm but I *cannot* do *this*. Perhaps it is a guilt feeling from childhood. Without this [guilt] feeling, I think I could have been a "sexy lady" and given my husband much enjoyment. As it is, I am a nervous woman and often take tranquilizers because of my "keyed up" feeling.

A Louisiana wife of 66, married to a husband of 64, says they have sex together once a week but she doesn't enjoy it very much. She and her husband both say that they feel uncomfortable talking about sex together. Asked what she'd do differently, she replies, "I'd discuss my feelings about sex with my spouse so that we could understand each other's likes and dislikes more."

A Pennsylvania husband, aged 65, says he is very comfortable discussing sex with his wife — but it makes *her* very uncomfortable. "I would love to discuss our sexual life but she wants no part of it," he writes. "I would deeply appreciate my wife taking the initiative more often; it would give her an opportunity to express her wishes."

There are two points in particular on which he would like his wife to speak frankly. One is her answer to the question, "What really turns you on?" He thinks this Consumers Union study should "encourage wives to be more specific about this with their husbands and *vice versa.* . . . Maybe before-and-after cases could be detailed where the sex of a couple was 'all right,' satisfactory in every respect, but then after [frank talks about sex] it was so much more [enjoyable] that it became unbelievable — and why didn't it happen sooner?"

The other issue on which he would like his wife to speak frankly concerns her orgasms. After forty years of marriage, he is still puzzled about this. "I, of course, experience orgasm every time," he writes, "but I can't speak for my wife. . . . She gives a good indication [of orgasm] every time — but there is never any comment from her." Since he has never had sex with any other woman, it is impossible for him to know whether her "indication" is really an orgasm or not.

We cannot get the answer from his wife's questionnaire; she answered none of our questions about sex. According to him, "She feels that [answering CU's sexual questions] would not be 'nice and proper.' . . . I am afraid that after all these years that attitude would be very difficult to change. Any suggestions in your book would be appreciated. Thank you."

A 66-year-old husband observes: "Most partners go through life playing a guessing game. By the time they really know what turns [each other] on, it's turn-off time."

A 72-year-old widower, living alone, recalls with sadness the years of his marriage:

> I regret the lack of open and frank discussion with my wife about many of our problems, sexual and otherwise. If she were here, I would correct that unfortunate situation. I have learned much from other partners since she died; they have been better informed, and [have] free and open personalities. My wife, too, was a dear person — but we were uneducated about physiological matters.

A dramatic example of failure of sexual communications which seems *not* to have impaired overall marital happiness is supplied by a 62-year-old Iowa wife. She has been married for forty years to a husband also 62. Both rate their marital happiness as 1. The husband says he is "uncomfortable" discussing sex with his wife, but supplies no details. The wife writes that she is "very uncomfortable" discussing sex with him — and she provides a wealth of details:

"Our love is very real . . . ," she writes.

> We admire each other and take pride in our accomplishments. We are affectionate and rarely have any bad disagreements. I'm happy when he comes home from work and he says he looks forward to it with joy. I would say our love is deeper and steadier than when we were younger.

Nevertheless, she continues, there is a major flaw in their relationship. "We have never *talked* a lot about our feelings and I don't think we ever will (I wish it were otherwise but don't have much hope). So I have learned to interpret his actions and hope he understands mine."

If she could start her marriage over, she continues, she

would try to talk and explain [my sexual] likes and dislikes more; but [my] husband was always of the opinion that it was "crude" to talk about it, even with me, or especially with me. Once I wrote him a letter — two pages — to try to make him understand my feelings. He must have thought I had flipped — no response, no change in anything. Silence. [I] have wished he was more aware of my needs, but have settled for what I can get.

This wife also tells us exactly what she would tell her husband if she could. Sometimes, she writes, sex with him is wholly rewarding and results in simultaneous orgasm —

but more often than not my husband has ejaculated and is spent while I am still needing action. Frustration for me is the result — which doesn't make me want to try again soon and can spoil my whole next day unless I work hard to overcome it.

Is this the way it is with the average man and woman? He is quick to arouse and goes rapidly to fulfillment. And often, even when I have a good start, and am building strongly toward a wonderful, delicious finish, he is *done*, leaving me with nothing.

I find this very hard to deal with. Is it possible for a man to delay his climax so as to bring his partner along better? If not, can't he wait to enter until she is closer to fulfillment? "Good guys finish last" would be a nice motto.

I'm afraid he thinks of me as cold, unresponsive, etc., etc., when it is just that I need more preparation than he does — *much more.*

One other thing: In the intensity of his need and with the strength of his muscles, I get a massage more often than the light, tender stimulation I need. This is one thing I have tried to tell him, but he forgets. . . . All my sensitive nerves seem to be on the surface; . . . hard rubbing, digging, or squeezing turns me off. *Depth* of thrusting does not help, rather the repetition of the motion — not speed, either, just more of it.

In fact, I would rather be on top and control that myself. I
hate to be mashed and held down hard.

She concludes: "I wish something could be done short of *talking* about it. That would be disastrous. I have hopes that this survey will result in better experiences for us. He reads everything
CU publishes! So write it all! We need it!"

One Midwestern respondent, a 58-year-old wife married for
sixteen years, writes that she is very uncomfortable talking about
sex with her husband and doesn't enjoy sex with him:

I try to psychoanalyze myself. Why am I so reluctant about
sex now? I mentally fight sex most of the time, avoid situations that could lead to sex. Yet I'd love to have a good sex
life — it's written about enough! He fantasizes and talks
about it and I'm turned off. I detest the awkward positions,
and when I find a comfortable position, it doesn't last long
and he is moving me.

The only time I "cooperate" sometimes is to help him
get it over with. That's wrong, and I know it. I feel so "used"
when it's over. At night I can sort of sleep it off and forget it;
but if it happens in the morning, I'm depressed and withdrawn for days, it seems (like now).

He upsets easily, and things can throw him off — like if
I'm "over-helpful" or . . . if I do start to think I can bring it
off and work hard. So I don't tell him what he does wrong
for me. I guess I feel he should sense what pleases and
doesn't please me. I know that's dumb — but I can't hurt his
pride by saying anything, I just can't.

I don't think he knows whether I'm fulfilled or not. Once
in a great while I can climax — but it is work and such an
effort of concentration, and then he's usually bruised. And I
wonder why he can't tell that that time it's "different" for
me! So I just go along, and will probably end up being coun-
selled some day.

I seem to find fault a lot during everyday living — so
how can I tell him about sex? Of course they're tied to-

gether; . . . if I were happier with sex I wouldn't be fault-finding during the day, so there's a nice circle. At least I know it and can work on improvement.

I'm depressed just writing about all this, but it seems a good opportunity to get it off my chest.

Interest in sex

We asked:

"How would you describe your present interest in sex?"

Husbands with a strong or moderate interest in sex and those whose interest is weak or absent are equally likely to be happily married:

Husbands	Interest strong or moderate (N=1,586)	Interest weak or absent (N=224)
Happily married	87%	87%
Unhappily married	13	13
	100%	100%

Among wives, in marked contrast, interest in sex, or lack of interest, is a powerful predictor of marital happiness. Among wives whose interest in sex is weak or absent, the proportion reporting a happy marriage is strikingly low:

Wives	Interest strong or moderate (N=831)	Interest weak or absent (N=338)
Happily married	91%	76%
Unhappily married	9	24
	100%	100%

Ease of sexual arousal

We asked:

"How easily do you become sexually aroused at the present time?"

Like interest in sex, ease of sexual arousal appears to have no association with the marital happiness of our husbands. Among our wives, however, those who can become sexually aroused only with difficulty, or who do not become sexually aroused at all, are much more likely to report an unhappy marriage than wives who readily become sexually aroused:

	Very or moderately easy	*Difficult, or don't become sexually aroused at all*
Husbands	(N=1,400)	(N=390)
Happily married	88%	87%
Unhappily married	12	13
	100%	100%
Wives	(N=692)	(N=417)
Happily married	92%	79%
Unhappily married	8	21
	100%	100%

Who usually initiates the activities leading to sex?

In the generation now over 50, most males were brought up to take the lead in everything from dancing to sexual intercourse; most females were brought up to wait until they were asked — and then to follow. We still find strong reminders of that tradition in current marital behavior.

One thousand fifty-eight wives and 1,551 husbands answered both the who-initiates-sex and the marital-happiness questions.

Sixty-three percent of these wives and 68 percent of these husbands say that in their marriage, the husband always or usually takes the sexual lead. Only 5 percent say that the wife always or usually takes the lead. The remainder — 32 percent of the wives and 27 percent of the husbands — report that wife and husband take the lead about equally often.

As shown in the table below, marital happiness is most commonly reported in marriages where the initiation of sexual activities is shared about equally.

	Wife always or usually initiates	Husband always or usually initiates	Wife and husband initiate about equally often
Wives	(N=57)	(N=655)	(N=330)
Happily married	84%	86%	94%
Unhappily married	16	14	6
	100%	100%	100%
Husbands	(N=68)	(N=1,053)	(N=419)
Happily married	85%	90%	93%
Unhappily married	15	10	7
	100%	100%	100%

A wife of 63, married for forty-one years, writes: "It would please me to initiate sexual activity — but [I] know my husband prefers otherwise. No doubt at times I do initiate it, but not as a direct approach."

A 71-year-old husband, married for thirty-eight years to a wife now 61, explains why he lets his wife make the first move:

Since my wife has to use vaginal treatment [lubricating jelly], it is better that she decides time of contact. Also, since her sexual receptivity is more variable than mine, better rapport is achieved if she decides.

Satisfaction with variety of sexual activities

We asked:

"How do you feel about the variety of sexual activities in your relationship?"

Only nineteen of our wives and five of our husbands say that they would like *less* variety in their sexual activities. Twelve percent of our wives and 35 percent of our husbands would like *more* variety.

As might be expected, the wives and husbands who are satisfied with the variety of sexual activities are much more likely to be happily married than those who would like more variety:

	Like things the way they are	Would like more sexual variety
Wives	(N=858)	(N=146)
Happily married	91%	79%
Unhappily married	9	21
	100%	100%
Husbands	(N=868)	(N=662)
Happily married	95%	85%
Unhappily married	5	15
	100%	100%

In sum, we have found that all ten of the sexual factors reviewed above are associated with marital happiness and unhappiness for wives; eight of the ten are associated with marital happiness and unhappiness for husbands. The strongest association for both wives and husbands is between enjoying sex with one's spouse and marital happiness. The association with marital happiness is also strong for having sex with one's spouse, satisfaction with frequency of marital sex, and feeling comfortable discussing sex with one's spouse. The association with marital happiness is clear but less strong for frequency of sex with one's spouse, frequency of orgasm during marital sex, initiation of marital sex by both spouses about equally often, and satisfaction with variety of activities in marital sex. Having a strong or moderate interest in sex and becoming sexually aroused easily are associated with marital happiness for wives; they appear to make no difference in the marital happiness of husbands.

We reported earlier that only 12 percent of our husbands and 25 percent of our wives consider the sexual side of their marriage to be of little importance. Let us now reconsider the importance of marital sex from a fresh perspective: How do the happily married differ from the unhappily married with respect to the importance they give to marital sex? Here are the data:

Wives	Happily married (N=1,004)		Unhappily married (N=156)	
Marital sex very important	33%	} 80%	13%	} 46%
Moderately important	47		33	
Of little importance	21		54	
	101%		100%	

Husbands	(N=1,587)		(N=217)	
Marital sex very important	48%	} 88%	49%	} 84%
Moderately important	40		35	
Of little importance	12		16	
	100%		100%	

Note that the vast majority of both our happily and our unhappily married husbands consider the sexual side of their marriage important. The same is true for our happily married wives. Among our *unhappily* married wives, however, the data are strikingly different:

   Most of our unhappily married wives consider the sexual side of their marriage to be of little importance. No other factor in this study, sexual or nonsexual, even approaches this sex-is-not-important factor as a predictor of marital unhappiness for wives. Nor is there any factor for husbands that even approaches this as a predictor of marital unhappiness.

FAITHFUL VERSUS ADULTEROUS MARRIAGES

Adultery is commonly believed both to cause and to arise out of marital unhappiness. Do the experiences of our husbands and wives confirm these beliefs?

Marital fidelity is the common pattern of behavior among our married respondents. Many factors buttress that fidelity.

One is the explicit vow, "forsaking all others," in the traditional wedding ceremony. Adultery is a sin in most religions, prohibited by the Seventh Commandment for Catholics, Protestants, and Jews alike. Until the 1960s, adultery was also a criminal offense in all states — and it remains a criminal offense in most states, though the adultery laws are rarely enforced. In the states now lacking laws against adultery, the state legislatures have not overtly repealed the old laws; instead, in the course of a general revision of their criminal codes, they have incidentally and quietly left out of the new codes criminal penalties for adultery, oral and anal sex, homosexual acts, and other sexual acts between consenting adults in private.

Adultery, moreover, is still a ground for divorce in states that have not abolished all grounds for divorce and substituted "no-fault" divorce procedures. In several states, indeed, adultery was for many years the principal ground for divorce.

Wives and husbands known to be engaged in adultery have been subject to widespread social condemnation. Traditionally, this has fallen much more heavily on the adulterous wife — but husbands have not escaped unscathed. Some employers have fired or refused to promote adulterous husbands, and some insurance companies have refused to insure them. (This is no doubt less common today than a generation ago.)

With all these religious, legal, social, and economic penalties against adultery, it is hardly surprising that only 95 (8 percent) of our 1,245 wives report engaging in adultery since 50. Among our husbands, adultery is nearly three times as prevalent — but still a minority activity: 429 (23 percent) of our 1,895 husbands report adultery since 50.

No doubt our adultery rates for both wives and husbands would be higher if many who formerly engaged in adultery had not by now secured a divorce or been divorced by their spouse. Moreover, we did not ask about adultery before age 50; no doubt some wives and husbands engaged in it then but abandoned the practice before 50.

When we compare our adulterous and our faithful wives on seven measures, as shown in the table below, we find the biggest difference to be between wives who report a very high (1 on our 1-to-7 scale) enjoyment of sex; the proportion of adulterous wives is much larger. Somewhat larger proportions of adulterous wives also report an annual family income of $25,000 or more, college degrees, and excellent or very good health. There is no appreciable difference between adulterous and faithful wives with respect to life enjoyment. Being happily married appears to be a strong deterrent to adultery among our wives, and being religious an even more powerful deterrent. In the table the factor most closely associated with adultery comes first and the factor most closely associated with fidelity last:

	Adulterous wives (N=95)	Difference in percentage points	Faithful wives (N=1,097)
Very high enjoyment of sex	54%	−20	34%
Annual family income of $25,000 or more	60%	−12	48%
College graduate	55%	−10	45%
Health excellent or very good	71%	−10	61%
Very high enjoyment of life	87%	−1	86%
Happily married	72%	+15	87%
Very or moderately religious	38%	+22	60%

Among our husbands, as shown in the table below, the differences between the adulterous and the faithful are smaller than among the wives, and the order of factors is different. An annual family income of $25,000 or more is the factor most closely associated with adultery; a happy marriage is the factor most closely associated with fidelity. Among husbands as among wives, similar proportions of the adulterous and the faithful report a high enjoyment of life. Being religious seems a less powerful deterrent to adultery among husbands than among wives:

	Adulterous husbands (N=429)	Difference in percentage points	Faithful husbands (N=1,392)
Annual family income of $25,000 or more	60%	−10	50%
Very high enjoyment of sex	57%	−7	50%
Health excellent or very good	70%	−6	64%
College graduate	65%	−5	60%
Very high enjoyment of life	89%	0	89%
Very or moderately religious	42%	+9	51%
Happily married	75%	+16	91%

Why some wives and husbands stay faithful

The religious, legal, social, and economic penalties against adultery cited above no doubt help keep some spouses from engaging in extramarital sex. Dearth of acceptable or available partners may be another factor. But the reasons given by our respondents are for the most part much more personal; they seem to arise directly out of the circumstances of each particular marriage.

"I cannot approve of sex outside marriage," writes a wife of 54. "That is 'defiling' my marriage bed whether it be done by my husband or me."

A second 54-year-old wife echoes these views: "Sex is such an intimate part of our marriage, I could not help but feel the marriage diminished if either of us had sex with someone else."

A 65-year-old wife writes:

I find my love for my husband has more depth, a stronger feeling and mellowed like rare wine. If either partner of the marriage has to seek outside for sex, then that marriage should be ended.

Other wives report that they have remained faithful — but express some small regrets. An example is this 70-year-old wife: "At times I regret having known only one man sexually; but if I had my life to live over, I would probably do the same."

"I sometimes wish I had had more heterosexual experience," a 56-year-old wife writes. "I have not done so out of loyalty to my husband but would have liked to."

A 67-year-old wife recalls:

I tried to get my husband's permission for outside sex after he could no longer function. He was shocked — and refused! I have too much respect for him, and we together have other "fun activities" — so it isn't important. Our being together *is* important.

A 52-year-old wife muses:

Even now, I feel sometimes I would like to have known what intercourse would have been like with another man — other than my husband. Maybe I would have had an orgasm. I never have with my husband.

Our faithful husbands express a similar range of views. One writes, at age 59, that "trust and fidelity outweigh the satisfaction of conquest and change of partners that seem so attracting." Another, 55, says:

I have a very healthy and active sex life with my wife. After being married for 35 years, I feel that my sex life now is better than ever before. In view of this situation, I have never found it necessary to seek activity outside my marriage.

A husband of the same age writes:

If the husband wishes sex outside of marriage . . . the wife should have the same prerogative, which I doubt many men would accept. Marriage is more fruitful and fulfilling if there is no outside sex by either spouse.

A deeply religious 60-year-old Georgia husband begins by expressing a very strict moral code. He is one of the few who cite a religious basis for his continuing fidelity:

I believe strongly that the moral rules of the Bible were given to us for our own good in *this* life. . . . I condemn adultery, and annulment if there has been sexual intercourse.

He then backtracks a step or two:

In certain circumstances, I concede that bigamy, if it could be accepted by the original wife, might be practical if it were not illegal. . . . I'm thinking of cases where a wife becomes insane, or becomes physically incapable of a wife's role — and the husband still needs a wife.

He does not comment on the converse situation — a wife who "still needs" a husband if her husband should become "physically incapable."

He also notes: "I admit [I] probably would enjoy a new relationship if it could comply fully with my Biblical moral standards."

A faithful 50-year-old Chicago husband says he would engage in extramarital sex if the opportunity came along:

[My] wife never was enthusiastic about sex. About five or six years ago, she began to say it was "undignified" or "like animals" or "not suitable at our age" and gradually stopped completely. . . . Because of the above, I would feel justified in having sex with someone else, but never have — mainly because I don't know how to find a partner without fear of discovery, embarrassment, etc.

A 70-year-old husband whose wife has been physically unable to engage in intercourse for some years writes from New England:

I have had opportunities to meet women for the purpose of sexual liaisons but have neglected to do so for fear or lack of courage. I regret not having availed myself of these opportunities and vow in the future to be more forthright, but. . . .

A 52-year-old New York City husband describes his wife as "a cook supreme . . . wise, frugal, level-headed, a wonderful mother, never a nag, hard-working, healthy, trusting, never demanding . . . all these good things but NOT sexy." She just doesn't like sex, he says. Under these circumstances, should he seek sex outside his marriage? His answer:

Religious and moral feeling conflict with personal feelings. . . . Adultery is the breaking of a promise or vow not just to the partner but more important, to yourself. A man's word should be the most sacred and honorable thing a man possesses. . . .

Then he turns from ethical to practical considerations:

If your wife finds out, everything's gone. The "other woman" is never satisfied with what she has. Altogether too many problems. "Thus conscience does make cowards of us all."

He adds one more detail: "Have I ever fantasized sex with another? You bet!"

A 54-year-old Texas husband sadly reports that his wife is not sexually aroused by his efforts. He continues:

It has occurred to me many times to have an affair but I have never done so. My reasons for contemplating this action are (1) to prove that I am still viable sexually; (2) [to prove] that I could be attractive to another female; (3) [to prove] that my technique was adequate . . . ; (4) to test my theory that some other woman would be more easily aroused by my sexual advances. I also fear this sort of encounter to the extent that I cannot tolerate rejection in any form. On a higher level, I firmly believe in the institution of marriage, family and all that this entails. Furthermore, my wife would not be understanding or compassionate to this sort of frailty.

He sometimes fantasizes sex with another woman. Why does he not live out this fantasy? "Too timid, I guess."

Next, let us quote from an unhappily married 55-year-old husband whose chief regret is that he married the wrong woman, and who appears to be on the verge of his first affair. His is an almost classic statement of what is often called the male "midlife crisis":

At the present stage of my life I am preoccupied with desires and fantasies of having a tempestuous, passionate affair with a beautiful, sexy young thing before it's too late. This is due not only to normal resistance to aging but [to] the gnawing feeling that I've missed something important in my younger years.

A happily married 57-year-old husband reports similarly on *his* midlife crisis:

After 50 you begin to feel you're missing something [if] you've never had any extramarital relationships. Even when [a] teenager, no sex with opposite sex until marriage. You feel you may not have much time left and you want to try something different and dangerous. It makes you feel excited and young again. It also does cause some problems of getting involved with other people and their problems. It also increases your responsibilities.

In short, the reasons given by our respondents for not engaging in adultery range from love and honor to timidity and lack of opportunity. While there may be subtle differences in detail and emphasis, the fidelity of wives and of husbands appear to have much in common.

Why some wives and husbands seek (and find) extramarital sex

We had expected to compile an anthology of reasons given by our adulterous respondents for engaging in outside sex — paralleling the reasons given above for refraining. Such reasons might include a spouse who is no longer physically able to have sex, marital incompatibility, boredom with marriage, a desire for variety, a feeling that life is slipping past, and so on. Some respondents, as we shall see, do give such reasons, but for quite a few others, adultery "just happens" — and for still others, it arises out of a complex set of circumstances that cannot be summarized simply.

Adultery takes two markedly different forms. Many of our adulterous wives and husbands have engaged since 50 in the activity commonly known as *cheating* — sex outside marriage without the knowledge or consent of the spouse. Others have engaged in sex outside their marriage with the knowledge and sometimes with the consent of their spouse. In a few marriages, indeed, adultery is a mutual and cooperative enterprise. We shall consider these forms of extramarital sex separately.

Wives who cheat

By far the longest-lived extramarital affair in our sample was described in chapter 1 — that of the 74-year-old widow whose affair has lasted for fifty-two years so far, "through two marriages on my part, one on his, and long, long separations in distance and time."

Another long-lived affair is described by a wife now 75, married for fifty years and living in an apartment on the West Coast. Early in her marriage, she and her husband both engaged in extramarital sexual adventures. "At first we were quite frank about these, but later, realizing that it did no good to tell and [that telling] tended to make us insecure and jealous, [we] kept any such extramarital activity from each other. The extramarital affairs were good experiences, and brief" — with one exception.

Back in 1939, during the eleventh year of her marriage, when she was 36, she had a full-fledged, romantic, falling-in-love experience with a married man of 29. They launched an affair, which has so far lasted for thirty-nine years. He is still married to his wife and she to her husband. Our respondent and her husband discontinued sexual activities eighteen years ago because of her physical changes (she has diabetes) and because both lost interest — but at 75 she continues to have sex with her 68-year-old lover once a month (mostly) or several times a month (when possible). She reports he always reaches orgasm; she, about half the time.

Neither she nor her partner, she says, "want to upset the applecart or hurt current spouse. We manage." She describes her marriage as "moderately satisfactory, happy," rating it as 2. Her enjoyment of sex with her lover, "is highly satisfactory, and private." She rates it as 1.

During the thirty-nine years of her affair, she has "cheated" on her lover on only one occasion. It "occurred many years ago when both marriage relationship and love relationship were at very low ebb with uncertainty for the future." She regrets this one slip from fidelity to her lover, and says that she now has no interest in outside sexual activity with anyone except him.

She ends with a general comment:

Morton Hunt in *The Affair* has a lot to say about extramarital activity which is interesting and valid; yet my experience is counter to his . . . thesis that affairs never last. That mine has [lasted thirty-nine years] is probably due to the fact that two intelligent people, loving their sex life, have rare and precious meetings, have used restraint, and have nourished other than sexual subjects of interest between them. There's conversation as well as love-making — every time!

Several of our wives report taking lovers when their husbands stopped having sex with them. One 50-year-old wife, for example, notes that her 52-year-old husband never had a high sex drive, and recently became impotent. Her immediate response was to fall in love with another man and launch an affair. "My sex outside marriage has made me realize what I'm missing," she writes. "I'm considering divorce in the hope I can find a partner who can offer opportunity for good sex."

A 62-year-old wife, married for thirty-five years to a husband now 73, has a more complicated story to tell. Eleven years ago her husband announced that he was impotent because of his age. She "didn't believe that for a minute" and concluded instead that he just didn't want to have sex with her anymore; hence she "had little compunction about taking a lover — and almost left my husband to marry him." Indeed, she took two lovers, "one regularly — I loved him; one occasionally — he was fun." She was then about 50.

Three years ago, she learned that her husband had a neurological disease — and that his sexual problems were a side effect of this illness. This changed her attitude toward her own infidelity. "[I] felt as if I were kicking him when he was already down. Out of pity I stayed with him and have never been unfaithful since." Instead, she masturbates once a month or so "to relieve tension." Sometimes she has orgasms in her sleep. She isn't happy this way — she feels "smothered" by her husband's "possessiveness" — but she is now doing her best to be a good (and faithful) wife.

A husband's invalidism was the occasion for adultery in several marriages, including that of a Cleveland woman whose husband entered a nursing home for terminal care when she was 59 years old. Shortly thereafter, she fell passionately in love with a married man four years her junior — and he fell in love with her. Now, after more than seven years, she and her married lover have sex about once a week; both reach orgasm on every occasion. She rates her enjoyment of sex at age 67 as 1, and describes her extramarital relationship as "the most fulfilling experience in my life . . . a really close relationship and really ongoing love affair —

which we know will continue to the end of our lives and maybe beyond!"

One wife, now aged 55, is married to her second husband, also 55. She and her first husband, she writes, "were physically and psychologically incompatible. I was not the wife to him that I [am] to my second husband." Thirteen years ago, she took a lover. The relationship has never ended — though it is no longer an affair. She and her lover married four years ago, shortly after her husband died. She writes:

> We're even more in love now than we ever were. For both of us, it's a second marriage. As happy as we are now, though, we've wondered whether our present feeling for each other could have survived the trials of most marriages — children, each other's families, late working hours, financial vicissitudes, and all the abrasions of everyday living. We doubt it. We're glad now that we weren't able to marry each other when we were young, and that we had a chance to practice on other partners. I'd really like to know what other people have to say about this.

Concerning the possibility of taking a lover during her present marriage, she writes:

> How could I? I'm already in love. . . . For me it would be unthinkable because I give myself completely to . . . my present husband — and there's nothing for anyone else to tap.

A 50-year-old Alabama wife reports that her husband, now 53, lost almost all interest in sex a quarter of a century ago. Since then she has had a series of lovers — including one currently — without her husband's knowledge. She explains:

> My sexual relations outside of marriage have been very pleasurable and long-lasting. They began as a result of my husband's loss of desire for sex. . . . I would get up and run around the block in the middle of the night just to release

the tension. I'm sure that our marriage would have ended if I had not found a relationship outside of marriage. . . . I do love my husband very much and enjoy our life together. I would not want to hurt him.

She then adds one more detail:

The past year, my husband has shown more interest in sex than he has [in the past twenty-five years]. I don't have any idea of the reason for this — but I'm very pleased.

A 55-year-old Philadelphia wife got married late in World War II, at the age of 22. "I was a poor judge of character when I chose my husband," she writes. "I did not know how violent a temper he had, or how overbearing and dictatorial he would become." She rates the happiness of her marriage as 6. She still has sex with her husband, but rates her enjoyment of it as 7, and comments: "I would like to *never* have sexual activities with him at all."

Despite all this, she rates her overall enjoyment of life as 2, and explains why. When she was 44, she took a lover:

I have had sex with this one man for the past eleven years. I am still in love with him and he loves me. My husband would never give me a divorce — said he'd kill me if I left him for another man. So I have sneaked off for all these years.

A 58-year-old Midwestern wife writes:

About one year ago I experienced a flaring love affair with a man eight years younger than I. It has continued sporadically . . . and has brought warmth and affection into my life. My sex life with my husband is satisfactory; but it is isolated from the rest of our co-existence. We quarrel and argue frequently. He is not affectionate and I was forced to squelch that part of my nature until I met someone who responded in that way. It is a very warm friendship — but there is sex involved, too.

But cheating by wives does not always grow out of marital unhappiness or dissatisfaction. A 57-year-old wife and her 60-year-old husband have been married thirty-eight years. They live in their own home in Georgia. She rates the happiness of her marriage as 1, and her enjoyment of sex with her husband as 2 — adding that it is "loving and wonderful and meaningful to us both." The problems in her marriage are financial, job, and health problems — not sex or jealousy problems. She rates communications with her husband as "very good," and she is "very comfortable" in discussing sexual matters with him. She also states that she is in love with her husband, and that he has not since the age of 50 engaged in extramarital sex.

This is hardly the kind of marriage in which cheating might be expected. Yet since age 50, she reports, she has had sex with three outside partners without her husband's knowledge. She comments:

> The value of extramarital affairs is often the excitement and the novelty. The sex is better — but if the couple were to marry, the same intensity, excitement, etc., would become routine. It is the newness that provides the heightened experience.

A 72-year-old wife, married for forty-two years, similarly reports that she is in love with her husband. They live in a condominium in Florida, and have sex together two or three times a week; both almost always reach orgasm. She rates both her marital happiness and her enjoyment of sex with her husband as 2. She adds, however, that she has had two outside affairs since 50 — one during the past year. She explains that her outside sexual adventures "stimulate response in marital sex."

Some wives look back on an extramarital affair with disapproval and regret. One of these, at 69, has been married for almost half a century to a husband now 76, and has been faithful through most of those years. *However* —

"For a few years during my middle 40's and very early 50's, I occasionally had sexual activities with one man with whom I considered myself to be in love at the time." The affair terminated when her lover died; she was then 53. Her husband has never learned of her one affair — nor, she says, has he ever engaged in extramarital sex.

"As I look back on this," she writes from a retirement community in the Southwest, "I realize that it was almost entirely physical and not really love. In other words, I thought that I was 'crazy about him,' and I was."

Following her lover's death, he continued to haunt her.

> The only sexual fantasy I can remember having is that I used to pretend I was having sex with my lover . . . when, in fact, I was having it with my husband. This went on for several years. . . .
>
> If I had my life to live over, I would not have had the relationship. . . . I consider now that it was degrading and not really love at all. But my husband and I were not that compatible at that time — and I was flattered at the attention I was receiving from a man whom I considered very attractive, and who also had a couple of other women interested in him. As I look back, he wasn't worth committing adultery for.

A 66-year-old woman, now a widow, similarly expresses regret for her one extramarital affair since 50. "Sex outside of marriage definitely weakens the marriage," she writes. "The game definitely is not worth the candle." She then reflects:

> If I had expended the same amount of effort in improving my relations with my husband that I spent sneaking around those afternoons for several years, my marriage would have improved a great deal.

Other unfaithful wives, however, express no regrets. Ten years ago a Washington State wife, now aged 56, married her second husband, now 72. They have sex a few times a month — but she doesn't enjoy it very much, rating it 5. Unknown to her husband, she has had two lovers. He, she says, has had none.

> With the advent of menopause, I feel liberated — and sex can be enjoyed for the enjoyment's sake alone. My sexual regrets during my lifetime are the regrets of omission — I would have shared much more with more partners. [Having no fear of pregnancy] makes *all* the difference to me. Now [sex] can be spontaneous and joyous.

Husbands who cheat

With relatively few exceptions, as the above accounts illustrate, adultery is a significant experience in the lives of our adulterous wives. It does not appear to have been a casual event to them at the time; and whether they look back with delight or with regret, many of them write about it at length and with feeling. They see the adultery in the context of their marriages and of their overall life patterns. This is also true of some, but not most, of our adulterous husbands.

One 66-year-old West Coast husband writes that he and his wife have had no sex for many years. Nine years ago he launched an affair with a young woman of 23. That affair still continues. He writes:

> My mistress . . . looks upon me as father, uncle, lover, and sometimes as little boy. I enjoy all roles. . . . Love in later years is comfortable, no sweat; we're never concerned about "the competition"; we've found what we want; we fulfill each other's needs; we're not afraid of losing each other. . . . The fact that sex *takes* longer is all to the good. We enjoy every minute of it. She helps it to be good — slowing down, speeding up, forgiving the occasional premature ejaculation. So *very, very* much depends upon the understanding partner. . . . When we are alone together, we move as we please.

We immediately speak up if we want something *not* done, or done differently. And it works. *That's* love in action!

His mistress is now aged 32. At 66, he refuses to obtain a divorce and marry her because when she "is in her 40's, still relatively young, I will be in my 70's. . . . She declares . . . age difference of no significance. I believe it will come to be; she's too sexy to be stuck with me forever."
Meanwhile, what of his wife?

My marriage could have been much better, if I had known what I need for sexual compatibility and what my intended wife needed. Despite problems, we have stayed together; but we have missed much — a fact that my mistress has made abundantly clear during the years of our affair.

Other adulterous husbands, in contrast, seem to view their extramarital encounters as casual, isolated events hardly worth mentioning. Some merely report, with little or no comment, the number of extramarital partners they have had since 50. Some are even vague about the number, writing "a few," or "several."
One 65-year-old husband, married for forty-one years to a wife now 59, says that without her knowledge, he has had three outside sexual partners since 50. His only comment is: "Every man and woman has the right to perform sexually as he or she desires as long as it doesn't interfere with others."
A husband of 60, married for thirty-two years, says he is in love with his wife and has sex with her once a week; in addition, he has had five or six partners outside his marriage since 50. His wife, so far as he knows, has had no outside sex. He comments: "Sex outside marriage is exciting and fun. Makes one feel younger for a while."
A happily married 56-year-old husband says that he and his wife experiment with all kinds of sex together, and that he is in love with her.
"The only sexual experiences I have had outside [my marriage]," he continues, "have been on two occasions (one experi-

ence each), and I feel these were . . . to prove I was attractive to someone else."

Sometimes a husband remains faithful decade after decade until, on a single occasion, an extramarital adventure simply "falls into his lap." That phrase is used by a 67-year-old husband in the Midwest, married for twenty-five years to a wife now 62. A few years ago, his wife decided to terminate sex. He writes:

"I have been faithful to my present wife since 50 except for one occasion which more or less fell into my lap. I was anxious to see whether I was still functioning — and very pleased with the results." His partner was also married. "We both decided not to continue [due to] the constant fear of being caught by one spouse or the other — and it really wasn't that much fun for a long-time relationship."

A somewhat similar — but ongoing — affair is described by a 68-year-old husband from Florida, very happily married for thirty-eight years. Last year, he reports:

An old friend with whom I had sex prior to my marriage lost her husband and looked me up. Association with her led to renewal of sex relations. She sometimes says she feels guilty about our relationship, but I do not have any feeling of guilt.

The oldest of our respondents engaging in adultery is a husband aged 84, long married to a wife now 80. They no longer have sex together, but his interest in sex remains moderately strong. He says he disapproves of extramarital sex — but he has had five extramarital partners since 50, and one of these relationships continues. He had his last falling-in-love experience twelve years ago, at age 72, and he is currently in love with his ongoing extramarital partner. He does not comment further.

Another 84-year-old respondent, recently widowed, gives a detailed account of his almost lifelong fidelity punctuated twice by brief affairs:

As was conventionally proper at the time, my wife and I were both sexually virgin when we married. I do not now recommend this kind of abstinence; but then I had the idea it might add to marital happiness. I am sure it didn't. My wife turned out to have little or no interest in intercourse, though she accepted it (too infrequently) as an expected wifely duty. I think she had never had an orgasm in her life when single; and she never had one with me until a weak one occurred [well along in] our marriage. Was it my fault? I believe I am sexually normal and capable of arousing females. Two girls whom I had dated before marriage had gone into orgasm in my company as we experimented, fully clothed, with the very earliest of preliminaries.

    .   Why didn't I recognize my mistake, get a divorce, and start over? Because it was far from a total mistake. My wife was everything a wife should be except an eager and skillful bedroom companion. We were fond of each other and suffered when we [were apart]. . . .

    When I was in my forties, she told me she would not be offended if I looked elsewhere for sexual variety. But when I tried it, she was [offended].

That was his first brief lapse. His second occurred more than twenty years later:

When I was nearly 70 (right now I am 84), a woman of about 40 . . . gradually entered my life. She said she had received twelve proposals in her girlhood and had accepted the wrong one. I knew her husband, and saw nothing wrong with him. She, indeed, liked most of his characteristics — but found him hasty, selfish, and inconsiderate in bed. She professed a deep love for me and would have been willing to divorce her husband and marry me; but this went beyond my interest, which was more of the immediate type. Also, it was too late in my life to break up a close familial structure (healthy and indispensable wife, devoted children and grandchildren). . . . For a period of a few months we were able to manage completely secret meetings and we did not waste the opportunities. We both had unpleasant feelings of guilt about it; but . . . I am glad I had it. I could have discussed it with my spouse, but [my partner] certainly could not have with hers. At that age, I could not have been a really good lover — but she found me satisfactory, and to me she was a bit of a revelation.

Like so many of our other respondents, this 84-year-old widower describes the change in his sexual views:

In earlier generations, the sound reasons against sexual freedom were three: It caused the spread of disease, it caused undesirable pregnancies, and it caused scandal and injury to reputations and personal sorrow. These objections are now inoperable or can readily be made so in the individual case. In a world with none too much joy, I think it indefensible to try to suppress or reduce an activity which combines the most intense pleasure possible to humans with complete lack of expense.

In recent years, sex manuals have described wives who really want to make love while their husbands only want to have sex. Several wives quoted earlier make this complaint, and some turn to extramarital sex for this reason. Some husbands also really want to make love — and turn to affairs when their wife refuses to engage in anything except a quick, perfunctory genital encounter in the conventional manner. A 60-year-old husband describes such a marriage. For thirty-nine years he has been married to a wife of the same age; they live in a suburb of Los Angeles.

"I enjoy variety," he explains. "My wife thinks all but kissing, breast stimulation, and genital stimulation with finger perverted. Then the missionary position, pump-pump-pump, hurry and reach orgasm. All else in her opinion is dirty. . . ."

This basic marital problem was exacerbated eight years ago when he first experienced prostate trouble. "I thought my sexual function was OK," he says, "until informed by my wife that I was no longer an adequate sexual partner for her. Since that time I have had trouble getting and maintaining as rigid an erection as before."

Rightly or wrongly, he blames his erectile problem on his wife rather than on his prostate condition. "Sex without orgasm is a total loss to her," he reports. "On the few occasions when ... I complained about her lack of response, she has said, 'Why should I get myself all worked up when you may not be able to do anything?' This has had a castrating effect on me."

He continues: "During the past two years, I have had infrequent [sex] with another woman who enjoys a variety of sexual activities. I find I enjoy these activities and function much better." His extramarital partner is five years older.

He says he is still in love with his wife. Then, paradoxically, he adds, "I am against affairs during marriage, for they are sure to destroy the marriage."

Another husband who complains that his wife wants only perfunctory sex is 68 years old and has been married for thirty-nine years. He and his wife live in the Chicago area. She is "unwilling to engage in sexual variations or extended foreplay," he says; indeed, she is "often reluctant to have sex" at all.

> Consequently, I seek variety from two widows about 50 years old — and [from] young prostitutes. . . . The widows are anxious for sex, want variety, no inhibitions. The young prostitutes give me the variety of youth, beautiful bodies — but the experienced widows give me much better sex.

A 66-year-old Florida husband, married for thirty-four years, writes that his wife and he were never compatible and that sex was never good between them:

> My wife . . . seemed to enjoy sex — but only on her own terms, no-variation-from-the-missionary-position, and don't mention any of those dirty perversions!
>   In the kitchen she was concerned and responsive to the foods I liked, and how I liked them prepared. Oh, that she could have been concerned and responsive to what I liked in bed.

He reports four extramarital partners since 50, and explains:

In my case, sex outside marriage provided a type of sex —
fellatio, cunnilingus, anal, "dirty" talk and wanton behavior — not available in my marriage bed. . . . [There the] sex
was nice, "clean," no variety. . . . With others there was a
wide variety of shared activity.

He adds that he and his wife are also incompatible in other
ways.

I'm not a slob. I have a wide range of interests in literature,
music, and the other arts. My tastes run to classical music,
hers to soap opera. In fairness, she didn't sail under false
pretenses; I simply was not sufficiently astute and observant
[before marriage]. I don't know how I could have been so
unaware. The signs were all there. I guess love is indeed
blind.

His extramarital sex nowadays is

the same as before 50, except that the pace may be relaxed
and time taken to be more discriminating. The emphasis can
be on quality rather than quantity, and the sex can be in
more comfortable surroundings in terms of creature com-
forts. The sex can be only a part — the best part, perhaps —
of an evening of good food, good wine, good music. After
50, the income may well be such as to afford some of the
other interests that were only the dreams of youth — travel,
art, fine home . . . etc. Sex, too, then should be a finer, richer
fabric. Why should all of the experimenting and imagination
in the household be limited to the kitchen and the flower
beds?

Having delivered himself of these marital complaints, our re-
spondent asks the same question other respondents ask: "Why do
I continue in a relationship that I would rather be out of?"
His answer is, in essence, similar to that of others:

What would she do? In her way, I think she loves me. She's
a good housekeeper and an excellent cook. We do not argue;
we do not fight. From the outside, it probably appears that
we have a good marriage — and by most standards, I suppose we do. And so . . . I cannot bring myself to leave a
woman who hasn't "done" anything to me.

He ends on a pensive note: "Wouldn't it be ironic if she would
like nothing more than to be rid of me? Shades of O. Henry!!"

When adultery is "found out"

As these life stories and quotations amply illustrate, some of our
husbands and wives report extramarital affairs lasting for years or
even decades without the knowledge of their spouses. None of our
respondents, however, explains in any detail just how this was ac-
complished. A spouse's discovery of a clandestine affair is rarely
reported.

One wife who did find out is 53 years old and has been married for twenty-eight years; she lives in New York City. Three
years ago, her husband discontinued sexual relations with her. As
a result, "[I] lost my self-respect, felt I wasn't enough of a woman
to be desired sexually."

After more than two years of this sexual estrangement, she
and her husband sought the help of a marriage counselor and
were encouraged to communicate more freely. They did — and it
was then that her husband's secret came out: He had been having
an affair with a much younger woman who had become pregnant,
and he had accepted financial responsibility for the young
woman's child. He was continuing to see her right up to the time
he and his wife entered marriage counseling.

Now, roughly a year later, this wife describes herself as "still
getting over the shock of learning of his affair and of others that
may have preceded it. Resentful of the stupidity of it all." She also
writes: "[I] doubt if I will ever get over the . . . terrible hurt of his
infidelity and lying."

There has been a reconciliation, however; and she and her

husband have resumed sexual relations. He says he reaches orgasm almost every time; she says she usually does. She rates her enjoyment of sex with him as 2, and he rates his enjoyment of sex with her as 3. She rates the happiness of their marriage as 6 — but she adds: "[I] have a feeling he's trying hard to make up for [those] barren years."

A husband aged 59, who lives alone in an apartment outside Washington, D.C., reports that he was faithful through twenty-five years of marriage. Then he discovered that his wife "had been sexual with a much younger man for three years. As a consequence, we separated nine years ago and my once-excellent health has failed me and I have to some degree withdrawn from most social activities and from cultivating new friendships."

He rates his enjoyment of life as 4, and says that he is often lonely. His only sex since his separation from his wife is masturbation once a week, and he explains why he has neither sought nor found a new partner since then:

> Although . . . she deceived me and left me broken in spirit, I also recall that before that bitter end and before she, in a moment of weakness, became slave of a much younger man, my wife was one of the finest human beings I have ever known.
>
> Having once intimately known the best, will I ever be able to accept less?

Only 5 of our 95 adulterous wives and 32 of our 429 adulterous husbands say that jealousy is a problem in their marriage. One reason for the relative infrequency of jealousy in these adulterous marriages may be that the cheating is successful; the unsuspecting spouse never does find out about it. Another reason may be that, following discovery, the marriage has terminated and is therefore absent from our marital data.

A third possible reason for infrequent reports of jealousy is that the spouse, consciously or unconsciously, *decides* not to be aware of the adultery. While we have no clear statements from respondents on this point, there are a few hints. One adulterous wife, for example, reports that her husband never did confront her with her decade-long infidelity — but "[I] think he was suspicious."

Some respondents write of how the wife or husband cheated, the spouse found out and engaged in extramarital sex in retaliation, and the marriage nevertheless survived. One such account comes from a wife, now 64, who is retired with her husband in a Florida condominium:

> My husband had an affair with a younger woman when I was in my mid-fifties — about ten to fifteen years ago. This was a traumatic, devastating experience for both of us — but particularly for me. He left me for about six weeks and wanted a divorce — then later, he returned, deciding he loved me and hated the younger woman. During the time we were separated, in a sense, I grew up. I was surprised to find that I was attractive to other men. A few men wanted to marry me. My husband had destroyed my ego so thoroughly that, I suppose, I had to find out that I was still desirable. A woman sends out unconscious signals when she is available. When my husband and I got together again, I stopped sending out signals to other men.
>
> Sex with other men was not satisfactory. My husband is a much better lover than any of my partners.

Her husband's adultery terminated more than a decade ago — yet her feelings are still intense:

> Infidelity . . . is a most traumatic, devastating experience for a person whose mate has been unfaithful. The scars never really heal. Trust and faith are never established. There is always a lingering doubt about whether your mate ever really loved you.

She adds: "I realized later that my husband's infidelity sprang from his feelings of inadequacy about himself — but I am not sure that I accept that deep down. It made me feel that I was inadequate as a woman."

The converse situation of a husband who enters into an extramarital affair when he learns of his wife's infidelity is described by a husband now 68. He and his 61-year-old wife have been married for thirty-eight years; they live in Arizona. He recalls:

> In my growing-up years, the word "unfaithful" conjured up a terrible trauma — which I experienced when I learned my wife was active in that field. After a cooling-off period, I evaluated the pluses and minuses and the bottom line said: Stay married.

He did stay married, and he says he is still in love with his wife. Shortly after he learned of her outside affairs, however, "I had a five-year affair, very satisfactory, with my secretary — which ended when she left to marry an old sweetheart."

After that, since he "no longer wished to become emotionally involved" outside his marriage, he "went the prostitute route," as he puts it. During the past year, he has had sex with a particular prostitute on twenty occasions, at a cost of $50 each.

Twice, this 68-year-old husband continues, his favorite prostitute "has included a friend of hers [so that] one of my fantasies came true! Having sex with two women! I've never had so good a time." He adds: "If my spouse was as good in bed, I never would spend $50."

"Consensual adultery," "open marriage," and "swinging"

This leaves for consideration here a small number of marriages in which extramarital sex has been engaged in since 50 with the spouse's knowledge, and often with the spouse's consent as well. Here are the statistics:

• Twenty-six of our wives report having had sex outside their marriage with their husband's knowledge.

• Forty-nine of our husbands report knowing that their wives have had sex outside their marriage. Presumably, these two figures overlap somewhat.

• One hundred of our husbands report having had sex outside their marriage with their wife's knowledge.

• Seventy-one of our wives report knowing that their husbands have had sex outside their marriage. Here, too, there is some overlap.

Summing up, at least 149 of our wives and husbands have, since age 50, had sex outside of marriage with the spouse's knowledge. The true number is probably considerably more than 149 but fewer than 246, which would be the total if there were no overlap between wives' and husbands' accounts.

These figures, moreover, are for *currently married* wives and husbands. Some of our divorced and remarried respondents — we don't know how many — were no doubt formerly parties to such marriages. The essential point here is that somewhere between 149 and 246 of our respondents know of their spouse's adultery and have *not* separated or secured divorces.

In some of these marriages, both husband and wife have, since 50, engaged in extramarital sex with each other's knowledge. Here are the statistics:

• Eighteen wives report that both she and her husband have engaged in extramarital sex, with the knowledge of both.

• Twenty-nine husbands report that both he and his wife have engaged in extramarital sex, with the knowledge of both.

Here, too, some of these wives and husbands are reporting on the same marriage. Thus the number of marriages in which both parties have had extramarital sex with the knowledge of both parties must lie somewhere between 29 and 47.

In marriages in which a wife or husband engages in extramarital sex with the spouse's knowledge, the adulterer may also have the spouse's consent — a situation sometimes called *consensual adultery*. One example is reported neither by the husband nor the wife. Instead, it is described by a 67-year-old Baltimore widow who is the husband's outside partner.

After her children left home, this widow writes, she began

taking in roomers. One was a young man of 24. She was then 54 and had been widowed for seven years.

After he had lived in her house for a year, "we began sex relations at his request. I was his first woman. Three years later, I introduced him to a young woman friend of mine. They married the next year. The three of us talked about our relationship all along, and we have continued our close association. There is no feeling of jealousy or competition."

Our respondent, though she has been playing the role of "the other woman" in her lover's marriage for the past eight years, does not feel that she is in any sense an intruder:

> My partner and his wife are happily married, love and care deeply for one another, share a good sex life together. She can not take as much sexual activity as he can, and I serve as a harmless outlet for his sex urges. It seems beneficial to all three of us.
>
> To outsiders, I appear as the mother image. We are very discrete. We keep our private lives to ourselves.

She continues:

> I spend about one night a week in their home, and I sleep with him. We take baths together, then go to bed, have intercourse with orgasms for both of us, and sleep well. Next morning we sometimes have quick intercourse, with orgasm for him. This was the same pattern when we started fourteen years ago in my house — except then it was every night. Most sessions last an hour or more. He is very articulate about sex experiences. He likes sex magazines and shows me pictures. . . . Although my husband and I were completely satisfied with our sex life and loved each other devotedly, my present partner has better sex technique and concentrates more fully on the sex act when it is happening. I naturally respond more. . . . [He] is the most perceptive man I've ever known. He enjoys seeing me have an orgasm, and will do anything to intensify my feelings.

Her 37-year-old partner, moreover, does not expect fidelity from her. He "likes to hear about [my] encounters [with others], does not object."

She sums up: "My life has been good. I've been very lucky. I'm grateful for true friends." She adds that she does not plan to buy this book — "I'd rather experience sex any time than read about it" — and she quotes Christopher Morley as saying, "Books are a mighty bloodless substitute for life."

A 55-year-old Pennsylvania husband and his 54-year-old wife have been married for twenty-one years. He says he has had sex outside his marriage with his wife's consent but without her knowledge — a curious situation which he explains as follows:

[My] wife has little sex drive and I have lots of sex drive. Solution is extramarital sex which my wife and I condone as long as it is not known to [her].

He adds, however: "I find extramarital sex hard to obtain, since women are normally looking for marriage or a lasting relationship — which I cannot give since I am married and would like to stay so."

In this situation, this husband had his first extramarital experience last year. It was with a prostitute, and he writes: "Sex with prostitute not satisfying. Prefer sex with willing partner doing it for fun rather than money."

Eight years ago, a 67-year-old husband, married for forty-six years, was placed on anti-hypertensive medication. As a result, he writes, he lost his appetite for sex — and since then, "my wife has my permission to have sex elsewhere. Yes, I gave her permission. I don't know if she ever did or not — but she had the opportunity." Despite absence of sex with his wife (or anyone else) for eight years, he rates his marital happiness as 1, and adds that "rapport between us is very strong."

A 55-year-old husband, married for twenty-one years, writes from New England:

My wife is grossly overweight and sexually unattractive to me. She seems to want it that way. I need and want sex, but

not with her. On the rare occasions when she wants it, I
enjoy it — but otherwise, I have no sexual desire for her.

He adds that his wife does not permit him to try to arouse her
sexually, and he describes "her desire to avoid sex except on the
rare occasions when she wants it. . . . My wife simply does not
want orgasms more than once a month."

Thirteen years ago, he began having sex outside his marriage — with five partners since 50. This is with my wife's knowledge. Indeed, he writes, "my wife almost seems to want me to
have sex outside as long as it does not impinge on her time. . . .
When [with a] girl friend . . . my sex is as often as twice a day for
four or five days. At home it is once a month."

He rates the happiness of his marriage as 3. When asked what
he would do differently if he had his life to live over, he replies: "I
would be unfaithful at a much earlier age." He does *not* mention
marriage to a different wife as a preferred alternative.

One wife reports that she received her husband's permission
to have sex outside their marriage forty-three years ago. She is 72
years old and has been married for forty-eight years to a husband
now 80. They live near St. Louis. From the beginning of their
marriage, she recalls, she wanted and needed much more sex than
her husband,

which was keeping me awake, tense, and bothered. . . .
When we first discussed the matter, during the fifth year of
our marriage, I . . . said to him, "You get all [the sex] you
want, but I get about a quarter of what I want — so I think I
have a right to get more if I can do it without creating emotional storms."

He reluctantly agreed, only asking me not to make him
conscious of it. And, of course, I loved him all the more for
his great-souled understanding and lack of petty *macho* pride.

Instead of extramarital sex, however, she soon found another
solution to her problems of tension and insomnia. "I was seeing a
physician about constipation, and I also asked him what I could
do about reducing my sexual desire."

The physician replied that there wasn't much she could do.

But then he said, "You could take bromides; they are supposed to quiet the nerves. Get the Burroughs-Wellcome tablets that come in a glass tube." Then he had a certain intense look in his young face. "Don't get the small ones, the diameter of a quarter. Get the largest — the size of a 50-cent piece."*

Well, when I got the stuff later, I found the tube, gently rounded, was an ideal masturbator. I think the doctor was trying to tell me, in those days when nobody was frank about such things, that I could stand my condition if I masturbated.

Now, forty-three years later, she continues to rate her marital happiness as 1, and she continues to supplement with masturbation her highly enjoyable but too infrequent sex with her husband.

A 66-year-old widow writes that nine years ago, "it was my husband's idea to exchange partners" with another couple. She and the other husband fell in love. Their affair has continued ever since:

I felt guilty and really wanted to stop seeing him during the time my husband was still living, but I feel no guilt now that I am a widow — and I enjoy my relationship with him even more.

I do not feel that I am cheating his wife of his affections because she really doesn't want them. She was more interested in my husband when this affair all started. . . .

His wife is my best friend. She admittedly does not like sex with him and, although I don't think she knows about us, I think she is happy when he can get satisfaction somewhere else. She is really frigid, a pretty weird situation.

---

* This was in 1934, when bromides could be legally purchased without a prescription.

This respondent reports that the sexual side of their relationship is important both to her at age 66 and to her lover at 64. They have sex together about once a week, which is about right for her; both reach orgasm almost every time. Her interest in sex is now strong — stronger than at 40 — and she enjoys sex more with her lover now than she did with her husband at 40. The only problem in the relationship, she says, is "one wife too many."

In addition to her nine-year-long relationship with her lover, she has had sex with two other men. She explains:

> Since my relationship with my partner will probably never lead to marriage, my outside sexual activity with two other partners has been because each of them really wants to marry me. . . . I am reluctant because I am really in love with my present partner and do not want to give him up.

We have several descriptions of "open marriages" — that is, marriages in which both wives and husbands engage in extramarital sex with mutual knowledge and consent. One account of such a marriage is supplied by a widow now 84.

> Since my husband had been too timid to have much experience with women before I married him, [she writes from the Gulf Coast,] he found, with the advent of considerable prestige in his field, that now women were easily available to him. Who could blame him for taking advantage of this? So, disdaining the double standard, I also had some lovers during marriage — not only before 50 but after 50. There were 15. (I have stodgily kept a list, and some were only once.)

The most significant of these fifteen relationships, she continues, was "a thirteen-year-long affair with a man fifteen years younger, who wanted to marry [me] — but I had seen the results of this with a couple where she was 75 and he 50. . . . It was the most intense experience of my life and I was shattered when we both felt it should end. Women usually feel worse anyway. In the above case, there's the feeling that everything is slipping past you, inexorably, and it's later than you think."

At 84, this widow no longer has sex with a partner, but she masturbates a few times a month — more frequently than at age 40 — and reaches orgasm every time. She sometimes dreams about sex; and on two occasions during the past year she had an orgasm when asleep or while waking up.

Another open marriage is described briefly by a 57-year-old wife married for thirty-three years to a husband now 58. Both have had outside partners; she has had three since age 50, one of them currently. She rates the happiness of her marriage as 2 and her enjoyment of sex with her husband as 3. She and her husband have sex from four to six times a week. She believes that "it is not necessary to be emotionally involved to enjoy sex," and she continues:

> My husband and I feel it is acceptable if either of us has a sexual experience outside of marriage. We do not believe in getting involved emotionally with another partner, though.

A 55-year-old wife has been married for thirty-seven years to a husband now 59. They live in New York City. She reports sex with "three or four" outside partners since 50 — with her husband's knowledge and approval. He has also had sex outside their marriage since 50 with her knowledge and approval. "We both find it rather exciting," she writes, "increasing rather than inhibiting our sexual activity together." She says she is in love with her husband; and she rates both the happiness of their marriage and her enjoyment of sex with him as 2.

A 56-year-old husband lives with his second wife, aged 45, in a Philadelphia suburb. He writes:

> I have tried open marriage and it doesn't work. A friend of mine said, "Anyone who can handle open marriage doesn't need it." It is too threatening and destructive.

The alternative options are either total monogamy or secret sex elsewhere. I have chosen the latter, and it works fine.

He reports fifteen extramarital affairs since age 50 — including his current one, of six months' duration so far, with a 35-year-old partner. He says that as compared with open marriage, his extramarital cheating "has improved my marriage relationship, both emotionally and sexually. . . . For a number of years after open marriage, I went through spells of impotence — with my spouse only! — but these have nearly vanished. The pressure is off." His only erection problem nowadays is the first time with a new partner. "Once that's out of the way, things are fine."

At 56, he has no difficulty in finding new extramarital partners. "With decrease in anxiety with regard to women, it has become easier to accept rejection. At the same time, it has become easier to proposition a woman, and — surprise! — acceptance rate has improved greatly."

In a philosophical mood, he continues:

Young people need to be reassured that life is not — after 50 — a downhill slide. [Simone] de Beauvoir, in her inimitable grimness, stated in her . . . *Coming of Age* . . . that once the libido fades, life acquires the taste of ashes. De Gaulle (I believe) said that "envy is the passion of the old." This may be true for Frenchmen — and women; [but] I more agree with the statement that the 40's are the old age of youth; the 50's are the youth of old age.

Any regrets? This respondent, at 56 with a 45-year-old wife and fifteen extramarital partners since age 50, replies: "The only sins I regret are the ones I failed to commit. 'An opportunity passed over never comes again,' my grandfather said."

What might be called an open marriage-*plus* is described by both the wife and the husband. She is 58 and he is 59. They have been married for thirty-seven years and live on the West Coast. He reports ten partners outside the marriage since age 50; she reports "many." Both rate the happiness of their marriage and their enjoyment of sex with each other as 1.

She explains:

> I seem to have the capacity to love and enjoy my husband increasingly over the years AND to develop what I consider to [be] love (affection, respect, intense physical attraction) with other men as well — ongoing relationships.

She adds that her "husband initiated my seeing other men. He is stimulated by it. He sees other women" but has "less activity than I have since opportunities are less easy to come by for men."

She wonders whether other couples in open marriages talk frankly about it to family, friends, co-workers, or therapists, and sees an advantage in doing so. "Being open and honest in a tasteful way helps set precedents for others who wish to do and be the same." She explains that her friends and her husband's friends tend to be divided into either "straight and professional" or "sex-centered" friendships. Only her straight and professional friends "have no knowledge that I have sex outside marriage. Two of our grown children know and seem to accept."

She notes that she is hardly ever lonely because of "family, friends, lovers, pets, and more work than I will ever finish. . . . Some sex partners have been very good friends. I have more time to devote to friends now than I had during very busy years of child-rearing, grad school, house remodeling, job and professional responsibilities." And she sums up: "Sex without love but with mutual affection and respect can be very rewarding and enriching."

The husband's report on this marriage is similar in many respects, but he also comments on *swinging* — engaging in group sex activities:

> Both my wife and I find variety in sex partners stimulating to the sex between the two of us. She is fairly at ease if she sees me have sex with another woman but I very much

enjoy watching her have sex with another man. She enjoys it and is very vocal. This excites me. In addition to the sex I have with other women, I enjoy holding and caressing [without sex]. I also have several women friends I have not had sex with but very much enjoy their company.

Asked about his sexual fantasies, he replies: "I sometimes think about my wife having sex with another man and sometimes with me and another man." Asked what he would do differently if he could start over, he replies, "I would not be as inhibited about having sex before or after marriage." And he sums up: "I believe in sex freedom but believe it should be practiced in such a way [that] it does not harm others."

Another swinging couple, both 56, have been married for thirty-four years and live in the Southwest. Both say they are now happily married and in love with one another. The wife adds, however, that things were not always so agreeable.

One problem was that her husband drank excessively for twenty-five years. Another was that he had a series of outside sexual affairs. "He did this for many years (with my knowledge)," the wife reports, "but I found it stressful to my security and ego needs." Her husband also "had one serious affair . . . which nearly drove me to suicide — and which caused a rift [that] took almost five years to heal." He, however,

was never threatened by my sexual activities outside the marriage — obviously much more secure than I am or was. . . .

[I] feel strongly that most marriages can make it if people try hard enough. [I] was determined to make mine work because my parents failed. This effort paid off. Compromise and the willingness to keep some independence are part of the key — and a sense of humor is elementary. We both know we can count on one another. I was fairly insecure about this during [my] early years [of marriage], which caused friction — but [I] am now aware that *loving* doesn't mean *owning* someone.

Since 50, this 56-year-old wife reports, she has had sex with "15 to 20" men outside of her marriage — and with one woman. The woman was 21 years old, and the episode lasted ten minutes. This "was at [my] husband's insistence in a swinging situation. [I] definitely did not like it."

Currently, the two attend "swings" — group-sex parties — together three or four times a year. She says:

> The swinging scene on occasion . . . relieves his tensions and adds novelty. . . . [I] feel more comfortable in a swinging situation than [when] my husband [is having affairs] alone. . . . I am a "closet swinger," meaning I don't mind other partners but like to be alone with them. [My] husband is an open-group person; he loves watching me with another man — which I've learned to tolerate on occasion but don't care for.

She says she is in love with her husband, and rates the happiness of her marriage as 2. She sums up:

> Love that survives stress, anxiety, trauma, and time is to me more deep. [I] also feel that it is possible to love more than one person — each differently, as one loves each child differently. This should not "unseat" one's "significant other."

The 56-year-old husband in this marriage gives a considerably more enthusiastic account of it:

> I persuaded my wife that extramarital sex was good (about 25 years ago), and since then we've had extramarital sex when we were together and apart. During [the] last ten years we've engaged in "swinging" and we both enjoy it very much. I would like to try swinging more often (e.g., once a month) but cater to my wife, who only likes it once every two or three months.

He reports "70 to 100 or more" sexual partners since age 50, and he continues:

We ... love threesomes very much for the combination of
excitement and intimacy. Although neither of us is bisexual
or homosexual, we enjoy seeing our spouse seduce and
enjoy sex with a member of the opposite sex.

He concludes: "Love in the later years is deeper, more meaningful, less erratically emotional, more rationally based."

A 59-year-old husband, married for thirty years to a wife now
57, says his fantasies involve "group sex, seeing other people
make sex; being seen." He has actually had this experience once,
with his wife and another couple. "I like it much; my wife does
not," he writes — and it has never happened again.

The longest-lasting experience with swinging is reported by a
husband now 74, retired in Florida on an income of more than
$50,000 a year. He married his second wife, he recalls, when he
was 38 and she 24. He writes:

Every facet of our life together has been a joy, presumably
because we have been able to communicate our ideas — sexual desires, financial problems, etc. — with each other. . . .

My wife and I have been "partying" [that is, swinging]
since we were married two or three years. In spite of our
deep love, we have enjoyed sexual contacts with other persons — but always when we are *together*.

We have partied with one man, or one woman, or one
couple — but never more than two other persons at a time.

Currently, at ages 74 and 60, this couple

are partying with a couple about 50 years old. This has gone
on for about four years, probably four times per year. It is
very satisfying to both of us (all of us).

My contact with *men* has been only when partying *with
my wife present* — and is part of the good time we are having.
I have never been with and have no desire to be *alone* with a
man. . . .

I think sexual inhibitions break up more marriages than sexual infidelity. . . . The secret is to make your wife #1.

He adds that "when we have a party with another person, it rarely ends in coitus. Usually my wife and I save that until we are alone." Now, after thirty-six years of marriage and thirty-three years of "partying," this husband observes:

Sex with one person may become old hat and jaded. They are tired of looking at the same breasts and genitals. The sex act (even with people in love) loses its excitement. But inject another person and make it a threesome or foursome and an entirely new element — one of adventure, newness — surfaces, leading to [youth-like] stimulation and satisfaction for all concerned. The main thing is: DO NOT SPLIT INTO SEPARATE ROOMS — STAY TOGETHER!

Summary

Reviewing the patterns of marriage from fidelity to consensual adultery, we find a broad spectrum of beliefs and practices. Our respondents range from faithful wives and husbands who would consider their marriage bed defiled by any outside sex by either spouse to those who engage in outside sex in the same bed along with their spouse and others. The former are far more common. A much larger proportion of husbands than of wives are adulterous.

For most of our adulterous wives, sex outside marriage seems to be a serious, significant experience. For many of our adulterous husbands it appears to be a considerably more casual matter.

Most of the wives and husbands in our study now adhere, both in principle and in practice, to a single standard: fidelity for both. But a double standard — adulterous husbands with faithful wives — still survives in some marriages; and there are also some adulterous wives with faithful husbands. A single standard of a new kind — consensual adultery for both partners — is found among our respondents but is infrequent.

The great majority of our faithful wives (87 percent) and husbands (91 percent) rate their marriages as happy. But a substantial proportion of our adulterous wives (72 percent) and husbands (75 percent) also rate their marriage as happy.

Of the fifteen nonsexual factors reviewed in this chapter, only one appears to be strongly associated with marital happiness: quality of communications between spouses. Six others show a modest association: health, education, religious commitment, employment versus retirement, first marriage versus remarriage, and marrying before or after 50. The other eight nonsexual factors have no meaningful relationship to marital happiness.

All ten of the sexual factors reviewed above are associated with marital happiness or unhappiness for wives; eight of the ten are associated with marital happiness or unhappiness for husbands. The strongest association for both wives and husbands is between enjoying sex with one's spouse and marital happiness. The association with marital happiness is also strong for having sex with one's spouse, satisfaction with frequency of marital sex, and comfort in discussing sex with one's spouse. Having a strong or moderate interest in sex and becoming sexually aroused easily are associated with marital happiness for wives; they appear to make no difference in the marital happiness of husbands.

❧ 3 ❦

Unmarried Women and
Unmarried Men

I'm just so old and lonely that sometimes I think I just don't give a damn what happens to me any more. Nobody else cares, and it's a very lonely road you can't see till you get there.

So writes a 61-year-old widow who has raised three children on a farm in the Southwest, on an annual family income of less than $5,000. Her husband died last year after ten years of being an invalid. She continues:

I do the same work I've done ever since I married 30 years ago. I keep house, do farm chores, and look after the needs of [my youngest child], a 17-year-old high school student. Now is that retired or just *tired*? I've had to work for anything I got all my life, and I don't see anything better coming up for me. I am a poor person — come from poor people and married a poor man. Get a little social security, but who in hell can live on that? Can you?

She rates her enjoyment of life as 7, and says she is almost always lonely, "especially nights." She would like to make new friends but is prevented by inadequate transportation, poor health, not enough money ("for sure"), and shyness. "I never did make friends easy," she writes. "I am Indian."

Following menopause at age 51, "I just lost interest" in sex. "We were so poor and I was tired all the time. I had just had it by then."

One reason she was often so tired and depressed was no doubt her health. She suffers from a thyroid deficiency. "My doctor died two years ago," she explains. "I was taking thyroid but I ran out and I can't afford to go to a new doctor. He was an old doctor and [charged] cheap prices." (Lack of thyroid medication could help explain at least some of the problems in her life; an untreated thyroid deficiency may lead to fatigue and mood depression as well as other symptoms.)

Her husband, she says, was the only man she ever loved.

> Love in youth is an exciting, passionate experience with no thought of self. If I ever marry again, it will be to better my circumstances — material, financial, etc. I've had it with this passionate stuff. Quiet companionship and a good friendship and comfortable support is what I want now. If I can't have that, or a good prospect of it, I'll go it alone. I don't want some old, penniless, broken-down guy to wait on. I want somebody to wait on me for a change.

She strongly believes that masturbation is not proper for older people, "or anybody else." However, she masturbates two or three times a year, always with sexual fantasies.

> What else is there to do under the circumstances? I get so lonely and sometimes a book or picture excites me a little and I'm alone and then I [masturbate] and then I am so ashamed of myself because I know by past experience I could have gone outside for a walk or something unless it's raining (and then I want to masturbate). Reading this stuff arouses me some, and when I see a vibrator advertised I'd like to try one but I don't know where or how I'd hide it. Any suggestions?

I don't really crave sex; I crave companionship mostly. . . .
Today's world is so cruel and self-centered and you have
got a dirty mind or you wouldn't be sending these [question-
naires] out and so have I or I wouldn't answer.

A 67-year-old widower in Indiana writes in a similar mood:

I have been widowed, alone, for eight years, so my sex life is
zero — nothing. My wife was sick nine years, so there have
been 17 years of inactivity. I'm sure I am useless for there
hasn't been erection for years. I would go to a prostitute but
I live in a small town where there are none (that I know of).
I couldn't afford one anyway, as I have [only] a very small
pension and Social Security [totaling less than $5,000 a year].
But sometimes I am so lonely I would pay for feminine companionship: to kiss, or hug, or just to hold her hand. Being
old . . . . and ugly is a terrible combination—so I keep busy
in my yard, reading, [attending] adult education classes at a
high school, and a hobby (carpenter work). But I *do* miss a
woman, very much. . . . Being lonely and old is just as bad as
being lonely and young. I know both. . . . No love, not even
anyone to touch, or hold their hand.

Such unhappiness could hardly be more poignantly expressed. Lonely, sad, embittered, resigned, cut off from life's re-
wards and enjoyments, these two respondents seem to epitomize
the tragedy of the unmarried elderly — not only spouseless but
partnerless and friendless, socially isolated and emotionally
alienated, trapped in poverty and either chronically ill or threatened by chronic illness.

Unquestionably, there are in the United States some very unhappy unmarried men and women over 50 — widowed, divorced
or separated, or never married. We shall meet some in this chapter, and they are worthy of serious concern. But they are very
much in the minority among our 512 unmarried women and 413
unmarried men. Another much larger but less frequently publicized segment comes into focus when we consider our life-
enjoyment statistics.

THE UNMARRIED AND LIFE ENJOYMENT

Of 492 unmarried women who rate their life enjoyment on our
7-point scale, 80 percent indicate high enjoyment and 20 percent
low enjoyment. The proportions for the men are similar: of 402
unmarried men, 83 percent report high, and 17 percent low, enjoyment.

A larger proportion of men than of women in their fifties report high enjoyment of life — but this is not true for the sixties:

Age and life enjoyment

	In their 50s	In their 60s	Aged 70 and over
Unmarried women	(N=176)	(N=177)	(N=139)
Life enjoyment high	79%	81%	81%
Life enjoyment low	21	19	19
	100%	100%	100%
Unmarried men	(N=148)	(N=126)	(N=128)
Life enjoyment high	84%	81%	83%
Life enjoyment low	16	19	17
	100%	100%	100%

Our unmarried women and men enjoy life less than do our
married respondents. The same difference — seven percentage
points — separates the unmarried from the married women and
the unmarried from the married men:

Marital status and life enjoyment

	Married	Unmarried
Women	(N=1,196)	(N=492)
Life enjoyment high	87%	80%
Life enjoyment low	13	20
	100%	100%

	Married	Unmarried
Men	(N=1,853)	(N=402)
Life enjoyment high	90%	83%
Life enjoyment low	10	17
	100%	100%

Of our unmarried women, more than half are widowed and one-third are divorced or separated. The proportions for our unmarried men are reversed:

	Women	Men
	(N=512)	(N=413)
Widowed	55%	34%
Divorced or separated	33	52
Never married	12	15
	100%	101%

Very similar proportions of our widows, widowers, and divorced and separated women and men report a high level of life enjoyment. Never-married men are the most likely and never-married women the least likely to report high life enjoyment:

	Widowed	Divorced or separated	Never married
Unmarried women	(N=265)	(N=168)	(N=59)
Life enjoyment high	81%	80%	76%
Life enjoyment low	19	20	24
	100%	100%	100%

Unmarried men	(N=135)	(N=207)	(N=61)
Life enjoyment high	82%	80%	93%
Life enjoyment low	18	20	7
	100%	100%	100%

A further comparison is of interest: 30 of our 61 never-married men consider themselves homosexual — but only one of our 59 never-married women considers herself a lesbian.

Income and employment

The incomes of men, as is well-known, exceed the incomes of women throughout our economy. This inequity is clearly visible in our income data. Three-fourths of our unmarried women are at the low end of the income scale, as compared with only one-half of our unmarried men:

Annual income	Unmarried women (N=504)		Unmarried men (N=407)	
Under $5,000	10%		8%	
$5,000–9,999	22%	76%	12%	50%
$10,000–14,999	28%		16%	
$15,000–19,999	16%		14%	
$20,000–$24,999	10%		13%	
$25,000–34,999	8%	24%	18%	49%
$35,000–49,999	4%		10%	
$50,000 and over	2%		8%	
	100%		99%	

The disparities shown in the table above no doubt result from at least two factors: Men who are employed earn more than women who are employed, and men retire on higher retirement incomes.

Some of our unmarried women and men depend on their work not only for income but for life enjoyment and for staving off loneliness; and some derive deep satisfaction from working. For example, a 60-year-old divorcée writes:

"I need full-time employment to be happy with myself. A few days of idleness make me very nervous and dissatisfied with life."

A 53-year-old never-married man writes: "I'm alone. My job gives me a reason for living."

An 82-year-old widow writes from New York City:

When I reached the then mandatory age of retirement, I was really at the height of my career. I was in a very satisfying position. Salary was begining to be commensurate with work, so to quit was preposterous! The "stupid" pension plan halted, but a blessed executive of a private agency said, "keep on." This I did — 7 years after retirement time. Then it was done in easy stages — first, part-time work, then I joined Vista. Somehow, with a still alert, active, curious mind, I could not see myself "on the shelf." Few volunteer jobs could really make use of my capabilities. Vista/Action is a blessing. I am still on their rosters doing work that a city should be hiring for — and paying for. [It] keeps me alive. Life is fun — in spite of an arthritic knee.

A 69-year-old divorced man who lives and works full time in the Midwest supplies some details:

When the company [I worked for] was sold, I was 60. The new management did not want me. Seven months of rejection by every conceivable potential employer made me so fired-up mad, I took over a bankrupt (Chapter 10) company and [now] make $150,000–$200,000 yearly. I didn't thank them then, but now I am "happy I was too old."

A 70-year-old widow writes from Virginia:

Every time I try to retire, someone says, "Come and help me part time, I need you." So I keep working — just got a raise in salary. Sometimes, on a tired, dreary AM — like a rainy Monday — I wish I didn't have a job, but I think that has nothing to do with age. A job keeps one active and stimulated and using one's powers constantly. And it *makes the world a better place for everyone.*

When no work for pay is available, some older women move on to unpaid volunteer work in search of the same kinds of satisfaction. An example is a 66-year-old Florida widow who writes:

Having worked when young, later in marriage (when children were older), I found retirement (widowed by then) left too much time with no feeling of accomplishment of any sort. Also, felt I had much to offer to seniors (much younger than I chronologically) by services for their benefit, consequently mine. Am now employed in an agency which is unique in that no remuneration is given — services by seniors for seniors only. My work is friendly visitation, telephone reassurance, editing a monthly communication for seniors — endeavoring each month to have items of interest as well as constructive suggestions. This work is fulfilling to me — gives me a feeling I have a "place in the sun." I suppose it could be considered as an "ego trip" of sorts — at least I'm not sitting on my feathers, becoming *self*-centered and ill because of bordeom!

But a 70-year-old Texas widow who also does volunteer work still regrets the loss of her occupation:

My husband and I owned a cattle and grain ranch. When our son grew up, he was taken in as a partner. I worked in the fields and with the cattle, so I suppose I was self-employed. My husband died [of a stroke], quite suddenly. . . . My son is doing a good job and I have no complaints about the way he is running the ranch. But besides losing my husband, I lost also my occupation. Now I keep busy doing volunteer work. Running here and there — but it seems rather useless.

Other unmarried respondents express quite different feelings about working — and not working. Thus a 65-year-old widow writes: "I *didn't* have a long, all-consuming, completely satisfactory career in business; therefore, [I] was rather glad to retire."

Retirement

For many unmarried respondents (as for many husbands and wives), retirement is a mere bugaboo — distressing to look forward to but enjoyable after it occurs. In the table below, as in the similar table for husbands and wives in chapter 2, the proportion of respondents reporting positive feelings toward retirement rises sharply after retirement — while the proportions reporting mixed or negative feelings drop very substantially:

	Employed	Retired
Unmarried women	(N=184)	(N=188)
Positive feelings toward retirement	43%	73%
Mixed feelings	47	24
Negative feelings	10	3
	100%	100%

	Employed	Retired
Unmarried men	(N=168)	(N=181)
Positive feelings toward retirement	39%	76%
Mixed feelings	48	20
Negative feelings	13	4
	100%	100%

The statistics here as elsewhere are confirmed by the accompanying comments. There is an almost gleeful attitude toward retirement in the comments of some of our men — including a 70-year-old retired widower who writes: "Now that I have retired and someone asks, 'Do you miss your job?' I reply, 'Immensely! Particularly on weekends and holidays!' "

"Retirement is great," writes a 57-year-old retired widower. "I'm so busy doing things I want to do, when I want to do them, that I don't know how I ever had time to go to work."

And a never-married retired man, aged 63, observes, "It took me a long time (about half a minute) to 'adjust' to retirement."

A 70-year-old Rhode Island widow who has retired writes: "I enjoy having all this time to myself — to do with as I wish, and [I] find that time is not heavy on my hands. It passes all too swiftly. It's good not having to go to work. . . ."

Only seven of our retired unmarried women have negative feelings about retirement, and even in some of these cases the problem is money rather than the state of being retired. A 69-year-old widow who has retired in Arizona on an income of less than $10,000 a year writes:

"I love retirement, but deeply resent the starvation income. [I] am frightened to death of the future. Expenses have gone up almost 100 percent and my retirement [income] has gone up two percent . . . for the last four years." Her plight is made worse by major surgery, from which she is now recovering.

Another 69-year-old widow, retired on an income of less than $10,000 a year, reports from the Midwest:

When I retired nine years ago, I expected to be able to live comfortably and carefully on my pension. I even expected to be able to travel a bit and enjoy my retirement. But, with inflation, I'm barely able to get along. My car . . . is wearing out. I need a winter coat, rugs [are] worn, etc. I've developed diabetes, had a heart attack last year — so my medical bills are large. I . . . don't have social security. . . . I do have Part B of Medicare — for which I pay a considerable sum. I live to pay medical bills, taxes, insurance, etc. It's a terrible way to live.

Loneliness

Of the many problems that confront older men and women in our society, loneliness is often seen as the most widespread and the most distressing. The portrait of Whistler's mother, impassive and alone, is a symbol deeply etched in our consciousness. Similarly, the elderly man is often seen as a lonely figure — or perhaps not seen at all.

Our data do not confirm the loneliness stereotype. Only two percent of our unmarried respondents report that they are "almost always" lonely; half of them say they are "hardly ever" lonely. The proportions for our unmarried respondents are compared with those for husbands and wives in the table below:

	Unmarried women and men (N=915)	Wives (N=1,234)	Husbands (N=1,883)
Almost always lonely	2%	1%	less than 1%
Often	14	6	4%
Sometimes	35	29	23
Hardly ever	50	64	73
	101%	100%	100%

How do so many unmarried women and men manage to minimize loneliness and to enjoy life so fully? Not surprisingly, there is no one answer to the problem, but rather a wide range of ways. As we shall see, some methods of staving off loneliness are used by many of our women, others by many of our men.

The dearth of unmarried men

As is well known, unmarried women far outnumber unmarried men. According to the official figures, the ratio was 2.7 unmarried women for every unmarried man over 50 in the United States at about the time of our study. From age 65 on, the official figures gave a ratio of 3.3 unmarried women for every unmarried man.

The official figures, however, seriously understate the problem. They take no account of the fact that more unmarried men than women (57 percent versus 33 percent in our sample) are already involved in an ongoing sexual relationship and are therefore unlikely to be available; nor do they take account of the fact that more unmarried men than women (10 percent versus 1 percent in our sample) consider themselves homosexual. If these percentages from our sample are applied to the official data, the ratio that emerges is more than five unattached heterosexual women over 50 for every unattached heterosexual man over 50.

This gender imbalance profoundly affects many crucial aspects of life for our unmarried women. The lives of older men are also profoundly affected by the imbalance — but in a quite different direction. Our data make it possible for us in subsequent sections of this chapter to explore the *impact* of the gender imbalance on both our unmarried women and our unmarried men.

Quite a few of our unmarried women describe at length the impact of the gender imbalance on their own personal life. A 67-year-old San Francisco widow eloquently sums it all up:

> Lack of male companionship, friendship, being cherished, is the biggest blank in my life. I resolutely turn away from all advances, flirtatious or sexual, from *married* men. No friends ever invite me to meet an interesting man or even fill in as a dinner partner, and I am not aggressive socially. Seeing six blue-haired women competing for the attention of one overweight male on a cruise or at a gathering turns me off. I have noticed that a man my age or older, vigorous and intelligent enough to be attractive to me, is invariably going out with a 35-year-old "chick" with false eyelashes.
>
> In the ten years since I was widowed, numbers of married men have told me how attractive I was and that I should marry again — but when I once asked "Who? Where do I meet him?", the reply was a weak, "At dances and parties."

(I always had to have a date to go to a dance or party as a teen-ager; I can't seem to force myself out on the town [alone] now!) Statistics, I realize, are against me. . . . I am not interested in a fireside companion or someone looking for his mother or [a] housekeeper.

Friendships

One obvious solution to the problem of loneliness is to have close friends. To distinguish close friendships from sexual relationships and also from mere acquaintanceships, our questionnaire carried this instruction:

"We would like you to think about the people with whom you feel especially close, to whom you can confide your innermost feelings but with whom you do not have a sexual relationship.
"Do you have any such close friends?"

Of the 502 women who answer, only 14 percent say they have no close friends. Of the 407 men who answer, 28 percent report no close friends. (Instead of close friends, as we shall see, more men report sexual partners.)

As might be expected, the dearth of available men profoundly affects the gender patterns of close friendships. Unmarried men have mostly women friends — and unmarried women, too, have mostly women friends. Here are the details, as supplied by 434 unmarried women and 294 unmarried men:

• Only 61 percent of these women report even one close male friend — while 85 percent of the men report one or more close women friends.

• Nine percent of the men but only 1 percent of the women report that all of their close friends are of the opposite gender.

• Only 60 percent of the women but 76 percent of the men report having close friends of *both* genders.

• Finally, 39 percent of the women report that their only close friends are women — as compared with 15 percent of the men (including the 10 percent who consider themselves homosexual) who say their only close friends are men.

In addition to answering our statistical questions on close friendships, an astonishingly high proportion of our unmarried respondents — more than 90 percent — chose to contribute comments on the role of friendships in the later years and in their own personal lives; only about 8 percent of our married respondents commented on friendships.

A theme recurring in many comments is that close relatives also function as close friends, particularly among our unmarried women. Thus a 55-year-old divorcée writes from Florida: "An important part of my life is being friends with my grown children and their spouses. That is one of the joys of being a parent."

A never-married California woman of 66 writes: "My close friends are two: one of my brothers and [a woman] with whom I have been 'best friends' since I was 14. My two sisters are very close seconds."

The two quotations above make another important point: While 61 percent of our women report that they have one or more close male friends, this total includes close male relatives — sons and sons-in-law, brothers, and so on — who function as close friends in the absence of unattached men.

Other respondents who rely on close relatives to function as close friends include a 73-year-old widow who writes from Baltimore:

Close friendship with my . . . granddaughter is a real joy. We visit each other three or four times a year. Visiting my children and their families is always a pleasure but they live [hundreds of] miles away.

A 77-year-old widower comments similarly: "My close friends are members of my family, plus a few I correspond with."

A 52-year-old widow, who lives in a New York City suburb, gives a moving account of intergenerational friendships with both her parents and her children:

My parents died within the last fifteen months — my father after lengthy physical ill health and my mother in an advanced state of mental decay. Their plights were bad enough, but what they would have been like without [children and grandchildren] in the same city, and [others] willing and able to fly in fairly often, I cannot bear to imagine. Our love and care, and that of more extended family members, certainly meant a lot to their emotional and physical well-being. My own [children] are now in their twenties and their love is immensely important to me. Seeing how good [they] were with their grandparents encourages me to believe that they will do whatever they can for me.

A retired 65-year-old social worker, who has never married and never had sex with anyone, lives in her own house in Connecticut. She reports that until retirement her work was a major source of satisfaction — but she doesn't miss it:

I am thoroughly enjoying my retirement. I moved to a community where I had vacationed with my sister and her husband for 20 years (they lived here; my widowed sister still does). I chose to retire three years before mandatory retirement. I live independent of my sister, yet enjoy her companionship. I have made many new friends in the past year and have found a supporting community in a church. To be able to participate/contribute to community groups — League of Women Voters, agency boards — without the pressure of administrative responsibility has brought a great sense of release, and I believe has freed me to enter into new relationships more easily. Understandably, these relationships do not have the depth of some of those which developed over the years but I have some new friends with whom I share; and [I] maintain an ongoing relationship with old friends in spite of distance.

Nine percent of our unmarried women and 5 percent of our unmarried men describe themselves as "very religious," and several associate their religion with their friendships. A 70-year-old widow says: "My relationship with the Lord Jesus Christ and with my children (I have six) are very satisfactory. People are . . . likely to seek me out as a special friend."

One of the men comments that "since I became a Christian, I have found it easier to make friends."

A 69-year-old widower in the Southeast writes:

> I have many good and true friends, and make more every year through my [work]. However, my closest are my three daughters and their fine husbands. How fortunate I am that all six of them are born-again Christians, and the husbands all in Christian service, and my daughters very supportive and teach Bible studies. . . . I am probably uniquely blessed with children, grandchildren (whom I frequently babysit), and . . . friends. . . . For the first few months [after my wife died], I considered finding someone to share my interests — but decided I did not need another marriage with all the blessings of family and [career] the Lord has given me.

Several respondents report that the continuing-education courses they are taking provide a rich source of friendships — such as a 62-year-old widow in Colorado, who writes:

> I have been a college student . . . for the last five years (just got a master's degree . . .) and have therefore mingled with a great many young people. I try not to force myself on them [or] act as if I were their age [but] we have lots of fun — occasionally going out [together] or visiting one another. . . . I've found that age doesn't really matter . . . much to most people; it's your personality that counts.

Finally, let us consider the words of a widow of 75 in the Midwest, who writes that she has no close friends. She begins her comments with a poignant look back: "Love in one's later years can be beautiful. It's no longer wine and roses and heights of passion; it's steady, tender, reliable, supportive, gentle. I miss it dreadfully."

She continues:

Death, illness and moves to other areas of the country all
have contributed to reducing my circle of close friends. I
have acquaintances where I live but no close friends, no *real*
friends. . . . My male friends, excepting for one cousin, were
the husbands of my women friends; all have died. . . . I
haven't been to the theatre since my husband's death — a
form of recreation we used often to enjoy with other couples.

I wish I had a man friend to share things such as theatre,
concerts, stimulating conversation, dinner out, etc. Probably
I have always enjoyed male companionship a bit more than
female companionship; but such unattached males as there
are in this retirement community are boring and dull.

She concludes with observations about widowhood:

The older we are, the more difficult meeting those needs becomes. As I contemplate my own experience and that of
friends, relatives and acquaintances who lost their husbands
after they were 60, it seems to me that the trauma of widowhood is deeper and longer-lasting than that of women who
have lost their husbands when they were younger. A younger woman may compensate to some degree, *via* a job or
caring for young children. Such compensations are often de-
nied . . . to older women.

Just as our unmarried women tend to comment on the dearth
of close men friends, so our unmarried men tend to comment
on the plentiful supply of close women friends. Here are three
examples:

A 60-year-old widower in Oklahoma writes that "most of my
close friends are women, and though the relationships are not —
at present — overtly sexual, there is a lot of sexual drive behind
them. I [suspect] the women realize this. Something keeps the
drive from turning into action. I *think* I am in some way sexually
unattractive to those persons, perhaps because I am seen as want-
ing/needing too much from a relationship."

A never-married male observes:

A male 50 or over can have male-female friendships with women with whom he has never had sex, women with whom he does have sex, and women with whom he used to have sex — all agreeably, since the hot eagerness of youth and desperate sexual seeking seems to disappear . . . with middle age.

Our third example is a 50-year-old widower who writes:

All of my closest friends are female. For whatever reasons, I find women generally are easier to talk with. I generally care for women more than men. I believe that frequently they got "the dirty end of the stick" from lovers and/or uncaring husbands who seem to be emotionally dead.

A 76-year-old New England widow writes about the importance of male friends: "Friends are always important — especially male ones. As one gets older, one needs them more for they understand one's life — and are easier to talk to."

And a 66-year-old widow writes from Ohio about the importance of friends of both genders:

I have several beautiful and meaningful relationships (nonsexual) with men one-half my age. They take me to lunch or theater. We exchange gifts, books, thoughts and ideas. We enjoy being together. I have much the same relationship with several women half my age, and also several younger couples.

Making new friends after 50

Approximately half of our unmarried respondents, both women and men, report that they have about the same number of close friends now as at age 40. About a quarter of our unmarried women and a third of our unmarried men report fewer friends now.

When we asked how easy it is to make new friends compared with age 40, about 50 percent of the women and 55 percent of the men reply "about the same"; the rest are equally divided between those finding it easier now and those finding it harder.

A 74-year-old widower in New Jersey writes:

Making new friends in later years is difficult. My wife passed away a year and a half ago. Most of our close friends have died or moved away or become alcoholic. Being alone, I find it difficult to make new friends. Shyness seems to be a problem. I seem afraid to get involved.

I would like to be able to fall in love again, but most ladies my age turn me off. I do not want to get married again. If one takes [a woman] out to dinner and entertainment a couple of times, [she becomes] possessive.

A widow, who lives in San Diego, begins her detailed comments with a complaint:

At 70, I'm tired of television's portrayal of the old as either (1) grinning, garrulous, bouncy bores, or (2) doddering old darlings with full cookie jars and a store of folk wisdom, yearning to cook a big dinner and dandle somebody's baby. *Don't they know any of us?*

She continues:

I can make friends more easily now than ever, for several reasons: (1) I am less shy than when I was younger. (2) Other people are lonelier than when *they* were younger. (3) I have learned more of the social graces. (4) I know more about psychology, understand others better, and can usually make them like me if I want to.

The other side of the coin: (1) I need people less. (2) I have less energy for friendship. (3) There is no readily accessible place [for us] to meet again as friends — we all live, it seems, miles from everywhere we want to go and [at 70] we have little business driving the [highways]. (4) Worst of all, everybody but me has some sort of ailment — and old people don't appeal to me very much. I don't want to see the pictures of grandchildren, or to hear-or-tell what the doctor said. My friends are old friends; we were young together (with the exception of one friend I made more than ten years ago). I don't *want* any new friends — except that I miss having a close man-friend. I had a few, but they died or moved away; and the old men I meet do not attract me — we have nothing to remember together. I would like some *casual* friends in a square-dance group, maybe; but there aren't enough men left in my age group — and anyway, how would we all get there? I don't really mind a lot; just a little. My days are full, and I'm not the lonely type.

A 59-year-old never-married Colorado man comments:

The tragedy of age 59 is the loss of dear and old friends. Just the past ten days, phone calls told me of the death of two friends — one going back 42 years and one 32; thus my circle of friends tightens. . . . Friends who die cannot be replaced, for they became friends at certain moments of my life; . . . those moments are forever gone.

I would certainly like to meet a woman who is as free of responsibility as I am. Somehow all of the widows [and] singles I know are involved with children, family, jobs — thus are not free to travel, to vacation, etc. Example: I am now preparing another coast-to-coast trip. . . . I would love a companion (female) on the trip, a pleasant, educated person with her own resources — but, alas, I cannot find her. I vacation in Palm Beach, Lauderdale, and in New England and California, and meet many lovely women but . . . have not [yet] found a winning companion. I might add [that] this is a problem of retiring before 55 and being single.

A 54-year-old widow writes from St. Louis:

Due to widowhood and living alone, I seem to have more time to pursue and commit myself to friendships. They are like marriages — each one is demanding in its own way. My age and status (widow) make me more reserved and it does take longer [to establish a new friendship] than during the marriage years — but I'm doing it!

But a 76-year-old widower comments:

There are two categories of friends: the old ones who are slowly dying off and the young ones who are constantly moving to greener pastures. Each time you lose a friend it is harder to replace them.

In marked contrast is the 72-year-old widower in the Midwest who reports:

As I grow older, I find friends far easier to acquire. I am not a "joiner." Never attend old folks' meetings, etc., but I constantly make new friends and do it easier than when younger because I don't feel so self-conscious — am more outgoing.

And a 52-year-old woman who has never married writes from New Orleans:

Close friendships are very important. These involve primarily friendships of long standing. Meeting new friends (as opposed to acquaintances) becomes more and more difficult, but the effort should not be abandoned. Many of my friends [now] live at great distances; but [this] in no way impairs the meaningful relationship.

Some unmarried respondents report special relationships which in some ways go beyond close friendship.

A 64-year-old widow writes from North Carolina:

Since being widowed . . . (children grown and flown), I have very much enjoyed having a male graduate student at the house. I enjoy the illusion of "family" and within the year or so that he lives here we become good friends. Several of them come back to see me occasionally. I have always preferred men's conversation to women's, and having a man to talk with (when he has time) is a real pleasure. This is a strictly platonic relationship, but I wouldn't consider having a girl roomer, regardless of her conversation. I like a man's voice and his shoulders under the T-shirt; and I don't mind cleaning up after him as I would after a girl. My daughter says, "A student at your house is halfway between a son and a boyfriend." I don't deny it. There are all degrees of interplay between men and women.

The 66-year-old Ohio widow, quoted earlier on the importance of having friends of both genders, writes:

I recently started taking massages from a young man who is a licensed Swedish masseur — very proper — as a relaxant and in furtherance of my health goals. To my surprise, I find myself enjoying the whole "touching" process in a very erotic way as well. It fills in all the "touching" I am not getting in my mostly-single state.

We asked our unmarried respondents whether they would like more opportunities to meet a man or a woman who might become a close friend. When it comes to meeting someone of the same gender who might become a close friend, 48 percent of our women say yes — but 30 percent say no. Similarly, 49 percent of our men say yes to meeting a potential male friend — but 32 percent say no. The rest didn't answer.

Meeting someone of the opposite gender who might become a close friend is more interesting, particularly to our unmarried women: 66 percent say yes to meeting a man, while 23 percent say no. And 60 percent of our unmarried men say yes to meeting a woman, while 32 percent say no. Again, the rest didn't answer.

Seventeen of our unmarried women and 39 of our unmarried men say they neither have a close friend nor want to meet one.

The excess of men in this comparison may well be due, at least in part, to the fact that more unmarried men than women are involved with an ongoing sexual partner — and may therefore have no room in their life for a close friend.

Barriers to making friends

We asked:

"Which, if any, of the following now interfere with your making new friends?"

Nineteen percent of our unmarried respondents, both men and women, do not report any barriers to new friendships. The remaining 339 men and 414 women cite one or more deterrents, distributed as follows:

	Unmarried women (N=339)	Unmarried men (N=414)
Not enough social activities	47%	46%
Not enough time	35%	32%
Shyness	25%	29%
Not enough money	18%	14%
Inadequate transportation	17%	8%
Health	13%	9%
Lack of privacy	3%	4%
Other	13%	13%

The lack of social activities, cited by almost half of the unmarried respondents who answer the question, is a clear statement of need for both unmarried men and unmarried women. One striking difference between the women's and men's responses: Twice as high a proportion of unmarried women as men cite "inadequate transportation" as a barrier to making new friends. The disparity calls attention to a major handicap many older women face: lack of driving licenses and cars. Indeed, around the period of our study, about 37 percent of women aged 50 and over were not licensed drivers — as compared with about 5 percent of men.

Living arrangements

As might be expected, the dearth of unmarried older men has a substantial impact on the living arrangements of both our unmarried women and our unmarried men. Of the 912 who tell us whom they are living with, more than twice as many unmarried men as women (29 versus 14 percent) say they are living with a sexual partner.

This, in turn, affects our loneliness data. Among our unmarried men living with others — including the 29 percent living with a sexual partner — the proportions reporting loneliness are substantially lower than among our unmarried men living alone.

Among our unmarried women, there is no difference in loneliness between those living alone and those living with others. The frequency of loneliness for unmarried women is less than for unmarried men living alone but more than for unmarried men living with others (including the 29 percent living with a sexual partner):

	Unmarried women living alone	Unmarried women living with others	Unmarried men living alone	Unmarried men living with others
	(N=352)	(N=153)	(N=279)	(N=131)
Almost always feel lonely	1%	2%	3%	0%
Often	13	10	20	6
Sometimes	35	36	35	32
Hardly ever	51	52	42	62
	100%	100%	100%	100%

Enjoyment of life among those living alone and with others is also affected by the gender imbalance. A much larger proportion of unmarried men living with others (including the 29 percent living with a sexual partner) report high life enjoyment than is the case for unmarried men living alone, unmarried women living alone, or unmarried women living with others:

	Unmarried women living with others	Unmarried men living alone	Unmarried women living alone	Unmarried men living with others
	(N=148)	(N=275)	(N=344)	(N=127)
Life enjoyment high	78%	79%	81%	90%
Life enjoyment low	22	21	19	10
	100%	100%	100%	100%

To sum up, our unmarried men living with others (including the 29 percent living with a sexual partner) report less loneliness, and a larger proportion of them report a high level of life enjoyment, than is true of our other unmarried respondents — men living alone, women living alone, and women living with others.

THE SEXUALLY ACTIVE AND INACTIVE

Just as more unmarried women than men appear to rely on close friendships for their life satisfactions, so more unmarried men than women appear to rely on sexual activities for their life satisfactions.

A substantially greater proportion of our unmarried men than women are sexually active — that is, they are currently masturbating and/or have an ongoing sexual partner and/or have had sex with at least one casual partner during the past year:

	Unmarried women	Unmarried men
	(N=512)	(N=413)
Sexually active	68%	86%
Sexually inactive	32	14
	100%	100%

The proportions sexually active decline with age (see chapter 8); yet it is a notable fact that 50 percent of our unmarried women and 75 percent of our unmarried men aged 70 and over remain sexually active.

A higher proportion of our unmarried men than women (62 versus 54 percent) are currently masturbating; a higher proportion (57 versus 33 percent) have an ongoing sexual partner; and a higher proportion (34 versus 13 percent) report sex with one or more casual partners during the past year. The second and third of these disparities are clearly traceable in substantial part to the prevailing gender imbalance — the excess of unmarried women and the dearth of unmarried men.

Our divorced and separated women are substantially more likely to be sexually active than our widows and never-married women; the three subgroups of our unmarried men are separated by somewhat smaller differences:

	Divorced or separated	Widowed	Never married
Unmarried women	(N=171)	(N=282)	(N=59)
Sexually active	84%	60%	56%
Sexually inactive	16	40	44
	100%	100%	100%
Unmarried men	(N=213)	(N=139)	(N=61)
Sexually active	89%	80%	85%
Sexually inactive	11	20	15
	100%	100%	100%

It is possible that some of our sexually inactive unmarried men and women feel that they are sexually frustrated — that they want but can't find a sexual partner, and do not masturbate because of inhibition or taboo. But we fail to recall even one sexually inactive respondent who expresses sexual frustration in her or his Comment Pages. Frustration is expressed mostly by those who do masturbate and who want but can't find a sexual partner.

There are several reasons why the sexually inactive rarely appear to be sexually frustrated. Many report that they consider sex of little or no importance; that they have little or no interest in sex; that they never get sexually aroused; and that they experience little or no discomfort at going for prolonged periods — or even indefinitely — without a release of sexual tension.

One example is a 69-year-old divorcée who is now retired in Alabama. "I looked forward to retirement," she writes,

> and have enjoyed it even more than I anticipated, since I have no financial problems. I have always saved money for my retirement and also receive a generous annuity. I remain busy doing what I want to do when I want to do it. I do my own housework and all my yard work and spend most of my leisure time reading. I realize I am unusually fortunate in having the health and good vision to make these pursuits possible.

She has no men friends, and fewer women friends than at 40; but she hardly ever feels lonely, and has no desire to make additional friends of either gender. In addition to her former husband, she had several lovers in the past; but she is now sexually inactive, reporting neither sex with a partner nor masturbation. She explains:

> I never really *had* any sexual interest. I liked to feel that I was attractive to men, and enjoyed male companionship over female — [but] as for sex, I just went through the motions. . . . It was less trouble that way, and didn't really matter much to me one way or the other.

She describes her present interest in sex as "absent," says she never becomes sexually aroused, and adds that she can comfortably go without release of sexual tension "from now on."

Asked what she would do differently, she replies, "I probably would have far fewer sexual relationships than I had, although I don't especially regret any of them." She rates her enjoyment of life as 1.

One sexually inactive man who is enjoying life greatly without feeling sexually frustrated is a very religious widower of 83. A retired engineer, he lives alone in New England on an income of less than $5,000 a year. He neither has sex with a partner nor masturbates. Asked how long he can comfortably go without a release of sexual tension, he replies, "40 years." He has no children and no close friends, female or male — nor does he want any. He explains:

The days of my retirement are devoted to my own personal matters and [to] the contemplation and enjoyment of my God-given seclusion amidst the miraculous marvels of His own creation totally surrounding me on all sides. I have [a river] for my back yard, and I never attempt to kill any of its abundant denizens of all sizes. . . . This is the second year I have been burning wood in my oil-burning heating stove, to stretch my scarce and expensive heating oil. I hoist drift logs from the [river] up onto a sawing rig and chain-saw them to proper lengths. I rigged the hoist and the sawing outfit with my own sweat and brawn — good exercise physically and mentally. . . . I have chest-freezer space to hold enough . . . perishables to last me one year. When I have [it] filled, I "hole up" — hibernate, so to speak. I do a lot of talking to and thanking God for all the miracles He is bestowing on me to keep me fit and feeling that perhaps all my future is not yet behind me.

He never sees a physician and he describes in some detail, with much pride, how he has twice operated surgically on himself to remove growing tumors from his left forearm and his left hip joint.

He adds that he still has his fourteen-year-old car, but drives it only

> to pick up my 1) pears, 2) peaches, 3) tomatoes, 4) lettuce, 5) spinach, 6) ground beef, 7) beef liver, 8) vinegar, 9) whole-grain wheat (for my grinder to convert into whole-wheat flour), 10) whole-grain yellow field corn (for the same grinder), 11) nonfat milk powder, 12) sugar (no salt or pepper). . . . I checked my diet against [a nutrition guide], and now I know I am getting all the chemicals my body needs for fitness in accordance with the Recommended Daily Allowances [RDA] specified by the guide. . . . Just to be certain, I am consuming even more than the RDA — but not enough more to make me feel wantonly wasteful.

In addition to diet, he attributes his excellent health to keeping away from people — "a very effective barrier against colds" — and to refraining from sex in any form.

"In my view," he writes, "masturbation is not only an indication of base mental and physical depravity . . . ; it is wasteful of the body's 'seed' material. When left within the body, it is my view that this fluid is the most important contributor to the body's total . . . vigor [and] vitality." He continues:

> The lack of female image or person in my life serves . . . to keep my sex feelings well under control. Under this circumstance, one should conclude that the proper ingredients for dreams that result in orgasms are truly non-existent. I did, however, have an orgasm five years ago (at age 78) while sleeping; [I] wasn't even dreaming about anything. . . . I am 83 now, and that one will, probably, be my last one. (So what else is new?)

A third example of a respondent who is unmarried and sexually inactive but not sexually frustrated is a 55-year-old never-married attorney in upstate New York. She rates her health as excellent and her enjoyment of life as 1. She reports neither masturbation nor sex with a partner at any age, and she does not answer our questions on degree of sexual interest or sexual arousability. "Sorry — no sex experience whatsoever!" is her laconic but comprehensive comment.

One of our sexually inactive women tells a life story that might have come straight out of a novel by Nathaniel Hawthorne. She was born in a small New England town and has lived there all her life. Now 65, she lives alone in a private home in that town — perhaps the home in which she was born. She says that her present interest in sex is "absent." She has had only one sexual relationship, nearly half a century ago:

> When I was 19 and muchly in love, I had sex with my boy friend. This relationship did not work out. I simply could not marry another and have him think me second-hand. I was reared strictly.

She is not, however, wholly forlorn. She has a number of women friends — as many as when she was 40. She thinks it is easier for her to make new friends now than at 40. The only barrier to making new friends is absence of social activities in her small town. She is deeply religious. She has retired voluntarily from work, and views her retirement as "fulfilling and enjoyable. I travel [and] have become greatly involved in civic activities and my church." She is sometimes lonely — but not often. Indeed, she rates her overall enjoyment of life as 1.

How readers perceive such sexually inactive women and men may depend in part upon the attitudes, needs, and preferences of each reader. Some may see exclusion from sexual satisfactions as tragic — a tragedy exacerbated rather than alleviated by the fact that many of the sexually inactive report they are not interested in sex and are rarely or never sexually aroused. Other readers may see abstinence from sexual activities as a viable and potentially rewarding life pattern.

Our life enjoyment statistics shed some light on this issue.

Among both our unmarried women and unmarried men, high life enjoyment is reported by more of the sexually active than the sexually inactive. The difference is substantial for the women and even larger for the men:

	Sexually active	Sexually inactive
Unmarried women	(N=337)	(N=155)
Life enjoyment high	81%	74%
Life enjoyment low	19	26
	100%	100%
Unmarried men	(N=345)	(N=57)
Life enjoyment high	86%	65%
Life enjoyment low	14	35
	100%	100%

One argument frequently offered against sexual inactivity is summed up in the old adage "Use it or lose it" — meaning that those who remain sexually inactive for a substantial period find after a while that they have lost the capacity for sexual function. We have no statistics on this issue; but we do have in our sample several women and men who have successfully defied the adage, resuming sexual activity after a prolonged hiatus. Perhaps the most striking example is a 78-year-old Midwestern widow who neither masturbated nor had sex with a partner for 27 years after her husband died. What happened next, when she was 77, is eloquently narrated in her own words:

This is difficult for me to write and perhaps more difficult for you to believe — but it is true. About a year ago, out of curiosity, I read an "educational" article that very clearly explained intercourse, masturbation, effect of stimulating nipples, breasts, clitoris, genitals, nudeness and everything! I was home alone when I read it. I could not believe what was happening to this old body of mine while reading it. Your words "sexual arousal" describe it. There was actually vaginal moisture and the desire for intercourse! . . . It was after I read the article that I did masturbate . . . just to experience the effect of "playing" with nipples and clitoris! And I actually reached orgasm two of the times. Isn't it unbelievable?

Masturbation

The proportions of unmarried women and men who masturbate decline from decade to decade; but even in their seventies and beyond, 43 percent of our unmarried women and 54 percent of our unmarried men still masturbate.

We asked our respondents who masturbate to indicate for which of nine reasons or circumstances they do so. The most obvious answer is also the most frequent: "absence of acceptable partner." Many say they masturbate as a method of releasing sexual tension or as a major source of sexual enjoyment. One woman who makes this point is a New England widow of 54:

I did not learn to masturbate until my early forties. It has added much pleasure to my life and the fantasies I have developed have added to my overall desire for, and pleasure in, sexual activities. I believe middle-aged persons, especially sexually deprived persons, should have courses available which teach about fantasy, masturbation, and homosexual activity so that each can make an educated, informed choice.

Masturbation is the only sexual activity of a never-married 72-year-old male respondent who writes:

Because you will not know my name, I am going to admit that I have never really performed the sex act with a woman. In other words, I am still a virgin although a number of times and for different reasons the act failed. The reasons were never for lack of desire or ability to perform. As I passed 35 years old, only younger women appealed to me sexually. So . . . my opportunities are nil — and I have no desire for a young prostitute. I still have strong sexual desires for a young girl and very frequently fantasize.

He masturbates three to six times a week, less frequently than at age 40, and he seldom experiences orgasm. He comments: "My lack of sex life has, since I was sixteen, given me a serious inferiority complex." He also reports:

At least once every night I awaken with a very stiff throbbing penis, even after I've been to [the] bathroom and urinated. I can't understand how this can be, when I'm unconscious and not even dreaming about sex — also why . . . during the day, I cannot achieve that extreme stiffness. I know you can't write and tell me; but perhaps you can mention it in the eventual publication.*

He concludes:

My only regret is that fate failed so completely to cooperate with me in achieving sexual relationships. Mostly it was not my fault.

Another never-married respondent for whom masturbation has been the only sexual activity in his entire life is quite serene about it. Aged 83, he has retired on an income of between $10,000 and $15,000 a year and lives in a home for the aging in Illinois. He writes:

I am an 83-year-old virgin male, with many friends, male and female, who considers himself a "liberal" — and would not want [life] to be other than it is. . . . I have been happy in my retirement, keeping very busy. The last 15 years [have] been the best.

He hardly ever feels lonely, and rates his enjoyment of life as 1.

---

* Firm erections during sleep are a common experience for men of all ages. They occur mostly during a particular kind of sleep known as REM (rapid-eye-movement) sleep. *Why* they occur is unknown.

He masturbates once a month or less — less frequently than at 40 — "to release tension," and he comments: "Masturbation is almost a necessity for a single man who elects not to engage in sex with a partner." He usually has sexual fantasies when he masturbates, and he always reaches orgasm.

Asked if there is anything he would change in his life, he answers: "No. My way of life is the best *for me.*"

Some of our unmarried men have conflicting feelings about masturbation. One is a 76-year-old respondent who has retired in Florida on an income of between $10,000 and $15,000. He describes himself as "recently widowed," and rates his enjoyment of life as 5. He reports masturbating two or three times a week, and comments:

> Since early adolescence, I have been pathologically addicted to masturbation. This has caused me a great deal of suffering through guilt feelings and the self-hate that comes from being unable to escape from an addiction. I ascribe all this to the lack of sex education I had in pre-adolescence.

Sexual relationships

As noted earlier, our unmarried men are more likely to have a sexual partner than our unmarried women. Here are the details:

	Unmarried women	Unmarried men
Ongoing sexual relationship	(N=480)	(N=374)
Yes	33%	57%
No	67	43
	100%	100%
Casual sexual partner in past year	(N=367)	(N=213)
One or more	13%	34%
None	87	66
	100%	100%

We also determined the proportions of unmarried women and men who had sex with a partner at all last year — *either* with an ongoing partner *or* with one or more casual partners, *or* with both. The proportion of women who had sex of either kind last year was much lower than the proportion of men:

	Unmarried women	Unmarried men
Sex with a partner in past year	(N=483)	(N=376)
Yes	38%	65%
No	62	35
	100%	100%

The dearth of available men over 50 — and the excess of available women—is no doubt largely responsible for the differences in the above three tables.

A striking statistical note: Among our unmarried respondents with an ongoing sexual relationship, 20 percent of the men and 14 percent of the women also had one or more casual sexual partners during the year.

Solving the dearth-of-men problem

Despite the shortage of unmarried men, 160 of our unmarried women report an ongoing sexual relationship and 48 report one or more casual partners last year. Where do they find their sexual partners?

In the sections that follow, we shall discuss four possible solutions in order of their frequency:

First, 40 percent (60) of our unmarried women with ongoing sexual partners have taken a *married* man as a lover.

Next, a substantial but smaller number are making do with a male lover much older than they are.

Third, a suprising number have a much younger male lover.

Finally, there is a solution that is often discussed nowadays but is exceedingly rare in our sample. With so devastating a short-age of unattached older men, it is asked, why shouldn't older women team up with one another as sexual partners?*

We shall also discuss in the four sections that follow the sexual partner choices of our unmarried men. A few have chosen married women; many have chosen women much younger than they are; and some have chosen older women or other men. Note, however, that for most unmarried men, these are matters of choice, not of necessity. Instead of being loaded agaisnt them, the dice are loaded in their favor by the demographic facts of gender imbalance.

Partner married

A 51-year-old divorcée lives near Washington, D.C., on an annual income of between $20,000 and $25,000. She writes: "I feel great that I have handled my financial affairs so well I [was] able to re-tire prior to 50 — and I love it!"

Three years ago, she launched an affair with a married man nine years older than she. Her affair is not going too well these days; she rates the happiness of the relationship as only 4. "I don't think I love the man I am currently seeing," she writes, "but I feel I do need him — at least for now."

The two are not living together, she says — "but we do spend a lot of time with each other, [including] sleeping together 98 per-cent of the time." Concerning marriage, she writes:

> I do not feel the need to marry. I am quite independent, emotionally and financially, and feel marriage could add nothing worthwhile to my life. Conversely, it might termi-nate a lovely romance. My partner is married but has indi-cated he would divorce and marry me if I would have him. True? Who knows?

---

* "Two women? Impossible!" Queen Victoria is alleged to have remarked when asked to sign a law making lesbian activities a criminal offense.

A 58-year-old widow lives in the South on an income of between $35,000 and $50,000 a year. She writes: "I haven't time enough to do what I want to do — sculpture, painting, sports, nature, dog and children, garden, canoeing, flying, skiing, tennis, etc., etc. . . ."

She continues:

> I love life; it's excitement and [I] regret nothing. My double pneumonia made me realize others liked me. My touch with polio gave me courage and will power. My many allergies (wheat, milk, etc.) showed me discipline. My diabetes and . . . muscle problems turned me to vitamins. . . . Even had cancer.

She describes a sexual relationship with a married man that has lasted six years so far. In addition, she has had many casual sexual partners — five during the past year. "I do not feel it is wrong to 'help out' married men," she writes, "if [they are] not in the same city or work. One must be careful *not* to hurt the wife!! Some wives hate sex; what is a man to do?"

A 50-year-old divorced man in Connecticut tells us he has been married three times — "once legally, twice common-law." For the past five years he has been involved in an affair with a married woman now 36.

> Masturbation has become the mainstay of my sexual life now. This, I suppose, is due to my partner's not being readily available — since she is married and since her husband is not privy to our affair. I would rather sleep with my partner than masturbate, but I do not feel guilty about masturbating.

Neither he nor his partner, he notes, considers their relationship an exclusive one:

> My partner sleeps with her husband and with one other man. I'm jealous of the other man but not of the husband. I

sleep occasionally with [another woman]. My partner knows of it but she does not seem to mind.

This respondent also reports ten sexual encounters with men before the age of 50 and one since, none of which lasted more than a day.

Several respondents report that an "absent lover" who is married is the most meaningful relationship in their lives. A 52-year-old never-married woman in New Orleans, quoted earlier on the difficulty of meeting new friends, supplies a particularly moving example. For eleven years she has been in love with a man now 59. He is married and lives in another state:

> Many months, often one to two years, go by between meetings. During these intervals we correspond occasionally and my sex life comes to a standstill — not because I have a formal or informal commitment to him, but because casual sexual encounters (without affection) have no meaning to me, and at this time and for the last several years, I have not known any other men who have interested me.
>
> My relationship is of necessity clandestine, as my partner is married, but I have learned to accept this condition as better than no relationship with him. The relationship has great meaning to us both, provides something we both want and need. . . .
>
> While the long separations are difficult, it would not be possible to sustain this relationship without eventual detection if the opportunities for meeting were more easy and frequent.

A 52-year-old divorcée who separated from her husband six years ago lives in Texas and is employed full-time, with an income of between $15,000 and $20,000 a year. She writes: "Don't want to retire, can't afford it, and would feel useless and much more lonely. [At work] I interact with people. I love my work."

She has close friends, both men and women, about as many as

at age 40; but she is sometimes lonely, and would like opportunities to meet new friends, both women and men. She explains:

> Women friends are very important, even just to talk on the phone if we can't see each other. But married women tend to be jealous and see me only when husband is away. Couples I was friends with when [I was] married have ceased to be friends. All my [current] friends are *mine*, independent of my husband, or I met them after we separated.

Of her men friends, she writes: "Usually the sexual question comes up. Have three men friends at work; but their wives are jealous, [too]."

Thirty years ago, when she was 22, she met and fell in love with a visitor from Canada, then 32. They launched an affair which continued throughout her marriage and continues today. She wants to get married but he doesn't; he is married to someone else. She and her lover are able to see each other three or four times a year for visits of from three to fourteen days. On these occasions, she writes, she and her 62-year-old lover "have a lot of sex. When it's three days, many times a day. When it's [a longer visit] we slow down — but still at least once a day."

In addition to her lover, she has had sex with five other men since age 50. "Sex outside my relationship [with my primary lover] is rare," she writes, "[and] *always* initiated by the man. . . . He has a hard time convincing me. I may never do it again. My lover leaves me free — just wants me to tell him the truth."

When her lover is away, she masturbates once a week or so. "It releases tension," she explains, "and sometimes I can go to sleep — but I'm as lonely after as before."

A 70-year-old Massachusetts widow has been having an affair for the past four years with a married man. She tells her story succinctly:

> I have been without a husband for many years and have had only one other partner. . . . Since he is married, our times together are infrequent but most enjoyable when we do get to-

gether. He is exactly my age and believes older men who go for younger women are darn fools.

A 53-year-old divorcée has an ongoing sexual relationship with a married man — and with his wife as well. This is the only ménage à trois in our sample.

The husband is 57 and his wife 50. They and the divorcée live together in a condominium in Maine, the married couple on an income of between $20,000 and $35,000 a year, and the divorcée on less than $10,000 a year.

The divorcée reports that the three have sex together from four to six times a week. She says that all of them reach orgasm on all such occasions. In addition, this respondent masturbates once a week or so. She rates her enjoyment of life as 3, the happiness of the ménage à trois as 2, and her enjoyment of sex with her two partners as 1. She leaves our Comment Pages blank.

The wife in this threesome confirms most of this information, and adds several details. She says her present husband is her second; they were married fifteen years ago when he was 42 and she was 35. She had had two sexual relationships with other women before her marriage — one at age 20 with a 40-year-old woman and one at age 30 with a 22-year-old woman. She and her husband, she says, took in the divorcée as the third member of their household four years ago. Asked how often the three have sex together, she checks both "4–6 times a week" and "once a day or more." She confirms that the other two reach orgasm every time and reports that she reaches orgasm almost every time. She writes:

> One male (husband) and two females (friend and I) share same household. We all share in sexual activities — sometimes all at once. Other times, just two of us, in [any] combination (male-female, female-female, husband-wife, husband-friend). We have also been casually involved with others.

She had one sexual relationship outside the threesome last year — a relationship known to her two regular partners.

She concludes:

Glad to have a chance to "tell the world" how nice sex life can be in "later years." Sex and life are what you make them! . . . My two partners (husband and friend) are also completing these [forms], so you will get all three opinions. (Each of us is writing in private, by the way. . . .) Thank you for giving us a voice.

The husband in this ménage à trois, aged 57, confirms many of the statements of his wife and their friend. He reports two signs of diminishing potency: when fully erect, his penis is not as stiff as before, and his refractory period is longer. He says that he has sex with his wife and partner once a day or more, and that he reaches orgasm on every occasion. He reports "10 to 12" outside sexual partners, in addition to his wife and their regular partner, since age 50 — including a few brief sexual encounters with men. Asked if there is anything he would change or do differently with respect to love and sexual relationships if he had his life to live over, he answers simply: "No."

In addition to these and similar examples, we have a number of women whose sexual partner is not only married but also much older (or much younger) than they are.

Woman partner much younger

Of our unmarried respondents in ongoing heterosexual relationships, 167 men and 148 women tell us the age of their partner. The data yield two findings of special interest.

Note, in the top two lines of the table below, that the men's reports confirm the conventional view; more than two-thirds report that their partner is five or more years younger than they are. A much smaller proportion of women report that they are five or more years younger than their partner. The explanation for the discrepancy seems clear: many of the men with younger sexual partners have a partner ineligible for our study because she is under 50.

Note also, in the bottom two lines of the table below, that a remarkably high proportion (29 percent) of our unmarried women report a partner five or more years younger than they are. The men's reports show a much smaller proportion of men-younger relationships. The discrepancy here can be similarly explained; many of the women with a younger partner have a partner ineligible for our study because he is under 50.

The table confirms, in short, that unmarried men seek and find younger partners; but it demonstrates in addition that they also seek and find (or are sought and found by) older women. If there were a 2.7-to-1 excess of unmarried men rather than of unmarried women, more women than men might end up with much younger partners.

Here are the details:

Relative ages	Reports from unmarried men with women partners (N=167)	Reports from unmarried women with men partners (N=148)
Women 10 or more years younger	43%⎱ 69%	14%
Women 5 to 9 years younger	26 ⎰	11
Women 1 to 4 years younger	16	22
Partners same age	4	6
Women 1 to 4 years older	10	19
Women 5 to 9 years older	2	14 ⎱ 29%
Women 10 or more years older	1 man	15 ⎰
	101%	101%

A striking example of a relationship between an older man and a much younger woman is reported by a 50-year-old Illinois divorcée who is employed full-time as a bookkeeper and looks forward with positive feelings to retirement.

"[I] don't understand people who retire and have nothing to

do," she writes, "no hobby, no interest, no goal. If you have a desire to live in retirement, there is *so* much to do to make yourself sufficient, worthy, self-satisfied." Here, as we shall see, she is thinking of her lover who has been retired for many years.

She has a number of close friends, both men and women, and is hardly ever lonely. She would like to make new friends but she is too busy.

During her marriage, she writes, "I was unaware . . . that I should have an orgasm" — and she never did. At the age of 47, following her divorce, she entered into a sexual relationship with a man who "was very concerned and with time taught me how to feel an orgasm and enjoy it." He was then 79 years old.

That was three years ago. Nowadays, she and her 82-year-old lover have sex together from four to six times a week. She reaches orgasm almost every time, and he usually does. "[I] feel that he *should* reach orgasm more often."

They are now planning to get married. "I used to think an older man should not marry a much younger woman," she writes, "[but] I changed my mind. [It] is okay as long as they meet each other's needs physically and emotionally."

This 50-year-old woman says she is in love with her partner, and she comments:

> Love after 50 is great. You don't play as many "games" in
> courting. Communications are greater, and down-to-earth.
> More comfortable. You don't have the image of tall, dark,
> and handsome; you are more realistic — seeing the person
> inside and outside. Much more deep feelings and less super-
> ficial feelings.

She describes three problems in their relationship:

"Financial problems. Maybe I'm selfish; but I feel that [with] all I am putting into our relationship . . . he should provide *more* finances toward my expenses and living." With her full-time job and his present contribution, her income is between $10,000 and $15,000 a year.

"Also, my leisure time is [dependent] upon what *he* likes to do.

Hopefully, we can reach a decision where we can both have 'equal time'."

The third problem is that she would like more variety in their sexual encounters. "Being stimulated, genitals with mouth or tongue, would be most sensational," she writes. She has never had this experience. Also, "my stimulating his genitals [orally] would be stimulating to him." But alas, she writes, "older people . . . were born and reared with a lot of no-no's. . . . There should be sex education for older people; [it] might 'loosen' them to appreciate what sex is all about — even at their age."

Despite these reservations, she rates the happiness of her relationship with her partner as 2, and her enjoyment of life and of sex with him as 1.

A San Francisco man provides the classic example of a midlife crisis resolved by casting off a wife and taking up with a much younger woman. He was divorced three years ago, at the age of 50. "I could never discuss sex with my wife," he recalls, "and would never think of having sex in any other way than face-to-face intercourse. . . . During my marriage we never indulged in any oral sex, nor employed the use of vibrators, etc." Since his divorce, "all this has changed. . . . I have become more sexually aware and . . . sexually liberated."

His primary relationship since his divorce is with a woman eleven years younger. They cannot marry because "we both have dependent children . . . and cannot have them live together at this time." At 53, he rates both the happiness of this relationship and his enjoyment of sex with his 42-year-old partner as 1. He says he is very comfortable discussing sex with her; the sexual side of the relationship is very important for him and moderately important for her. They have sex together two or three times a week, which he thinks is about right. In contrast to his experiences during marriage, he now enjoys both active and passive oral and manual stimulation of the genitals, use of a vibrator, reading sexually explicit material and viewing hard-core pornographic films and photos. He has never watched people have sex or engaged in group sex — but he would like to. "[I] probably would have answered differently before my divorce," he notes.

After his divorce but prior to acquiring his current partner, he had sex with three other women. "I am interested in women who are much younger than I am only because I am single and they are so available," he writes. "Once a person is married to someone, I think that he/she should not be involved sexually with others; but where there is no commitment, then I think sexual involvement with others should be pursued."

An 80-year-old widower lives alone in Baltimore and is still employed part-time, with an income of less than $10,000 a year. He reports five of the six signs of declining potency. He does not masturbate currently, and he says he could comfortably go without sexual release for "several months."

When he was 76, however, he launched a sexual relationship with a woman of 56, and this relationship still continues. They don't get married because neither wants to give up a separate home. They have sex together a few times a month; both reach orgasm almost every time. "It is a fine and tender relationship," he comments. He rates the happiness of the relationship as 2 and his enjoyment of sex with his partner as 1.

A 65-year-old widower in Bakersfield, California, is working part-time with an income of between $20,000 and $35,000 a year. He reports three of the six signs of declining potency but does not consider any of them a serious problem. He comments: "Have had prostate trouble. Had transurethral operation [prostatectomy] which did not affect sexuality or sex functions or pleasure."

For the past three months, he has been having sex with a 35-year-old woman. He says that the sexual side of their relationship is very important to them both and that he is very comfortable discussing sex with her. They have sex two or three times a week; both always reach orgasm. Asked why they don't get married, he replies that he wants to but his partner doesn't.

An 81-year-old Minnesota widower is still employed part-time, with an income of less than $10,000 a year. He describes his health as excellent, and says he is moderately religious. He reports all six signs of declining potency; but this does not seem to impair his enjoyment of sex, which he rates as 1.

He has had "6 to 8" sexual partners since 50, including one

currently. He was 76 years old when this relationship began and she was 48. Now, after five years, they live together "part-time." He rates the happiness of the relationship as 2 and his enjoyment of sex with his partner as 1. They have sex together four to six times a week. He reaches orgasm about half the time; she seldom does. He says that she usually initiates the activities leading to sex, and that he likes it that way. The only problem in the relationship, he says, is that his partner is an alcoholic. Concerning masturbation, he writes:

"Even though [I have] good sex available just around the corner, I feel the urge and necessity [to masturbate] every so often. Perhaps every 60 days."

An unmarried man now 80 tells of falling in love at 78. The object of his affections was a woman of 54. "We 'hit it off' from the beginning," he writes.

The difference in age — 24 years — made absolutely no difference. She had guessed I was ten years younger, and was amazed (and pleased) that I could "deliver" all she wanted — which was two or three times a week. She remarked, "If I *told* anyone, they wouldn't believe it."

This went on for 18 months and then she wanted to get married. There was, I believe, love enough for that on both sides — but my income [less than $5,000 a year] would not support two; and also I felt she should have a husband nearer her age and said so.

She said, "I'll continue to work," and I said, "Not for me — that's not my idea of marriage."

The final outcome of this was an agreement on my part to be strictly a temporary "boy friend" who would "step aside" the minute she saw or met someone she thought she would like, hopefully for a husband. Two months later, she said, "I've met someone I want to date" — and, as we had agreed, she and I had no more dates. *Finis.* She dated him three months and then "ditched" him, saying "He was no good" etc. Then she met another [man] and later married him. I wish her well. I feel I did the right thing.

What's really important about this whole story is an answer to the question so many younger men have asked me — men in their 40's and 50's. *Question:* How old are you before (or when) you can't get an erection? That's what they are all *really* concerned about.

When I was in my late 70's, I told them the truth: "Up till now I really don't know." I'm sure some of them did not believe me. How anyone writing a book will convince them, I'm really at a loss to know.

Woman partner much older

A 50-year-old Massachusetts divorcée includes in her detailed typewritten comments a discussion of the role of friendships in her life:

> Life is extremely enjoyable to me now. I have more friends than when I was 40 (and married) because they are friends that suit me and my life-style. I have them as friends because they are interesting and we communicate well — not because of business or social purposes. Because I am small and care about my appearance, have an open mind, and "think young," my friends are ten to twenty years younger than I am. Young men are still attracted to me. I really feel at this point in my life that age is about 80 percent mental and 20 percent physical. I have seen and known people in their late 20's who are old simply because they are bored with life, have closed their minds to all the exciting possibilities out there.

In addition to her many friends, she has enjoyed a variety of sexual partners:

> During my marriage I had no outside sexual partners, even though I had a very frustrating sex life with my husband. Since I have been divorced, I have been with men in a very

wide age range — from 18 to 75 — and [I've] come to the conclusion that age difference has little to do with a couple's happiness. In fact, the young man who was 18 when I was 43 was the one I was most compatible with. We lived together for [a year and a half], and he wanted to marry [me] — but I finally sent him away to find someone near his own age. A couple of years later, he married a girl his own age and isn't happy because she acts "like an old woman" who doesn't want to go out, doesn't like sex, and with whom he can't communicate. He and I had sex every night and there was never a problem. So I would never say what is right and what is wrong for someone else.

I do believe that much younger men are better for me than older ones. The older men are, the more inhibited they seem to be. They lack imagination and excitement.

Her current lover is 38 years old — twelve years younger than she. Their affair began six months ago. She says she is not in love with him, and she complains that the affair is taking up too much of her time. She rates the happiness of the relationship as 4.

The two of them have sex together two or three times a week — which, she says, is not often enough for her. In addition, she masturbates once a week or so. She usually reaches orgasm during sexual encounters with her lover and always when she masturbates.

Despite the shortcomings of her relationship with her 38-year-old lover, she rates her overall enjoyment of life as 1, and she concludes on an optimistic note:

It is good to come to a point in my life where I feel I can pretty much do as I please, be pretty much in control of my own life and not feel dictated to by a husband or "society." I like myself and enjoy people immensely but enjoy being alone at times. I have developed an inner peace and strength and finally come to the place where, even though I am quite fond of men, I don't need one beside me to feel like a complete woman.

Another divorcée is 54 and lives in the Midwest on less than $5,000 a year. She is employed part-time but is seeking a full-time job. She describes a somewhat humdrum marriage: "My husband was never fantastic in bed but was interested." A few years ago, her husband began experiencing problems with erection; this "led him to seek new diversions, greater excitement — e.g., he [wanted] three-way sex with very beautiful young women." She did try group sex with her husband and others on one occasion, but didn't enjoy it. "Without judging the activity," she writes, "I find it isn't for me."

Last year, she and her husband separated — "his idea, though I was ready for separation." Almost simultaneously, she fell in love with a man of 35, and they launched a love affair which is continuing. She has known her lover since he was 15 years old.

She and her young lover, she reports, now have sex once a day or more — in the morning, after 10 P.M., and at "odd times, too." Her lover, she adds, is one of those rare males who can have multiple orgasms — and so can she. She reaches orgasm during each of their daily encounters and he almost always does. In addition, she masturbates once a week or so. She says that since menopause she is experiencing vaginal atrophy, a condition "interfering with my sex life." She also reports "not enough vaginal lubrication" during sexual arousal.

She checks 1 on our life enjoyment scale, 1 on our happiness-of-relationship scale, and 1 — indeed, she makes three check marks at the 1 — on our enjoyment-of-sex-with-your-partner scale. But she does note one flaw in her relationship with her eighteen-year-younger lover: communications between them are only "good." She explains: "How he lives and age difference leaves so much we cannot share."

She has never had a sexual relationship with another woman — but she has been sexually attracted to other women both before and since 50. She writes: "I believe I am, and all people are, potentially bisexual. Pleasure is pleasure, and given the appropriate cultural and personal stimulus, how can the genitals tell the difference?"

She concludes:

Women seem to have sexual capacities more suited to younger partners. . . . [I] would like to see stigma of older woman
with younger men reduced. That stigma is less if the older
partner is the male — and that's archaic and echoes chattel-
hood.

A 61-year-old widow in the New York City area began living
with a 26-year-old man when she was 41. Now, twenty years later,
they are still together. They have sex together a few times a
month; he always initiates the sexual activities. She seldom
reaches orgasm and she rates her enjoyment of sex with her partner as only 4. Nevertheless, she comments:

> I have never been happier than I am now. He loves me. . . . I
> am . . . doing the things I had to postpone for the years I was
> raising a family. Now I am really living.
>   Sex is OK but having each other is more important, and
> having fun together, and just having each other instead of
> being alone.

She rates the happiness of the relationship as 1, and explains
that she and her lover, now 61 and 46, don't get married because
"we prefer things the way they are."
  A 52-year-old Atlanta widower fell in love a year and a half
ago with a widow now 66. He rates both the happiness of this relationship and his enjoyment of sex with his partner as 1. They both
consider the sexual side of their relationship very important, and
they have sex together two or three times a week. He reports all
six signs of declining potency, but he says these changes

> are no handicap. I can have many *orgasms* on the way to one
> *ejaculation.* An hour of sex is much, much better and more re-
> warding than a four-minute quickie.

He says that his partner wants to get married but that he
doesn't because he likes things the way they are and doesn't want
to give up his separate home. "Also, my partner is [so much] older
than I. . . ."

He concludes on a happy note: "Love and sex is getting better and better all the time — but then, I have a very loving and encouraging partner."

A 66-year-old retired schoolteacher with a much-younger lover lives in an apartment in a New Jersey retirement community on an income of less than $10,000 a year. She was widowed four and a half years ago. She writes:

In the last 34 years [of our marriage], there was from very little sex to none at all. . . . My husband was semi-invalid to invalid for 12½ years, [including] the last very difficult four years of his life and the living nightmare [of] his last six months.

She dealt with this situation in part by seeking and finding satisfaction in her work. "Sex drive can be changed into physical energy," she writes, echoing Sigmund Freud's theory of sublimation, "and there are a lot of boys and girls who remember a warm, loving teacher — which is a lot more important than whether or not I got laid." She also found great satisfaction in her family, including her three granddaughters and her grandson.

She masturbates two or three times a week, but her comments on masturbation are hardly enthusiastic. She quotes Xaviera Hollander on the subject: "Once you've mastered the finger exercises, it's time to get on with the main piece," and she adds: "According to the literature, one should get a more volatile orgasm [from masturbation]. Not me. Stop-gap aid only."

In addition to her many other sources of life satisfaction, she has had four lovers since the age of 50, one of them currently. She met her present lover thirty-five years ago, when she was 31 years old and he was 16 — perhaps he was one of her students. They did not, however, launch an affair at that time; thirty-four years elapsed before he came back into her life as a lover. That was one year ago, when he was 50 years old and she 65.

During the past year, she and her new partner have been having sex about once a week. Both of them reach orgasm on every occasion. She describes her present interest in sex as strong, and says she becomes sexually aroused "very easily." She rates her present enjoyment of sex with her lover as 1. They don't get married because they both prefer things the way they are, and neither wants to give up a separate home.

Her children know about her sexual liaisons and she finds their reactions to her life-style "interesting, amusing, and touching. . . . Their major concern has been that I might get hurt, or be too generous with my material possessions." The only family problem that has arisen was a minor one: Her young grandson was visiting and her lover was there, too. Her grandson, she reports, behaved like "a brat. He was jealous. Granny was supposed to be *his* for three weeks. I've read of this happening to young . . . mothers, but certainly never expected to encounter it at 66. My [lover] and I were most amused."

Asked what younger people should know about sex and aging, she replies: "That sex is not only for the young. It is integral for life. Not everyone remains interested — but those who do live more fully. Quality — not quantity — [counts]. There are many dividends to aging." Then she concludes:

> Sure, I'm a 1912 model and some of the parts are wearing — but I still water ski. [Recently] learned to snow ski. Plan to take up scuba diving when I can . . . find the time. Celebrated my sixty-fifth birthday last year on the banks of the Colorado River at the bottom of the Grand Canyon. . . . My daughter and grandson were with me. . . . After we'd camped in the sand . . . they brought from the raft a decorated birthday cake with candles, tablecloth, and pink champagne. My sixty-sixth [birthday] didn't compare — but my grandson served me breakfast in bed.

A 75-year-old widow, thrice-married, has been involved off and on since the age of 35 in a love affair with a married man ten years her junior.

She was a teacher in a New England private school for thirty years until her voluntary retirement at the age of 61. Her retirement income is less than $10,000 a year — but she is glad to be retired.

> I was a dedicated teacher, in the generally accepted meaning of that term. That meant long hours of work. . . . Before I retired, meetings, meetings, *ad nauseam* had become established. I was glad to get away from that part, but still miss the children. I *liked* teaching, and extra work on behalf of the children was no hardship. . . . I did look forward to retirement, but had been alone too much and at the beginning of freedom felt lonely. [Now I] have a yard to take care of, books to read, correspondence to keep up, and seldom feel lonely. I have [a television set] but watch it evenings only.

She had a hysterectomy, with both ovaries removed, which brought on menopause at 39. She took estrogen briefly for hot flashes, but stopped at age 40. At age 75, she still has hot flashes, but describes them as "no problem." Some years ago she had a double mastectomy. She takes medication for diabetes and for high blood pressure. She suffers from otosclerosis (a loss of hearing function); and she comments: "You'd be surprised to know how impatient some people are with the 'hard-of-hearing.' I'm not deaf, but definitely have impaired hearing. It's a nuisance."

Despite all these health problems, she describes her present health as "very good" — better than average for her age.

She says that her third husband was impotent. "Because of his impotence we used mutual manipulation, and that was pleasurable. He could not have an erection, but could, and did, have an orgasm and ejaculation."

She met her present "regular partner" forty years ago, when she was 35 and he was 25. She would not marry him then because of "the age difference" — but over the years, "as opportunity allowed, he and I had sex. This continued for twenty years — some years none because of distance between us, some years six times." Recently he became her "regular partner," and still is.

She describes in some detail their love-making at the ages of 75 and 65:

[Manual stimulation], gently done, gives me great pleasure and satisfaction. My regular partner and I usually use this method of love-making [nowadays]; and when I have had one orgasm [in this way], he enters me and I have a second orgasm when he has his. We discovered this [technique] early in our relationship — 41 years ago. How time does pass!!

Though she enjoys mutual manual stimulation of the genitals, she does not like having her genitals stimulated orally by her partner. Asked about her enjoyment of orally stimulating her partner's genitals, she checks both yes *and* no. She enjoys stimulating her partner's breasts or nipples during love-making — and she reports that since her double mastectomy, "oddly, where the breasts used to be, the sensory response remains!" She doesn't like being seen naked by her partner because she is "too fat." (She makes no reference here to her double mastectomy.) She has tried masturbating with a vibrator, but doesn't enjoy it.

In addition to her "regular lover," this 75-year-old widow with otosclerosis, diabetes, hot flashes, and high blood pressure, and with her uterus, both ovaries and both breasts removed, reports that during the past year she had sex three times with another man, aged 60, whom she calls her "outside partner." She explains:

The outside partner knows of my regular partner, but not who he is. The outside partner is no lover, but is a nice, decent man. . . . After six years of saying no, I agreed [to have sex with him] but do not approve. He is 14 years younger than I. I am fully aware of his reason for coming to see me, and avoid it whenever possible. He does pay me the compliment of saying that I give him *great* pleasure.

A 55-year-old Florida widow who is employed full-time with an income of between $15,000 and $20,000 a year writes: "At this point, I have no plans to retire. I think it is wrong to think of quitting work and vegetating — which happens to a lot of old people.

Part-time work [with] flexible scheduling is a much better alternative."

She has many close friends, all women — more now than at 40. She would like to meet a man who might become a close friend, but she is too busy. She is sometimes lonely, but not often.

Asked what she regrets, she replies, "I regret being such a prude. I never experimented or enjoyed sex much until after I was [widowed] at 52. I always believed that one man was much like another — and that ain't true."

Since 50, she has had sex with seven men — and has tried almost everything including active and passive oral sex, anal sex, rough sex, being watched while having sex, mutual masturbation, using a vibrator, and viewing pornography. She has liked them all. The only activities on our list of twenty she has not tried are watching other people have sex and having group sex — and these she does not want to try.

Her current ongoing sexual relationship is with a 35-year-old married man. They have sex together about once a week — which isn't often enough for her — and they both always reach orgasm. She also masturbates once a week. She rates the happiness of her relationship with her twenty-year-younger lover as 3, but her enjoyment of sex with him as 1. She concludes: "As my friend said after a wonderful two hours of love-making, 'If the kids only knew!' For us, anyway, it is so much more wonderful now than when we were young."

A 70-year-old widow lives alone in her own house in Rhode Island on an income of less than $10,000 a year. She rates her health as fair, explaining that she suffers from emphysema and a thyroid condition. She rates her enjoyment of life as 4.

For the past three years, however, she has had a continuing sexual relationship with a married man now aged 63. They have sex only a few times a month, which, for her, is not often enough. She masturbates two or three times a week in addition and remarks that "it keeps the genitals supple." She also has sex occasionally with another married man.

I'm not satisfied with the way things are with me. I prefer someone for myself alone. My partners are married — supposedly happy. We never discuss this. Both are quite a bit younger than I and both keep calling quite frequently but I put them off because I don't want to be regarded as too available. They do not tell me of their sexual habits with their wives. I would like to know but can't bring myself to ask. I want to know whether it is better with me and how so.

Asked about regrets, she replies:

I regret not being more sexually active in my younger days, but there were too many taboos. If I had it to do all over again, I'd experiment more and my late husband, who was also inexperienced, would have been happier also. This new freedom came too late for me.

A 66-year-old divorcée lives in her own home outside St. Louis and works at a full-time job, with an income of between $10,000 and $15,000 a year. She writes:

Our generation was raised in sexual ignorance. What little we learned in school was strictly biology. My parents were of little or no help. The most I seem to have learned was that neither a boy nor I was ever to touch me "down there." As a result, my teachers were immature young men — and a husband who, like the young men, tended to the "wham, bam, thank you ma'am" technique. Young people should be taught that there is much more to sexual fulfillment and enjoyment than just the act of fucking.

She reached menopause at 48 and thereafter, she writes:

I had the feeling more and more that I was merely a mechanism for my husband to satisfy his sexual wants. He resented a slight vaginal dryness I had developed [and] he didn't want to take the time to arouse me to achieve natural lubrication. He would smear a little surgical jelly on me and bang away. I started to masturbate to achieve my own orgasms but . . . was ridden with guilt because I had to resort to this "unnatural" practice.

When she was 61, after thirty-eight years of marriage, "my husband divorced me to marry a younger woman. I was forced to go back to work." Her self-esteem and self-image survived that potentially crushing blow, however, for she writes:

> . . . I can still look into a mirror and see an attractive woman with a still lovely figure. I can see no reason why a man younger than [I] should not find me attractive; and if he and I were like-minded, I would not hesitate to marry a man much younger than I.

The man who did revolutionize her life was five years younger — and married.

When she took a job after her divorce,

> I found myself working for a man who was not only a wonderful supervisor but a wonderful person. A relationship developed that eventually led to sexual activity. Maybe what I have experienced is not love. Whatever it is, it [is] so different from my marriage that it has given me new life. . . .
>
> At our very first experience, my partner displayed a gentleness and patience I had never experienced with my former husband. He encouraged me to talk about the frustrations of my marriage. This provided a sort of catharsis. He approached our union with patient understanding of my need to be aroused. He expressed delight at viewing my body. When I raised the prospect that my vaginal dryness might be a problem, his response was to apply his mouth and tongue to my genitals. Initially, this act was a shock to me. While I was aware there was such a thing as cunnilingus, this was my first experience — after age 60! He told me my cunt was beautiful, which was a surprise to me. My former husband had never described it as other than ugly. Before I knew it, the act had proceeded beyond its original purpose — to enhance my lubrication — and I was experiencing an orgasm. Only then did he penetrate me and, for the first time in God knows when, I had not just one, but multiple orgasms from intercourse.

He has now broken down all my inhibitions and my sexual life for the past three years has been glorious. I avow all my lusts to him, in the earthiest of language, and he responds to whatever I ask.

She then adds a word of advice to other women: "The woman who lets her wants be known is the woman who has her wants fulfilled."

This 66-year-old divorcée reports that she and her 61-year-old married lover now have sex together from four to six times a week; he always reaches orgasm and she almost always does. She says, however, that this is not often enough for her; so, in addition, she masturbates two or three times a week. Her lover has completely eradicated her former feeling that masturbation is "a degrading practice" and "unnatural."

"Masturbation is fun!" she now writes.

Today it is just fun and another way of coming. Most often I masturbate in the morning when I awake from erotic dreaming about sex. It seems a natural finish to my dream. I fantasize that what began in the dream is being completed while I am awake. The most frequent fantasy is of '69', [mutual oral stimulation] with my partner.

Asked what she would do differently, she refers back to the desolate years of her marriage. "I would, if I had to do it again, be a more aggressive partner. I would have stated my wants and insisted that these wants be satisfied. While I have enjoyed much fulfillment in the past three years, I feel cheated of so much I could have enjoyed if I knew then what I know now."

She concludes with some general observations:

Obviously, as my experience shows, old folks can and do have a full sexual life. The young should learn that sex is a dynamic activity that can continue so long as the body is willing. For some reason, older men are able to be accepted as having a continuing sex drive and are often pictured as "rutty old goats." [In contrast,] there are . . . many old wives' tales about what happens to women at menopause and, as a result, many women approach menopause as the end of their sex lives. I think young women need to be reeducated to the fallacy of this approach.

Partners of the same gender

As we have seen, most of our unmarried women with an ongoing sexual partner have found that partner by pairing up with a married man or with a much older man, and a surprising number have paired up with a much younger man. One additional way to find a partner despite the dearth of men is often discussed: pairing up with another woman.

While several mention this possibility in their comments, only three of our 512 unmarried women report that they are currently engaged in an ongoing sexual relationship with another woman. In marked contrast, thirty of our unmarried men report that they are currently engaged in an ongoing sexual partnership with another man. Thus, so far as our respondents go, same-gender relationships are not a solution to the dearth-of-available-men problem; they are a part of the problem.

Old friends make good partners

One bit of practical advice on how an unmarried older woman can find a partner comes from several of our unmarried women: Look up friends from your past, even your distant past. Examples include a 71-year-old widow who launched an affair in 1968 with a man she first met back in 1919 or 1920; a widow who at 52 fell in love and launched an affair with "a former suitor" she had met when she was 18; and a woman who launched an affair at the age of 62 with a man she had fallen in love with when she was 30. Other examples of this phenomenon appear throughout this book.

Each such experience taken by itself seems a mere coincidence. But the *multiplicity* of these reports indicates that much more than mere coincidence is involved. Rather, we have here a theme that recurs, with variations, in the lives of many older women.

Much the same is true, of course, of older men; every time a woman enters into an affair with a man she has not seen for many years or decades, there is also a man involved who is entering into an affair with a woman he has not seen for many years or decades. Such meetings, however, are usually initiated by women because it is women who are vastly outnumbered and who therefore have to go far afield to seek out acquaintances, friends, or lovers from their earlier years.

But sometimes men take the lead. A 78-year-old divorced man living in Southern California writes that at 68, "I rediscovered a . . . school companion who was a widow, and a 60-year friendship grew into something more for both of us." Now, ten years later, the two are still together and have sex a few times a month — which he considers "about right for 78 years." He rates both the happiness of the relationship and his enjoyment of sex with his partner as 2.

Very often, of course, a woman or man who meets an old friend finds that the attraction they formerly felt for each other no longer survives; but we have no reports of such cases for an obvious reason. People are always running into old friends they haven't seen for years or decades; there is nothing worth recording in such encounters unless the old mutual attraction *does* survive and *does* lead to a significant new relationship.

Multiple relationships and group sex

Two percent of our unmarried women and 6 percent of our unmarried men report having engaged in group sex since age 50.

One of our divorced men, now aged 59, remained a faithful husband through most of a twenty-six-year marriage. Then he moved to the Chicago area and discovered group sex — swinging. He reports "between 90 and 100" partners since 50. For the past two years he has had a primary relationship with a 53-year-old woman and her husband.

Our respondent does not consider himself a homosexual, and

had no homosexual relationships before 50; but he has had "six or eight" since then — all of them, apparently, in swinging situations. "Basically, I do not have the capability to become in love with a man," he states. Besides, "as I grow older and my capacity decreases, I am hard put to keep up with my female lovers. So I don't cultivate male partners — except the married couple who are my closest friends."

A 51-year-old divorcée lives in New Jersey and works part-time, with an annual income of less than $10,000. She writes:

> My job is not very important, but even so, I feel I'm contributing to my community by being employed. I feel somewhat useful to society; and although I don't now have enough time to do everything I want to do, I think that if I retired, I'd have too much time even with hobbies.

This respondent rates her current health as good, rather than very good or excellent; she is taking anti-hypertensive medication, and suffers from menopausal hot flashes. She reports no close friends except her daughter and son-in-law; but she is hardly ever lonely. She masturbates two or three times a week, and cites four reasons: "I enjoy it. It releases tension. It's an additional source of sexual satisfaction. My partner likes to watch."

Until about two years ago, she explains, she felt guilty about masturbating. Then she launched a continuing love relationship with a married man of the same age — and her sexual attitudes changed. Nowadays, "I really can't see that there is any harm in [masturbation] for young or old people — but it still seems to be a taboo subject and practice."

In addition to changing her views about masturbation, her married lover has introduced her to swinging, and she reports that she enjoys it. During her two-year affair with him, she has had sex with eight other partners, both male and female. "My partner initiates outside sex," she explains. "I'm really not interested in sex with any other men but sometimes I've gone along with it. My few sexual encounters with other women have been very casual — certainly not what I would call a 'relationship' — but I've enjoyed them."

This respondent rates her enjoyment of life, the happiness of her relationship with her partner, her enjoyment of sex with him, and her enjoyment of sex in general all as 1.

Another unmarried woman with multiple partners and group sex experience recounts a life story that is unusual in several respects. A 58-year-old Midwestern divorcée, she reports a conventionally puritanical upbringing: "Earlier religious teachings (a pox on them!) limited my masturbation (I worked it off making cookies in those days)." An unhappy marriage, with children, followed, during which she worked off excess energy by intensive volunteer work for her religious denomination.

In her forties, she recalls, she worried that life would become even more dismal for her after 50, with her children gone and no role left for her to play in the world. She dreaded the "empty nest." Shortly before her fiftieth birthday, however, she experienced what might be called a "religious deconversion." That was in the late 1960s, when the women's movement was giving voice to the view that a life such as hers was frustrating and a waste of woman's talents. She listened, agreed, and made revolutionary changes:

> I divorced at 49, ill-prepared to earn my living, . . . without alimony and [with very little] child support. I took out loans, went to school full time (slept part time), got professional training.

The years since then "have been my very best years in that they have been personal growth years. I loved raising my children, too, but that was another era — now over. I'm proud of my efforts in my own behalf, in becoming a trained professional, in earning much more money [between $25,000 and $35,000 a year] than I would have guessed when I crawled out of that marriage. I am economically autonomous . . . able to choose."

A year after her divorce, she started dating and soon took a lover. He "bought me my first vibrator and encouraged me to become easily orgasmic. Masturbation (I still dislike the *word*) is a delight now. Some of my best sex is with myself. Long, tantalizing, fantasy-laced, varied, lovely sex — with all the atmosphere, the props, the whatever-I-imagine. Fits my schedule nicely, too." She currently masturbates two or three times a week, always with fantasies. She does not, however, describe those fantasies. "My sexual fantasies are the one thing I have never been willing to share with anyone," she explains, "which strikes me as strange. I'd probably *do* any of them with you; I just won't talk about them."

Asked how many casual sexual relationships she has had since 50, this respondent first wrote down "400." Then she crossed that out and wrote in "500?" "Approximately 40" of her 500 casual sexual partners, she adds, have been during the past year. She attaches a footnote:

> On the enormous number of men and women I have made love with: For openers, numbers are hard to figure, so let me tell you how it all came about. . . . The man who gave me my first vibrator was finally successful in talking me into trying group sex [at 50]. After a while I liked it better than he did. The learnings from these "swinging" sexperiences have been invaluable. I have met people different from me — culturally, economically, educationally, by age, religion, color — in the most "real" of ways, naked and in bed. I have learned that "making it" happily with another human being . . . is seldom related to the usual criteria of size, shape, age, great beauty — or to [their] cars, clothes, or bank accounts. . . . I've met some wonderful people in the very considerable cross-section I've rolled into during [my swinging] years.

She goes on to explain: "Swinging . . . means many partners each week. Varied experiences — varied rhythm of frequency — but always several times a month — love it!"

Asked about falling in love and being in love, she describes "the rush of infatuation — turn-on chemistry," and comments, "I can do that and get over it in an evening or two. I do not confuse that with loving. . . . I like loving more. (Falling in love would involve much mental obsession — louse up my work.)"

She says that she currently *loves* several men and women, and explains what she means by this:

Love now is not holding, owning, displaying, controlling, shoring up insecurity, insufficiency, getting. Love is an attitude, an appreciation of a different other, a joy in *"being with"* that is open-handed, not clutching. For me, this feels good — better than my 20's loves.

Love in a more encompassing sense, she writes, would be

delicious, but incompatible with all my life's interests, it seems. Where would I find the time?

In so much of these musings, I recognize some "typically male" thinking, in that professional excellence, learning, economic achievement — all those things that men do in their twenties and thirties are important to me [now]. "Making it" with a partner may be second to "making it" personally. I got a late start, you see, and I want everything *they* wanted. I'm just getting around to it two or three decades later.

She continues: "I have four ongoing sexual relationships, all males, whom I have known for [seven years or longer] and who are my friends and lovers." One of the four is her first lover, with whom she still spends a night from time to time.

Each has a permanent relationship [with another woman]. I know each of the women. Some of them are sometimes [my] lovers, too — yet the relationship with the males is something by itself, and each male is different, and each relationship is different — although all are sexual when we can find the time. . . . The frequency of sexual activity [with them] is not enough to suit me; but . . . my schedule is in *my* hands, and I choose schedule over sex pretty often.

She also finds time occasionally for sex with a widower nine years older than she, whom she met at a swing — a "friendship" that has lasted five years so far.

She was never sexually attracted to another woman before 50 — but she has often felt such an attraction since 50. Indeed, she estimates that of the five hundred people with whom she has had sexual encounters since 50, more than fifty have been women. Her one durable sexual relationship with another woman began eight years ago, when she was 50 and her partner was 24; this relationship still continues. Of her experiences with women she writes: "Lesbian relationships are, for me, part of caring, loving, [an] expression of affection, fun, . . . a fine idea for older women who may find women partners easier to come by."

Many of our other unmarried women say that the life they live today is quite different from the life they lived before 50. But none describes quite so complete or so dramatic a metamorphosis from devout, conventional housewife to successful professional woman and swinger.

Why sexual partners don't get married

When two unmarried people enter a sexual relationship, one polite way to refer to the liaison is to say that "they are living together." One of the unexpected findings of this study is the discovery that more than half of our unmarried women and men involved in an ongoing sexual relationship are *not* living with their sexual partner.

We did not ask respondents with sexual partners why they are not living together; but we did ask why they don't get married. Most of them responded, and close to half indicate that they prefer things the way they are — that is, unmarried. The biggest differences between the women and the men is that 43 percent of the women — but only 16 percent of the men — say they can't get married because their partner is already married to someone else:

Reasons for not marrying	Unmarried men (N=183)	Unmarried women (N=154)
We prefer things the way they are	44%	46%
We haven't gotten around to it yet but plan to	30%	19%
I don't want to be responsible for my partner's support or medical expenses	20%	6%
My partner wants to get married but I don't	14%	8%

My partner is married to someone else	16%	43%
Neither of us wants to give up a separate home	20%	19%
We don't want to lose economic benefits (social security, alimony, etc.)	14%	13%
My partner doesn't want to be responsible for my support or medical expenses	3%	4%
My children or my partner's children object	3%	4%
I want to get married but my partner doesn't	2%	4%

Some of our unmarried women complain that unmarried men are looking *only* for a casual sexual encounter, while the women want a solid, ongoing relationship, or marriage. There is a modicum of truth here — but it is far from the whole truth. Sometimes it is the woman who doesn't want to get married.

Two women who take this view are described by a Louisiana widower, aged 58. He writes that after his wife's death a few years ago, "I spent a year and a half without any sexual activities with a partner. [Then] I met a divorcée . . . and started a sexual relationship with her."

This first postmarital relationship, however, had a serious problem. Our respondent did not want merely a sexual partner; he wanted a wife.

"After 30 years of a very beautiful marriage relationship," he explains, "I think I subconsciously have been looking for a relationship [I] could closely identify with my marriage experience." His partner felt very differently about this. "She said that she could not and never would be interested in a love [or marriage] relationship because of the bitter experiences she had in her first marriage. I told her we were incompatible but . . . we continued our relationship for six months until I met my present partner."

This new partner is also 58 and a widow, and the two have been having sex together for the past year. "I think I have found the woman I want to be my second wife," he writes. Why don't they get married? He replies that he wants to — but, again, this partner doesn't. Her reason for preferring to have sex outside of wedlock involves a curious paradox. He explains: "My partner was raised a strict Catholic, [and she] taught her children a high moral standard." At the heart of that standard was her Church's opposition to divorce. "The religious stigma of divorce is so strong that she wants to be very sure" before she commits herself to marriage.

"Living with me on a trial before-marriage basis," he continues, "is causing more stress [for her]. She knows I am uncomfortable in a relationship outside of marriage, too; but I understand and appreciate the meaning of a trial relationship."

Asked what he particularly wants us to cover in this book, this respondent, who describes himself as moderately religious, suggests "the problems confronting widows and widowers in resuming a love-and-sex relationship, in or out of wedlock — perhaps exploring the morality involved and the Christian relationship to the sexual revolution. Is there a New Morality?"

From our statistical data and our Comment Pages, it is clear that most of our currently unmarried men, like most of our currently unmarried women, do want a durable relationship — and that some even want to remarry. The reason why many unmarried women doubt this, however, is also clear.

Since most of our unmarried men are already involved in an ongoing relationship, they are unavailable to unattached women. Many of the men who do "come buzzing around," "propositioning" older women, *are* seeking casual sex.

The same perception may also be encouraged by the tendency of older women and men alike to keep their sexual activities a closely guarded secret. Thus our many unmarried men who have been involved for years in stable ongoing sexual relationships are relatively invisible. Few people, including few older women, know of these enduring, mostly clandestine, relationships. As more and more members of the generation over 50 come out of the geriatric closet, these long-term nonmarital relationships rather than casual sex will be seen as the norm for unmarried women *and* unmarried men over 50 — that is, as the type of relationship engaged in by most of those who are having sex with a partner.

Sexual activity and life enjoyment

How is the sexual activity — or inactivity — of our unmarried men and women related to their enjoyment of life? More of the sexually active than inactive report a high level of life enjoyment. More of those who have a sexual partner than of those whose only sexual activity is masturbation report high life enjoyment. Sexually inactive unmarried men are by far the least likely to report high life enjoyment:

	Having sex with a partner	*Masturbating only*	*Sexually inactive*
Unmarried women	(N=168)	(N=169)	(N=155)
Life enjoyment high	88%	78%	74%
Life enjoyment low	12	22	26
	100%	100%	100%
Unmarried men	(N=225)	(N=120)	(N=57)
Life enjoyment high	88%	80%	65%
Life enjoyment low	12	20	35
	100%	100%	100%

SUMMARY

Unquestionably, there are many unhappy unmarried women and men in our society, but among respondents to our study they are a small minority. Contrary to conventional perceptions, chronic loneliness is also a minority experience among our unmarried respondents.

Women generally have a smaller income than men; this is notably true of the unmarried women in our study.

Most of our employed respondents, women and men alike, are worried about the prospect of retirement — but most of those who have retired are pleased with the experience.

Close friendships are important to many of the unmarried, especially the women. A supportive network of close friends helps to minimize loneliness and maintain life enjoyment. Many of the unmarried say they would like to meet new friends but are deterred by barriers, including not enough social activities, not enough money, and shyness. Some say they don't have enough time for new friends. Of particular interest is the larger proportion of women than of men who report that inadequate transportation prevents them from making new friends; lack of a driver's license and of access to a car can be almost crippling for some older people.

Like other women of their generation, our unmarried women were brought up to believe that the proper way to live is with a man at your side. About one-third of our unmarried women have managed to find a male partner despite the dearth of unattached older men; most of those male partners are either married or much older than the women — or both. A surprising proportion of older women, too, have a sexual partner much younger than they are. The other two-thirds of our unmarried women have had to adjust to a partnerless life-style for which few of them were prepared. Most of them have adjusted through work, supportive friendship networks, close family ties, or in other ways. Some now even prefer things this way. But many others suffer and bitterly protest the inequity.

Our unmarried men, too, were brought up expecting to go through life with a woman at their side. More than half of them do have such a partner. Our unmarried men adjust to their status about as successfully as do our unmarried women, but the men appear to rely more on sexual activities and less on friendship networks or family ties. In pursuing their sexual interests, they tend to seek out much younger women. Some of our unmarried men, too, long for a female partner but can't find one.

Substantially more of our unmarried men than of our unmarried women are sexually active. Sexual activity continues into the seventies and in some cases beyond for half of our unmarried women and three-quarters of our unmarried men. A major part of sexual activity for many of the men and women is masturbation;

for some, of course, it is the only sexual activity. The reasons for masturbating most commonly given by both women and men is that they lack a partner, that masturbation relieves sexual tension, and that they enjoy masturbating.

Quite a few of our unmarried women tell of finding a partner by looking up an old friend from years ago; this appears to be a promising approach for older women and men seeking a partner.

Unlike many of our unmarried women, some of our unmarried men want only casual sex and many of them find it; some want a solid relationship with a woman, and many find that. Some even want marriage, and most of them appear to find it. All of this contributes to the difficult odds confronting unmarried women who seek a partner. Yet, for many of our women, being unmarried and female is fully compatible with leading a rich, busy, happy, and — for some — sexually rewarding life during the later years.

❧ 4 ❦

Homosexual Relationships

ONLY FIFTY-SIX OF OUR MEN CONSIDER THEMSELVES HOMOSEXUALS; and only nine of our women consider themselves lesbians. This is hardly an adequate sample on which to base a review of homosexuality in the later years.

Hundreds of men and women who do *not* consider themselves homosexual, however, have provided us with data concerning their homosexual interests and experiences. These data illuminate three aspects of homosexuality that are often ignored in discussions of the topic:

• Reasons why so many more men than women report homosexual experiences — both before and after 50, both in our study and in prior surveys of human sexuality.

• The impact on later life of casual homosexual experiences during adolescence or earlier.

• The place of occasional homosexual experiences in the lives of older women and men who are in all other respects heterosexual.

WHY FEWER WOMEN THAN MEN HAVE HAD HOMOSEXUAL EXPERIENCES

The Kinsey study, and all subsequent surveys of human sexuality with which we are familiar, report a substantially higher propor-

212

tion of men than of women with homosexual experience. Our respondents confirm this.

We asked:

"Have you ever had a sexual relationship with a [person of your own gender]?"

Thirteen percent (301) of our men but only 8 percent (131) of our women say they have had one or more homosexual experiences.

If we limit ourselves to the years after 50, we find that nearly 4 percent (86) of our men but less than 2 percent (25) of our women report one or more homosexual experiences since 50.

This was to be expected. We received a surprise, however, when our respondents answered an additional question:

"Have you ever felt sexually attracted to [a person of your own gender]?"

Here 11 percent (196) of our women but only 8 percent (184) of our men answer yes.

A closely related finding was also a surprise:

Of our men who have been sexually attracted to a man, 72 percent have had a sexual relationship with a man — but of our women who have been sexually attracted to a woman, only 34 percent have had a sexual relationship with a woman.

If we limit ourselves to the years after 50, we find that 5 percent of our women and of our men have been sexually attracted to a person of the same gender. But when we consider their homosexual experience, the same remarkable disparity emerges:

Of respondents who have been sexually attracted to a person of the same gender since 50, 56 percent of the men but only 23 percent of the women have had a sexual relationship with a person of the same gender.

Why do fewer women act upon the sexual attraction they feel?

We offer two hypotheses to help explain this female/male disproportion. The first concerns the different ways in which our women and men have reacted through the years to the sexual upbringing they have shared.

Both the women and the men in our sample, for example, were warned as children against masturbation. In their later years, however, our women are more likely than our men to abide by the masturbation taboo they initially shared. Fewer women than men masturbate.

Similarly, both the women and the men in our sample were brought up to believe in faithful, monogamous marriage. In their later years, however, more wives than husbands continue to abide by the adultery taboo and to refrain from extramarital sex.

In much the same way, we believe, both the women and the men in our sample were brought up with a strong taboo against homosexual activity. And, as with masturbation and adultery, more women in our sample have continued to abide by that taboo — despite feelings of sexual attraction to other women.

Our second hypothesis concerns the *initiation* of sexual activities.

Among our respondents, the men were brought up to *seek* sex, the women to be *sought after*. And as our questionnaire returns show, our men are still much more likely than our women to *initiate* activities leading to sex. As a result, when two men find themselves sexually attracted to one another, there are three likely avenues to sexual activity. Either man may initiate the activities leading to sex, or both may engage in initiatory behavior. Sex is quite likely to follow.

When two *women* find themselves sexually attracted to one another, in contrast, each is likely — in accordance with their upbringing and with their custom through the years — to wait for the *other* to initiate the activities leading to sex. As a result, sex is much less likely to follow.

Several of our women respondents state quite explicitly that they approve of lesbian relationships, and are ready for one — if somebody else *makes the first move*. A 59-year-old widow with no homosexual experience writes:

I believe I would like to try a lesbian experience — but have no aggressive intentions toward fulfilling this goal. As a matter of fact, [I] wouldn't even know how to go about it.

A 70-year-old widow with two male lovers writes:

I have no experience *re* lesbianism or bisexualism. However, am curious. I do not seek it; but if it happens naturally, I'll try it.

A 69-year-old divorcée writes similarly:

I have thought that since men in their 60's and 70's are so rare, a lesbian experience might be a pleasant substitute — but [I] have not found a woman who attracted me enough or who made any advances.

A 66-year-old Ohio widow has never had a lesbian relationship, but writes:

I have gradually become very sexually attracted to a much younger woman friend who is an avowed lesbian and with whom I have a fine friendship. I would not make this known to her or impose myself on her.

The "avowed lesbian," in turn, may very well be thinking that she doesn't want to "impose" herself on our seemingly "straight" respondent.

Another widow, aged 64, has never had a lesbian relationship and has had no heterosexual relationship, either, since her husband died twenty-nine years ago. She writes from North Carolina:

Since age 50, I have had two "crushes" on women who are about my age. These were emotional attachments, but were not sexual; and since they were not returned, I soon got over them. The two women are still my friends.

If this respondent were a man accustomed to seek sex rather than to be sought after, the outcome of these two "crushes" might have been very different.

We offer our two hypotheses not as findings but rather to

stimulate further study. Our sample is small. No doubt there are some women as defiant of sexual taboos as any man — and some women as ready to initiate activities leading to sex as any man. But overall, we believe, for women raised by Victorian standards, these two hypotheses appear to be likely explanations for the very low level of lesbian activity (as distinct from lesbian attraction) reported.*

EARLY HOMOSEXUAL EXPERIENCES

A 56-year-old husband who lives in Washington State writes that he is still in love with his wife after thirty-five years of marriage. He says that their marital sex is very important both to him and to his wife; they have sex together two or three times a week and both always reach orgasm. He rates both the happiness of his marriage and his enjoyment of sex with his wife as 1.

"All forms of stimulation except pain . . . and group sex appeal to my wife and me," he reports. "Oral stimulation to orgasm is best of all!!! Masturbating together and each other is also a '9' on a scale of '1–10'." He continues: "I feel the sexual act is more exciting and more sensitive now than before. We (my wife and I) experiment all the time so that each time has its own excitement."

Here, in short, is a happily married, exclusively heterosexual male — except that at the age of 11, he had sex ("two or three times only") with his 25-year-old uncle. Asked what he would do

---

* A woman consultant to this study adds a third possible explanation:

"Gay men have bath houses, clubs, bars, etc., as well as particular neighborhoods in urban centers (such as Castro and Polk Streets in San Francisco) where they can meet and socialize. There are fewer social facilities (coffee houses, clubs, restaurants) for gay women even in large cities, and none whatever in most of the United States. The smaller number of avowed lesbians and their lower incomes as compared with gay men makes it difficult or impossible for them to establish such facilities; many efforts have failed. The absence of places where lesbian women can meet and socialize, in turn, makes it more difficult for women (especially older women) to find sexual partners of their own gender."

differently, he replies: "I would avoid the sexual encounter with my uncle (although I don't know how). . . ."

A 68-year-old New York City wife, married for forty-two years, stopped having sex with her husband ten years ago, when he became impotent. She writes, however, that "our sex life was great while it lasted." She rates the happiness of her marriage as 1, and says she is still in love with her husband. She has never had an extramarital partner. She continues:

I matured very young. Sex activities for me were with other girls. As I grew into my teens, I stopped all such activities. I wanted to be "wanted and loved" by a male. To me, that was normal and natural. Early experimenting with girls was a growing, experiencing phase that I outgrew. I never harbored the thought of lesbian sex after that.

The essential point of these two stories was documented by Kinsey a generation ago but bears repeating here: Casual homosexual experiences early in life do not brand participants as homosexuals and do not necessarily or frequently lead to subsequent impairment of heterosexual orientation. Here are three additional male examples:

A happily married 58-year-old husband recalls:

When I was about 15, the six or eight boys who "hung together" indulged in a summer of group masturbation (speed to ejaculation, accuracy in placing ejaculate in chalk circle on basement floor, etc.), oral sex, and attempts at anal sex. This passed as soon as we discovered girls, and I don't consider it a "sexual relationship."

A twice-married husband, 67, describes his only homosexual experience:

I was sexually abused by a larger boy when I was 11 and since that time the idea disgusts me. However, I have no ill feelings toward homosexuals *per se*.

A New England husband at 56, married for thirty-three years, rates both the happiness of his marriage and his enjoyment of sex with his wife as 1. His only homosexual experience was at age 17 and lasted five minutes. He explains: "[An] older man paid me for him to have oral sex with me."

Here are three examples from our women respondents:

A 62-year-old Indiana wife, happily married for 36 years, writes:

> The only physical contact (sexual) I ever had with another female was with my sister during the early teen years. We weren't permitted to have boy friends; consequently, we satisfied our desires by playing with each other. Since we have become adults, we never speak of it or have ever indulged again.

A 66-year-old widow also recalls that her only homosexual relationship was with her sister at an early age. It lasted for three years. "I outgrew it," she explains.

A 64-year-old widow, married for 35 years, writes:

> When I was 14 or 15, a girl friend and I used to sleep together and we would "pretend" we were lovers. She was always the man; I was the woman. We used to "pretend" movie plots; and we used to kiss and embrace (not very specifically!). We outgrew this, thought it childish, and gave it up — apparently with no lesbian urges [thereafter]. We both fell madly in love [with men] and married young.

Such anecdotal accounts, of course, have only limited value as evidence. Much more impressive, we believe, is what our respondents did *not* report. We invited them to comment on homosexual and bisexual matters, and many accepted the invitation. But we failed to find even one account by a respondent, male or female, who felt that his or her subsequent life was sufficiently blighted by an early homosexual experience to make the damage worth reporting on our Comment Pages.

HOMOSEXUAL EXPERIENCES OF HETEROSEXUALS AFTER 50

Our respondents were brought up to believe, decades ago, that the human species is divided into two quite disparate subgroups: homosexuals and heterosexuals. Since then, substantial numbers have learned through their own experience that this is not the case. Two hundred and forty-five of our men who do *not* consider themselves homosexuals nevertheless report one or more homosexual experiences; and 122 of our women who do *not* consider themselves homosexuals make the same report.

Many of these had only adolescent experiences of the kinds described above. However, 30 of our nonhomosexual men and 16 of our nonhomosexual women report one or more homosexual experiences since the age of 50. Ten men and 5 women, indeed, had their *first* homosexual experience after 50.

One of these is a 74-year-old widow who lives in the San Francisco Bay area. She writes:

> I was married very young (while in college) and my husband was about the same age. We had a satisfactory marriage, children, and a vigorous sex life — but he was killed after only a few years of marriage. I had little financial resources and small children, so my next marriage was virtually an economic necessity. My second husband was very, very much older. Although frequent jibes are made at May-December marriages, ours was quite good. Although he did not achieve an erection frequently enough for my needs, he was not averse to, in fact rather enjoyed, cunnilingus, so I had ample orgasmic satisfaction. After he died, I was affluent enough to live comfortably.

Since her second husband's death, she has had numerous sexual partners — six of them during the past year. Instead of categorizing them as either "ongoing sexual relationships" or "casual partners," she writes:

> I have some difficulty with the distinction. . . . Neither is quite accurate. If "ongoing" means "exclusive," the answer is

no. If "casual" means picking up a stranger at a bar, the answer is no. Specifically, I have sexual relations with several men from time to time who are friends or persons I know very well.

She denies that she has had any sexual *relationships* with other women, but reports ten sexual "episodes" with women — all of them since 50. She explains:

During the past years I have had only a very few sexual episodes with women, brought on, not by me, but by the partner — as a result of excessive persuasion, suitable juxtaposition, personalities, and with no current date for that time, *"faute de mieux."* These women generally were seeking an exclusive, prolonged relationship which I rejected, so the episodes were not frequently repeated. Such episodes were not objectionable physically, but rather mildly pleasant, usually with mild orgasmic sensations — [unlike] those with a man, which Linda Lovelace described in *Deep Throat* as "bells ringing and rockets and bombs exploding."

A 63-year-old husband, married for forty-one years, rates his current enjoyment of life and the happiness of his marriage as 2. He and his wife have not had sex together for six years. They both lost interest, he says, and he explains:

After 35 years of "going in the same hole the same way every time," and my wife's putting on weight and losing her figure, she no longer sexually arouses me. However, we still love each other and get along just fine.

He reports only one sexual relationship outside his marriage; it began a year or two after he and his wife discontinued sex, and it still continues. It is with a man: "My brother-in-law is in the same boat I am" — that is, no sex with his wife — "so we have developed a sexual relationship with each other."

Here are other examples, both female and male, of heterosexually oriented respondents who have had occasional homosexual encounters since 50:

A 61-year-old New York wife rates both the happiness of her marriage and her enjoyment of sex with her five-year-younger husband as 1. They have sex together only rarely — once a month or less; they both always reach orgasm on these occasions. She masturbates once a month or less in addition — and she has had sex since 50 with four partners outside her marriage, without her husband's knowledge. Three of her outside partners were men. Her one sexual encounter with a woman occurred when she was 57 and her partner 50; it lasted two hours. She leaves her Comment Pages blank.

A 52-year-old Alabama husband, married for twenty years, has sex with his wife two or three times a week — but rates his enjoyment of sex with her as only 4. He always reaches orgasm on these occasions; she never does. He has also, with his wife's knowledge, had sex with seven outside partners in the two years since his fiftieth birthday. Five of his outside partners were women, two of them prostitutes. The other two were men involved in swinging situations. Each lasted half an hour or less.

One wife reports that her only homosexual experience was in a swinging situation, with her husband present, when she was 55 and the other woman 45. She does not comment.

Another wife reports that her only homosexual experience occurred when she was in her fifties; the other woman was 22. It lasted ten minutes. "Do not enjoy homosexual activities," she writes. "My only experience was at [my] husband's insistence in a swinging situation. Definitely did not enjoy it."

A 56-year-old husband, married to his second wife for sixteen years, rates both the happiness of his marriage and his enjoyment of sex with his wife as 1. He reports only one extramarital relationship since 50. It was with a 40-year-old man, occurred three years ago, and lasted two months. He comments: "With family relationships to maintain and protect, it is difficult to gain satisfaction through bisexual or homosexual relationships."

A 54-year-old divorcée is a retired college professor with a Ph.D. degree. She has been married three times, and for eight years she has lived with a male lover. She rates as 1 her overall enjoyment of life, the happiness of her relationship with her lover, and her enjoyment of sex with him.

In addition to him, she reports *"circa* sixty" other sexual partners, male and female, during the four years since age 50 — with her lover's knowledge, support, and often cooperation. She had sexual relationships with "about five" women during the five years before age 50, and with "about 20" since then. She comments:

> Since the age of 50, I've been involved in sex research and am now better informed and freer about sex than I was before. I was always very active sexually — but have now come out of the closet and proclaimed myself a sexually active older woman. This has had some interesting social and professional repercussions!!

Sex after 50, she continues, "is more enjoyable and less anxiety-producing than when we were young." Asked what she'd do differently if she had her life to live over, she replies: "I'd have allowed myself to express my sexuality more openly and honestly earlier. And I'd not have waited till the age of 45 to explore sex with other women."

Note that in many of these examples, and in others elsewhere in this study, primarily heterosexual respondents who engage in occasional homosexual activities tend to see such encounters as an additional rather than an alternative form of sexual activity.

HOMOSEXUALITY AND AGING

As noted earlier, our population of avowed homosexual respondents is too small to permit statistical analysis.*

---

* Fortunately, a broader study of the impact of aging on male homosexuals was published in 1982: *Gay and Gray: The Older Homosexual Man,* by Raymond M. Berger. We have found no comparable work on lesbians and aging.

A few of our men and women who consider themselves homosexuals do comment on their feelings about aging. For example, a 54-year-old divorcée, the mother of two children, began her third lesbian relationship six years ago with a partner then 32. The relationship is continuing. She comments:

> I have loved both men and women, and feel greatly enriched by the experiences. . . . Women supporting one another in areas of work, love, marriage, concerns about aging, death, loss of parents, growth of children, etc., has been very beneficial to me. I think both men and women can be more open with one another as they become older. Pretenses take up too much energy.

About aging, she writes: "I have been very fortunate in my relationships and [in having] a satisfying vocation. Some women are frantic when they perceive themselves as aging. . . . Aging has never frightened me."

A 64-year-old never-married man writes from Indiana: "I am a homosexual and have lived with my partner thirty years." His partner is 66. Our respondent states that he is in love with his partner, and rates both his enjoyment of life and the happiness of his relationship with his partner as 1.

Some heterosexual marriages, it will be recalled, continue to thrive long after husband and wife have discontinued sexual relations. This happily paired homosexual male similarly reports that he and his partner have not had sex together for the past ten years. He has hypertension, but he says that discontinuance of sex was his partner's decision, and was caused by his partner's physical changes — his partner has diabetes and takes an antihypertensive drug. Our respondent's interest in sex, however, remains moderately strong, and he masturbates two or three times a week.

Reviewing his life, he reports that his homosexual relationships have been "very rewarding," and have not been a handicap in achieving his life goals. Like many heterosexual wives and husbands, he is concerned about the future: "Loneliness could be a big problem for a homosexual if his partner died; but, if emotionally stable, no more so than [for] a heterosexual — possibly less."

A 60-year-old never-married, out-of-the-closet lesbian lives alone in upstate New York and is employed full-time, with an income of between $10,000 and $15,000 a year. She reports "numerous" women sexual partners before age 50 but none since. Her only current sexual activity is masturbation once a month or less.

"While not now active," she writes, "I am now and all my life have been homosexual, and my situation is entirely so directed. At my age, and in the *very* conservative community that I now live in, it is unlikely that I shall form another [lesbian] relationship."

She makes it clear that life without a partner is not her first choice:

> I would like nothing better than having a permanent relationship with another woman — for the companionship as much as for the sexual satisfaction. As a recent "refugee" from [Chicago] where there is an overt gay women's community, I find small town gay life so covert as to be all but invisible.

She does not, however, bemoan her fate: "I have (thank you) many other interests and pursuits and find that I manage very nicely without a partner." And she concludes: "I have been something of a loner all my life, and expect to survive to a ripe old age as a celibate — not out of choice, to be sure, but there are worse things in life."

A 59-year-old male homosexual, in answer to how many homosexual partners he has had, replies: "Dozens ... scores ... maybe even hundreds." He does report one relationship lasting ten years — but he adds:

> The "10 years" refers to the period of time during which I had casual sex periodically with the same person — but not to the exclusion of other persons, and not . . . a very close relationship in other ways over this period of time. In other words, almost all my sex life has been a casual thing, with

whomever was there and willing. I cannot say I've ever had
an "enduring sexual relationship" with anyone for any period of time.

He is one of a very few who report: "I have never had a heterosexual experience and have never wanted one."

This respondent rates his enjoyment of life as 2, and states
that "my sex life has been quite satisfactory." Like several other
men who rely on casual sexual relationships, he sees aging as a
problem:

Getting older for the homosexual probably means — at least
it has for me — that casual partners are less available, and
those that are available are less desirable. . . . The younger
one keeps himself looking as he grows older, the easier it is
to find casual sex partners if that is what one is interested in
(as I am).

A related comment comes from a gay respondent in California. Now that he is in his sixties, he writes, "things are more difficult. There is much more rejection by other gays. . . . A plus is that
I find [younger] gays are attracted to me and seek my counsel and
friendship — but not sexually. I am able to accept this. . . ."

Another respondent, aged 63, adds:

I'm not sure older men are less welcome in [homosexual]
bars and baths, except in the sense that there are likely to be
fewer people there at any one time who will be interested in
sex with them. (I go to bars very seldom, baths more often.)
I think it is true that only a minority of people are able to
think of a person much older than themselves as a sex partner; on the other hand, I've made some very satisfactory
pick-ups of younger men in bars, and have had some lovely
experiences in baths — partly *because* of a white beard I wore
for two years. But such episodes do become less frequent as
one grows older.

A 72-year-old respondent reports a hundred homosexual partners before age 50 and thirty more since then. He does not comment on the problem of finding casual partners at age 72 — but he does report that he had sex with five men during the past year.

Finally, a 50-year-old widow in San Diego reports that she has come out of the closet and publicly identified herself as a lesbian. She writes: "[I] was married for 14 years, and thoroughly enjoyed the first ten of them."

She has had three women sexual partners, one of whom is still her sexual partner. This partner is now 43 years old and the relationship has lasted three years. Both are employed; they live together in a private home on a joint income of between $20,000 and $25,000 a year.

Our respondent and her partner have sex together about once a week; both always reach orgasm. She feels that this is about the right frequency for her. She does not currently masturbate. She rates both her enjoyment of life and the happiness of her relationship with her partner as 2, and her enjoyment of sex with her partner as 1. Of the effects of aging, she writes:

> On the positive side of aging as a lesbian, I would place the fact that, as a group, lesbians place less emphasis on looks and more on character than does most of society. I don't believe there is the same premium on youth that there is in most of society.
>
> On the negative side, social disapproval must become harder and harder to take as one's friends die off. I suppose that the absence of a socially approved support system will become very difficult. I can hardly imagine sitting in the Golden Age Club and talking about *my* good old days!

SUMMARY

Only a minority of our respondents report any homosexual experience; and even fewer report such experiences since 50. More of our women than men report being sexually attracted to a person of the same gender, both before and after 50 — but more men, both before and after 50, report having had a sexual relationship with a person of the same gender.

Both our statistical data and the comments of our respondents make it clear that there is no sharp dividing line between "homosexuals" and "heterosexuals." Quite a few report enjoying heterosexual relationships throughout their lives — except for a few homosexual encounters during adolescence or earlier; others report lifelong heterosexuality except for one or a few homosexual relationships after 50. As Kinsey observed a generation ago:

The world is not to be divided into sheep and goats. . . . It is a fundamental of taxonomy that nature rarely deals with discrete categories. Only the human mind invents categories and tries to force facts into separated pigeon-holes. The living world is a continuum in each and every one of its aspects. The sooner we learn this concerning human sexual behavior the sooner we shall reach a sound understanding of the realities of sex.*

---

* *Sexual Behavior in the Human Male*, p. 639.

PART II

HOW HUMAN SEXUALITY CHANGES IN THE LATER YEARS

⊱ 5 ⊰

Changing Sexual Attitudes
and Activities

QUEEN VICTORIA REIGNED OVER BRITAIN FROM 1837 TO 1901. THE attitudes and standards of behavior promulgated in her name profoundly influenced the world's morality well into the twentieth century. Sexual "Victorianism" has come to mean a set of rigid, repressive rules that forbid, among other things, masturbation, sex outside marriage, "unnatural sex acts" such as homosexual contacts, and even public displays of affection.

Our oldest respondents — those aged 77 through 93 — were born in Victoria's reign. Both they and our younger respondents learned about life from their parents, many of whom were Victorians born and bred. Many of our men and women refer to their Victorian background in their Comment Pages.

To what extent have our respondents now departed from Victorian sexual opinions? This chapter is concerned mostly with changes in their views on five emotion-laden topics: masturbation, sex without marriage, sex without love, pornography, and homosexuality.

MASTURBATION

Victorian parents had a very clear idea of what was right and what was wrong, often founded on religious doctrines; and they fervently inculcated their values in their children. The masturbation taboo was the keystone of their entire system of child-rearing — and no wonder.

Many Victorian parents had themselves been taught when young, and continued to believe, that masturbation is both a sin leading to damnation and an inexorable destroyer of both mental and physical health — leading to insanity, blindness, stunted growth, acne, and moral and physical "degeneracy." The most eminent physicians of the age, as well as religious leaders, reinforced these views. Even Sigmund Freud taught — until he changed his mind at the age of 69, in 1925 — that masturbation is the cause of what he called "the actual neuroses." It is hardly surprising, then, that Victorian parents concerned with the welfare of their children both in this life and in the hereafter focused their most intensive efforts on maintaining the masturbation taboo.

Those efforts began while infants still lay in their cribs. The "snuggle bunny" and other infant harnesses were designed in considerable part to prevent babies from touching their own genitals. Diapers were folded wider than necessary, and were pinned in a particular way, as a further barrier to the infant's genital explorations and manipulations.

Often this vigilance was maintained throughout childhood, at puberty, and into adolescence. Freud himself records the case history of an adolescent girl who — on his prescription — was placed under prolonged round-the-clock surveillance so that she would have no privacy for masturbation. Prostitution was tolerated throughout the Victorian era in part because it helped save boys and men from masturbation. There are records of wealthy and eminently respectable Victorian mothers who, when all other efforts failed, with heavy hearts hired mistresses for their teenage sons in order to save them from the disastrous consequences of "self-abuse." Readers will hardly be surprised, then, to find that the effects of the masturbation taboo are still evident among many of our respondents. What may be surprising is the large proportion of our respondents who do *not* hold the Victorian attitude toward masturbation.

We asked whether respondents agree or disagree, strongly or moderately, with the following statement:

"Boys and girls need to be reassured that there is nothing wrong with masturbation."

Among the 78 percent of respondents who take a stand, those who agree that children need reassurance about masturbation outnumber those who disagree by almost four to one:

	Women's and men's opinions	
	(N=4,140)	
Strongly agree	33%	62%
Moderately agree	29	
Neutral	21	
Moderately disagree	8	16%
Strongly disagree	8	
	99%	

We also asked our respondents to indicate their degree of agreement or disagreement with this statement:

"Masturbation is not proper for older people."

Seventy-seven percent of our respondents take a stand, and those who approve of masturbation for older people outnumber those who disapprove by roughly the same four-to-one ratio:

	Women's and men's opinions	
	(N=4,149)	
Strongly agree	8%	} 14%
Moderately agree	6	
Neutral	24	
Moderately disagree	20	} 63%
Strongly disagree	43	
	101%	

More of our women and men (62 percent for each) approve of masturbation for older people than engage in masturbation (41 and 53 percent, respectively).

Interestingly, a substantial proportion of our respondents who disapprove of masturbation for older people do in fact masturbate. Of our 253 women who disapprove, 19 percent report that they masturbate; of our 309 men who disapprove, 28 percent say they masturbate.

The incidence of masturbation among both our men and women declines with age. A substantially greater proportion of our men than of our women — at all ages — report they masturbate:

	Proportion currently masturbating
Women in their 50s (N=801)	47%
Women in their 60s (N=719)	37%
Women aged 70 and over (N=324)	33%
Men in their 50s (N=823)	66%
Men in their 60s (N=981)	50%
Men aged 70 and over (N=598)	43%

Married women are the least likely to report masturbation and unmarried men the most likely:

	Proportion currently masturbating
Married women (N=1,245)	36%
Married men (N=1,895)	52%
Unmarried women (N=512)	54%
Unmarried men (N=413)	63%

Our respondents contribute numerous comments, both for and against masturbation. One 69-year-old husband and father writes:

> I cannot agree with condoning masturbation for boys and girls. Undoubtedly it does take place but condoning it puts the stamp of approval on it and encourages other acts which turn out harmful for our society.

He does not elaborate.

A 68-year-old wife no doubt speaks for many others when she sums up her own attitude toward masturbation in a single word: "Disgusting."

At the other extreme is a 77-year-old widow who writes:

> I believe wholeheartedly that the change in social attitude toward masturbation is one of the few very healthy aspects of our society during the late 20th century.

It is this sense of *change* in attitudes toward masturbation that leaps most conspicuously from the comments of our respondents, as the following quotations illustrate.

> When I was young, I was told that [masturbation] was wrong and it would affect my health and harm my brain. As a re-

sult, my school marks suffered because I could not stop masturbating and thought I just couldn't succeed in school. Boys
should be helped through this difficult period.

— Husband, aged 66

I used to feel a bit guilty about masturbation but now see
nothing against it and much for it. Sex is a normal function
and should be exercised — if not with a partner then without
one.

— Widow, aged 65

I was brought up by my mother to believe masturbation
would drive me crazy. It hasn't yet.

— Husband, aged 68

My mother listed masturbation as a sin — but *she* never experienced a single orgasm. I would have found the life of a
divorcée impossible without this outlet.

— Divorcée, aged 52

The sense that we are watching a continuing process of change
in the attitudes and opinions of many of our respondents is confirmed by the somewhat longer replies penned by some of them.
A 56-year-old wife and mother in Georgia begins:

Masturbation has always seemed repulsive to me, I guess because of my strict upbringing. I reared six sons; and during
their growing-up years, we had to deal with masturbation.
Tried to tell them it was harmful to their bodies and [that]
their needs would be satisfied in the realms of marriage.

Like many of our other respondents, however, this woman's
views have recently undergone change. She herself still does not
masturbate, but she now thinks girls and boys need to be reassured that there's nothing wrong with it. She describes her own
earlier stance as "pretty Victorian," and explains: "I have changed
my views since freedom of discussion of sex has become so universal. So I say, to each his own."

A 70-year-old San Diego widow manages to express four separate attitudes toward masturbation in a single paragraph. She begins with open hostility:

Of course there's something wrong with it! Narcissism is a major sickness of our time, and masturbation is an aspect of narcissism. Besides, it's too easy; sexual pleasure should require effort, commitment, interaction, emotion — not just a solitary, mechanical relief.

She then retreats one short step:

As an occasional relief, masturbation is perhaps valuable; but it leads inward, not outward — and sexual pleasure should have *something* to do with love of someone else.

A confession follows:

I have masturbated since I was four years old; I don't think it was to my advantage, for I have never had an orgasm except in that way, and have no doubt missed something in life.

She concludes with a fear, also expressed by others, that masturbation may get out of control:

Such an easy, instant pleasure is likely to become an obsession with youngsters and preclude other interests.

A Kansas woman, now aged 58 and divorced, reports that she married at the age of 28 and had five children in rapid succession — whereupon her husband discontinued vaginal intercourse to avoid further pregnancies and demanded only oral and anal sex. "No fun!" is her comment. "I very much disliked [that]." At age 34, accordingly, she began with some trepidation to masturbate.

Masturbation was probably considered the major SIN when I was young. Turning to it for my needs took some mental hassle. I was angry that I had sexual appetites that could no longer be satisfied [through intercourse with my husband]. So — I turned to masturbation, first with loneliness as a strong element as well as all the physical urges. I am no longer haunted; it is a way to solve the problem, not so dishonorable after all.

A 66-year-old widow with a 62-year-old lover writes from California:

I have learned more about sex in the past three years than in the preceeding sixty-three. I [used to masturbate] only with deep feelings of guilt, brought on by my upbringing. Today I find it pleasurable and do so without any feeling of guilt.

Then she adds:

Because most older folks of today had their sexual learning neglected when they were young, most older people . . . are in need of sexual instruction. The myth that masturbation is a degrading practice that can cause insanity needs to be destroyed. Old and young should be informed that there is nothing . . . wrong with the practice.

Some respondents who continue to condemn masturbation no longer insist that it is a sin or that it will lead to physical or mental disease. They cite more mundane reasons for refraining:

I do not masturbate and never have. I have more interesting and worthwhile things to do with my time — like reading, sewing, gardening, etc.

— Divorcée, aged 58

I think masturbation might make a person become preoccupied with sex and if the person should become senile as they grow older, it might be hard to control.

— Widow, aged 61

I've decided it's too much work for so little pleasure.

— Divorcée, aged 51

I find masturbation to be the most intensely lonely occupation in the world. I would much rather lie in bed with a man with no love-making (i.e., intercourse) than masturbate by myself.

— Divorcée, aged 50

Masturbation at this time in my life is a waste of time. I am sure I would feel ashamed of myself if I should try it just for the hell of it — which I have no intention of doing.

— Husband, aged 78

A 70-year-old New Orleans husband who has had no sex with his wife for twenty-four years but who continues to have sex with his mistress, now aged 63, asks:

"Why waste the sexual potency that's left on masturbation?"

Among our respondents is a 60-year-old psychiatrist in the Southeast whose opinion on masturbation is essentially negative — but a far cry from the view of Victorian psychiatrists that it inevitably leads to insanity: "Thumb-sucking, smoking, masturbation, and other infantile substitutes for adult sexual experience may well be tolerated in adults but can hardly be encouraged."

In contrast, a 68-year-old divorcée in Buffalo says *her* physician warned her that an *absence* of sexual release was damaging her health:

My husband's health failed many years before he died. . . . He thought all sex was "dirty" and he tried to be as good as possible by indulging in sex as seldom as possible. He drove me "up the wall." I wanted much more frequent sex, and

more fun, more time spent in sex. Finally, my doctor told me
the extreme frustration was damaging my health. After six
years, love had disappeared so I walked away. It was much
easier for me to live without sex when I was not sleeping in
the same bed with a man who kept pushing me away.

Her life at age 68 is quite different. A few respondents are
worried about *too much* masturbation — but not this one:

At present, I masturbate at least once a day, and have several
orgasms each time. I use Vaseline as a lubricant to prevent
chafing. Sex with a man I care about is much better but
when I don't have a man partner, I need something.

A 53-year-old never-married respondent in Phoenix similarly
calls attention to what he calls the "therapeutic value" of masturbation:

It is just as necessary for older people as for young ones —
perhaps more so, to keep the spark of sex and zest for living
alive. Masturbation should be discussed openly with children, without condemnation or guilt association. It is as natural as going to the bathroom, but shouldn't be indulged in
public. My own generation is so narrow-minded about sex,
they should be educated as to the therapeutic value of masturbation, among other things. . . . It is a reasonably satisfying and completely harmless outlet. Thanks to Mom . . . I
spent half my life feeling inferior and guilty about it. No
more!

A 61-year-old North Carolina widow writes: "I never masturbated until I read the *Hite Report*. The orgasm is stronger than in a
conventional sexual position, but the same as in oral sex." But she
adds: "It's no fun in the fun house alone!"
Eloquent praise of masturbation comes from an 82-year-old
widow in New York City.

To be able to successfully masturbate in the later years . . .
gives one a continued feeling of being a person . . . still a
woman, still a man . . . It keeps a necessary spark burning
which says, 'I'm yet alive — all of me!'

Two major generalizations emerge from this brief overview,
both worth repeating once more: All older women and men are
not alike. Moreover, many older people differ from themselves
when they were younger. It is this range of variation and this current of change in attitudes that emerge most clearly from our
questionnaire returns — with respect not only to masturbation
but also to the remaining topics treated in this chapter.

SEX WITHOUT MARRIAGE

As noted in earlier chapters, many hundreds of our respondents
frankly report to us on their premarital, extramarital, and postmarital sexual activities since reaching the age of 50. Some describe these activities at length and in detail. But few bother to
write out their abstract *opinions*, either pro or con, about nonmarital sex. Our respondents are much more interested in, and write
much more fervently on, the issue of sex with or without love (see
below) than on the issue of sex with or without marriage.

We believe that this lack of interest in the morality versus the
immorality of nonmarital sex in itself marks a major change in attitude since Victorian times, when sex outside of marriage was
both a sin and a criminal offense.

We presented respondents with this statement:

**"It's okay for older couples who are not married to have sexual re-
lations."**

A majority of our women and an even larger proportion of our
men agree:

It's okay for older couples who are not married to have sexual relations

	Women's opinions (N=1,782)		Men's opinions (N=2,375)	
Strongly agree	36%	} 57%	48%	} 72%
Moderately agree	21		24	
Neutral	21		14	
Moderately disagree	7	} 23%	5	} 13%
Strongly disagree	16		8	
	101%		99%	

SEX WITHOUT LOVE

The Victorian maiden was expected to remain not only physically chaste but sexually unaroused until the Prince Charming of her life — her "intended" — hove into view. Immediate attraction was expected to ripen quickly or slowly into true romantic love; and, following marriage, sex became possible. Sex without love or sex with a stranger was unthinkable — or so the socially accepted scenario read.

How do our respondents feel about such matters today? We used two questions to determine their views. First, we asked whether they strongly or moderately agree or disagree with this statement:

"Sex without love is better than no sex at all."

Second, we asked whether, since age 50, they have had "sex with someone you don't know very well," whether they enjoyed it — and, if they have not done so, whether they would like to try it.

These issues cut to the heart of a question that is very much alive today among people of all ages. Several of our respondents told us that it made them look closely at their own current beliefs about sexuality.

"That one about sex without love . . . is hard," writes a 60-year-old widower in Oklahoma.

> At times of great frustration (often!) I think that's true; but [sexual] experiences with no love feelings turn out themselves to be unsatisfactory and frustrating. I guess I want to "make love" in the most real sense of the word: make love happen through sex — and it doesn't, of course. On the other hand, a number of sex relationships — brief, infrequent, single episodes at times — have been with persons with whom I have intellectual or long-standing friendships of a "loving" if not "love" nature and are thus not unpleasant or threatening (implying that when there is not this quality of closeness, things can be unpleasant and/or threatening — which I guess is true).

A 70-year-old widow writes:

> *Re:* sex without love. I believe if you can't get the love you want, take the love you get — if you *like* the person.

Another widow, aged 71, writes:

> I believe that sex without love is better than no sex at all because the definition of love is so personal and indefinite. I would have sex with anyone whom I liked, respected, or even enjoyed for the moment.

Whether our respondents express themselves as favoring or opposing sex without love, almost all of them approach the question as a matter of personal taste and preference rather than as a moral issue. This is a striking change from Victorian times. Here are some examples:

In the absence of the person I love and cannot have sexual
relations with, I prefer masturbation to having sex with
someone I don't care for.

— Divorcée, aged 55

I cannot conceive of having sex with someone I don't know
very well. Casual sex is alien to my thinking and feelings. I
must know a woman well to have sexual relations with her.
And the better the knowing the better the sex.

— Widower, aged 50

If sex without love is the only thing available to an individual, then I see no problem — but it should never be under-
stood as more than half a loaf.

— Wife, aged 51

Sex with a stranger would be an adventure and exciting; but
I find I need rapport first — or think I do.

— Widower, aged 62

Sex without love but with mutual affection and respect can
be very rewarding and enriching.

— Wife, aged 59

One unhappily married 66-year-old husband puts a subtle
twist on the issue: "Love without marriage is better than marriage
without love."

A 62-year-old widow says she approves of sex without love. "I
mean with liking — mutual attraction — not just anyone. I may
not have morals, but I do have taste!"

A 67-year-old widower who lived for many years in an "open
marriage" recalls his late wife's views on sex without love: "She
was a Quaker; and sex without warm rapport, empathy, intimacy,
mutual affection, was simply unthinkable." He adds with amuse-
ment: "It sometimes took her as long as 45 minutes to establish
that ambience."

Sex without love is the only opinion question in our questionnaire on which our women and men take opposite sides. Among

our men who take a stand, those who agree that sex without love is better than no sex at all outnumber those who disagree by nearly four to one. Among our women, those who disagree substantially outnumber those who agree:

Sex without love is better than no sex at all

	Women's opinions	Men's opinions
	(N=1,789)	(N=2,377)
Strongly agree	10% } 28%	33% } 67%
Moderately agree	18	34
Neutral	20	15
Moderately disagree	18 } 51%	9 } 17%
Strongly disagree	33	8
	99%	99%

What proportion of our respondents have actually engaged in sex since age 50 with someone they didn't know very well? What proportion would like to try it? Almost 3,000 women and men answer these questions. A much higher proportion of men than of women say they have tried it. Of those who have tried it, a somewhat higher proportion of men say they enjoyed it. Of those who have not tried it, a much higher proportion of men say they would like to try having sex with someone they don't know very well:

	Women	Men
Among all our women and men, how many have tried it?	(N=1,844) 4%	(N=2,402) 10%
Of those who have tried it, how many liked it?	(N=79) 62%	(N=250) 88%
Of those who have not tried it, how many would like to try?	(N=1,133) 4%	(N=1,530) 28%

PORNOGRAPHY

Back in 1978, when our questionnaire was drafted, the term *pornography* generally meant sexually explicit verbal or visual materials specifically designed to produce sexual arousal. That was the way we used the term in our questionnaire. Our respondents, too, use the term in that way — as shown by the discussions of pornography on their Comment Pages.

Since our questionnaire was drafted and our questionnaire forms were filled out, however, a new meaning of *pornography* has arisen. It is now sometimes used to mean portrayals of violence toward women, and materials designed to foster violence toward women. Throughout this report, the term pornography is *not* used in this sense. Rather, it carries its original meaning of materials designed to produce sexual (not violent) arousal. In their comments, our respondents, too, make no references to portrayals of violence against women as "pornographic."

The Victorian concept of pornography is hard to recall today. Almost everything having to do with sex and the human body was deemed improper and excluded from Victorian writings. Unmarried people did not even kiss in respectable Victorian novels, except perhaps for one chaste touching of the lips at the moment of betrothal. Children were born in those novels — but the sexual activities leading to pregnancy and birth were not even hinted at, much less described. Writers used the terms "white meat" and "dark meat" to avoid having to mention the *breast* or *leg* of a chicken — and even the legs of chairs were decorously hidden by skirts in Victorian illustrations. Yet, at the same time, hardcore Victorian pornography, printed and sold through underground channels, was as bluntly frank and detailed as the rawest of contemporary publications. Reprints of popular Victorian erotica are currently being sold in adult bookstores and by mail order.

Victorian taboos, let us add, did not disappear with the death of Queen Victoria. Books were "banned in Boston" and even in New York City as late as the 1950s. A 75-year-old Wisconsin physician who was formerly a theology student recalls:

When I wanted a book on sex and contraception before [my wife and I] were married, it was illegal to sell them. To get Margaret Sanger's book [on contraception], I climbed a back stairway in New York [and] knocked on a door. A view panel was opened and someone asked, "What do you want?" I said, "The Book." The person looked out at me, then said, "That will be four-fifty." I handed the money through the panel and the book was handed out and the panel closed. The knowledge of the book and where and how to get it was common knowledge at the Union Theological Seminary.

We've come a long way!*

As might be expected, our respondents differ widely on the issue of pornography. One position is presented by a 65-year-old husband who begins:

I approve of the sexual revolution, but I despise pornography in all types of media. Public displays or media displays have never been my cup of tea. Sex is a private matter to me.

He adds, however, that he does enjoy "off-color" writings "if they are clever and entertaining, not just dependent on my 'prurient' interest." Then, apparently after a bit more thought, he adds: "I guess there are more people who have interests in pornography than there are people like me. So perhaps I am not so 'normal'?"

A frequently expressed view is presented by a 61-year-old respondent who considers himself a homosexual: "I . . . disapprove

---

* In 1937, the year after its founding, Consumers Union published a booklet on contraceptive materials. It was addressed to physicians and social workers and to married couples "who have been advised by their physicians to use contraceptives." The booklet created a furor, which culminated in 1941 with a Post Office order barring it from the mails. Consumers Union filed suit, and in 1944 the Court of Appeals of the District of Columbia upheld Consumers Union's right to use the mails to disseminate information that "vitally concerned the lives and health of those to whom it was directed." [Consumers Union of United States, Inc. v. Walker, 145 F.2d 33 (D.C. Cir. 1944).]

of all the hard-core printed pornography available to those under 21."

A 52-year-old wife and mother in Omaha expresses a vigorously hostile attitude toward pornography. "I have had a surfeit of sex in TV and magazines," she writes.

> People have a choice concerning movies and books; but . . . sex in magazines (pretty girls — legs spread while they display their genitalia) disgusts and dismays me. I have found this sort of thing in my 17-year-old son's possession and feel it will not enhance his attitude toward women. We have a lot of sick people who push and publish this garbage.

A 68-year-old Texas wife, however, takes a quite different position:

> I used to find pornographic material under my son's mattress. I would put it back. It did not bother me as I was raising my sons and daughter to enjoy every minute.

A 54-year-old divorced man writes:

> I think [pornography] should only be available to adults and from restricted locations. In other words, the average citizen should not have to be exposed to it everywhere he turns because it is an affront to many people.

Some respondents do not complain about pornography *per se* but about the quality of the pornography currently available. As one 71-year-old husband puts it: "Some of the literature makes sex as exciting as fixing a tractor."

Some respondents voice their approval of sexually stimulating material:

> I approve of [pornography]. Left alone, like water, it will seek and find its own level. It will not hurt anyone, and people would be happier and better off. I and most everyone I

have known have been exposed to pornography as far back as I can remember — and I never knew of a case where it was harmful to anyone.

— Husband, aged 66

I think some of the X-rated movies can be helpful and can bring more joy and less guilt to sex.

— Husband, aged 54

Pornographic material or sex movies could be used to help educate people to enjoy sex life more.

— Husband, aged 70

The . . . four older gals I know enjoy *Playgirl* and Xaviera Hollander's book now and then. One is 87 and another 79; the other two are in their 60's.

— Wife, aged 55

Some feminists take strong exception to the anti-female aspects of much current pornography. An 83-year-old widow who lectures annually at a medical school makes this point vigorously: "I went to only one pornographic film but found it so degrading to women I never wanted to go to another." She continues, however:

I read *Playboy* and look at pictures for identifying with women (I am lusty) and other erotic magazines for fantasies; but [I] do not think others come up to the standard of *Playboy*. I wish *Playgirl* did. I do not like *really* pornographic magazines. The women look like pieces of meat."

We sought to gauge views on pornography by asking respondents whether they agreed or disagreed with the statement:

"Communities should have the right to ban all pornographic materials."

Thirty-eight percent of our respondents agree that communities should have that right; 47 percent are opposed; and the remainder are neutral:

	Women's and men's opinions	
	(N=4,172)	
Strongly agree	23% ⎫	
Moderately agree	15 ⎭	38%
Neutral or undecided	14	
Moderately disagree	16 ⎫	
Strongly disagree	31 ⎭	47%
	99%	

Those in favor of community power to ban apparently thought their reasons were self-evident, for they did not add comments; those opposed, however, commented at some length.

> What is "pornographic" material? And how to avoid the banning of pornography from leading to censorship of important educational materials — e.g., sex education? Rather than have the latter development I would prefer no legal banning of "pornography" and [to] leave it to the people generally to avoid using offensive materials — that is, materials offensive to them as individuals.
>
> — Husband, aged 68

> Even the Supreme Court can't decide what is pornographic so why should a community be allowed to?
>
> — Husband, aged 63

> I am particularly squeamish about laws or restrictions on the flow of written and filmed materials, whatever the justification. Thus, though I abhor some of the films, literature and other vehicles of a plainly porno sort, I would not have them

banned. We must not legislate personal taste except to protect children and the less competent adults.

— Husband, aged 65

Only those communities [that] can muster a 100-percent
positive vote on a definition of pornography should ban it.

— Husband, aged 52

Banning attempts do more harm than the porno material itself. Driving it underground puts it in the hands of unsavory
people who produce low quality. In Denmark all bans were
removed and after an initial flurry no demonstrable harm
has resulted. Their main market is to repressed tourists.

— Husband, aged 56

One 66-year-old husband recalls that he was formerly very
much opposed to pornography. "I remember writing to the *Saturday Evening Post* in the 1930's complaining about a full-page portrait of a girl in a bikini. (That was before *Hustler*.)" Now his view
has changed:

Pornography has its uses. It cannot really be banned because
whatever exceeds the permitted limit becomes pornography.
Perhaps it ought to be taxed like liquor so that most of the
profits accrue to the state.

The *use* of pornography by our women and men respondents,
as distinct from their opinions about pornography, is discussed in
chapter 9.

HOMOSEXUALITY

The only taboo to rival the masturbation taboo in Victorian times
was the one against homosexuality. The Oscar Wilde case in 1895
shocked the Western world; and the murder of 14-year-old Bobby
Franks by Nathan Leopold and Richard Loeb in 1924 went even

further in establishing homosexuality as the aberrant form of sexuality most to be dreaded and guarded against. Our respondents were reared in the shadow of one or both of these *causes célèbres*. Many of them were taught that sex is for procreation only and that all other sex is "unnatural"; sex with a person of the same gender was viewed as the most unnatural of all the known vices. Thus, it is hardly surprising that a marked degree of hostility toward homosexuality survives among some of our respondents.

Even as late as the 1960s, the penalties (imprisonment, social ostracism, unemployability, and others) for homosexual acts that came to public attention made it essential for persons who engaged in such acts to be particularly secretive about them. As a result, many people have never personally known a male homosexual or lesbian whom they recognized as such. A further effect of this secrecy was to leave the impression that "homosexuals" must be altogether different from other people. This is far from being the case. Most of those who engage in homosexual activities occupy the broad middle ground between the exclusively heterosexual and the exclusively homosexual. They are human beings who rarely, sometimes, often, or always engage in short-term or long-term relationships with others of the same gender.

In this chapter, however, we are considering *attitudes* toward homosexuality; and those attitudes, as we shall see, are for the most part based on the view that the human species comes with only one of two labels attached — heterosexual or homosexual.

Some respondents write more heatedly on homosexuality than on any other topic in our questionnaire. We attribute this in part to the fact that opinions on this subject are rapidly changing, and in part to the fact that our questionnaires were filled out during the fall and winter of 1978–79, when proposals to broaden or curtail the civil rights of homosexuals were being angrily debated in many communities — and when Anita Bryant's anti-gay crusade was under way.

Let us consider first the attitudes of respondents who state that they personally know one or more homosexuals. One is a 50-year-old Delaware widow who writes:

The only lesbian I know well is a 78-year-old aunt, an alcoholic, who is an impossible human being and always has been. [Other homosexuals] I know, or have known slightly, have been just like all the rest of us — some good and some bad qualities. I'm sure it's not an easy life whether they're in or out of the legendary closet, but I strongly feel they should have the same rights as heterosexuals.

A 68-year-old never-married woman writes from Oakland, California:

I don't know any [male homosexuals or lesbians] really well but there are some in the nursing profession (I am an R.N.). I think they are as moral as anybody, as interested in long-term alliances as anybody, as little likely to rape or procure as anybody. It is no worse to recruit a boy than to recruit a girl; either is a reprehensible crime, but I do not think homosexuals do more than their population-ratio amount of this. We all know there are plenty of male attacks on young females and I would guess a few older females enjoy "educating" young males.

A 68-year-old widow writes from Florida:

I was a Principal of a Federal Prison Women's Education Department for ten years, while married to my second husband. . . . I met and worked in the midst of many lesbians. This neither attracted nor repulsed me. Rather, I was concerned . . . to listen and learn about their initial and continuing sexual activities. I was totally satisfied and gratified in and with my heterosexual life. If aging women find happiness and emotional security in lesbianism, I say, "Let them do so!"

A 62-year-old Iowa husband writes:

The two homo men who have lived next door to us for years seem to have a very good relationship after 20–25 years. . . .

They don't fight as they used to. They are as dependent on each other as any older man/woman couple.

A 77-year-old Connecticut widow writes:

The acceptance of lesbian and [male] homosexual relationships [seems] to me a giant step toward sexual sanity despite the fact that I have some [personal] revulsion toward any possible [sexual] relations with other women.

Another 77-year-old widow writes:

Although never engaging in lesbian practices, I have known some [lesbians] — also some of the male counterparts. I have done some studying on the matter. Those persons I have known have been attractive, talented, sensitive, artistic persons. There are perverts in all walks of life. The usual homosexual that I have known has not been a pervert (in the sense of criminal). They have different life-styles from me and I accept them as friends if I am attracted.

She then adds:

I'm turned off by a self-righteous zealot like Anita Bryant. I am a professed Christian and as such I endeavor to live in a loving relationship with myself, my neighbor, my enemy, those different from me in color or creed.

A 60-year-old Texas husband specifically notes a recent *change* in his opinions:

I have full respect for homosexuality and bisexuals, believing it to be as "normal" as my own preference for our marital heterosexuality. As a career military officer, I had an early aversion to any homosexual acts and investigated and prosecuted a couple of cases successfully. But in later years, I developed acceptance of alternate life-styles as long as children

aren't *directly* influenced — one way or the other — believing
(as I myself feel) that development of sexual preference is
fairly fixed at birth . . . and we find our preferences without
being influenced by our casual observations of men or
women who happen to be gay . . . or straight. I likewise feel
that a late-blooming *change* in preference might be a great
thing for an elderly person who might otherwise find themselves lonely and frustrated after the loss of their mate.

A 63-year-old wife comments specifically on the effects of
aging on homosexual partnerships:

Having observed two long-term homosexual relationships for
several years each, I would say that if two members of a pair
are well-suited to each other, and stable, aging would have
about the same effect as with heterosexual pairs. If the relationships formed, either homosexual or heterosexual, are
casual or short-lived, aging will, at best, discourage liaisons;
at worst, [it] can be devastating. It seems that the most comfortable condition of aging is in the company of another,
either of the same sex or opposite. In time, other factors
such as familiarity, agreeableness, common experience or interests are important.

A 69-year-old Boston widow comments similarly on aging and
homosexuality:

I grew up knowing that one of my . . . aunts was a lesbian. . . . My view is to treat an aging lesbian the same way I
would any aging woman — with respect and affection if that
was normal. I did not note any difference in my own family
in regard to my aunt and her "mate" and their behavior. . . .
    I think her close friends included widows, bachelors, un-
married young professional people — and when she was an
old lady, they, too, were old men and women and still close
friends.

A 70-year-old widow writes:

I am against discrimination towards homosexuals. Why shouldn't they teach children? They always have.

Not all our respondents, of course, are so accepting. Here is a sampling of contrary views:

Homosexuality, or what might be termed "homo," is found in nature only in the lowest forms of life and that is exactly what it is, *"the low form of life."* These people are sick, *very sick.* They should be treated as any other person with serious mental problems.

— Widower, aged 63

I do not think God meant us to be lesbians. He made woman as a helpmate for the man, not for another woman, no matter what age we are. Our society is becoming another Sodom and Gomorrah and if we are so blatant as to flaunt homosexuality openly, I think God will use His power to destroy the nation.

— Wife, aged 53

[I] had "blow jobs" twice when very young, very single, during military service [in] World War II — before I received Jesus Christ as my personal Savior. I regret not being intelligent enough at the time to know that such activity is against God's principles and wish I had known Christ earlier. Any homosexuality is immoral and sinful at any age.

— Husband, aged 55

I still think homosexuality and lesbianism [are] against God's plan. If people must be these types, I think it should not be made public — like it is now. I think it is not something to be proud of — but rather to be ashamed of. Perhaps I was born 50 years too soon, but that is the way I feel. I would not want to be a lesbian.

— Wife, aged 65

A 67-year-old husband objects even to our including questions about homosexuality in our questionnaire:

> Sex is related to reproduction. People like the ones who drafted this questionnaire have distorted its primary function. Until recently homos were regarded as sick, exhibitionists, or child molesters and were treated accordingly. You are equating deviance of a minority with the norm of the majority and are helping borderline people go off the deep end. You have been encouraged by phony nonsensical psychologists and psychiatrists who stand to benefit from the number of off-balance people they can produce. You may consider yourself liberal; [but] you not I will pay the bill in the years ahead for treating these mental cases you have helped create.

Even more extreme are the remarks of a 70-year-old husband who writes:

> In my view, every homosexual should be put to *death*. That is how I actually feel about it. It violates all the teachings of Christianity (*Romans* 1:26–32).

But a never-married 66-year-old man, who reports "hundreds" of homosexual partners before 50 and "hundreds" more since then, comments:

> I have nothing but contempt for those prudish, medieval, bigoted heterosexuals who think God made the world just for them. They want all kinds of rights for themselves but are too small-minded to grant the same rights to homosexuals. . . . Fortunately, there are increasing numbers of . . . heterosexuals who realize that God created both gays and straights and [that] a nation's laws should permit both groups to co-exist side by side in complete equality.

In addition to our questions about homosexual experiences (reviewed in chapter 4), we asked two opinion questions. The first concerned law enforcement. At this writing, only about a dozen states have repealed their laws making homosexual acts felonies punishable by long terms of imprisonment. Even where these laws are still on the books, however, they are only rarely and only selectively enforced. We asked respondents whether they agree or disagree with the statement:

"Laws against [male] homosexual and lesbian acts should be enforced."

Our other opinion statement about homosexuality shifted the ground of discussion from law enforcement to personal privacy:

"[Male] homosexual and lesbian relations between older people are nobody else's business."

Some respondents agree with both statements and comment on the seeming contradiction:

In an apparent contradiction, I indicated that laws against homosexuals should be enforced but that acts between consenting homosexuals are nobody's business. All laws should be enforced or repealed. In this case, the latter is recommended.

— Husband, aged 51

I believe we should enforce our laws; otherwise why have them? But I think there is no need for laws against homosexual or lesbian acts between consenting adults.

— Wife, aged 69

Laws against "forced" homosexual acts should be enforced; but if it is between two consenting adults, it's nobody's business — if it is in private. (I do not like to hear them bragging about it, though.)

— Divorcée, aged 52

All laws should be enforced. Laws against homosexuality
should be repealed.

— Divorcée, aged 53

Subject to these and similar qualifications, respondents who
favor enforcement outnumber those who oppose enforcement by
almost two to one:

*Laws against [male] homosexual and
lesbian acts should be enforced*

	Women's and men's opinions (N=4,109)
Strongly agree	35% ⎫ 50%
Moderately agree	15 ⎭
Neutral	22
Moderately disagree	12 ⎫ 28%
Strongly disagree	16 ⎭
	100%

When we consider the responses to the second question, we
find a shift of opinion, as might be expected — but the magnitude
of the shift was unexpected. Of our respondents who take a stand,
those who agree that homosexual relations between older people
are nobody else's business outnumber those who disagree by five
to one:

[Male] homosexual and lesbian relations between
older people are nobody else's business

	Women's and men's opinions	
	(N=4,163)	
Strongly agree	49%	70%
Moderately agree	21	
Neutral	17	
Moderately disagree	6	14%
Strongly disagree	8	
	101%	

Taken together with the comments of many of our respondents, the two tables above express strong opinions on two bastions of Victorianism. On the one hand, respect for law receives firm support; on the other, acceptance of homosexuality as a private matter, beyond government purview, receives overwhelming support and represents a dramatic departure from Victorian standards. Indeed, this acceptance appears to be the high-water mark of our respondents' departure from Victorian sexual attitudes:

It seems only fair and honest for people to have the right and freedom of choice as to their sexual preferences, whether "straight," lesbian, or homosexual. I happen to be "straight" — but I would *deeply* resent it if someone told me I *had* to be so!

— Wife, aged 62

I find the present campaign against homo and lesbian lifestyles very objectionable and do not feel such persecution belongs in the political arena.

— Widow, aged 69

I am not homosexual and I do not understand [homosexuality]; but I am not God to say what someone else should do and neither is the government.

— Widower, aged 57

I'm very old-fashioned. I don't read sexy novels; I don't enjoy sexy movies. I know there are homosexuals. They should have the same freedom heterosexuals have. Maybe I believe this because I am so opposed to Anita Bryant. What she's for, I'm against; and what she's against, I'm for.

— Divorcée, aged 50

Our society is too uptight about homosexuality. A lot of us fight against homosexual behavior because we have to some degree homosexual attractions within us and we think they are wrong and try to suppress them.

— "Bisexual" husband, aged 53

People have no right to decide what is "sinful" and then punish people who sin — even though there is no victim. Bloodthirsty Christians are the bane of our society. Homosexuality, as an example, is no threat to the general public, and — even though one may think it sinful — there is no need to suppress or punish it.

— Husband, aged 70

I am totally indifferent to the hue and cry *in re* [homosexuality] and the concerted effort by so many to keep sex issues alive. To me the "crusaders" in matters of sex . . . would be better off saving their strength to improve the socioeconomic conditions of our poor and distressed.

— Unmarried male, aged 59

Even some respondents personally sympathetic to homosexuals are strongly opposed — as in several of the examples above — to homosexuals making their sexual preferences publicly known. "Let them do what they please — but keep quiet about it" summarizes a common attitude. This attitude misses an important point. So long as homosexuals did in fact keep quiet about it, they remained a misunderstood, slandered, and discriminated-against minority, subject to long terms of imprisonment and socioeconomic ostracism. The common stereotype of the homosexual in those days was of a sinister figure lurking around school grounds or ice-cream wagons for little boys to seduce or rape. Only after homosexuals began to come out of the closet, so that people could see what they are really like, did public opinion shift toward a more accepting position.

VICTORIAN AND NON-VICTORIAN RESPONDENTS

What kinds of people still hold Victorian sexual opinions and what kinds do not? To find out, we assigned numerical scores to each of the questions discussed in this chapter — on masturbation, sex without marriage, sex without love, pornography, and homosexuality, with high scores indicating support for Victorian sexual views and low scores indicating support for non-Victorian sexual views. We next divided our respondents into two equal groups, labeling the half with high scores "Victorians," and the half with low scores "non-Victorians." We then determined how our "Victorians" differ from our "non-Victorians" with respect to gender, age, education, income, marital status, and four other factors.

We found that among our respondents, Victorian sexual views are more often expressed by women; by older respondents, both men and women; and by those reporting less education, less income, low enjoyment of sex, and low sexual frequency. Non-Victorian sexual views are more often expressed by men and by younger respondents, both men and women. The unhappily married are slightly more likely than the happily married to express non-Victorian views; those with low enjoyment of sex are slightly more likely to express Victorian views. Those who report having sex more than once a week are by far the most likely to express non-Victorian views.

Here are the details:

	Proportion tending to hold to Victorian sexual views	Proportion tending not to hold to Victorian sexual views
Women (N=1,650)	58%	42%
Men (N=2,303)	46%	54%
In their 50s (N=1,552)	44%	56%
In their 60s (N=1,570)	52%	48%
Aged 70 and over (N=831)	65%	35%
Education not beyond high school (N=874)	67%	33%
Education beyond high school (N=3,060)	53%	47%
Income under $10,000 a year (N=450)	61%	39%
Income $10,000 or more a year (N=3,384)	50%	50%
Married (N=2,939)	53%	47%
Unmarried (N=859)	54%	46%
Happily married (N=2,915)	51%	49%
Unhappily married (N=486)	47%	53%
High enjoyment of sex (N=2,814)	47%	53%
Low enjoyment of sex (N=607)	59%	41%
Sexual frequency:		
More than once a week (N=1,197)	36%	64%
About once a week (N=1,397)	50%	50%
Less than once a week, not at all, or no answer (N=1,359)	67%	33%
High enjoyment of life (N=3,351)	50%	50%
Low enjoyment of life (N=512)	55%	45%

Summary

Most of our women and men were exposed to repressive Victorian standards of sexual behavior during their formative years. These standards continue to determine the opinions of some of our respondents, but most respondents now express non-Victorian opinions on most of the seven sexual statements here reviewed.

On one statement — that homosexual relations between older people are nobody else's business — seven out of ten of both our women and our men express non-Victorian views. Majorities of both women and men also express non-Victorian views on masturbation for children, masturbation for older people, and sex without marriage. On pornography, a plurality but not a majority of respondents express non-Victorian opinions. On the issue of enforcing the anti-homosexual laws, half of our men and women express Victorian opinions and the other half either express non-Victorian opinions or say they are neutral. On only one issue — that sex without love is better than no sex at all — do women and men take different sides. Here half of our women express Victorian views while two-thirds of our men express non-Victorian views.

In short, some older people — like some younger people — cling to the views they were brought up with. Many others have come a long, long way.

❧ 6 ❦

Health and Sexual Changes

SOME WOMEN AND MEN REMAIN IN EXCELLENT HEALTH INTO THEIR eighties and perhaps beyond — but some do not. Some women and men remain sexually active, and maintain a high level of sexual enjoyment, into their eighties and perhaps beyond — but some do not. The data supplied by our respondents make it possible to trace the course of both health and sexual function through the decades after 50 in a population that is on the whole healthy and sexually active — but that includes many respondents who are neither.

We find that impaired health, as anticipated, has a measurably adverse impact on sexual function. This impact, however, is quite modest — smaller, for example, than the adverse impact of aging on sexual function. This is true both for impaired health in general and for the seven specific health factors for which we have sexual data: heart attack, diabetes, the taking of anti-hypertensive medication, hysterectomy, ovariectomy, mastectomy, and prostate surgery. Some adverse health factors can in isolated cases be devastating sexually and in other respects. But *most* of our women and men continue to enjoy life, and to enjoy sex, despite these and other health impairments.

People often talk about their operations; but they rarely confide in one another concerning the sexual effects — or absence of sexual effects — of surgery. There is a similar reticence concerning the sexual effects of heart attacks and of diseases such as diabetes. As a result, the whole subject is surrounded by an aura of mystery and dire foreboding. We hope that the data here presented — including the frank statements of patients who have abandoned all reticence on their Comment Pages — will clear up much of the mystery and dispel unwarranted forebodings.

HEALTH AND AGING

Ninety percent of our women and men are enjoying excellent, very good, or good health:

	Women (N=1,833)		Men (N=2,385)	
Health excellent or very good	63%	} 90%	65%	} 90%
Good	27		25	
Fair or poor	10		10	
	100%		100%	

As might be expected, the proportions reporting excellent or very good health decrease and the proportions reporting only good, fair or poor health increase as the decades roll by:

Women	In their 50s (N=799)	In their 60s (N=714)	Aged 70 and over (N=320)
Health excellent or very good	69%	60%	51%
Good	24	29	31
Fair or poor	7	11	18
	100%	100%	100%

Men	(N=816)	(N=977)	(N=592)
Health excellent or very good	74%	63%	57%
Good	20	26	30
Fair or poor	6	12	13
	100%	101%	100%

We shall have much to say about aging and sexual function in chapter 8.

HEALTH AND SEXUAL FUNCTION

We measured the impact of health on sexual function using three yardsticks:

• The proportion of respondents who are sexually active — through masturbation or sex with a partner or both.

• The proportion of those sexually active who report high sexual frequency — that is, who report masturbation or sex with a partner or both once a week or more.

• The proportion of those sexually active who report high enjoyment of sex.

We found, as might be expected, that impaired health adversely affects *sexual activity*. Here are the proportions sexually active among our women and men:

87 percent of our women in excellent or very good health
79 percent of those in good health
72 percent of those in fair or poor health

93 percent of our men in excellent or very good health
87 percent of those in good health
82 percent of those in fair or poor health

Note particularly the high proportion sexually active (72 percent of the women and 82 percent of the men) despite fair or poor health.

The figures above, moreover, tend to overstate the impact of health on sexual activity. When our statisticians "controlled" for age — that is, when, within an age group, they compared the proportion sexually active at each health level — they found only small differences in sexual activity among the health levels. Thus, most of the decline in sexual activity appears to be due to aging rather than to health impairments *per se.*

Impaired health, of course, may adversely affect a man's or a woman's sexual function without terminating sexual activity altogether. Our second and third yardsticks were designed to explore this possibility.

We found that *sexual frequency* also tends to decline with impaired health. Here are the proportions of those sexually active who report having sex at least once a week:

69 percent of our women in excellent or very good health
63 percent of those in good health
54 percent of those in fair or poor health

80 percent of our men in excellent or very good health
72 percent of those in good health
60 percent of those in fair or poor health

Here again, controlling for age shows that the above figures overstate the impact of health on sexual frequency; most of the differences shown are due to aging rather than impaired health *per se.*

Our third yardstick, *enjoyment of sex,* tells the same story. Among the sexually active, the following proportions report high enjoyment of sex:

70 percent of our women in excellent or very good health
64 percent of our women in good health
53 percent of our women in fair or poor health

89 percent of our men in excellent or very good health
81 percent of our men in good health
70 percent of our men in fair or poor health

And, once again, controlling for age reveals that most of the differences shown are due to aging rather than to impaired health *per se.*

We conclude that impaired health does indeed have an adverse impact on sexuality — but only a modest one. Differences due to aging loom much larger.

While the differences in the three tables above appear to be due primarily to the adverse impact of poor health on sexual function, another factor may be at work. Perhaps sexual activity, frequency, and enjoyment have a favorable effect on health.

SEXUAL CHANGES ASSOCIATED WITH SPECIFIC HEALTH IMPAIRMENTS

Does having a heart attack increase the likelihood that a woman or man will become sexually inactive? How does it affect frequency of sexual activity? Enjoyment of sexual activity? What about the sexual effects of taking anti-hypertensive medication? Mastectomy? Hysterectomy? Prostate surgery? These are the kinds of questions to which we now turn.

While we cannot here survey the entire field of sexual dysfunction, we can at least indicate its boundaries. Dr. Helen Singer Kaplan, clinical professor of psychiatry and director of Human Sexuality Teaching Program at the New York Hospital–Cornell Medical Center, has pioneered in the study of sexual problems and sex therapy. Like many of her peers, she recognizes sexual dysfunctions as having psychological roots, physiological roots, and often a combination of both.

In her book *Disorders of Sexual Desire,** Dr. Kaplan devotes some twenty pages to long lists of drugs, physical conditions, and diseases that may impair sexual function. Some drugs are exonerated of having adverse sexual effects; others only "may" have such effects. "While the specific mechanisms of action are not clear in all cases," she writes, "clinical evidence suggests that some drugs may produce a diminution of sexual desire" as well as impotence and orgasm problems. Among the drugs cited are "certain centrally acting antihypertensive agents."

Physical conditions that may lead to pain during intercourse

---

* *Disorders of Sexual Desire,* by Helen Singer Kaplan, M.D., Ph.D. (New York: Brunner/Mazel Inc., 1979), pages 80, 81, 203–222.

or other sexual activities, Dr. Kaplan indicates, include genital and prostate infections, hernias, prolapse of the uterus, post-hysterectomy scarring, and many more.

Dr. Kaplan exonerates some diseases, like some drugs, of having adverse sexual effects, and indicates that some diseases, too, only "may" have such effects. Among the diseases she categorizes as a "frequent cause of sexual difficulties" are diabetes, multiple sclerosis, thyroid deficiency, and alcoholic neuropathy (a disease of the nervous system caused by alcohol).

"Chronic alcoholism," she states, "may result in permanent neurological damage and consequent impaired genital functioning." Elsewhere, she describes depression as "perhaps the most common physiologic cause of [reduced sexual desire]." "Musculoskeletal disorders of the pelvis and lower back," including arthritis of the hip, "make sexual activity and intercourse painful or difficult."

While we cannot report on these three very common causes of sexual dysfunction — chronic alcoholism, depression, and musculoskeletal disorders such as arthritis — we can report on the sexual effects of seven other common health factors covered by our questionnaire. Of these seven, three affect both men and women, three are exclusively female, and one is exclusively male. They are listed below in order of frequency; respondents reporting two or more health factors are counted two or more times:

Health Impairments

Of 1,844 Women

Hysterectomy (surgical removal of the uterus), reported by 34 percent (635)

Ovariectomy (surgical removal of both ovaries), 18 percent (339)

Anti-hypertensive medication, 18 percent (336)

Mastectomy (surgical removal of one or both breasts), 5 percent (93)

Diabetes, 4 percent (74)

Heart attack, 4 percent (66)

Anti-hypertensive medication, reported by 18 percent (433)

Prostate surgery, 13 percent (302)

Heart attack, 10 percent (251)

Diabetes, 6 percent (136)

Anti-hypertensive medication

A Seattle widower married two years ago, at age 58, a woman then 41.

Until six months ago, he and his wife had sex together two or three times a week; he considered this "not often enough," and masturbated a few times a month in addition. Both he and his wife, he writes, almost always reached orgasm He felt uncomfortable and restless if he went without sexual release for more than three days. He describes his interest in sex as strong — indeed, stronger than at age 40 when he was married to his first wife.

All this, he goes on to explain, describes how things were six months before he filled out our questionnaire. Then a marked change occurred. He now finds that it is taking him longer to attain an erection. When fully erect his penis is less stiff then formerly. He more often loses his erection during sex. It takes more vigorous stimulation of his penis to reach orgasm. His refractory period is longer. He rates all five of these changes as "serious problems," and describes them as "all very new (last six months) and very upsetting."

In some cases, a complete medical and psychosocial evaluation may be necessary to determine the cause of such a sudden decline in potency. This respondent, however, considers the explanation in his case obvious: The changes occurred shortly after he began taking medication for high blood pressure — hypertension.

Different patients respond in different ways to the adverse sexual changes noted while taking anti-hypertensive medication. A 70-year-old Nevada husband comments:

Use of [medication] for hypertension loused up my sexual performance. . . . Penis not as stiff as before. However, without [the medication], I might not be around to worry about it.

A 74-year-old Oregon husband taking anti-hypertensive medication says he "lost interest" in sex,

due to inability to perform, and [it] doesn't bother me at all. I'm not hung up on sex — which no doubt makes me un-American! Please do not send the CIA or FBI to check. I feel that sex belongs largely to youth. Of course, if one never grows up, then no doubt one is hung up on it into old age.

A quite different adjustment to anti-hypertensive medication is reported by a 65-year-old divorced man who writes that three years ago he launched a sexual relationship with a woman then aged 55. Now, he says, he is taking anti-hypertensive medication and is suffering from all six signs of impaired sexual potency. He considers all six "serious problems." Nevertheless, the relationship continues. He and his partner have sex a few times a month, using manual and oral stimulation. She always reaches orgasm; he seldom does — but he enjoys it anyway. "I believe taking medication against hypertension caused [my] problems affecting erection," he writes. "However, I sleep with her overnight three or four times a week." Despite his erectile and orgasmic problems, he rates his enjoyment of sex as 3.

A 70-year-old husband writes from Indianapolis:

I am taking a pill to control my blood pressure. I believe a good many men past age 60 take these blood pressure pills that make them totally impotent sexually or to some degree affect their sexual life. Of the 25 or 30 different pills available, are there any that will *not* affect one's sexual activity?

That question, of course, strikes at the heart of the matter. The answer comes in two parts:

• Different types of anti-hypertensive medication achieve their effects in different ways. A patient may experience adverse sexual effects from one type but not from another. Asking your physician to switch you to a different type of medication is thus a reasonable request if you believe your present medication is impairing your sexual response.

• Adverse sexual effects may also be related to the dosage of medication. Thus, before changing medication, you may reasonably ask to have your dosage reduced in an effort to find a level that controls blood pressure adequately without depressing sexual response unduly.

A 70-year-old West Virginia husband makes both points: "Some of the anti-hypertension drugs my doctor has prescribed have made me impotent, either from type or dosage," he writes. "My current [anti-hypertensive] medicine does not appear to bother me."

Eighteen percent of our 4,246 respondents are currently taking anti-hypertensive medication. What proportion of the 769 remain sexually active? Does medication affect their frequency of sexual activity? Their enjoyment of sex?

One way to find answers to these questions would be to compare our respondents taking anti-hypertensive medication with our respondents not taking such medication. This comparison might be misleading, however, since among our respondents not taking anti-hypertensive medication there are many who suffer from generally poor health or from specific causes of sexual dysfunction *other* than anti-hypertensive medication. Accordingly, in the table that follows, we compare our respondents on anti-hypertensive medication with a "healthy comparison group."

To identify this healthy comparison group, we first eliminated all respondents who rate their own health as fair or poor, or who do not answer that question. We similarly eliminated all men and women who report any of the health impairments listed earlier, as well as men who have prostate trouble (not just those reporting prostate surgery). Finally, we eliminated all respondents who are taking anti-coagulants or insulin. This leaves 1,191 men and 819 women in our healthy comparison groups.

As shown in the table below, a comparison of the anti-hypertensive medication groups with the healthy groups shows that smaller proportions of both women and men on anti-hypertensive medication are sexually active. In addition, fewer of the sexually active report having sex at least once a week; and fewer report a high enjoyment of sex. Yet it is noteworthy that substantial proportions of men and women on anti-hypertensive medication remain sexually active, report having sex at least once a week, and report a high enjoyment of sex.

Men	On anti-hypertensive medication	Healthy comparison group
	(N=433)	(N=1,191)
Sexually active	85%	94%
	(N=367)	(N=1,115)
Sex at least once a week	74%	82%
High enjoyment of sex	82%	87%
Women		
	(N=336)	(N=819)
Sexually active	78%	86%
	(N=262)	(N=705)
Sex at least once a week	59%	71%
High enjoyment of sex	59%	70%

The sexual effects of anti-hypertensive medication shown in the table above are dwarfed by the sexual effects of aging (see chapter 8). Moreover, because differences due to aging are included in these data, the differences attributable to health impairment are somewhat exaggerated.

In addition, the differences in the above table are exaggerated by a second factor: some of the respondents in the group taking anti-hypertensive medication also suffer from one or more *other* sex-affecting health impairments (such as diabetes or prostate trouble or both). Thus the differences due to taking anti-hypertensive medication *per se* are somewhat lower than shown in the table. The same two qualifications — differences due to aging and to multiple health impairments — hold true for all subsequent tables, both male and female, in this chapter.

Heart attack

In the past, many patients were warned following a heart attack that they should not engage in "strenuous activity" — and some interpreted this warning to mean that they should not engage in sex.

Within the past decade, however, medical opinion concerning sex after a heart attack has changed. Patients can now be assured that sexual intercourse places no more strain on the heart than climbing two flights of stairs. Most heart-attack patients can be encouraged to resume sexual activities at the same time that they resume other comparable physical activities. Consumers Union's medical consultants wholly agree with this advice — for women as well as for men who have had heart attacks.

What of the small group of cardiac patients who *can't* climb two flights of stairs safely without suffering cardiac pain or shortness of breath? Dr. Richard A. Stein, director of the Cardiac Exercise Laboratory and Medical Service, State University of New York–Downstate Medical Center, Brooklyn, advises patients in this category to take their usual dose of nitroglycerine fifteen minutes to half an hour before engaging in sex. Just as nitroglycerine enables them to walk farther and engage in other moderate physical activity safely and without pain, so it may enable them to engage in sex safely and without pain.*

Of our 317 men and women who have had a heart attack, the

---

* See "Sexual Counselling and Coronary Heart Disease" by Richard A. Stein, M.D., in *Principles and Practice of Sex Therapy*, Sandra R. Leiblum and Lawrence A. Pervin, eds. (New York: The Guilford Press, 1980).

vast majority remain sexually active. Among the men, the likelihood of being sexually active is somewhat less than it is for the healthy comparison group. High enjoyment of sex is only slightly less likely for the sexually active heart-attack men, but the likelihood of high sexual frequency is appreciably less.

	Men who have had a heart attack	Healthy comparison group
	(N=251)	(N=1,191)
Sexually active	86%	94%
	(N=215)	(N=1,115)
Sex at least once a week	68%	82%
High enjoyment of sex	83%	87%

Among our 66 women who have had a heart attack, 70 percent — 46 women — remain sexually active, as compared with 86 percent for the healthy comparison group. These 46 women are too few to permit useful statistical analysis. To the extent that the experience of these women tells us anything, we can say that sexual frequency and sexual enjoyment are reduced for at least a few of the 46 sexually active women who have had a heart attack.

Diabetes

Medical authorities are agreed that diabetes is a major cause of sexual dysfunction. Dr. Kaplan calls diabetes "a frequent cause of sexual difficulties" — including impotence and impaired ejaculation among men, and impaired orgasm among women. Indeed, diabetes is believed to be the most common medical cause of impotence, and impotence may be the first sign of diabetes to be noticed.

Two hundred and ten of our respondents have diabetes. Of the 136 men, substantial proportions report no adverse effects with respect to sexual activity, sexual frequency, or sexual enjoyment:

	Men who have diabetes	Healthy comparison group
	(N=136)	(N=1,191)
Sexually active	80%	94%
	(N=109)	(N=1,115)
Sex at least once a week	70%	82%
High enjoyment of sex	79%	87%

Among our 74 women who have diabetes, 73 percent — 54 women — remain sexually active, as compared with the healthy comparison group's 86 percent. As was the case with our sexually active heart-attack women, the 54 sexually active diabetic women are too few for useful statistical analysis.

Hysterectomy

Thirty-four percent of our women respondents (635 out of 1,844) have already had a hysterectomy (surgical removal of the uterus). The proportion rises decade by decade — from 31 percent for women in their fifties to 34 percent for women in their sixties and to 43 percent for those aged 70 or over.*

Many women in the past, reared in ignorance of even the simplest facts about sex, feared that removal of the uterus was like male castration, "desexing" a woman and making sexual intercourse impossible. This, of course, is not true; hysterectomy only makes pregnancy impossible.

Some women who have a hysterectomy report decreased sexual response, and physicians have usually attributed this to psychological causes. However, as Masters and Johnson reported

---

* Hysterectomy is likely to become considerably less common, for at least three reasons: First, many women in past decades underwent hysterectomy in order to prevent future pregnancies; tubal ligation, a simpler and safer procedure, is now commonly used for this purpose. A second reason is the effectiveness of the campaign of the women's movement against unnecessary female surgery of all kinds. Finally, there is the growing tendency of women — and men — to secure a second opinion before submitting to major surgery.

back in 1966, the uterus and other pelvic structures undergo a series of rhythmic contractions during orgasm, occurring at eight-tenths-of-a-second intervals like the orgasmic contractions of the male penis. Following hysterectomy, the uterine contractions are, of course, absent.

Whether and how hysterectomy affects the quality of female orgasm as it is *experienced* has not, so far as we can determine, been studied. Our questionnaire returns throw no light on the issue — except for a comment by a 62-year-old widow who had a hysterectomy at age 41:

> I felt no diminution in my *femaleness* and *femininity* after the operation — but I noticed a pronounced difference in my *interior* at once. Only males have averred to me that the operation itself has *no* effect on sexual response. As a woman, I go on record as saying the uterus plays a secondary or accompanying role in coitus — acts or functions as a *sounding board* does in a piano. It reflects the orgasmic contractions, intensifying the sensations.

As shown in the table below, the impact of hysterectomy on sexual activity and enjoyment is quite modest, with small-to-negligible differences:

	Have had a hysterectomy	Healthy comparison group
	(N=635)	(N=819)
Sexually active	82%	86%
	(N=519)	(N=705)
Sex at least once a week	64%	71%
High enjoyment of sex	68%	70%

Surgical removal of both ovaries

The operation known as *ovariectomy* or *oophorectomy* involves the removal of either one or both ovaries. Three hundred and thirty-nine of our 1,844 women respondents (18 percent) have had both ovaries removed. The proportion rises from 16 percent for women in their fifties to 19 percent for women in their sixties and 22 percent for those aged 70 or over.

Just as surgical removal of both testicles (castration) leads to dearth of the male hormone testosterone, so removal of both ovaries is followed by dearth of a female hormone, estrogen. This promptly brings on menopause — often called surgically induced, or surgical, menopause — even among women who have the operation in their teens, twenties, or thirties. Dearth of estrogen, whether from surgical or from natural menopause, may have specific sexual consequences; these are discussed in the next chapter.

For the record, we present below our usual table showing the impact of ovariectomy on sexual activity, frequency, and enjoyment. Note, however, that the ovariectomized women in this table include two disparate groups of women.

One group is composed of ovariectomized women who are taking estrogen; they are quite similar to our healthy comparison group with respect to sexual activity, frequency, and enjoyment. The other group is composed of ovariectomized women not taking estrogen; they show adverse effects on all three sexual measures. The table below combines the two groups:

	Have had both ovaries removed	*Healthy comparison group*
	(N=339)	(N=819)
Sexually active	81%	86%
	(N=273)	(N=705)
Sex at least once a week	63%	71%
High enjoyment of sex	67%	70%

Mastectomy

Five percent of our women have had one or both breasts surgically removed. The proportion rises from three percent for women in their fifties to six percent for women in their sixties, and to nine percent for those aged 70 or over.

Mastectomy is performed almost exclusively for breast cancer. Like hysterectomy, the operation is likely to become less common in future years. More and more surgeons are recommending removal of the cancer, with preservation of the remainder of the breast, as an alternative to mastectomy in early breast cancer cases.* Such surgery is usually followed by radiation, delivered in a way that results in an excellent cosmetic appearance in many cases.†

The table below shows mastectomy to have only a moderate impact on sexual function:

	Have had mastectomy	Healthy comparison group
	(N=93)	(N=819)
Sexually active	81%	86%
	(N=75)	(N=705)
Sex at least once a week	59%	71%
High enjoyment of sex	64%	70%

Prostate surgery

The major function of the prostate gland is to provide the bulk of the fluid content of semen. (The remainder comes from the testicles and seminal vesicles.) As the prostate gland ages, its contractions at the time of orgasm become less vigorous and less fluid is ejaculated.

The prostate gland surrounds the portion of the urethra that is nearest the bladder. In older men, the gland often increases in

* See "Breast Cancer: The Retreat from Radical Surgery," in *Consumer Reports*, January 1981, pp. 24–30.
† We also call attention to the increased availability in recent years of plastic surgery for the reconstruction of breasts and the replacement of nipples following mastectomy. Several of our respondents report post-mastectomy breast reconstruction.

size, causing what is commonly known as "prostate trouble." The enlarged prostate slows the flow of urine and urine is left in the bladder at the end of urination. This residual urine increases the likelihood of bladder and kidney infections. A man with prostate trouble may urinate more frequently, and the feeling of urinary urgency may be intense. Total blockage of the urinary channel may follow — an extremely painful emergency requiring insertion of a catheter to drain the bladder. Surgery is commonly performed before total blockage occurs.

Three hundred and fifty-three of our men (15 percent) say they have prostate trouble, and 302 (13 percent) have had prostate surgery. The surgery figures are much more impressive, however, when we note that only 3 percent of our men in their fifties have had prostate surgery, as compared with 12 percent in their sixties, 24 percent in their seventies — and 42 percent in their eighties.

Prostate surgery may be performed for either of two quite different conditions. The first is "prostate trouble," as described above. The medical name is *benign prostatic hypertrophy* or *hyperplasia* (BPH).* The other common reason for prostate surgery is cancer. We shall discuss the two separately.

Surgery for benign prostatic hyperplasia (BPH)

In the early days of surgery for BPH, the nerves leading to the genitals were cut in order to reach the prostate; impotence or inability to have an orgasm or both were virtually unavoidable as a result. Then, about 1910, a novel approach to the prostate through the urethra was introduced — thus sparing (in most cases) the nerves essential to sexual function.

One of the first American surgeons to perform this type of operation, known as a transurethral resection, or TUR, was Dr. Hugh H. Young of the Johns Hopkins School of Medicine in Baltimore. One of his first patients to have a TUR was Diamond Jim Brady, a wealthy and flamboyant locomotive salesman internationally re-

---

* *Hyperplasia* is the correct term; but *hypertrophy* is the term commonly used by physicians and by our respondents.

nowned as the lover of a celebrated actress of that era, Lillian Russell. Following his TUR, it is alleged, Brady first spent a weekend with Lillian Russell and then asked Dr. Young:

"How much do I owe you?"

"Whatever you think it's worth."

"I can't afford that," Brady is said to have replied, "but here's a check for a million dollars."

The story is not altogether apocryphal. Dr. Young reported in his autobiography and elsewhere that he did perform the operation and that he received $220,000 from Diamond Jim — a substantial surgical fee in those days — to build a new urological center. The center was (and still is) named the James Buchanan Brady Institute of Urology in honor of Diamond Jim.

A disadvantage of the TUR is that it sometimes results in retrograde ejaculation — that is, a discharge of the semen back into the bladder instead of out through the urethra. This change, some of our respondents report, also affects the subjective *sensation* of ejaculation (see below).

Another operative approach to the prostate is through the lower abdominal wall and is called a suprapubic prostatectomy. Sexual function, including ejaculation through the penis, is usually preserved.

Several of our respondents who have had prostate surgery for BPH discuss the sexual effects on their Comment Pages. Some report no adverse effects whatever:

Had transurethral operation which did not affect sexuality or sex functions or pleasure.

I had a suprapubic prostatectomy . . . for benign prostatic hypertrophy in October 1977. No negative after-effect on sexual or urinary control functions.

Prostate partially removed in July 1978 — through penis [TUR]. No ill effects. Full recovery. Sexually OK.

Quite a few others, however, complain of retrograde ejaculation:

Following prostate surgery, I have ejaculation retrograde. Now, that may be a more hygienic method for one no longer wishing fatherhood — but it is hardly as satisfying!

[Following prostatectomy] I no longer ejaculate, but rather "ooze," which detracts considerably from the satisfaction of an orgasm.

Another comment begins in much the same way:

Before prostate surgery, orgasm and ejaculation coincided. Since the operation, I have not ejaculated. This lessened the enjoyment of sex.

But matters improved: "At first, after the operation, I did not enjoy sex. I do now. The change was very gradual."

Finally, let us cite without comment the complaint of an Indianapolis widower:

I am now 86, will be 87 in a month. Have had a normal sex life — always have satisfied my partners. Two years ago, I had a prostate operation. After it had all healed, I . . . did not shoot my sperm. My urologist was surprised that I had [even] had an erection. [He] said I was shooting backward and that the sperm was going backward into my bladder and would be absorbed in my urine.

I just get a partial erection since the operation. But when it is inserted in my partner's vagina, it comes up and I get some pleasure. My partner [aged 57] is happy. But I do not [reach orgasm] very often and [when I do] it is not like it was before the operation. Before the operation [at age 84], everything was normal and pleasurable.

Surgery for prostate cancer

The prostate is the second most frequent site of cancer in men. (Lung cancer remains number one.) A radical prostatectomy, as distinct from a transurethral resection or suprapubic prostatectomy, is often performed for prostate cancer. Radical prostatectomy is invariably followed by erectile impotence.

In recent years, efforts have been made to find an erection-preserving alternative to radical prostatectomy for early prostate cancer cases. One such alternative consists of removing the lymph nodes near the prostate and implanting pellets of radioactive iodine in the cancer. One of our respondents in Washington State who underwent this procedure back in 1975 reports:

> I have been operated on for [a] tumor in my prostate. The operation . . . involved the injection of pellets of radioactive iodine into the tumor and the removal of lymph nodes in the abdomen in the area of the prostate. There was none of the radical surgery often performed for cancer of the prostate. . . . At the present time I am assured by my surgeon that there is no evidence of any kind of the existence of the tumor. . . . I have had no interference with any sexual function or any other function since — except for the first month following the operation.*

Consumers Union's medical consultants believe that patients facing prostate surgery should explore the available alternatives — transurethral resection (TUR) or suprapubic prostatectomy for BPH, radical prostatectomy or retropubic implantation of radioactive pellets or some other alternative for prostate cancer. If a patient has any doubt, a second opinion should be secured. Patients with prostate cancer can consult both a urologist concerning radical prostatectomy and a radiotherapist concerning radioactive pellet implantation or some other form of radiation therapy.†

---

* In one study, 41 patients with prostate cancer had been having sexual relations prior to implantation of radioactive pellets. Thirty-seven of them resumed sexual relations within two months after implantation; three others resumed during the following four months. The one patient who did not resume sexual relations had adequate erectile function but expressed a disinterest in sex. Harry W. Herr in *Journal of Urology*, 121 (1979): 621–623.

† The issue of radical prostatectomy *versus* radioactive pellet implantation for

Sexual effects of prostate surgery

While some of our respondents state on their Comment Pages whether they were operated on for BPH or for prostate cancer, many others do not; hence we cannot separate the two groups for statistical purposes. For the two groups combined, we can say that despite the adverse effects of prostate surgery, substantial proportions of men are sexually active, engage in sex at least once a week, and report a high enjoyment of sex:

	Have had prostate surgery	Healthy comparison group
	(N=302)	(N=1,191)
Sexually active	83%	94%
	(N=251)	(N=1,115)
Sex at least once a week	64%	82%
High enjoyment of sex	81%	87%

prostate cancer was debated at some length in a 1980 issue of *Medical World News.* The debate was triggered when two radiologists, Dr. Morris J. Wizenberg of the University of Oklahoma and Dr. Robert G. Parker of the University of California at Los Angeles, called for a "men's liberation movement" to cut down on radical prostatectomies. "Until women began asking if they had to have their breasts removed," Dr. Parker was quoted as saying, "most surgeons didn't ask that question. Now it's time to ask the same question about prostate cancer because the surgical method, which is no better than radiotherapy, causes impotence in virtually 100 percent of the patients and incontinence in about 10 percent."

A third radiologist, Dr. Bernard Roswit of the Bronx (N.Y.) VA Hospital, added: "The time has come for patients to become aware of the fact that they can be successfully treated by radiotherapy without risk of mortality, incontinence, or impotence."

Urologists, however, promptly replied that these views were slanted. Dr. Patrick C. Walsh, chairman of the James Buchanan Brady Institute of Urology at the Johns Hopkins, for example, stated that following radical prostatectomy, patients still have normal feeling in the penis and normal orgasm; "they just don't have enough of an erection for vaginal penetration, and that can be restored with an implant." Another urologist, Dr. David F. Paulson of Duke University, said that 80 percent of the patients at Duke who have radical prostatectomies get a penile implant and resume sexual activities. *Medical World News,* 21 January 1980, pp. 27–28.

SUMMARY

Impaired health in general as well as the seven specific health impairments reviewed in this chapter have a measurably adverse effect on the proportion of women and men who remain sexually active. Among the sexually active, these health impairments have a measurably adverse effect on frequency of sexual activity and on enjoyment of sex. Even the largest of these impacts of health on sexuality, however, is smaller than the impact of aging on sexuality.

Remarkably large proportions of respondents, both men and women, report being sexually active, engaging in sex at least once a week, and with high enjoyment of sex — despite only fair or poor health, and despite the seven adverse health factors here reviewed.

❧ 7 ❧

Menopause
and Postmenopausal
Hormone Therapy

THE TERM *MENOPAUSE* MEANS THE PERMANENT CESSATION OF MEN-struation. This can normally occur as early as the late thirties or as late as the mid-fifties. Only 80 of our women report they are still menstruating. In this chapter we are concerned with the women whose menstrual cycles have ceased.

Menopause has numerous and widely varying effects, both favorable and unfavorable. Thus when two women disagree concerning the effects of menopause, both may be entirely right. We shall repeatedly stress this wide range of variation among our women, as demonstrated by their answers to our menopause questions.

WHY SOME WOMEN WELCOME THE MENOPAUSE

One respondent, a 69-year-old Seattle widow, notes only one menopausal symptom — an *increase* in sexual pleasure:

> Menopause increased my sexual enjoyment because of not having to worry about getting pregnant — there was no birth control pill before I reached menopausal age.

A 54-year-old wife in Arkansas comments similarly that it "is great not getting pregnant or having monthly bothers."

A 51-year-old New Hampshire wife writes:

Menopause has brought with it a new freedom in sex with my spouse — as well as a feeling of control of my life and a new spurt of energy, never having those "tired" days. I love it! Also, I have led a group of women for the past three years in a creative maturity group, exploring life's changes and [how] we can grow in more ways.

Some writers wax almost lyrical about the benefits of the menopause. In *Every Woman's Book of Health* (1961), for example, Maxine Davis describes the menopause as "an event to which a woman can look forward with the happy anticipation of a child waiting for Santa Claus." She continues: "The menopause is a normal episode in the life of every woman, normal as morning and evening, normal as summer after spring."

ESTROGEN-ASSOCIATED MENOPAUSAL PROBLEMS

In addition to marking an end to "monthly bothers" and to the need for contraceptive precautions (although many authorities recommend that contraceptive precautions continue for one year after menstruation ceases), menopause reflects a gradual decline in the production of estrogen by a woman's ovaries. Estrogen is important for maintaining a variety of bodily functions. A decline in estrogen production is therefore followed by changes in those functions. It is important to distinguish these estrogen-associated changes from the changes due to aging as such — for the estrogen-associated changes can be forestalled or reversed. There are two ways to distinguish bodily changes due to lack of estrogen from changes due to aging:

• If a change occurs in *young* women following surgical removal of the ovaries (surgical menopause), then that change is clearly not due to aging *per se.*

• If, in addition, the change can be forestalled or alleviated by the administration of estrogen, then it is highly probable that it is caused by lack of estrogen. Four groups of changes have been shown to be associated with estrogen deficiency in both of these respects:

> hot flashes and hot flushes
> vaginal changes
> urinary tract changes
> bone changes

Many postmenopausal women, however, do not experience these changes to a bothersome or even a noticeable degree, for a reason that is not often mentioned in nontechnical discussions. Following menopause and the decrease in estrogen production by the ovaries, the adrenal glands and the postmenopausal ovaries continue to produce substantial quantities of another hormone, androstenedione. In some women enough of this hormone is converted to estrogen so that symptoms associated with lack of estrogen may not appear for many years. Most of this conversion of androstenedione to estrogen occurs in the body's fat cells; hence, in the experience of many physicians, obese women are less likely than thin women to experience symptoms of postmenopausal estrogen deficiency.

The hot flash syndrome

The temperature of the human body is held within a narrow range (normally 97 to 100 degees Fahrenheit) by a complex and sensitive system of checks and balances. Withdrawal of estrogen following either surgical or natural menopause may upset these thermostatic controls. There is first a sudden surge of heat through the body, known as a "hot flash." This hot flash is not just a subjective sensation of warmth but an actual heating of the body, measurable with a thermometer. To dissipate the excess heat, the body promptly goes through a pattern of protective changes, including flushing and often sweating — both heat-dissipating mechanisms. The hot flush and the sweat are thus the body's efforts to get rid of the excess heat generated by the hot flash. Sometimes too much heat is dissipated — whereupon the hot flush and sweating are followed by a chill. The chill, in turn, may be followed by shivering, a muscular reaction that generates heat and restores body temperature.

Some postmenopausal women report no hot flashes or hot flushes at all. "What's a hot flash?" one respondent asks. Others experience them only a few times a day for only a few weeks or months, and only in a mild form that does not impair functioning. Still others experience hot flashes and hot flushes many times a day, throughout the day and night, for years. A flash, flush, sweating, chill, and shivering episode may last for as long as half an hour and may be severe enough to prevent employment outside the home, interfere with household activities, and interrupt sleep throughout the night. The bed sheets may be repeatedly drenched with sweat. We need hardly add that the hot flash syndrome, especially if it occurs shortly before or during a sexual encounter, can seriously impair female sexual function.

Most postmenopausal women taking adequate doses of estrogen report that they rarely if ever experience hot flashes. Once estrogen therapy is started, hot flashes are terminated or moderated in a matter of days.

Vaginal changes

Prior to puberty — that is, prior to the time when the ovaries start producing abundant amounts of estrogen — the vaginal lining is thin, delicate, and vulnerable to both physical trauma and infection. At puberty, when the ovaries start flooding the body with estrogen, notable changes occur in the vaginal lining. It becomes thicker, and develops a tough outer layer of cells to protect the more delicate underlying tissues. The vagina becomes larger and its walls more elastic.

Following menopause, the vaginal lining, deprived of estrogen, may revert to its prepubertal state. The protective cell layer disappears; the lining becomes thinner and again vulnerable to infection and injury. Dryness, burning, itching, and pain sometimes accompany these changes, even in sexually inactive women.

In addition to changes in the vaginal lining, there may also be a shrinkage of vaginal capacity and loss of tissue elasticity. Both the depth and the diameter of the vagina may be reduced, along with a decrease in size of the clitoris and thickness of the labia. This kind of postmenopausal shrinkage and loss of elasticity can be a cause of *dyspareunia* — pain during intercourse. It may make intercourse impossible, even with a lubricant. These vaginal changes may not be noticeable to a troubling degree for several years following menopause; hence, many women fail to recognize them as menopausal or as estrogen-associated. They are called *vaginal atrophy* or *senile vaginitis* by physicians. Here are some examples among our respondents:

A 51-year-old wife in the Southeast had her uterus and both ovaries removed at age 34, and started taking estrogen at 45. Then she stopped because "I thought that the continued use of estrogen would give me cancer of the breast or other area." Without estrogen, however, "my sex life [was] hurt very badly because my vagina [became] very dry."

During this period without estrogen, she and her husband "tried K-Y [Jelly] and Vaseline, also saliva but nothing works for over five or six minutes. The saliva causes chapping." So this respondent resumed taking estrogen.

A 54-year-old New England widow with a lover she expects to marry soon writes that following menopause at age 46, she experienced vaginal dryness. She started taking estrogen at 47. She stopped for a time, but then started again, explaining:

> Onset of menopause caused dryness and thinning of vaginal membranes, and pain and bleeding with intercourse. Interest and desire were not decreased but pleasure was. [Estrogen] completely eliminated . . . senile vaginitis.

A 64-year-old wife reports that following menopause she experienced vaginal dryness, marked changes (shrinkage) of the clitoris, and a marked decrease in interest in sex. The estrogen helped; "as long as I took estrogen, there was only slight decrease in sexual interest and not too much vaginal dryness."

She then stopped estrogen "on advice of M.D.," and noticed "marked decline in sexual interest and ability to achieve orgasm." That, she says, is why she resumed taking estrogen, and continues to take it.

A 68-year-old wife near New York City describes the time that elapsed between menopause and her first estrogen prescription: "Until my need for estrogen supplement was discovered and prescribed for, I had several years of painful intercourse — naturally a handicap to conjugal life."

She stopped taking estrogen when menstrual-like bleeding occurred, then resumed estrogen in vaginal cream form — explaining: "[I] need it for lubrication of vaginal lining."

A 69-year-old Virginia wife had a hysterectomy at 43, with removal of both ovaries (surgical menopause). She also had a double mastectomy. Following surgical menopause, she experienced vaginal dryness. Menopause did not affect her sexual responsiveness, however — "unless perhaps to increase it."

She began taking estrogen twenty-four years ago, at 45; and she comments:

> With estrogen I lead a normal life; without it I am miserable. Since I have no breast tissue and no uterus . . . I am not considered at risk from breast or uterine cancer — so hope to continue estrogen therapy as long as I live. That is likely to be to about 90, if my heredity and present survival mean anything. Without estrogen, I would hope I didn't live that long and I have every sympathy for postmenopausal women who are no longer using estrogen because of the risk of malignancy.

During the twenty-four years since she started estrogen, she has tried going without it on several occasions, for reasons she does not state. "Vaginal dryness and inflammation plus hot flashes," she reports, "follow every attempt at going without estrogen."

Another 69-year-old wife, married for forty-four years and living near Chicago, experienced menopause at about age 48. She started taking estrogen for vaginal dryness, but stopped after one month. "I adjusted to its dangers to me and not being able to take it," she writes. The vaginal changes grew worse, however, so that she suffered "pain in [vaginal] wall, caused by extreme dryness — looked 'cracked,' the doctor said."

She accordingly started taking estrogen again in the form of a vaginal cream. She writes: "I was in great pain during sexual intercourse before using the cream, and uncomfortable even in ordinary activities."

Note that all six of the women quoted above are in a particularly favorable position to observe the effects on themselves of alternating periods of being off and on estrogen. They first experienced what the menopause was like without estrogen. They then started taking estrogen and could gauge the difference it made. Then they stopped, and again experienced what it was like without estrogen. Finally, they resumed estrogen and could make a fourth set of observations.

Anecdotal experiences and personal observations such as these can never prove the efficacy or safety of any medication. However, these and many similar comments from our respondents are confirmed by the findings of clinical studies. Some women suffer vaginal changes to a marked degree, resulting in pain during intercourse and other adverse affects. Such changes are in whole or in part alleviated by taking estrogen.* Most women do not experience such marked changes, or experience them only in their very late years.

We asked our postmenopausal women whether they have experienced vaginal dryness since menopause; 612 (35 percent) answer yes.

---

* One physiological study has documented the expected improvement in the vagina of postmenopausal women treated with estrogen. Blood flow, vaginal fluid, and vaginal acidity were measured in 14 postmenopausal women before and after they began estrogen replacement therapy. Taking estrogen resulted in increases in these measures in the direction of the values seen in premenopausal women. "Estrogen Deprivation and Vaginal Function in Postmenopausal Women," James P. Semmens, M.D., and Gorm Wagner, M.D., in *The Journal of the American Medical Association*, 248 (1982): 445–448.

We also asked:

"How adequate is the vaginal lubrication you produce during sexual arousal?"

Six hundred ninety-nine (40 percent) of our postmenopausal women check "not enough lubrication."

Urinary tract changes

Just as lack of estrogen adversely affects the lining of the vagina in some women, so it may also adversely affect the outermost portion of the urethra (whose opening is above the vaginal opening), making it prone to infection. Frequent infections of the urethra and bladder may follow. Intercourse can initiate infections in women with urinary tract changes, leading to discomfort during intercourse. A 60-year-old New Jersey wife who does not take estrogen notes an additional sexual problem associated with postmenopausal urinary tract changes:

> The ease with which a bladder infection can occur has dampened the pleasure of oral sex for me. Unfortunately, . . . invading organisms are a constant situation and after several such infections, [my husband and I] stopped [cunnilingus].

Urinary tract changes due to lack of estrogen usually respond favorably to estrogen administration.

Many women do not experience urinary tract changes, or experience them only infrequently, or only in their very late years.

Bone changes

The bones of the human body are composed of living cells. Throughout life, these cells are continuously replacing old bone with new bone. A number of nutrients and hormones, including estrogen, are needed for this bone-maintaining process.

If nutrients such as calcium or vitamin D are lacking, new bone is not produced as rapidly as old bone is lost. Lack of estrogen produces a quite different effect. New bone may be produced at the normal rate, but bone *loss* is speeded up. As a result, the bones become thinner, more brittle, and more readily fractured. Bone thinning of this kind is called *osteoporosis.*

Osteoporosis may be accompanied by chronic bone pain, most commonly manifested by backache. Indeed, when a post-menopausal woman complains about her "arthritis," the cause of her discomfort may actually be osteoporosis. (Pain, of course, can be a major inhibitor of sexual enjoyment.) About one postmeno-pausal woman out of four eventually suffers from osteoporosis to a serious degree.

Bones thinned by lack of estrogen are easily fractured. One kind of fracture that is rarely recognized by women as estrogen-associated is the "wedge fracture" of the vertebral bones in the upper spine. These wedge fractures are not the result of injury. Instead, portions of the backbones, weakened by osteoporosis, simply collapse. Wedge fractures can cause the loss of height and the characteristic "dowager's hump" of some postmenopausal women.

Spontaneous vertebral fractures also occur in the middle and lower spine of women with osteoporosis. These "crush fractures," as they are called, also contribute to the loss of height of some postmenopausal women. One-quarter of all women are said to suffer from wedge or crush fractures due to osteoporosis by the age of 75.

In addition, bones thinned and weakened by osteoporosis are easily fractured by falls or other trauma; hence hip fractures and wrist (Colles') fractures are much more common following meno-pause. One estimate is that osteoporosis is responsible for 700,000 bone fractures of all kinds among postmenopausal women in the United States each year. Hip fractures are commonly the most disabling.*

---

* "Twenty percent of all women will have suffered a hip fracture by the time they reach age 90; and of these, 90 percent will be found to have osteoporosis." Often hip fractures require prolonged hospitalization; "as a result of complications [such as blood clots or pneumonia] stemming from the hip fracture, 16

Lack of estrogen may not be the only or even the most important factor in a particular patient with fragile bones. Cancer, lack of calcium or vitamin D, or excesses of hormones such as cortisone or parathyroid hormone may weaken bone despite adequate estrogen levels.

Prescribed estrogen, if taken early, can delay bone loss due to lack of estrogen; and it can curb additional loss after some loss has occurred. If a patient with osteoporosis takes estrogen for a period of time and then stops taking it, bone loss sets in again.

REASONS FOR TAKING ESTROGEN

In addition to the four reasons for taking estrogen cited above — to forestall or minimize hot flashes, vaginal changes, urinary tract changes, and bone changes (osteoporosis) due to lack of estrogen — a fifth reason is cited by some of our respondents: They "feel better" when on estrogen.

A 60-year-old wife with six children reports from the Northwest that following menopause she experienced vaginal dryness and fatigue. "With three of six children still to raise," she writes, "a physical exam showed no evident reason for my inability to work through the day. The doctor . . . suggested estrogen. . . . The effects for me have been the difference between day and night."

She continues: "Five years ago, a doctor told me to discontinue the [estrogen] pills. I did for four or five months." During those months, "I felt terrible. I would prefer to take estrogen and feel better while I live, even if it costs me a longer life." Accordingly, "I looked for a new doctor and now take [a smaller dose]."

Another 60-year-old Virginia wife with twenty-one years of postmenopausal experience on estrogen, off estrogen, and then on again, comments: "When I stopped taking [estrogen], I was really irritable, grouchy, and 'bitchy' to everyone."

We have no doubt that some postmenopausal women on es-

---

percent of the women die within three months." "Benefits of Estrogen Replacement," by Isaac Schiff, M.D., and Kenneth J. Ryan, M.D., a paper presented at the Consensus Development Conference on Estrogen Use and Postmenopausal Women, National Institute on Aging, Bethesda, Maryland, September 13–14, 1979.

trogen do in fact feel better than they do when not on estrogen. We wonder, though, whether this is a direct or indirect effect of estrogen. After all, a woman who finds that sexual intercourse is no longer painful, that she is no longer subject to repeated infections of the urethra and bladder, that she no longer experiences debilitating hot flashes, hot flushes, or bouts of sweating, chilling, and shivering, and that her "arthritis" — that is, her osteoporosis — is no longer as painful, is quite likely to experience an enhanced sense of well-being.

SEXUAL EFFECTS OF POSTMENOPAUSAL ESTROGEN

In addition to its vaginal effects, estrogen may have other favorable effects on postmenopausal sexual functioning. Among our respondents are 408 postmenopausal women taking estrogen and 1,356 not taking it. When we compare the two groups, we find that 93 percent of the estrogen-takers are sexually active as compared with 80 percent of the nontakers.

Among the sexually active, we find small but consistent differences between postmenopausal women taking and not taking estrogen on eight out of ten measures of sexual function:

Those taking estrogen are more likely to report high enjoyment of sex, high or moderate sexual frequency, sometimes waking up feeling sexually aroused, sometimes having an orgasm when asleep or while waking up, a strong interest in sex, and about the right amount of vaginal lubrication. Estrogen-takers are also more likely to report that they are currently masturbating, and that they experience orgasm more than 90 percent of the time when they masturbate. Wives on estrogen are somewhat more likely to be having sexual intercourse with their husbands.

We find no differences between estrogen-takers and nontakers with respect to frequency of orgasm during marital sex or ease of sexual arousal.

Our postmenopausal women taking estrogen are somewhat younger on the average than those not taking estrogen. This may account for some of the differences between estrogen-takers and nontakers.

When we limit consideration to our 339 women who have had surgical rather than natural menopause, we find that 94 percent of our ovariectomized estrogen-takers, as compared with 72 percent of nontakers, report being sexually active. Among these sexually active ovariectomized women, a larger proportion of estrogen-takers than nontakers report high or moderate sexual frequency, sometimes waking up feeling sexually aroused, sometimes having an orgasm when asleep or while waking up, a strong interest in sex, and about the right amount of vaginal lubrication. The ovariectomized women taking estrogen are also more likely to report that they are currently masturbating.

We find no differences between ovariectomized estrogen-takers and nontakers with respect to enjoyment of sex or ease of sexual arousal.

We have also compared our ovariectomized women on estrogen with our healthy comparison group, which includes both estrogen-takers and nontakers. Ninety-four percent of our ovariectomized estrogen takers, as compared with 86 percent of our healthy comparison group, report being sexually active. Among these sexually active women, our ovariectomized estrogen-takers score about as high as the healthy comparison group on four of our ten measures of sexual activity. They score a bit lower with respect to enjoyment of sex and frequency of sexual activity, and a bit higher with respect to waking up feeling sexually aroused and sometimes having an orgasm when asleep or while waking up. Overall, the difference between ovariectomized estrogen-takers and our healthy comparison group is very small.

Our ovariectomized women *not* taking estrogen, as noted earlier, are much less likely than the healthy comparison group (72 percent versus 86 percent) to be sexually active. Among the sexually active, the ovariectomized women *not* taking estrogen score substantially lower than the healthy comparison group on all ten measures of sexual activity.

There are two ways to interpret these comparisons between estrogen-takers and nontakers. Perhaps taking estrogen enhances the sexual functioning of postmenopausal women — or perhaps postmenopausal women who are functioning well sexually are more likely to be taking estrogen.

The former interpretation — that estrogen enhances post-menopausal sexual functioning — seems to us to be more plausible. In the first place, postmenopausal women who are functioning well sexually have *less* reason, not more, to take estrogen. Moreover, the comments of many estrogen-takers (some of them quoted above) make it clear that many postmenopausal women with sexual problems take estrogen specifically for that reason.

Despite the substantial likelihood that estrogen enhances postmenopausal sexual function, however, our data fall short of *proving* a causal relationship. Surveys of the kind we have made can never prove causality; other types of studies are needed to confirm survey findings.

Because of this lingering doubt concerning a *causal* relationship between postmenopausal estrogen and enhanced sexual functioning, we do not cite sexual benefits as a reason for taking estrogen postmenopausally. We prefer to limit ourselves to the four well-established benefits: effects on the hot-flash syndrome, on vaginal dryness and vaginal atrophy, on urinary tract problems, and on osteoporosis.

ESTROGEN AND DEATH RATES

Early estrogen studies seemed to indicate that postmenopausal women taking estrogen have a lower risk of heart disease and a lower death rate from all causes. These studies have been heavily discounted in recent years, in part because most of them were not prospective studies and in part because interest in potential estrogen benefits seems to have been buried under greater interest in potential estrogen hazards. In February 1983, however, a report of a study of 2,269 women at ten medical centers in the United States and Canada, published in *The Journal of the American Medical Association*,* rearoused the earlier interest in estrogen benefits.

The study was concerned with preliminary results of a project launched back in 1971 by a group of Lipid Research Centers seek-

---

* "Estrogen Use and All-Cause Mortality," Trudy L. Bush, Ph.D., et al., in *The Journal of the American Medical Association*, 249 (1983): 903–906.

ing to determine the effects of cholesterol and other fatty substances (lipids) on heart disease. The researchers had not intended to study estrogen effects; but since estrogen may affect blood lipid levels, the use or non-use of estrogen was recorded for each woman entering the study. These women, aged 40 through 69, were followed up once a year, for an average follow-up period of 5.6 years per woman.

Here is what has emerged from the computers so far:

When all estrogen users were compared to all non-users, the women taking replacement estrogens had an average annual death rate which was about one-third that in women not using estrogens (3.4 vs. 9.3 per 1000).

This LRC study is especially impressive because low death rates were enjoyed by various subgroups of women on estrogen, too. For example, a lower death rate was found among estrogen-takers who had had a hysterectomy or a hysterectomy and one ovary removed and among those who had had a hysterectomy and both ovaries removed — as well as among those who had not had these surgical procedures.

Could some factor other than estrogen account for the lower death rate? If LRC women taking estrogen smoked less than non-takers, for example, the nonsmoking rather than the estrogen might explain it. To check such possibilities, the LRC data were adjusted for cigarette smoking, alcohol intake, obesity (body mass), age, education, systolic blood pressure, and blood lipids. Even after allowing for these factors, women on estrogen continued to show a lower death rate than women not on estrogen.

The LRC study has not yet determined whether the low death rate among women on estrogen therapy is due to fewer deaths from heart disease (as seems likely) or from other causes. The study is continuing, and future reports may answer this question. The authors of the first LRC report on estrogen state:

Our results are consistent with those from several other prospective studies and should prompt further research designed to explore the complex relationships between estrogen use and risk of disease and death.

Meanwhile, since the findings of the 1983 LRC study are still preliminary, we do not cite a lower death rate as a reason for taking estrogen.

REASONS FOR NOT TAKING ESTROGEN

The medical reasons for not taking estrogen following menopause are few in number but important. Let us review them one at a time.

Estrogen and endometrial cancer

One widely publicized reason for not taking estrogen after menopause is the increased risk of cancer of the endometrium — the lining of the uterus. This is a relatively uncommon form of cancer among postmenopausal women who do *not* take estrogen; it is diagnosed in about one of them per thousand each year. Reports in the medical literature indicate that taking estrogen increases this risk to four or five per thousand each year. Evidence is accumulating, however, that there may be ways of minimizing the risk of endometrial cancer among women taking estrogen; six of these measures are discussed later in this chapter.

Estrogen and breast cancer

Laboratory studies in animals have shown a relationship between estrogen and cancer including breast cancer. But at least a dozen clinical studies have found no increased risk of breast cancer among postmenopausal women taking estrogen, and a few studies have even shown a lower breast cancer risk. Some studies, however, have shown an increased risk — and they should not be ignored.

Estrogen and gall bladder disease

There is evidence that postmenopausal estrogen use increases the risk of gall bladder disease and incidence of gall bladder surgery. The increase in gall bladder operations is about 1.7 per thousand women on estrogen per year.

Other possible side effects of estrogen

Some women taking estrogen may experience other significant, if less hazardous, side effects. These include nausea, vomiting, abdominal cramps, bloating, headache, dizziness, water retention, breast engorgement and tenderness, and increase in the size of preexisting fibroids (benign tumors of the uterus).

Undiscovered adverse estrogen effects

There is good evidence that postmenopausal estrogen in conventional dosage does not have an adverse effect on blood pressure, the heart, or the circulatory system. There is also no increase in the risk of blood clots. There is similarly good evidence that postmenopausal estrogen does not increase the cancer risk for any site except the endometrium. It is possible that additional adverse effects of postmenopausal estrogen will be discovered hereafter. But after decades of use by millions of women, estrogen is no longer a new drug. Intensive searches have already been made for adverse effects of all kinds. The research to date makes it likely that only relatively rare or relatively mild adverse effects remain to be discovered.

THE BOTTOM LINE: SHOULD A POSTMENOPAUSAL WOMAN TAKE ESTROGEN?

We wish there were a simple, universal answer to this practical question, but there isn't. Instead, the prudent course depends on a woman's own answers to two related questions.

Does she need estrogen?

As we stressed earlier, many postmenopausal women do *not* need estrogen; they have enough already. Estrogen should *not* be taken by any woman who doesn't need it. (The same is true, of course, of any medication.)

How can a postmenopausal woman tell whether or not she needs estrogen? Laboratory tests are available; but they can be expensive and are not always needed. The best way to determine a woman's need for estrogen is to consider the severity of her symptoms. Are her hot flashes impairing the quality of her life? Is she suffering from vaginal changes sufficient to make her uncomfortable or impair sexual function? Is she experiencing repeated urethral and bladder infections? Is she suffering from pain due to osteoporosis — or from a degree of osteoporosis that is likely to lead to or has already caused bone fractures? Is she losing height or developing a "dowager's hump"? If none of these factors is present, she probably does not need estrogen.

If she decides that she does need estrogen, yet another question must be answered:

Does she want to take estrogen?

Women vary tremendously in what they value. Some, for example, value their sexuality highly — as they have reported throughout this book. Some value freedom from pain. Some would not trade even a major sexual benefit or a major reduction in the risk of bone fractures for even a slight increase in cancer risk.

Some of our women report that they took estrogen for a time, then stopped — in some cases because they no longer felt the need, but more often because they were "concerned about cancer," or because "I think estrogen is dangerous," or because "I read numerous reports that it was harmful and could cause cancer." A 52-year-old Massachusetts divorcée reached menopause at age 44 and a year later began taking estrogen, which "vanquished all symptoms." She continues:

However, after seven years of estrogen, I thought it time to quit. I didn't ask my doctor if it was okay . . . I just stopped. I've had a few annoying sudden outbreaks of heat, but that symptom is abating, so I think I was right to stop. . . .

She reports vaginal dryness "since stopping estrogen."

One respondent who has never taken estrogen expresses her opinion quite emphatically:

My views on postmenopausal estrogen are violent enough to scorch this paper. I read a lot about it and the more I read the madder I get. Estrogens have been murderously overprescribed for women by thousands of uncaring and stupid doctors. They are still being overprescribed for the feeblest of reasons. . . . Words cannot describe my contempt and hatred for the doctors who persist in this and the drug industry fatheads who push it. Estrogens are definitely carcinogenic and cause uterine and breast cancer . . . and it is inexplicable to me that enormous numbers of uninformed women are still receiving this deathly stuff.

Some of our other respondents agree with this view — if perhaps somewhat less forcefully. Clearly these women should *not* take estrogen.

Other women, in contrast, are fully aware that estrogen may be increasing their cancer risk but decide to continue taking it anyway. Some of them state their reasons in a quite straightforward manner; here are half-a-dozen examples:

A 55-year-old wife in Colorado reports vaginal dryness following menopause at age 51. She started taking estrogen, but stopped because "[I] thought I could do without it. . . . Had concern over cancer warning reports for estrogen, too." Soon after stopping estrogen, however, "hot flashes [and] vaginal dryness recurred, so I started again. . . . I ceased worrying about cancer from taking hormones. I'd rather be comfortable now."

A 54-year-old Michigan wife started estrogen at age 42. After eleven years on estrogen, she "stopped briefly following surgery for malignancy, involving reproductive tract." She started taking estrogen again, however, because of "recurrence of hot flashes (quite severe)." She explains:

> The advantages of estrogen — reduction or elimination of hot flashes that can continue for years after last menses, the positive effect on osteoporosis, the fact that it helps with vaginal atrophy and lubrication — far outweigh the possible connection with cancer in my view.

Another 54-year-old respondent — a Massachusetts divorcée with a lover — had a hysterectomy at age 36. She later had a mastectomy. She started taking estrogen at 51 — but stopped because of "increasing side effects, and my physician preferred that I not take it because of mastectomy." After a period without estrogen, however, she resumed taking it, explaining:

> [Estrogen] would seem to be a possible danger to persons who have had cancer. I am in that category; however, I decided to take the risk in favor of quality rather than quantity of life.

A 56-year-old widow took estrogen, stopped, then resumed. She explains: "I'm taking my chances with cancer because I believe I'd be a bitchy old woman without estrogen."

A 62-year-old widow in Minnesota had her uterus and both ovaries removed at age 50, and was promptly placed on estrogen. When she developed a small breast cyst, however, her physician took her off estrogen. Thereafter she resumed taking it, explaining that "the side effects from lack of estrogen were worse than the possibility of developing cancer."

A 72-year-old Florida wife married for half a century reports that she experienced vaginal dryness following menopause at age 46. Her physician promptly placed her on estrogen. Subsequently, however, her physician — whether the same one or another is unclear — took her off estrogen because "he feared breast cancer." Despite his fear, she resumed taking estrogen because she "be-

came very uncomfortable — hot flashes, perspiration, fatigue."
She comments: "I do not believe doctors truly understand older
women's need for hormones. At my age (72), the danger of cancer
is less frightening than the extreme discomfort of not taking it."
Except for the period when her physician took her off estrogen,
she has been taking estrogen for twenty-six years.*

Note that all six of the women quoted above, like those quoted
earlier, are able to compare four distinct periods in their lives: an
initial postmenopausal period without estrogen; a period on estrogen; a second period without estrogen after they discontinued
it; a second period on estrogen after they resumed taking it.

We believe that each woman's own value system, as reflected
in comments such as those above, should be fully evaluated when
estrogen use is being considered. If a woman's major concern is to
minimize her cancer risk, that value judgment should certainly be
respected. So should the value judgment of women who are quite
prepared to run a modest cancer risk in return for estrogen benefits.

Fortunately, as noted above, there are ways to minimize the
risk of cancer.

How to Take Estrogen: Minimizing the Risk

We review here six ways of minimizing the cancer risk when estrogen is taken by postmenopausal women. None of these approaches, however, and no combination of them, is certain to reduce the risk to zero.

Dosage

With estrogen as with any other medication, there is a very simple
rule: *The dose should be the minimum needed to secure the desired benefits.*

---

* Our respondent who has been on estrogen longest is an 80-year-old registered
nurse in Pennsylvania, who started estrogen forty-four years ago and has never
stopped taking it. Our oldest respondent still taking estrogen regularly is 81. She
started taking it ten years ago when she had a hysterectomy and acquired a
lover. Her relationship with her lover continued, and continued to be sexually
fulfilling, until his death a few months before she filled out our questionnaire.

Conversely, there is little reason to take estrogen at all — or to take any other medication — if the dose is too small to secure the desired benefits. A woman who finds that estrogen is doing her no good and that her symptoms continue unabated should either discontinue estrogen altogether or else ask her physician to increase her dosage.

Vaginal estrogen cream

When the link between postmenopausal estrogen and cancer of the uterus was first discovered, some physicians (prudently, it seemed at the time) shifted their patients — including a number of our respondents — from oral estrogen tablets to vaginal estrogen cream, hoping in this way to secure local vaginal benefits and thus limit exposure of the rest of the body. Of our 408 postmenopausal women taking estrogen in 1978, 53 were taking it in vaginal cream form. It has now been established, however, that vaginal estrogen cream application results in rapid absorption of the estrogen into the bloodstream. Indeed, the *peak* estrogen level in the blood, for a brief period after use of the cream, may actually be higher than following the usual oral dose.

Several of our respondents report using an estrogen cream only on occasions when they have intercourse — perhaps once or twice a week. While studies have shown that it is *continuous* stimulation of the endometrium that leads to precancerous changes, there are no hard data either establishing or casting doubt on the safety of *occasional* vaginal cream use. Whether such use is sufficient to produce the desired benefits is also not known. Each woman using a vaginal estrogen cream must determine for herself whether its use is helping her, and whether it is worth whatever risk (if any) there may be.

Cyclic use

To avoid continuous stimulation of the endometrium, many physicians give estrogen cyclically — for example, daily oral doses for three weeks or longer, followed by a week or more off estrogen. The available evidence indicates that such a schedule offers some degree of protection against endometrial cancer — but, in the opinion of Consumers Union's medical consultants, not enough.

Progestin in combination with estrogen

Recent studies suggest that if estrogen is taken cyclically with a progestin — a synthetic hormone similar to progesterone — the endometrial cancer risk may be substantially reduced. In one study, indeed, women on an estrogen-progestin combination had a significantly lower endometrial cancer rate than women who took no hormones at all; this suggests that the progestin protects against naturally arising — as well as against estrogen-associated — endometrial cancer.

One objection to the estrogen-progestin combination for postmenopausal women is that its use has not yet been adequately studied. In particular, the long-term safety of the progestin has not been established.

A possible objection to the estrogen-progestin combination is that it may trigger menstruation in some postmenopausal women. In several studies, however, postmenopausal women proved quite willing to go back to the bother of menstruating in return for the estrogen benefits they were experiencing, and for an assurance that their endometrial cancer risk was minimized or eliminated altogether.

Periodic medical examination

A postmenopausal woman considering taking estrogen should first have a comprehensive medical examination (complete history, physical examination, and thorough laboratory evaluation), in order to detect any problems (such as a personal or close family history of breast cancer) that might preclude the use of estrogen.

Once estrogen has been started, a medical examination should be repeated at least twice a year for the first year or two, and annually thereafter. Physicians vary in their ideas about which procedures are necessary for follow-up examinations; no uniform guidelines exist. Consumers Union's medical consultants recommend the following:

1. A medical history, covering events since the woman's prior medical examination. The history should zero in on problems known to occur more frequently with estrogen use.

2. A physical examination with special attention to the breasts and pelvic area, including a Pap smear of the cervix.

3. Periodic measurement of height (the loss of which implies osteoporosis of the backbone).

4. Blood tests for sugar, cholesterol, high density lipo-protein cholesterol (HDL), triglycerides, and liver function.

Some authorities recommend, in addition, a sampling of the endometrium every year or two in an effort to detect the presence of endometrial cancer at an early stage, or of endometrial hyperplasia (believed to be precancerous). Some gynecologists, however, feel that periodic endometrial sampling may not be necessary if cancer of the endometrium is excluded at the time of the initial examination and a progestin is used with the estrogen.

Duration of estrogen use

No drug — and this includes estrogen — should be taken for a longer period than necessary. The shorter the period of estrogen use, the less the risk.

Some women whose primary reason for taking estrogen is the hot flash syndrome may be delighted to discover after some months or a year or two on estrogen that they can discontinue its use without a return of the hot flashes. Others, however, may discover that the flashes return when they discontinue estrogen, even after years of use.

With respect to vaginal changes and urinary tract changes, symptoms can be expected to return when estrogen use is discontinued. Bone loss also resumes after estrogen use is discontinued.

This can pose a dilemma for both the woman taking estrogen and the physician counseling her. While the risks associated with estrogen use are believed to increase over time, few studies go beyond a period of fifteen years. Thus, the full extent of long-term risk is not known.

In short, determining how long to continue the use of estrogen is rarely an easy decision.

SUMMARY

We know that this review of the pros and cons of estrogen use is not what many postmenopausal women readers would like us to provide. They would much prefer a few simple words of advice: "Take estrogen" or "Keep away from estrogen." But important decisions, alas, are rarely that simple. The best advice we can give is that each postmenopausal woman carefully review the evidence in this chapter and elsewhere,* discuss it with her physician, and then ask herself the two key questions: "Do I *need* estrogen?" and "Do I *want* to take estrogen despite the risks?"

---

* See, for example, "Estrogen Replacement Therapy," chapter 23, in *The Medicine Show,* by the Editors of Consumer Reports Books, 5th edition, 1980; updated January 1983.

❧ 8 ❧

Sexual Changes
Decade by Decade

WHAT PROPORTION OF MEN AND OF WOMEN EXPERIENCE A DECLINE IN sexual function after the age of 50? For men, the answer is: *all men.* What's more, for most men past 50, this is not a recent phenomenon. Most of them have been experiencing a progressive decline ever since sexual function peaked in their early twenties, or before. Most women, however, do not experience a peak in sexual function during their adolescent years or early twenties, and thus do not undergo a steady decline from then until old age.

THE KINSEY DATA

Evidence for the changes before age 50 comes from the pioneering data assembled by Dr. Alfred C. Kinsey and his associates a generation ago. Evidence for the changes after 50, suggested by the Kinsey data, is confirmed and enriched by the responses of our 4,246 men and women.

In its monumental second report, *Sexual Behavior in the Human Female,* the Kinsey group emphasized "the later development of sexual responsiveness in the female and its earlier development in the male:

... The male's capacity to be stimulated sexually shows a marked increase with the approach of adolescence.... The incidences of responding males, and the frequencies of response to the point of orgasm, reach their peak within three to four years after the onset of adolescence. On the other hand . . . the maximum incidences of sexually responding females are not approached until some time in the late twenties and in the thirties. . . .

The frequencies of sexual response in the male begin to decline after the late teens or early twenties, and drop steadily into old age. On the other hand . . . among females the median frequencies of those sexual activities which are not dependent upon the male's initiation of socio-sexual contacts [e.g., masturbation], remain more or less constant from the late teens into the fifties and sixties.*

Kinsey's data, however, do show a decline in female sexual activity in the fifties and early sixties. His tables stop at age 65.

While the Kinsey data for the years from puberty to age 50 or so were more than adequate to support these findings of male and female sexual activity, his data for the later years — particularly after age 60 or so — were drawn from a very small sample. Kinsey frankly disclosed the inadequacy of his data for the later years, explaining that he was publishing them anyway "because of the importance of information on those [much older] groups." His study, after all, yielded the only data then available.

Our data

Our 4,246 respondents constitute the largest geriatric sample ever assembled for a sexuality study — not only for the total period after age 50 but also for each decade from the fifties through the eighties. Our sample is the first one large enough to permit charting sexual changes between the fifties and the sixties, and between the sixties and subsequent years — for women and for men separately.

Our two central findings can be stated with confidence:

• Male sexual function undergoes a gradual, steady decline from the fifties on.

---

* *Sexual Behavior in the Human Female* (Philadelphia: W. B. Saunders, 1953), Alfred C. Kinsey, Wardell B. Pomeroy, Clyde E. Martin and Paul H. Gebhard, pp. 714–715.

• Female sexual function also undergoes a decline from the fifties on.

Here is how sexual activity declines with age among our 1,844 women and our 2,402 men:

	In their 50s (N=801)	In their 60s (N=719)	Aged 70 and over (N=324)
All women			
Sexually active	93%	81%	65%
All men	(N=823)	(N=981)	(N=598)
Sexually active	98%	91%	79%

Note that in the table above, and in other tables presenting sexual data for both men and women, the figures for men are higher than those for women — often substantially higher. This is true not only in our study but also in all other surveys of human sexuality with which we are familiar. The male figures are higher for young people as well as old people. They are higher for proportion masturbating, frequency of masturbation, frequency of orgasm during masturbation, proportion having sex with a partner, frequency of sex with a partner, frequency of orgasm during sex with a partner, interest in sex, ease of sexual arousal, and other measures.

In this study, there are some exceptions to the general observation that male sexual figures are higher. One set of exceptions concerns wives and husbands reporting on marital sex and frequency of marital sex. Another exception is frequency of orgasm when asleep or while waking up. In these exceptional cases, male and female figures are quite similar.

Our data cast no light on *why* male sexual figures are so often higher; nor have we found a convincing explanation in prior studies. Some have speculated that the difference must be genetic, or hormonal, or cultural. We don't know. Perhaps it is all three. In any event, readers can observe for themselves, in the table above and the tables that follow, both the existence of these gender differences and the size of the difference in each table.

The proportion sexually active declines, decade by decade, for married and unmarried women, and for married and unmarried men:

Sexually active women	In their 50s	In their 60s	Aged 70 and over
Married women	(N=590) 95%	(N=495) 89%	(N=160) 81%
Unmarried women	(N=179) 88%	(N=184) 63%	(N=149) 50%
Sexually active men			
Married men	(N=643) 98%	(N=811) 93%	(N=441) 81%
Unmarried men	(N=152) 95%	(N=131) 85%	(N=131) 75%

In addition to demonstrating the decade-by-decade decline in sexual activity, the table above has other features of interest. Note that the differences between our married women and our married men are negligible. Note also that the figures for our unmarried women and men in their fifties show the usual male excess — while the figures for the sixties and seventies show a much-larger-than-usual male excess. We attribute this at least in part to the shortage of male partners available to unmarried women in their sixties and beyond — and to the ready availability of female partners to men in their sixties and beyond (see chapter 3).

Further, note in the table above that our unmarried women in their fifties are only moderately less likely than married women in their fifties to be sexually active; but this difference increases markedly in subsequent decades. Finally, note that our unmarried men are less likely than our married men to be sexually active; but the differences are surprisingly small — much smaller than the differences between unmarried and married women. We believe that these differences, too, are attributable at least in part to the dearth of unattached men and excess of unattached women in the later decades.

The proportion of sexually active women and men who report having sex at least once a week also declines from decade to decade:

Sexually active women	In their 50s	In their 60s	Aged 70 and over
	(N=743)	(N=582)	(N=211)
Sex at least once a week	73%	63%	50%

Sexually active men			
	(N=804)	(N=893)	(N=473)
Sex at least once a week	90%	73%	58%

Note in the table above that the usual male excess, visible during the fifties and sixties, narrows after age 70.

In the table below, the proportion of sexually active respondents reporting a high enjoyment of sex declines markedly from decade to decade — but not as abruptly as the decline in sex frequency shown above:

Sexually active women	In their 50s	In their 60s	Aged 70 and over
	(N=743)	(N=582)	(N=211)
High enjoyment of sex	71%	65%	61%

Sexually active men	In their 50s	In their 60s	Aged 70 and over
	(N=804)	(N=893)	(N=471)
High enjoyment of sex	90%	86%	75%

A decade-by-decade decline is also shown on five other measures of male and four of female sexual activity:

All respondents

Women	In their 50s	In their 60s	Aged 70 and over
Orgasms when asleep or while waking up	26%	24%	17%
Women who masturbate	47%	37%	33%
Frequency of masturbation among women who masturbate	0.7 per week	0.6 per week	0.7 per week
Wives having sex with their husbands	88%	76%	65%
Frequency of sex with their husbands	1.3 per week	1.0 per week	0.7 per week

Men			
Orgasms when asleep or while waking up	25%	21%	17%
Men who masturbate	66%	50%	43%
Frequency of masturbation among men who masturbate	1.2 per week	0.8 per week	0.7 per week
Husbands having sex with their wives	87%	78%	59%
Frequency of sex with their wives	1.3 per week	1.0 per week	0.6 per week

Frequency of masturbation among women who masturbate is the only measure in the table above that does not show a decade-by-decade decline. As noted earlier, male-female differences are small or negligible for orgasm when asleep or while waking up, proportions having marital sex, and frequency of marital sex. Frequency of masturbation shows the usual male excess in the fifties — but this tapers off in the sixties and disappears thereafter.

SEXUAL FUNCTION: HEALTH VERSUS AGING

As noted in chapter 6, impaired health may adversely affect sexual function. Impaired health, moreover, becomes more frequent, decade by decade. To what extent are the decade-by-decade declines in sexual function portrayed in the tables above due to aging *per se*, and to what extent are they the result of the decade-by-decade increase in health impairments?

When we compare the 819 women in our healthy comparison group with our 1,025 other women, and similarly compare the 1,191 men in our healthy comparison group with our 1,211 other men, we find that sexual activity declines consistently, decade by decade, for all four groups. The rate of decline among the healthy is as steep as among the others. We can thus conclude that the decline in sexual activity, decade by decade, is primarily an aging rather than a health effect for both men and women.

We can test this conclusion by comparing the healthy with the others from decade to decade. Among our men, the healthy in their *sixties* are less likely to be sexually active, and those sexually active are less likely to report high sexual frequency, than the others in their *fifties*. The same is true for the healthy men *aged 70 and over* as compared with the other men in their *sixties*. Thus, it appears to be the inexorable march of the decades rather than increasing health impairments that is primarily responsible for the decline in male sexual activity and in male sexual frequency as well.

We can also confirm our finding that the decade-by-decade decline in *sexual activity* among our women is due primarily to aging. Sexual activity is less among our healthy women in their sixties than among our other women in their fifties, and less among our healthy women in their seventies than among our other women in their sixties.

We cannot, however, use this approach for *sexual frequency* among our women; the data are inconclusive. We attribute this to a well-known phenomenon: The sexual frequencies reported by women are profoundly influenced by the age, health, and level of sexual functioning of their husband or partner. (Male sexual frequencies are much less influenced by the female partner.)

Physiology of Sexual Aging

When a man suffers an abrupt decline in sexual activity, it is often easy to assign (rightly or wrongly) a cause — such as a heart attack or surgery, a quarrel with his wife or partner, a setback at work, an attack of acute depression, or any of a wide range of other common explanations. But no single circumstance nor any combination of such circumstances can account for the phenomena we have just reviewed: the steady and progressive decline in sexual function, including nocturnal emissions, masturbation, and sexual intercourse, affecting married and unmarried men, including those in good or excellent health, at all ages from adolescence on. Underlying each individual experience there must be a basic physiological pattern of male sexual aging — a lifelong pattern that may be altered, favorably or unfavorably, by particular events in the lives of particular men, but that nevertheless progresses inexorably even in the absence of such events.

It is all too easy for a woman to suspect, as her husband or partner exhibits this pattern of declining sexual function, that it must be because *she* is losing her attractiveness or because he no longer loves her. A woman may even suspect, at some stage in his sexual decline, that he must be having sex outside their relationship. She may think — or even complain — "You could have sex with me if you really tried, or if you really wanted to." But her husband or partner has long known, of course, that an erection or orgasm cannot be willed in the way in which a smile or a wave of the hand is willed. The sections that follow explain why.

Changes in erectile function

We asked our men which of these four changes in erectile function they have experienced:

"My 'refractory period' — the time it takes me to be able to have another erection after orgasm — is longer now.

"It takes me longer to get an erection.

"When fully erect, my penis is not as stiff as before.

"I more frequently lose my erection during sex."

Here are the answers we received:

	Men
	(N=2,402)
Refractory period longer	65%
Takes longer to get erection	50%
Penis less stiff when fully erect	44%
More frequently lose erection during sex	32%

Numerous physiological studies help to explain *why* these changes occur.

The erection of the penis is essentially a blood-flow phenomenon. During sexual arousal, an increased volume of blood flows into the tissues of the penis. Erection occurs when more blood flows into the penile tissues than out through the deep central vein of the penis.

During erection, the blood pressure within the penis rises above the blood pressure elsewhere in the body. As Dr. Helen Singer Kaplan phrases it: "The penis is maintained hard and erect by a high-pressure hydraulic system which uses blood as its fluid."*

As people age, the maximum blood supply available to the heart, the lungs, the skin, and other organs diminishes; the maximum blood supply available to the penis is similarly curtailed. Thus a decline in blood flow into the penis during sexual arousal is no doubt one factor in male sexual aging.

The rate at which the blood leaves the penis also affects erection. Thus a man may also have erectile problems because blood is draining out of his penis too rapidly. This, too, may be an aging phenomenon.

While the blood vessels are thus directly responsible for erection or the lack of it, they are not self-activating. Rather, the changes are *neurovascular*. They are under the command of the *autonomic nervous system*. Nerves of this system can produce either a widening of the blood vessels, which increases the flow of blood, or a narrowing, which curtails the flow. More important, they can and do produce a coordinated pattern of blood-vessel responses; the blood vessels supplying the penile tissues can expand while the vessels draining them are contracting, thus building up the blood pressure within the penis. The net effect, if all goes as scheduled, is engorgement and erection of the penis.

Since the autonomic nervous system is not under conscious control, an erection cannot be willed. Indeed, trying to will an erection is like trying to speed up or slow down the digestive system by an act of will.

In the female as in the male, blood-pressure changes profoundly affect sexual arousal. More blood flows into the genital system of the sexually aroused female through the pelvic arteries than flows out through the pelvic veins, raising the genital blood pressure. The clitoris and labia as a result become engorged with blood, just as the penis does. In addition, fluid exuded from the pressurized genital blood vessels seeps into the vagina; this fluid is the major source of vaginal lubrication. These changes are the female equivalent of penile erection. The vaginal lubrication is a

---

* H. S. Kaplan, *Disorders of Sexual Desire* (1979), p. 16.

sign that the sexually aroused female genital system is appropriately engorged with blood under high pressure.

In the female as in the male, these vascular changes are not self-activating but neurovascular — under the control of the autonomic nervous system. Autonomic centers in the female as in the male spinal cord send messages to the pelvic area instructing some blood vessels to expand while others contract, raising blood pressure within the genital system and producing vaginal lubrication.

Like other bodily systems, both the female and the male autonomic nervous systems are subject to aging. These aging processes may help to account for changes in vaginal lubrication and erectile function over the years.

What triggers erection? One answer is: messages from the penis. For example, tactile stimulation of the penis causes messages to travel from sensory nerve endings in the penis to the autonomic nerve centers in the spinal cord — and these centers respond by sending "Erect!" commands back to the penile blood vessels.

Sensory nerve endings are also subject to aging. Laboratory tests have shown that the penises of older men are less sensitive to tactile stimulation than the penises of younger men.

Of course, erection does not result solely from stimulation of the penile nerve endings. The nerve centers in the spinal cord also respond to messages from centers in the brain. These messages travel down the spinal cord to meet any messages that may be coming in from the penis. The sight of an attractive woman, or even the fantasy of one, may initiate such a message from the brain.

In young men, messages from the brain can by themselves trigger spontaneous erection in the absence of penile stimulation. Some older men, however, no longer experience spontaneous erection from psychological stimuli alone; they require tactile stimulation or a combination of tactile messages from the penis *and* messages from the brain. The brain centers are no doubt also subject to an inexorable aging process.

To carry the female-male parallel one step farther, tactile stimulation of the clitoris and other female erogenous zones, along with psychological stimulation, initiates messages to the nerve centers in the female spinal cord. These centers respond, as in the male, by sending commands to the pelvic blood vessels — thus triggering the swelling of the clitoris and labia and vaginal lubrication, much as erection is triggered. Aging no doubt affects these functions in the female as in the male.

Changes in vaginal lubrication

Here we must note a serious gap in our female data, and in the data of all prior studies concerning female sexual response. Erection in the male and vaginal lubrication in the female, as we have just seen, are parallel physiological responses to sexual stimulation. As men age, their refractory period becomes longer; it takes longer to get an erection; when fully erect the penis is not as stiff as before; and the erection is more often lost before orgasm. Do parallel changes occur among aging women? No one knows.

If asked, substantial proportions of women might well report that it takes more time (and more stimulation) before lubrication of the vagina begins; that when fully lubricated, the vagina is not as moist as in earlier years; and that the vagina more often goes dry again before orgasm. But we did not ask these detailed questions, and neither has anyone else. We hope that future studies will explore this area of female sexual response.

We have, however, taken the first step. We asked:

"How adequate is the vaginal lubrication you produce during sexual arousal?"

The proportion of our postmenopausal women who report "about the right amount" of vaginal lubrication during sexual arousal declines from decade to decade:

	In their 50s	In their 60s	Aged 70 and over
Postmenopausal women	(N=723)	(N=717)	(N=324)
About the right amount of vaginal lubrication	48%	35%	23%

Thus the female genital system involved in pelvic engorgement and vaginal lubrication ages much as the male erectile system ages. The decline with age in adequacy of lubrication may also be due in part, of course, to a decline with age in sexual stimulation, and, as noted in chapter 7, to reduced estrogen levels.

Just as a woman may misinterpret her aging husband's or partner's erectile problems as evidence that he no longer loves her or is having an outside affair, so a woman's decline in vaginal lubrication may be misinterpreted by a husband or partner. Understanding this phase of the physiology of female aging may prove helpful in forestalling such misunderstandings.

Changes in orgasmic function

A sharp distinction must be made between the physiology of erection and of lubrication, described above, and the physiology of orgasm. Quite different mechanisms are involved. For example, a person may experience orgasmic problems even though her lubrication system or his erectile system is functioning exceedingly well. Conversely, a person may experience orgasm even though she is inadequately lubricated or he is unable to achieve or maintain an erection.

When the male orgasm is triggered, it generally proceeds through two phases. In the first phase, semen enters the urethra. Masters and Johnson refer to this as the "point of no return" or the "moment of ejaculatory inevitability." Men who wish to delay orgasm must learn to do so before this point is reached. More specifically, they must learn to recognize the sensations that occur prior to the "point of no return" and to slow down *before* that point

is reached. The second phase of male orgasm consists of a rhythmic series of contractions of the penis, producing ejaculation of
the semen, and accompanied by pleasurable sensations. Female
orgasm also consists of a series of rhythmic contractions and
pleasurable sensations.

Following some forms of surgery and when certain medications are taken, older men may experience orgasm without ejaculation of semen — the so-called *dry orgasm*. In another form of dry
orgasm, retrograde ejaculation, the semen is ejaculated back into
the bladder rather than out through the penis. Some men can
learn to experience repeated orgasms prior to a single ejaculation.*

It takes longer — and it takes more stimulation — for most
older men to reach orgasm than it does for most younger men. We
need hardly point out that this male "orgasmic slowdown" can be
a blessing for some women. Some of our men respondents also
comment on how pleased they are that "holding back" is no
longer necessary. One husband, age 56, notes: "My main problem
in younger years has been very quick orgasm, which is now improved (due to age?)."

A 70-year-old husband similarly reports that his orgasmic
slowing-down is "no real problem. I have lost a tendency to premature ejaculation — a positive result."

A 51-year-old husband is just beginning to experience orgasmic slowing-down on some occasions — and he is glad of it:

> *Sometimes* it takes longer, but it is enjoyable and not a source
> of panic. I used to be a "Minute Man" but now the extra
> time [makes sex] more enjoyable. I look forward to the extra
> time. Years ago it was five minutes; now it is about fifteen.
> Nothing to worry about — and with my wife, once a night is
> enough.

Aging, however, is not always a cure for premature ejaculation. A few of our older men continue to be afflicted with it. A 56-

---

* See "Multiple Orgasms in Males" by Mina B. Robbins and Gordon D. Jensen,
in *Journal of Sex Research*, 14 (1978): 21–26.

year-old husband, for example, reports that it does not take him longer nowadays. "The exact opposite is true. Very little stimulation is required for orgasm. Most difficult to control or hold off until necessary."

Masters and Johnson and others have described other changes in the orgasmic machinery that commonly occur with age. Less semen is ejaculated. The series of penile contractions may be less vigorous, so that the semen is ejected with less force, and there may be fewer penile contractions in the series. The "moment of ejaculatory inevitability" may no longer be identifiable, so that the two stages of orgasm seem to be only one.

We asked our respondents:

"How often do you ... experience orgasm when you engage in sexual activities [with your spouse or partner]?"

Among the women who answer, differences from decade to decade are small and without a consistent pattern — except for a gradual increase in the proportion who seldom or never experience orgasm with a partner:

	Sex with partner		
	In their 50s	*In their 60s*	*Aged 70 and over*
Women	*(N=638)*	*(N=476)*	*(N=140)*
Orgasm every time or almost every time	52%	45%	49%
Usually or half the time	29	33	24
Seldom or never	19	22	28
	100%	100%	101%

Among the men who answer, the pattern is clear and consistent: a small-to-moderate decade-by-decade decline in the incidence of reaching orgasm during sex with a partner:

	Sex with partner		
	In their 50s	In their 60s	Aged 70 and over
Men	(N=705)	(N=780)	(N=369)
Orgasm every time or almost every time	92%	85%	70%
Usually or half the time	7	11	20
Seldom or never	1	4	10
	100%	100%	100%

Note that the male excess is much larger than usual in the fifties and sixties.

We also asked:

"How often do you experience orgasm when you masturbate . . . ?"

Here there is a steady decline from decade to decade for women and men reporting orgasm every time or almost every time, and an increase for those who seldom or never reach orgasm:

	In their 50s	In their 60s	Aged 70 and over
Women	(N=390)	(N=285)	(N=117)
Orgasm every time or almost every time	83%	79%	74%
Usually or half the time	9	11	12
Seldom or never	7	10	14
	99%	100%	100%

Men	In their 50s (N=568)	In their 60s (N=516)	Aged 70 and over (N=274)
Orgasm every time or almost every time	91%	84%	73%
Usually or half the time	5	9	14
Seldom or never	4	7	13
	100%	100%	100%

Note that the usual male excess disappears after age 70.

We sought to gauge orgasmic changes among our men with two additional measures:

"It takes more stimulation of my penis to reach orgasm now."

and

"I more often fail to reach orgasm nowadays."

Here are the answers we received:

	Men (N=2,402)
Takes more stimulation of penis to reach orgasm	46%
More often fail to reach orgasm	20%

Changes in sexual desire

Until a few years ago, sexual arousal (erection and vaginal lubrication) and orgasmic function were considered the most important, or perhaps the only, physiological factors involved in sexual response. Quite recently, however, increasing attention has been directed at a third factor — *sexual desire*. Among men and women aged 50 and over, our data indicate, changes in sexual desire are at least as important as changes in the other two factors.

Physicians occasionally encounter a patient who is emaciated, perhaps dangerously so, despite the fact that the patient's entire gastrointestinal system is functioning normally. The stomach is quite capable of digesting food and the intestines are also functioning properly — but the patient lacks appetite for food and therefore doesn't eat. Lack of sexual desire can be thought of similarly as a *lack of sexual appetite.* Having little interest in sex, a man or woman may rarely or ever engage in sex — despite sound erectile function and sound orgasmic function.

Attention was focused on this desire factor with the publication in 1979 of Dr. Helen Singer Kaplan's book, *Disorders of Sexual Desire.* Our discussion of sexual desire is based in part on Dr. Kaplan's text and in part on our own findings.

Dr. Kaplan defines "sexual desire" as "an appetite or drive which is produced by the activation of a specific neural system in the brain." It is very similar to what Freud called *libido.*

Sexual desire, Dr. Kaplan explains, "is experienced as specific sensations which move the individual to seek out, or become receptive to, sexual experiences." When the sexual desire center in the brain is "turned on," people may feel "horny," Dr. Kaplan notes, or they "may feel vaguely sexy, interested in sex, open to sex, or even just restless. These sensations cease after sexual gratification, *i.e.,* orgasm. When this system is inactive or under the influence of inhibitory forces, a person has no interest in erotic matters; he 'loses his appetite' for sex and becomes 'asexual.' "

Dr. Kaplan also notes that the centers in the brain that coordinate sexual desire are directly connected to the centers in the spinal cord that coordinate erection and orgasm:

Input from the higher centers can enhance or diminish the genital reflexes. Thus, when [sexual desire] is high, when a person feels sexy and sensuous, erection [is] full and rapid, and orgasm is easily achieved. In fact, erection and even orgasm may at times be achieved purely on the basis of external stimuli and fantasy without any physical stimulation of the genitals. But the opposite is also true. When desire is absent and the sexual experience is flat and joyless, the threshold for the genital reflexes is much higher. When one is not turned on it can take "forever" and the physical stimulus must be intense before the genitals will function.

Our respondents filled out their questionnaires before Dr. Kaplan's book on sexual desire was published. Yet several of them draw from their own experience the same distinction between libido and erection — between sexual desire and genital function — that Dr. Kaplan explains.

A 50-year-old wife, for example, reports that she and her husband have sex about once a week; she always reaches orgasm on these occasions. She says her vaginal lubrication is about the right amount — the same as at age 40. Thus she is functioning well with respect to both genital engorgement and orgasm. She rates her enjoyment of life as 1, and the happiness of her marriage as 2. Nevertheless, she writes:

> My problem . . . is a lack of interest in sex. I love my husband and enjoy his company; but in recent years I feel I could get along very well without sex. We had a very active sex life in earlier years and I never fail to reach orgasm, even now — but I would rather not *bother* at all!

That her problem is in fact a loss of sexual desire is indicated by her answers to desire-associated questions. She reports, for example, that she can comfortably go without sexual release for "a month or more." She says that the sexual side of her relationship is of little *importance* to her. She describes her present *interest* in sex as weak. She does not masturbate, and she considers her once-a-week sex with her husband "too often." She rates her *enjoyment* of sex (despite orgasm every time) as 4.

Some of our men similarly distinguish between sexual desire and genital function — but they tend to report continuing desire despite declining function. A 56-year-old husband, for example, describes how his erections have slowed down while his desires remain unchanged:

> I recall from age 11 the time our babysitter sat on my lap and showed me a "dirty book"; I had the stiffest hard-on

possible before she flipped to the second page. *Playboy* magazine used to provide sizable erections — often embarrass-
ingly so. Prior to age 45 or 50, sexual arousal was *synonymous*
with an erection.

Now *I* am sexually aroused by the same stimuli as before, but [my penis] may remain passive or semi-erect — not
very responsive, but . . . highly receptive to the idea of more
stimuli.

A 60-year-old respondent makes the same distinction when
commenting on how easily he becomes aroused these days: "By
'aroused,' if you mean mentally, there is no change. If physically,
i.e., erection, it is with some difficulty. The desire is as great as
ever and as quickly kindled."

Some women quite understandably fail to make this distinction with respect to their husband or partner. They know, of
course, that an erect penis is a highly reliable signal of male sexual
desire, and they therefore mistakenly infer that a limp penis must
signal an absence of desire. In fact, a penis may remain limp in the
presence of intense desire — limp but "highly receptive to the
idea of more stimuli," as our respondent quoted above phrases it.

We did not use the term "desire" in our questionnaire, but we
did ask several questions which, we believe, can serve as gauges of
sexual desire. One was:

"How would you describe your present interest in sex?"

Both men and women report a decade-by-decade decline:

	In their 50s	*In their 60s*	*Aged 70 and over*
Women	*(N=783)*	*(N=658)*	*(N=260)*
Interest in sex strong or moderate	75%	67%	59%
Weak	20	23	23
Absent	4	10	18
	99%	100%	100%

Men	In their 50s (N=820)	In their 60s (N=963)	Aged 70 and over (N=567)
Interest in sex strong or moderate	94%	88%	75%
Weak	5	10	18
Absent	1	2	8
	100%	100%	101%

We asked:

"Compared with when you were around 40, how would you describe your present interest in sex?"

There is a continuing decline with age for both women and men:

Women	In their 50s (N=777)	In their 60s (N=644)	Aged 70 and over (N=250)
Interest in sex stronger now than around 40	18%	11%	8%
About the same	47	39	34
Weaker now	35	50	58
	100%	100%	100%
Men	(N=819)	(N=981)	(N=598)
Interest in sex stronger now than around 40	11%	8%	4%
About the same	65	53	44
Weaker now	24	40	52
	100%	101%	100%

We asked:

"How important is the sexual side of your relationship to you . . . ?"

Once again, a decline with age is seen in both women and men:

	In their 50s	In their 60s	Aged 70 and over
Women	(N=689)	(N=555)	(N=187)
Sex very important	37%	30%	28%
Moderately important	46	43	35
Of little importance	17	26	37
	100%	99%	100%
Men	(N=757)	(N=890)	(N=495)
Sex very important	61%	46%	36%
Moderately important	35	42	40
Of little importance	4	12	24
	100%	100%	100%

Note that the male excess is even larger than usual during the fifties.

We asked:

"Some [individuals] become uncomfortable or restless if they go without a release of sexual tension for too long a period. For about how long can you comfortably go without a sexual release?"

Approximately half of our women and one-quarter of our men did not answer this question — a much higher frequency of "No Answers" than for most other questions. The "No Answers" ranged from 40 percent for women in their fifties to 70 percent for women aged 70 and over; and from 17 percent for men in their fifties to 35 percent for men aged 70 and over. Our respondents' Comment Pages do not indicate any reasons for these failures to answer. Because the "No Answers" vary so widely with age, we place little reliance on the answers we did receive.

We can report, however, that among men who answer, there is a marked decade-by-decade decline in the proportion who become uncomfortable after less than a week of abstinence — paralleled by a marked increase in the proportion who can comfortably abstain for a month or more. Our women's replies show no consistent pattern and yield no useful information.

"Response thresholds"

The Kinsey study, the physiological facts, Dr. Kaplan's clinical findings, and our own questionnaire returns are all compatible with a simple model of gradual sexual change as men age. The basic concept can be illustrated by an analogy.

Tap your finger gently with a hammer, and no unpleasant sensation is evoked. Bang your finger hard with a hammer, and the pain is intense. Somewhere in between the tap and the bang is a level of stimulation that just barely evokes the sensation of pain. Physiologists and psychologists call this level of stimulation the "threshold."

It is well-known that pain thresholds vary; one person may wince at a stimulus that another barely notices. Thresholds may also differ in the same person from time to time. That there are thresholds for human sexual response, too, and that these thresholds change with age, can be illustrated by following a more or less typical male through the decades from age 17 on.

At age 17, let us say, this hypothetical young man walks into a diner and sits down on a stool at the counter. A waitress comes over to him and smiles. His penis immediately rises in full erection. We can say of him at this stage in his development that he has a *very* low threshold for sexual arousal — a very low erectile threshold. Even so mild a stimulus as a waitress's smile and her proximity to him on the other side of the counter is sufficient to surmount the threshold — to trigger the complex set of neurovascular changes that raise his penile blood pressure and thus produce erection.

Our young man's erectile threshold is low in another respect as well. Let us suppose that as he sits on the stool at age 17, his jeans happen to rub against his penis. This degree of tactile stimulation of the penis, even before he catches sight of the waitress, may by itself trigger erection. Thus his erectile threshold is very low for tactile as well as for visual and other types of psychological stimulation.

By the time this young man reaches 27 or 37, his erectile threshold will have risen. The waitress who now comes over to take his order will not trigger a full erection, and may not stimulate any change at all in the state of his penis. She may be quite as attractive as the waitress who approached him when he was 17 — but *he* has changed. More specifically, the neurovascular apparatus controlling his penis has changed. His threshold for tactile stimulation will also have risen; it may at age 27 take considerably more than the casual friction of his jeans against his penis to trigger erection.

Nor is this the whole of the story. Sitting there waiting for his order at age 17, he may follow the waitress with his eyes and his hand may stray down to his crotch. Only two or three strokes through his jeans may produce orgasm and ejaculation. His orgasmic as well as his erectile threshold is very low. This threshold, too, will no doubt have risen by age 27 or 37.

All 17-year-olds, of course, are not alike in these respects. Some have higher and some lower erectile and orgasmic thresholds than is usual for their age — just as some men past fifty have thresholds that are higher or lower than is usual for *their* age.

By the time our 17-year-old has reached 47 or 57, a further change may have set in. He may find that erection is no longer triggered at all by psychological stimulation alone. One of our divorced men, aged 58, describes this change succinctly: "The sight of a pair of shapely legs or well-rounded buttocks no longer excites spontaneous erection." Most men in their fifties need at least a modest amount of direct tactile stimulation of the penis before erection occurs. Dr. Kaplan has described the not untypical case of a 55-year-old patient whom she calls Tony, who experienced this change, thought he had an erection problem, and developed "performance anxiety":

Tony revealed that he was upset because he required direct stimulation of his penis in order to have an erection. He believed he "should" erect instantly on looking at [his wife Teresa] and he had been ashamed to tell Teresa this. He was reassured as to the normalcy of his need [at age 55] for tactile penile stimulation and he soon learned that he could function well as long as she stimulated him. She loved to do this and his performance anxieties vanished. . . .*

At about this time — perhaps in his forties or fifties — our once-brash 17-year-old may reach what seems to him (and perhaps to his partner) the Golden Age of male sexuality. Erectile problems (except for a longer refractory period) have not yet set in, but orgasm and ejaculation are now somewhat delayed. Indeed, it takes a special additional effort, even after prolonged psychological and tactile stimulation, to reach orgasm. As a result, sexual activity can be continued indefinitely — yet can be terminated by orgasm whenever he chooses to make an additional effort. This Golden Age slowly fades as the additional effort necessary to reach orgasm increases, and as the tendency arises to lose erection prior to orgasm.

For some (perhaps many) men, a time eventually comes when sexual intercourse itself is not a sufficient stimulus to surmount the orgasmic threshold. These men now need manual or oral stimulation of the penis in order to reach orgasm — just as many women of all ages need manual or oral stimulation of the clitoris.

A time may also come for some men when erection no longer occurs despite high levels of both psychological and tactile stimulation. We have a few respondents for whom this is true. Even then, however, orgasm may in some cases still be experienced following skillful stimulation of the flaccid penis.

Both the Kinsey data and ours suggest varying response thresholds for women, too. Among women, however, the variations from adolescence to old age cannot be readily illustrated by a single hypothetical example because of the very wide range of variation among women *at any given age.*

---

* H. S. Kaplan, *Disorders of Sexual Desire*, pp. 105–106.

At one extreme, there are women of all ages who are quite as sexually responsive, readily orgasmic, and sexually active as most men. At the other extreme, there are women who have never experienced sexual desire, sexual arousal, or sexual activity (including masturbation) at any age. In between, there are widely divergent patterns and levels of desire, responsivity, and activity at all ages. Perhaps there is an underlying pattern of some kind among women, comparable to the male pattern illustrated by our story of the brash young man. But if one does exist, that pattern is masked by the wide range of variation (no doubt at least in part culturally determined) from woman to woman at all ages.

Men, too, differ from one another at all ages; but the differences from man to man are not sufficient to mask the underlying decline with age from adolescence on.

A NOTE ON MEN AND WOMEN AGED 80 AND OVER

Among our 76 men and 38 women age 80 and over, 46 men and 15 women report they are sexually active.

Of the 46 sexually active men, 25 report that they have sexual intercourse with a wife or partner, and 16 of the 25 say they reach orgasm about half the time or more. Four others say they have other types of sex with a wife or partner. Twenty-nine men say they masturbate, eight of them once a week or more.

Of the 15 sexually active women, three say they have sexual intercourse with a husband or partner and always or usually reach orgasm. Two others say they have other types of sex with a husband or partner. No doubt there would be more women having sex with a partner if more husbands or partners were available.

Of these sexually active men and women, 37 men and 12 women rate their enjoyment of sex on our 1-to-7 scale:

Sexually active men aged 80 and over

Very enjoyable	(20) □	(5) □	(5) □	(2) □	(1) □	(3) □	(1) □	Not at all enjoyable
	1	2	3	4	5	6	7	

Sexually active women aged 80 and over

Very enjoyable	(4) ☐ 1	(1) ☐ 2	(3) ☐ 3	(0) ☐ 4	(0) ☐ 5	(1) ☐ 6	(3) ☐ 7	Not at all enjoyable

We do not offer these data as an adequate account of male and female sexual activity after age 79. Our numbers are much too few (although our 76 men represent the largest such group yet assembled). What we can say, however is this: Sex does not inevitably stop after age 79. *Some* men and *some* women aged 80 or over continue to have sex with a spouse or partner, *some* continue to masturbate, and *some* continue to reach orgasm. Most of those in our sample who remain sexually active continue to rate sex toward the "very enjoyable" end of our scale. Future research should concentrate, not on a superfluous effort to determine more precisely the proportions of those sexually active and inactive, but on ways in which men and women in their eighties and older who *want* to enhance their sexual activity and enjoyment can achieve that goal (see chapter 9).

The statistics here, as elsewhere in this report, come to life in the comments of our respondents. A 60-year-old wife living near Los Angeles, for example, writes at some length about her 80-year-old husband who "had spinal surgery at age 72. It left him with paralysis and some permanently damaged autonomic nerves. . . . He walks now with effort and with a cane, but is on his feet much of the time."

Despite this —

My husband has a sex drive at 80, and is discontent if he does not have lots of love. It is relaxing to know after menopause that a wife can enjoy her husband's sexual attentions without fear of pregnancy.

She adds that she "would be happy with caresses" — but "he feels deprived if the affection does not end in intercourse." So they have intercourse together two or three times a week. She notes that both of them, at ages 80 and 60, reach orgasm almost every time. She rates both the happiness of her marriage and her enjoyment of sex with her disabled 80-year-old husband as 1.

Consider, next, this 85-year-old wife who lives with her 85-year-old husband in a retirement community in the Southwest on an income of less than $10,000 a year. After fifty-five years of marriage, both she and her husband rate their enjoyment of life and their marital happiness as 1.

The wife has high blood pressure. The husband is in good health but has had a prostatectomy. He reports all six signs of declining potency — and considers all six "serious problems." The wife confirms their presence, but considers only five of them serious problems.

Despite this, they continue to have sex together — once a week, according to the wife; two or three times a week according to the husband. Both enjoy stimulating each other's genitals manually and having their own genitals stimulated manually. They have tried oral sex, but the wife did not enjoy it. They both enjoy manually stimulating her clitoris during intercourse.

Both of them, at age 85, usually reach orgasm, and both rate their enjoyment of sex with one another as 1.

An 80-year-old husband in Virginia has been married to a wife four years younger for the past seven years. He rates his enjoyment of life, the happiness of his marriage, and his enjoyment of sex with his 75-year-old wife as 1. He reports that both he and his wife consider the sexual side of their marriage "very important." They have sex together about once a week; both reach orgasm about half the time. He becomes restless or uncomfortable if he goes without sex for more than a week. He comments: "Love is much more satisfactory in later years; no children to distract, no monthly periods to worry about, no pregnancy fears."

In addition to his once-a-week sex with his wife, he masturbates once a week or so and comments: "I think masturbation is good and useful and *very* much misunderstood."

An 83-year-old woman near San Diego has been married for fifty-four years to a husband ten years younger. She rates her enjoyment of life and the happiness of her marriage as 1, and her enjoyment of sex with her husband as 3. She says they have sex together about once a week; she almost always reaches orgasm. She reports "about the right amount" of vaginal lubrication during sexual arousal, and adds that she becomes sexually aroused "moderately easily" — but less easily than at age 40. Asked what younger people should know about love and sexual relationships after 50, she replies: "That sex relations may continue indefinitely."

An 80-year-old husband, married for fifty-four years to a wife six years younger, reports from Wisconsin that he has had no sex with his wife for 24 years: "My wife left with another man. I took her back. Now we are just living together for our children's sake."

He masturbates occasionally, and writes: "[Masturbation] takes longer and [is] more enjoyable than sex with women."

An 80-year-old wife, married to a husband of 81, writes:

I have been fortunate to have had a full and quite happy married life, still in force after 60 years. We have not had actual sex for some years because of my husband's impotence — although we enjoy sleeping together.

Then, thinking back, she adds:

I wish I might have had more sexual instruction and less rigid and ignorant upbringing . . . before my marriage, for this would have permitted greater pleasure and perhaps longer lasting afterward. . . . I would try more variation and experiment in sex with my husband. Also, at this advanced age, I am still uncertain if I should have had an extramarital relationship to have made me more whole and tolerant in my personal life.

In the past, she writes, she enjoyed stimulating her husband's genitals manually and having him stimulate her genitals manually and orally. She tried stimulating his genitals orally but did not like it. The only other sexual activity she tried but didn't like was having her anus stimulated during sex. The only activity she has not tried but would like to try is using a vibrator.

She still masturbates occasionally — once a month or less — and still reaches orgasm about half of the time.

A sexually inactive 81-year-old St. Louis woman rates her enjoyment of life as 1. She writes:

> I was widowed . . . at age 33. I was a virgin at marriage and have been celibate since my husband's death. . . . Lack of sex hasn't hurt me or my pleasant, busy life. Never needed analysis either.

A sexually inactive 82-year-old widow writes from the Pittsburg area:

> I was married to one man fifty-nine years. . . . I never had sexual relations with any other man, either before marriage or since. I never intend to.

One of our husbands, in Topeka, married his third wife when he was 45 and she was 25. Now, at ages 81 and 61, both rate the happiness of their marriage as 1 and their enjoyment of sex as 2. They have sex together about once a week, and both reach orgasm about half the time.

A never-married 81-year-old man recalls:

> My sex education — what little there was — was from an old book. Masturbation was bad, *very bad.* I tried not to, but my testicles got so full that it hurt. Usually spilled out in my sleep.
>
> Then, at high school age there was a little red book promoting medicine to cure sexual diseases. They were terrible. I would not dared to have sex if I had an opportunity.

Now this respondent describes himself as "age 81 and *never* had sex." He comments:

> What a lot I have missed due to my lack of sex education when I was young. Hope this may be of some use to you — this odd report.

An 84-year-old Maine widow recalls:

My husband died at 71, after forty-six years of marriage.
Ours was a mutually happy relationship. Our communications were good. We had a wonderful sexual relationship,
which continued up to a few weeks before his death. I don't
recall which one of us initiated having sex, it seemed to just
come natural after lying close together. We enjoyed sex several times a week, and he always experienced an orgasm. . . .
I didn't usually, but I just enjoyed being close to him and
giving him pleasure. . . .

I wonder if it was as often as he would have liked. Perhaps we should have indulged more often. It seemed satisfactory at the time, and I sure wish I could enjoy the experience now, as I do get terribly lonely and hungry for some
affection at times. Of course, it isn't possible, but I do wish
that there was some way a woman alone could have her
needs satisfied. [She does not masturbate.]

An 82-year-old Arizona husband, married for thirty-six years
to a wife seventeen years younger, reports that they have not had
sexual intercourse for the past nine years because "I have not been
able to hold an erection long enough." They do have other sexual
activities together, however. He explains: "In spite of my lack of
orgasm, I am able to produce an orgasm in my wife by manual
manipulation."

His wife, now 65, confirms that they have sex together several
times a month and that she always reaches orgasm. He rates his
enjoyment of sex with her as 1 and she rates her enjoyment of sex
with him as 2.

An 85-year-old Maryland widow writes:

My mother instilled a feeling of fear [of sex] and reluctance,
and that [sex] was to be never discussed. I did not understand until old age that really it was necessary to a man; he
could not help his natural urges.

Her marriage was "fairly compatible until about age 50 [when my] female organs seemed to dry up. . . . Intercourse was so painful [I] avoided it and in time ceased altogether. No desire, and husband had had operations, so we were in harmony — just companionship."

She also writes:

After I lost my husband (after fifty-six years of marriage) did I remember and regret I had not been more loving. In old age one should show affection to each other and it does not necessarily mean sex at all — only a deep love and understanding and need for companionship.

That is what I miss — not sex but companionship. It is the loneliness one feels! Desire to have a close association . . . the knowledge you have someone you can feel completely honest with and depend on. Man or woman misses that when they lose their partner by death.

An 82-year-old Pennsylvania husband, married for fifty years, says that his wife lost interest in sex three years ago, when she was 67. They have not had sex together since. He now masturbates several times a month to relieve tension, always reaching orgasm.

An 85-year-old widow living in a retirement home in Florida writes:

I enjoy man talk, and am glad there are both men and women here. . . . I'm hostess in this corridor and take new residents to the dining room, introduce them and help them get acquainted. I prefer having at least one man at the table where I eat. There have been at least three weddings here, and I approve, since they were people who seemed to need close companionship. My feeling has been, "Who wants a sandwich after a banquet?" My husband died at 48; we had been very happy, and for perhaps a year I could feel myself close enough to him to have an orgasm. I became involved in volunteer work and my children's social life — and tried to be very tired at night. I continued seeing our friends, but

seldom for dinner, since it had been a joke in our dinner
club that we had to sit together or we would be so unhappy — that gives you some idea of our love for each other.

I still enjoy reminiscing with people who knew him, and
I feel, sometimes we will start right where we left off, when I
get to heaven, too.

An 85-year-old widow in North Carolina reports a wholly
conventional life:

I had the happiest marriage for fifty-two years — wonderful
strong feeling of love and trust. . . . Am sure I sound
old-fashioned — never had sex with anyone except my husband. . . . I would not marry again . . . do not need sex —
would not live with any man — do not masturbate — have a
full, happy life — do not need male companionship.

Her opinions, however, are much less conventional:

I believe gays and lesbians should be allowed to live in
peace; do not approve of Anita Bryant's crusade . . . I believe
in legal abortion . . . and I work for abortion council. Believe
until we get a *reliable* contraception method, abortion is a
must! Had one child.

She rates her enjoyment of life as 1.

An 87-year-old man in Pasadena, California has been married
four times. He describes his present relationship, entered into
when he was 81, as "common-law type." His partner is 69. He and
his partner have sex together several times a month; he never
reaches orgasm during sex with her, and he explains why: "Mutual until 83. Now [I] come too slowly, so give partner orgasm and
get mine separately" by masturbation.

His partner confirms all this, and adds:

He can give me a lot of pleasure simply *because* he takes so
long to come. I am not hurried or worried. His gentle rub-

bing against the clitoris is very exciting. I miss nothing, and neither does he — except that, at age 87, he would like more of it, and I have become more interested in writing stories, making gardens, music, keeping a large correspondence going, etc.

One of our two 90-year-old women lives in California. She skipped over our sexual questions, explaining: "I have never had sexual relations with anyone but my husband, and that was only after we were married. That was a long time ago. In later years my interests have been intellectual."

Our other 90-year-old woman lives alone in New Hampshire on an income of less than $5,000 a year. She rates her enjoyment of life as 1, and says she is rarely lonely. She writes:

I think that trying (and succeeding!) to appear younger than we are has kept older women *feeling* younger than we are, and that makes all the difference between us and our mothers' generation! We still tint our hair, wear makeup, adopt younger clothing (pantsuits are a boon, keep us warm and hide some of our physical deficiencies) and join in our daughters' activities — all helpful in making us feel like *persons* not *old* people.

Of sex she writes:

I found sex important in my marriage; but unselfish love was much emphasized by my parents, and much more important. If we think of others first, things usually work out well in other respects. . . . Many modern sexual ideas are not acceptable to me, but I try to understand the good points and keep my opinions to myself.

She also writes:

I have enjoyed friendships with older men as I have aged, but still could not consider sexual affairs. My marriage was

ideal, and although it ended with the death of my husband
at age 55, every day I have wonderful memories of those
years. That may be the reason I have not remarried. If I were
younger, I would consider remarriage, as one certainly
misses a companion.

Our oldest respondent, it will be recalled, is a 93-year-old
husband. He has been married for fifty-nine years to a woman
sixteen years younger. He rates his current enjoyment of life as 1
and the happiness of his marriage as 2. He does not masturbate
and he no longer has sex with his wife; they stopped some years
ago because he lost interest.

That sexual desire may survive in a very old woman until
death itself calls a halt is attested to by a 74-year-old minister in
our sample. He recalls that some time ago, he paid a pastoral visit
to a woman lying on her deathbed in a nursing home.

She was approaching death from old age. In fact, she opened
her eyes only long enough to see who I was. Her limbs were
already stiff — but she reached out a hand, took mine in
hers, and, pressing it against her chest, firmly pushed it toward her [genitals]. Because we were in a nursing home
where a nurse might come in at any time, by the time our
hands reached her navel I panicked, resisted her, and took
my hand away. Two days later, she was dead.

THE BOTTOM LINE: SEXUAL ENJOYMENT

Readers who have come this far may be perplexed or even distressed by the apparent inconsistency between what so many of
our men and women tell us on their Comment Pages and what
their responses to the objective questions seem to be telling us.
Does sex "get better and better," as so many respondents al-
lege — or is there progressive, decade-by-decade deterioration, as
the statistics seem to show?

We think that both perspectives on sexual aging are sound

and significant, and much less in conflict than might appear — for at least two reasons.

In the first place, much (though not all) of the sexual decline among our sexually active men and women is concerned with the *frequency* of various sexual activities. The enjoyment of sex can and sometimes does increase with age even as the frequency may decrease. The 68-year-old widower quoted earlier makes precisely this point: "To sum up succinctly, I indulge less and enjoy it more with a partner of similar tastes and interests."

A 58-year-old wife, married thirty-one years to a husband of 59, writes from Pittsburgh: "The sexual relationship can be just as enjoyable, or better, as when young, with less frequency perhaps."

A 59-year-old San Francisco husband, married for thirty-two years to a wife now aged 58, is equally succinct: "Sexual activity may decrease but the pleasure doesn't diminish."

And a 63-year-old Michigan wife comments on her marriage of forty years to a husband the same age: "Although sex in later years may not happen as frequently as earlier, . . . it can still be as intense and rewarding when it does happen."

In the second place, and perhaps more important, some of our respondents have chosen not to be mere passive observers of the rising sexual response thresholds they experience from decade to decade. They have instead sought and found techniques for maintaining, or in some cases even enhancing, their enjoyment of sex despite the progressive physiological changes described in this chapter. These techniques for learning to live with and even benefit from the changes brought by sexual aging are the focus of chapter 9.

❧ 9 ❦

How Our Respondents Compensate for Sexual Changes as They Age

A 61-YEAR-OLD DALLAS WIDOWER IS RETIRED ON AN INCOME OF BE-
tween $25,000 and $35,000 a year. His wife died two years ago —
but she is still very much on his mind. Asked why he doesn't remarry, he replies: "I am emotionally resistant to marrying anyone
again. I still love my wife. . . ."

Thinking back over his lengthy marriage, he continues: "I
could not duplicate that experience. I do not have the physical or
emotional resources to duplicate it."

His physical resources in particular are far below par: He reports all six signs of declining sexual potency, and says they are so
severe that he is no longer able to have sexual intercourse. He has
discussed his potency problems with a physician, a psychiatrist,
and a sex therapist, but none of them was helpful. He no longer
masturbates.

Here is the prototype of the aging, impotent male, suffering
from the physiological changes described in chapter 8 to a degree
much more severe than is common among men his age. His physiological changes, moreover, are complicated by his continued
mourning for his wife. Yet this impotent 61-year-old widower
who no longer even masturbates rates his enjoyment of sex as 1.

How does he do it? His method is similar to those developed
by many other respondents, women and men, who have learned

that the enjoyment of sex need not be dependent on genital performance.

Shortly after his wife died, he launched a sexual relationship with a 40-year-old woman. He is not in love with her, but he rates the happiness of their relationship as 2.

He and his partner do not have sexual intercourse; his penis, he says, is too limp for that. But they engage in just about everything else, including manual and oral stimulation of each other's breasts and genitals. They have sex together two or three times a week. During these encounters, he reports, she almost always reaches orgasm and he usually does. When he doesn't, moreover, he isn't bothered in the least: "I no longer care whether I have an orgasm. It interrupts the pleasure."

Hundreds of other respondents similarly describe the methods they have discovered for maintaining or even enhancing sexual enjoyment despite the rising sexual response thresholds and the other changes wrought by illness and by aging.

Physiological approaches to sexual enhancement

The techniques our respondents use can be sorted into two overlapping categories: *physiological approaches* (such as manual and oral stimulation of the breasts and genitals), and *psychological approaches* (including sexual fantasy, the use of pornographic materials, and the stimulation that comes from sex with a new partner). Many activities, of course, provide both physiological and psychological stimulation.

Nudity

A wife and husband who have for decades engaged in sexual intercourse with their bodies discreetly covered or partially covered may be surprised at the intensity of psychological response when they abandon the nudity taboo; the absence of clothing may bring freshness to an experience that has become routine. In addition, there is a physiological response to warm body-to-body contact without intervening barriers.

A 75-year-old widow asks in her Comment Pages:

Heavens to Betsy! Do you really think that today there are
sexual partners who do *not* see each other naked? My husband, children, and I always went around the house without
regard to clothing. I am not ashamed of my body!!!

There are indeed wives and husbands in our sample, married
for decades, who have never seen one another naked — for readily understandable reasons.

Many little girls and little boys during the Victorian era and
thereafter were taught that they should always put on their night-
gowns or nightshirts before taking off their clothes, even when
they were alone, in order to spare even themselves the sight of
their naked bodies. This attitude toward nudity, instilled at a very
early age, sometimes lingered on into marriage, even during sexual intercourse. Indeed, some Victorian prostitutes refused to take
off all their clothes in the presence of a patron — and patrons, too,
often remained partially clothed.

How many of our respondents still cling to the Victorian na-
kedness taboo? We asked whether, since 50, they have engaged in
the following activities:

"Seeing your partner naked

"Being seen by your partner when you are naked"

Four percent of our wives and husbands report they have not
seen their spouse naked; 5 percent say their spouse has not seen
them naked.

A 74-year-old clergyman, married for forty-three years to a
wife of the same age, comments from Southern California:

When [my wife] sees the strong body of Atlas, she is turned
off by it; in fact she does not appreciate the body of any
man. She is enthusiastic about a man's sense of humor, his
excellent use of the English language, or any excellence in
his manner, thoughtfulness, and other mental virtues. Body

hair is also repulsive to her. We have never bathed together or undressed each other — or slept in the nude. Such things would offend her sensitive nature, I guess.

A 61-year-old Illinois wife is pleased that she eventually overcame her own nudity taboo. Asked what she would do differently if she had her life to lead over, she replies: "I'd . . . have allowed myself earlier to sleep in the nude with my husband. I thought I'd be too cold during the winter months — but there wasn't that much difference, and the skin contact made it worth it."

Breast stimulation

The female breasts and nipples have intimate neural and hormonal ties to sex centers in the brain and spinal cord. Hence stimulation of the female breasts and nipples can, and often does, trigger or enhance sexual desire, engorgement of the female genitals, and vaginal lubrication. For some women on some occasions, it may even produce orgasm.

Seventy-one percent of our heterosexual women* say that a partner has stimulated their breasts or nipples since 50; and 81 percent of our heterosexual men* say that they have stimulated a partner's breasts or nipples since 50. Thus stimulation of the female breasts is an accepted feature of lovemaking after as well as before 50.

More surprising is the extent to which stimulation of the *male* breast is also common practice after 50. Thirty percent of our men say that a partner has stimulated their breasts or nipples; and 31 percent of our women say that they have stimulated the breasts or nipples of a partner.

More than 90 percent of men as well as of women who have

---

* We were concerned, when drafting this chapter, that gay men and women might prove different from heterosexual men and women with respect to such activities as stimulation of the male breasts, anal stimulation, and perhaps others. Accordingly, our fifty-six men and nine women who consider themselves homosexual have been eliminated from some of the statistical tables in this chapter.

tried it, moreover, say that they enjoy stimulating a partner's breasts and having their own breasts stimulated:

	Proportion who say they enjoyed it
Women who have stimulated their partner's breasts or nipples (N=573)	93%
Women who have had their breasts or nipples stimulated by their partner (N=1,297)	93%
Men who have stimulated their partner's breasts or nipples (N=1,911)	99%
Men who have had their breasts or nipples stimulated by their partner (N=703)	91%

Five percent of our women have had a mastectomy and several of them (or their partners) say this prevents breast or nipple stimulation. As noted earlier, however, at least one woman who has had a double mastectomy reports that "oddly, where the breasts used to be, the sensory response remains!"

Manual stimulation of the genitals

The role of the clitoris as the site, or at least one site, of female sexual arousal — closely paralleling the penis as the major site of male sexual arousal — has been known to both women and men since time immemorial. It took Victorian repression to erase this knowledge — or almost erase it, for no doubt countless men and women rediscovered this truth for themselves even during the depths of the repression. Since the 1930s and 1940s, sex educators led by Dr. Robert Latou Dickinson and Dr. Alfred C. Kinsey have done their best to make the importance of clitoral stimulation known to both women and men — and the information has also been circulated by countless sex manuals and by the Masters and Johnson studies.

Our data demonstrate that the lesson has been learned by the vast majority of our respondents — and that many have also learned (with much less encouragement from the professionals) to engage in manual stimulation of the aging male's genitals. An example is the husband quoted in chapter 1 who writes that he and his wife, at 80 and 75, "keep our interest [in sex] alive by a great deal of caressing and fondling of each other's genitals. We feel it is much better to wear out than to rust out."

The 74-year-old clergyman quoted earlier in this chapter recalls:

> Some ten or fifteen years ago, [I discovered] I could [no longer] reach orgasm with intercourse alone; I needed a little extra stimulation. [My wife] supplied it by caressing my scrotum. She also needed some extra stimulation about the same time, so I stroked her clitoris with a finger. . . . I have not discussed these matters with anyone else, so I do not know about the experiences of other couples. I am eager to see your report.

A twice-married 65-year-old Georgia husband says that when he was 57, "I became impotent." Soon thereafter his wife died. At age 60, he married a woman of 43. "Since remarriage I sometimes have difficulty [getting] sexually aroused. Occasional manual sex (usually my wife stroking my penis) reestablishes potency."

A 73-year-old Detroit widower had a prostatectomy at 65 and has not had an erection since. Two years ago, however, he launched a sexual relationship with a never-married woman, now 82. Despite absence of an erection, he explains,

> [I] do enjoy orgasm by hand stimulation, using a special process developed by myself. Actually, it is a form of masturbation. By hand manipulation, I arouse my partner to orgasm and she fondles my genitals. After she has been satisfied, then I masturbate myself to orgasm with her help.

He rates his enjoyment of sex with his partner as 1.

An 81-year-old husband, married for fifty-one years to a wife now 80, writes:

Make it clear to women that handling of their male partner's "private parts" in a really positive way, even leading to masturbation, is pleasant to him and can be done vigorously without damage. My wife knows this now, but it took her a long time to find out. A very pleasant supplement to intercourse or attempts at intercourse.

A 70-year-old widow recalls: "When my husband was alive, mutual masturbation was pleasurable. Now [solitary] masturbation is my only form of sexual pleasure."

A 69-year-old New Jersey widower writes:

When I was in my early 60's, a young feminist friend of mine introduced me to a new form of sexual activity which she called "You do you, I do me." To my surprise, I found it very enjoyable. Since then, I have introduced several women friends to it, especially in situations where they were sexually turned on but loath to engage in intercourse with someone they didn't know well enough.

When sexual intercourse is no longer possible at all, orgasm through manual stimulation may still remain possible — and enjoyable. A 66-year-old Idaho husband reports: "Since my wife had a hysterectomy operation, it became difficult for [her] to have an orgasm — and I had a bad back; so manual stimulation was our form of sex for about 15 years."

A 77-year-old husband writes: "I really have no erection but I have a [manual] release which is satisfying. Since I am unable to have normal sex, I enjoy this as a substitute."

A 70-year-old New England husband, married for forty-four years to a wife now 66, writes:

Sex with my wife has developed serious drawbacks. For over five years, I have been unable to enter her because she suffers pain. If my penis were the size of my forefinger, I would have no difficulty. And [my forefinger] is what I use — first lubricating her vagina with Vaseline jelly. I manage [in this

way] to arouse her to orgasm, and she arouses me to orgasm
by stroking my penis.

A 72-year-old Missouri wife married for forty-eight years tells
us: "My husband's joints are painful — so that limits his activity,
but his mind and disposition are fine so I am lucky." She adds that
her 80-year-old husband "has not had a full erection for at least
eight years"; hence they no longer engage in sexual intercourse —
but they continue to have sex together. At 72, she reaches orgasm
almost every time. She explains:

> He is such a delightful, delicious caresser that he can give
> me an orgasm without [intercourse]. He does not crave this
> activity as often as I do, but the quality is worth waiting for.
> In any case, I can piece out with masturbation.

We remind readers of the 75-year-old widow who reports:
"Because of [my husband's] impotence, we used mutual manipulation, and that was pleasurable. He could not have an erection,
but could and did have an orgasm and ejaculation [through mas-
turbation]."

Thirty-eight of our men and thirty-one of our women report
that one of the reasons they masturbate is because "my partner
likes to watch." One of these is a 76-year-old husband, married
for forty-two years to a wife now 63, who writes from Florida:

> My wife and I frequently masturbate together. I particularly
> like to watch her reach orgasm. Also, I usually masturbate
> her before indulging in oral sex; it heightens her anticipation
> and increases her vaginal lubrication, which I love.

He adds that he masturbates two or three times a week and almost always reaches orgasm.

His wife reports that she also masturbates two or three times a
week — because she enjoys it, because it is an added source of
sexual satisfaction, and because "my partner likes to watch" —
and she, too, almost always reaches orgasm.

According to our respondents, mutual masturbation may take

any of several forms. The woman may masturbate the man to orgasm while the man is masturbating the woman to orgasm, or they may take turns, or each may engage in self-stimulation within the lovemaking setting — and be aroused by observing their partner's arousal as their own is occurring simultaneously. Masturbating within such a mutually acceptable, mutually arousing, lovemaking framework can be an altogether different — and for some women and men a far more rewarding — experience than solitary masturbation.*

The statistics confirm the comments:

• 64 percent of our women say a partner has manually stimulated their genitals since 50.

• Of those women who have experienced it, 96 percent say they enjoyed it.

• Similarly, 78 percent of our men say they have manually stimulated a partner's genitals since 50.

• Of those men who have done it, 98 percent say they enjoyed doing it.

• 64 percent of our women say they have manually stimulated a partner's genitals since 50.

• Of those women who have done it, 91 percent say they enjoyed doing it.

• Similarly, 74 percent of our men say a partner has manually stimulated their genitals since 50.

• Of those men who have experienced it, 99 percent say they enjoyed it.

Manual stimulation of the clitoris during intercourse

Hundreds of young women cited in the *Hite Report* (1976) testify to the importance of manual stimulation of their clitoris not only prior to but also *during* sexual intercourse. Some of Hite's respon-

---

* Some respondents report that manual stimulation is facilitated, and the sensory response intensified, if a lubricant is used.

dents say they can reach orgasm during intercourse only by manually stimulating their own clitoris during the act; others have partners who manually stimulate their clitoris during intercourse.

How widespread is acceptance of these techniques among *older* women and men? Here is what our respondents report concerning their own activities since age 50:

• 27 percent of our women have manually stimulated their clitoris during sexual intercourse.

• 94 percent of the women who have tried it say they enjoyed it.

• 69 percent of our men have manually stimulated their partner's clitoris during intercourse.

• 97 percent of the men who have done it say they enjoyed doing it.

Some of our women not only enjoy manual stimulation during intercourse but (like some of Hite's younger respondents) cannot reach orgasm without it. An example is the 65-year-old wife who writes: "I have *always* needed manual stimulation of my genitals by my partner to reach an orgasm."

The so-called missionary position — sexual intercourse face-to-face with the man on top — is perhaps the only position in which manual stimulation of the clitoris during intercourse may be difficult or awkward, especially if both partners are obese. In almost any other position, partners can readily discover how either of them can manually stimulate the clitoris while intercourse is under way.

A female sex therapist who has served as a consultant to this study confirms the importance for many women of manual stimulation of the clitoris during intercourse — and adds a related comment:

I have found that my women patients are most easily able to have orgasms during intercourse if they lie in the same position they use when stimulating their clitoris manually during masturbation. A woman who usually masturbates by rubbing her clitoris while lying on her stomach, for example, may be most readily orgasmic while rubbing her clitoris in the same position during intercourse. The "missionary position," with the woman lying on her back, knees spread, and the man between her knees, is ideal for the woman who masturbates in this position.

Some women masturbate by rubbing their hand against the stationary clitoris; others move the clitoris up and down against a stationary hand or object. Using the same technique (whatever it may be) during intercourse may facilitate orgasm. Thus, a woman who masturbates by moving her clitoris up and down against her hand or an object can, during intercourse, move her clitoris up and down against her hand, her partner's hand, or his pubic bone.

Earlier researchers have reported that many young women reach orgasm more readily, more securely, and on a higher proportion of occasions when masturbating than when having sex with a partner. We find the same to be true for *older* women.

We asked our frequency-of-orgasm question for masturbation and for sex with a partner at different places in our questionnaire. Thus women filling out the questionnaire did not have the comparison in mind when they answered the two questions. When we compared the answers, we found that 61 percent of our 525 women who answer both questions report a higher orgasmic frequency during masturbation — as compared with only 16 percent reporting a higher orgasmic frequency during sex with a partner and 24 percent reporting the same frequency for both.

We had expected that. What surprised us was the fact that 26 percent of our 1,024 men who answer both questions also report a higher frequency of orgasm when they masturbate. Fifty-six percent report the same frequency for both and only 18 percent report a higher orgasmic frequency during sex with a partner. Thus the greater orgasmic efficacy of manual stimulation than of intercourse for most women turns out to be true for some men as well.

Oral stimulation of the genitals

The Victorians considered oral sex to be an unnatural act or perversion. Victorian physicians hesitated to mention such matters even in medical textbooks, and therefore used Latin terms — *fella-tio* for oral stimulation of the male genitals and *cunnilingus* for oral stimulation of the female genitals. Indeed, in some textbooks entire paragraphs were printed in Latin, so that innocents happening upon them would not understand what was being said. The fact that a husband had demanded either fellatio or cunnilingus from his wife was sometimes cited by the wife as a ground for divorce.

Today, under the laws of some states, fellatio and cunnilingus are still included in the definition of sodomy* — that is, they are felonies punishable by long terms of imprisonment, even when engaged in by a consenting wife and husband in the privacy of their bedroom.

There is some evidence that men have been more accepting of and desirous of oral-genital sex than women. Prostitutes, for example, have long reported that some married men come to them for oral sex because their wives refuse to engage in it; many of these men want fellatio but quite a few want cunnilingus.

Some of our women and men still think that fellatio and cunnilingus are perversions or otherwise unacceptable. Others now accept either active or passive oral sex, or both; and some report these practices to be a particularly enjoyable and effective part of their lovemaking. Here are the relevant statistics for our respondents' activities since age 50:

Fellatio

• 43 percent of our women report that they have orally stimulated the genitals of their partner.

• 75 percent of those who have tried it enjoyed doing it.

• 49 percent of our men report that their partner has orally stimulated their genitals.

• 98 percent of those who have experienced it enjoyed having it done to them.

---

* In some states, legislators were too prudish to use the term *sodomy* in the law; a euphemism, "the crime against nature," was used instead.

Cunnilingus

• 56 percent of our men report that they have orally stimulated the genitals of their partner.

• 95 percent of those who have tried it enjoyed doing it.

• 49 percent of our women report that their partner has orally stimulated their genitals.

• 82 percent of those who have experienced it enjoyed having it done to them.

These statistics lead to three observations:

First, more respondents, men and women alike, report having engaged in cunnilingus than in fellatio.

Second, more men than women enjoyed fellatio.

Finally — and this is surprising — more men than women enjoyed cunnilingus.*

One Kentucky husband, aged 54, explains why he enjoys cunnilingus but not fellatio:

I have indicated a negative answer [to enjoying fellatio] only because I know my wife detests the activity and only does it once in a great while to please me. Under [those] circumstances, I can't enjoy it. I wish passionately that she enjoyed being the active agent in oral sex [to] a fraction of the degree that I do.

Our respondents use oral sex as either a preliminary or an alternative to sexual intercourse. Oral stimulation of the penis may be begun while it is still flaccid, in order to produce an erection, or it may be used to facilitate orgasm, or both — or just for fun. Similarly, oral stimulation of the female genitals may be used to facilitate either vaginal lubrication or orgasm — or just for fun.

The Florida couple quoted earlier in this chapter about masturbating together because "my partner likes to watch" also report

---

* A woman consultant to this study comments: "Many women have told me that they would enjoy receiving cunnilingus more if their partners were slower, gentler, and didn't press stubbly, unshaven faces against their thighs and genitals."

on their oral-genital activities. The 63-year-old wife says that she enjoys both the active and passive forms. Her 76-year-old husband supplies the details:

> I have a moderately severe emphysema, and the physical exertion of penile-vaginal sex imposes rather severe breathing problems. Also, both my wife and I have put on weight [so that] it is physically difficult to achieve satisfactory insertion of the penis (despite 7-inch erection). So, consequently, my wife and I almost exclusively indulge in oral sex. We [formerly] did . . . about 50 percent of each; now almost 100-percent [oral]. . . . We are finding improved techniques greatly increase pleasure — and the enjoyment of tasting vaginal secretions and ejaculate. [Oral sex is] far less physically tiring; and the depth of orgasm and frequency [for] my wife [is] quite marked. Also, this activity seems to have brought us more closely together and [made us] less intolerant of each other.

A 62-year-old Montana husband with a 61-year-old wife gives their views after thirty-seven years of marriage:

> [We] have found oral and manual stimulation of genitals to orgasm a most pleasant experience. About one-third of our sexual activity is by these methods. I believe it is good to have variety in your sexual activities. . . . I would recommend starting oral sex in marriage when the novelty of routine sex begins to wear off. It would help to keep a man and wife interested in each other and eliminate looking outside of marriage for stimulation.

A 70-year-old Rhode Island widow with two lovers writes:

> I like having my genitals mouth-stimulated even more than intercourse — although I will not stimulate [their] genitals by mouth. I find this unsanitary and somewhat repulsive and wish they wouldn't keep coaxing me. I try, but it's no good. I dislike this and stipulate now it's a no-no.

A 51-year-old husband writes from New York City:

The physical structure of my wife's vulva does not allow friction between the penis and clitoris during coitus. Experimenting, we could find no position that would enable penile stimulation [of the clitoris] that wasn't uncomfortable. As a result, I resorted early to manual or oral stimulation to ensure my wife's full enjoyment of intercourse. I usually bring her to orgasm by manual or tongue stimulation before entering her at all. In return, she plays the game with me; often mutual masturbation replaces the first session of sex with us. . . . It would seem that this technique might become more important as erection becomes more difficult to achieve and hold in later years.

A 59-year-old husband writes from San Francisco:

Although my wife and I have stimulated each other's genitals orally, it hasn't made my sexual response more vivid — but I think my wife reaches orgasm more easily.

A Phoenix husband, aged 53, writes:

I enjoy performing oral sex on my wife, but she doesn't particularly like it — and at times dislikes it. That is the major problem area in our sex life. Otherwise, it is very satisfactory.

A 54-year-old husband in Washington, D.C., is somewhat tentative:

Of course, some of the new methods of sex, such as oral sex, arouse one's curiosity; but you more or less stay with the methods that have become natural to you. I might be tempted to try other methods with a mutually agreeing partner — but that is the only way. As the saying goes, "Try it, you might like it."

A 71-year-old widower with a "lady partner" aged 63 reports from the Midwest that the two of them met "through an old folks' correspondence club" about a year ago.

As neither of us had ever had a sex relation outside of marriage, we have explored various sex activities with the enthusiasm of teenagers — and [we] both find oral sex to be ideal. We find in it a close relationship far superior to "normal" sex. Also far less exhausting — and always successful, so there is no frustration.

A 62-year-old widow in suburban Chicago comments: "Do not approve [of oral sex]. Sex is beautiful if done as nature intended — there is no reason for position 79 [sic] or whatever — just act as nature intended."

A 60-year-old Trenton wife, in contrast, reports that for the past two years she has suffered "decrease of interest in sex due to dryness and pain even though [a lubricant] was provided." As a result, she now finds "oral sex for both partners to [be] a most enjoyable variation."

A 75-year-old Boston widow, who for the past two years has had a lover four years younger, writes:

The only thing that shocks me about this [questionnaire] is the question about "stimulating partner's genitals with mouth or tongue." I thought only dogs did that. . . . When I showed my son that, he said, "Mother, you have lived a sheltered life."

Let us here quote again the 51-year-old wife, married for twenty-six years to a husband sixteen years older, who recalls that late in their marriage, "He started stimulating my genitals with [his] mouth, which brought me to more multiple orgasms. [I] wish I had let my husband stimulate my genitals orally early in our marriage."

Readers may also recall the 70-year-old Boston widower who describes his own "limited virility," and who says that his sexual relations with his 65-year-old partner "are almost exclusively based on my caresses, leading to cunnilingus and to repeated orgasms on her part."

A 77-year-old husband in Harrisburg, married for nine years to a wife now 83, recalls his first experience with cunnilingus not so long ago:

> The idea of touching a woman's genitals with my tongue was revolting to me until I finally did it just to convince myself. Then I discovered it to be most pleasant. There was absolutely no offensive taste or smell. Her nether lips were just as sweet as the upper. Furthermore, I was able to give her an orgasm — and that pleased me too. It was like payment for all the orgasms she had given me.

Finally, readers may recall the 74-year-old widow who writes:

> My second husband was very, very much older. Although frequent jibes are made at May-December marriages, ours was quite good. Although he did not achieve an erection frequently enough for my needs, he was not averse to, in fact he rather enjoyed, cunnilingus, so I had ample orgasmic satisfaction.

Anal stimulation

Stimulation of the anus during sex is often considered an exclusively homosexual activity. Our data show that assumption to be a mistake: 16 percent of our heterosexual men and women report that, since age 50, they have had their anus stimulated during sex. Of those who have tried it, 86 percent of the men and 67 percent of the women say they liked it.

Here we must report a curious phenomenon. Despite the fact that 16 percent of our women and men report having engaged in anal stimulation during sex since age 50, and despite the fact that most of them say they enjoyed it, we failed to find a single discussion of anal sex on our Comment Pages. Apparently anal sex —

unlike masturbation, cunnilingus, and fellatio — is still taboo as a topic of discussion, even among those who engage in it and enjoy it.

Using a vibrator or massager

Ever since the invention of the electric motor, women here and there have discovered that the vibration produced by a motor can provide an efficient and prompt method of reaching orgasm. A 69-year-old New Jersey widower writes, for example:

> When my wife and I were in our 50's, I came home one day and told her that there was a gismo called a vibrator, a sort of quivering electric motor, and that when a woman pressed it against her clitoris, she got orgasms.
>
> "Pouf!" my wife replied, "that isn't news. I learned it on the shaky old Thor washing machine in my mother's kitchen when I was ten years old."

Three pioneering American gynecologists — Drs. Robert Latou Dickinson, W. F. Robie, and LeMon Clark — learned independently from their women patients of this method of sexual stimulation. All three recognized the importance of this discovery as an aid for women unable to reach orgasm through other means, or able to reach orgasm only rarely and with great difficulty. All three — and many of their successors in the field of sex therapy — accordingly proceeded to recommend the use of the vibrator as a learning device. They reported that some patients who experience orgasm with a vibrator initially are subsequently more likely to reach orgasm in other ways as well.

By the 1960s, a number of brands of small massagers — driven by 120-volt house current or battery-powered* — were being sold at some drugstores and department stores and by mail, as well as at sex shops and adult bookstores. One observer has called the

---

* A woman sex therapist who served as consultant to this study writes: "Battery-operated vibrators don't really provide enough power for most women; the plug-in kind should be recommended instead."

vibrator the only real advance in the field of human sexuality since the days of the Greeks and the Romans. According to one estimate, 1,300,000 vibrators were sold in the United States in 1979.* (Some, of course, may have been purchased for nonsexual massage.)

A 60-year-old wife in Fresno, California, married for thirty-nine years, writes that her 62-year-old husband has "serious problems" with erection. It takes him longer to erect, and when fully erect his penis is not as stiff as before. He more frequently loses his erection during sex nowadays, and his refractory period is longer. She adds that it takes her longer, too, to become sexually aroused these days — and her husband is unable to sustain an erection that long.

In that situation, her husband bought her a vibrator — and at 57, she learned how to masturbate with it. She had never masturbated before. "My husband is very happy and insists I use the vibrator," she writes, and she is happy, too.

An 83-year-old widow with numerous sexual partners since 50 writes:

> As I grow older, I am more discriminating [and] can't be bothered getting ready and spending time with a person who is not interesting or amusing. At present, frankly, I prefer the vibrator, which needs only desire and fantasy. I use it for self-pleasure about once a week.
>
> Believe it or not, masturbation is tiring for an older person. Therefore, vibrators are a blessing. Until that time, masturbation [by hand] is better because there is flesh-on-flesh pleasure.

Thirteen percent of our women say that they have tried a vibrator since age 50; and of these, 81 percent say they enjoyed it.

Among our men, 15 percent say they have used a vibrator; and of these, 90 percent say they enjoyed it. Quite a few of them note that they use the vibrator on their wives rather than on themselves. An example is a 68-year-old St. Louis husband who writes:

---

* *New York Times*, February 9, 1981, page B-1.

Although I must admit anxiety with [respect to] erections, etc., my wife seems not to mind — seems to enjoy sex more. We use a vibrator for added clitoral stimulation on all meetings. . . . Wife's orgasm seems livelier with [penis and vibrator] together.

Several men report using a vibrator on themselves. One is a 66-year-old divorced man in Delaware who has had no sex with a partner for years and who reports five of our six signs of declining potency — three of them "major problems." Even his masturbation is adversely affected; he describes how disappointing it is "trying to draw a little off by hand — and finding that the well is dry." With a "buzzer," however, he reaches orgasm "every time." His suggestion for other older men: "Advise 'em to buy and use a buzzer!"

An 84-year-old widower recalls:

I accidentally discovered at a late teen age that a rubdown vibrator had a striking effect on the penis. . . . For several decades thereafter, I took a lively but only theoretical interest in mechanical substitutes for intercourse. Some time in my 50's, I began to feel that something of the kind would be useful or at least desirable in my life. Since I certainly would not have been brave enough to look into the market for such apparatus, I constructed my own, which I still have and use. It is an electrically powered unit which combines vibration with a reciprocal vagina-[like] stroking movement. Even at my advanced age, I get from it a more intense local pleasure than any woman ever gave me. Of course that localized pubic sensation is not all that good intercourse provides.

The proprietor — a woman — of a store that sells vibrators has inquired into why some men *don't* get pleasure from the vibrator. Her findings:

First, the sensation is too intense for many men. They might do better if they try using it through several folds of soft cloth or toweling.

Second, they usually apply it to the most sensitive parts of the penis — the glans, or head, and the corona, or groove behind the head. They should try other places on the penis or nearby.

Third, they expect the vibrator to produce orgasm all by itself — which it rarely can. Being in the *mood* for sexual arousal, and using sexual fantasy or other forms of pyschological stimulation, is as important with a vibrator as with hand stimulation.

Using a vaginal lubricant

A 52-year-old Cincinnati wife experiences inadequate vaginal lubrication during sexual arousal. "Lately," she writes, "my husband applies lubricating jelly to me before intercourse. I find this very pleasurable, and he seems to enjoy the application equally well."

As noted in chapter 8, vaginal lubrication is the female physiological equivalent of erection of the penis; and, like erection, it tends to become more of a problem during the later years. Almost 700 of our women report inadequate vaginal lubrication during sexual arousal.

One approach to the problem is extended foreplay, including manual and oral stimulation of the breasts and clitoris, for a considerable time before an effort is made to introduce the penis into the vagina. Readers may recall the 74-year-old widow who reports adequate lubrication — "more with plenty of foreplay." For some older women, however, no amount of foreplay is enough.

A second approach is to apply a lubricant to the vagina, or to the penis before it is introduced into the vagina.

"Stuffing"

Sex therapists sometimes recommend a simple approach to the limp-penis problem: The man, or his partner, or both of them simply "stuff" the limp or inadequately erected penis into the vagina. For some men on some occasions, the sensations engendered in the limp penis as it lies encased in the warm, moist vagina may be sufficient to trigger full erection even when all else fails.

A 60-year-old Oklahoma widower reports that "stuffing" is a necessity for him: "During intercourse, entry of a half-aroused penis seems necessary for the organ to become fully hard."

A 60-year-old husband who occasionally resorts to stuffing writes from northern California: "I did not marry until age 44 and had never had a sexual experience before then; in fact, I never even masturbated. I was late maturing physically."

Nowadays, he continues:

> By the usual definition I am impotent — cannot sustain a hard-enough erection to copulate. My wife tries hard to help and with her help I can occasionally penetrate. However, without copulation we usually have good sex. She always makes sure I have an orgasm and I strive to give her an orgasm.

He estimates that she does reach orgasm about half of the time.

Asked how often he and his wife have sex, he replies: "I circle dates on the calendar in my diary, and find we have averaged 20 times a year for the last three years."

Though sexual intercourse is thus both difficult and relatively infrequent, this impotent husband — like many others in our sample — continues to enjoy what remains. Indeed, he rates his enjoyment of sex with his wife as 2.

A lubricant may be helpful as part of the "stuffing" procedure. A 59-year-old Texas husband has made this discovery: "My inability to achieve a full erection is extremely frustrating for me. If it weren't for the help of an outside lubricant... I doubt if I could ever penetrate my wife."

A 74-year-old Minneapolis husband with an erection problem has not only discovered "stuffing" for himself but has combined it with a variety of innovations of his own. "I married a woman aged 36 when I was 65," he writes. "We have a wonderful marriage.... We have had a mutual love, trust, and understanding. We each enjoy our marriage."

He and his wife have sex together every Friday night; he supplies details:

> I think as a man get older, it takes more to stimulate him so that he can enjoy sex. There are things he can do to help the situation. I am a retired engineer and am used to solving problems.
>
> One thing I have done is to improve our bedroom facilities for making love. We sleep on twin beds. I fixed one bed so that a pair of footrests can be attached to the foot. . . . My wife can move down so that her hips are right at the end of the bed — with her legs spread apart and resting on the footrests.
>
> I get between her legs with my feet on the floor. The height of the bed has been adjusted so she is at the correct height. She is now completely exposed so that I can enter her easily, even without an erection. [This is the "stuffing" technique.] I also have a cross-piece down on the floor under the foot rests, that provides a place for my feet to push against.

While stimulating his wife orally in this position, he continues, "I watch her to judge when she is about ready to have an orgasm, and then make my penetration and we have our orgasms together — which is the ultimate in lovemaking." Using this technique, he adds, both he and his wife, now aged 74 and 45, reach orgasm on 100 percent of their lovemaking experiences.

This is his third marriage. The first two, it appears, were not as successful — for he writes: "It's a shame that a man lives most of his life before he learns how to treat a woman."

A divorcée in her late fifties says she greatly prefers intercourse with a limp penis. "I sit on his penis and let my partner have his orgasm in my vagina," she explains, "and then my turn comes. With his limp penis still inside me, I rub my clitoris up and down against his pubic bone while I enjoy a whole series of orgasms. With this technique, a partner whose penis is limp or who ejaculates prematurely is no problem at all."

Fatigue and coital positions

Some men find the "missionary position" (with the man on top) fatiguing. One writes:

> In my late 60's, I began to find sexual intercourse physically *tiring* — especially holding my body up off the bed when having intercourse in the missionary position. My partner and I tried it with her on top, but she weighs almost twice as much as she used to and that didn't work very well.
>
> Then I discovered how to plant one hip firmly on the mattress to support my weight, and to enter my partner sidewise. This proved to have many advantages — including the ease with which I could stroke her clitoris and she could simulate my penis with her fingers during intercourse. The main advantage, however, was that my leg, back, and arm muscles didn't get fatigued from holding my weight up in the air. Sex takes longer these days — and now that it is less fatiguing, it is also more enjoyable.

Sex in the morning?

We asked:

> "At what time of day do you most commonly have sex with your . . . partner?"

Some respondents didn't answer and many more said that it varies. Among those who did cite a particular time of day, the replies are quite consistent:

	Women (N=780)	Men (N=1,297)
Morning	29%	30%
Afternoon	9	7
Early evening	13	10
After 10 P.M.	50	53
	101%	100%

We also asked:

"At what time of day is your . . . partner most sexually arousable?"

Here the replies specifying particular times reveal an interest-ing gender difference: Among respondents citing a particular time, about half of the women report that their partners are more arousable in the morning, while about half of the men report that their partners are more arousable after 10 P.M.

	When male partner is most sexually arousable, according to women respondents (N=609)	When woman partner is most sexually arousable, according to men respondents (N=1,019)
Morning	49%	28%
Afternoon	8	10
Early evening	11	13
After 10 P.M.	32	48
	100%	99%

Quite a few respondents, especially those who no longer have to go to work in the morning, say they enjoy sex particularly dur-ing the morning hours. In addition to being fresh and untired, a man may then be able to take advantage of his "early morning erection." A 54-year-old husband writes from Maine:

Sex for an orgasm is almost always in the morning now. The old body is fresher then. In the evening, we both are too tired for much [sexual] activity except a little play.

But a 57-year-old wife writes from Santa Barbara:

[My husband] seems to think that sex only comes after the eleven o'clock news. I have tried in the morning, but it isn't usually successful. I really should try him in the middle of a dull TV program, but I haven't so far.

Fondling and cuddling

Let us conclude this discussion of physiological aspects of love-making after 50 by considering what happens in a relationship when neither partner becomes sexually aroused any longer. Even then, some women and men continue to experience the warm delight of sheer physical closeness — just lying together, cuddling and perhaps caressing, "enjoying the many 'touching' pleasures *this* side of orgasm" as one respondent phrases it.

A 72-year-old California husband whose wife is no longer physically able to have intercourse writes: "When actual sex copulation ceases in old age, sexual feelings do not cease. Kissing, fondling, touching are also expressions of sex and there's always the delight and joy of watching the young and admiring beauty."

He adds that, since his wife discontinued sex, "I'm gradually becoming impotent so it's not important to me any longer. Like Socrates in the *Republic,* it's a relief to lose the burden of sexuality in its virulent form."

He adds, however, that in his fantasies, "I'm young again, a straining, eager bull."

A 67-year-old Canadian widower describes the pleasure he continues to get "from the caressing and fondling and the feel of my partner's body" — even though he has been impotent for more than five years. His story warrants recounting at some length.

He married for the first time at 34. "I would say that I had a good marriage for over 30 years," but there were sexual problems.

I would definitely try to change the sexual pattern that my wife and I had IF I had the knowledge I now have when I was first married. My wife and I were both inhibited, she more so than I. We had difficulty in discussing sex. She gave me more pleasure than any woman will ever be able to do so again . . . but I think I failed to give her the same pleasure she gave to me. If I had given her this pleasure, our marriage might have been much better (although it was still a good marriage). . . . I had assumed my wife got the same pleasure I did. I now think I was wrong.

His wife died three years ago; in retrospect he writes regretfully:

If I had had more sexual experience when I married, I might have gotten over some of my inhibitions and been of greater help in ridding my wife of her inhibitions. But I accepted, pretty much, the social mores of my day. The mores of today hold out the hope for better marital and sexual attitudes. . . .

His regrets are deepened in part by the fact that after fifteen years of marriage, he and his wife discontinued sex altogether. He was then 49.

For the last five or six years, I have been impotent. There may be some slight stiffening of the penis at times — but not enough for penetration. Perhaps once in a couple of months I can masturbate and ejaculate, but with no erection.

But this story of a 67-year-old man, impotent since age 62 and widowed since 64, does not end here. There is another chapter. Shortly after his wife's death, and despite his continuing impotence, he found a number of sexual partners. He soon launched a continuing sexual relationship with one of them, a woman then aged 47. She "taught me how to *give* pleasure." Then he amends that statement. "I can't say that this . . . woman taught me, as actually we learned together how to give her pleasure. I enjoy the pleasure she gets."

The two of them now have sex together four to six times a week. She always reaches orgasm on these occasions; he never does — but he enjoys both manual and oral sex, both active and passive, without erection or orgasm. He rates his enjoyment of sex as 3, despite his continuing impotence. "Even with this problem," he explains, "I can still give some partners very strong, sustained, and repeated orgasms. I get pleasure from *their* reaction, as well as from the caressing and fondling and the feel of my partner's body. I regret my lack of capability, but accept it."

PSYCHOLOGICAL APPROACHES TO SEXUAL ENHANCEMENT

Those nerve centers in the spinal cord that control vaginal lubrication, penile erection, and orgasm, it will be recalled, respond to two quite different sets of messages. Some come from erogenous zones such as the breasts and genitals following *tactile* stimulation. Other messages reach the spinal cord centers from the brain; they are triggered by *psychological* stimuli — by sights and sounds and smells and narratives and memories and fantasies. Our respondents also make use of these psychological stimuli to surmount rising sexual thresholds. As one 55-year-old husband points out, "The Number One sex organ is still the brain." Or, as a woman consultant comments: "Sexual arousal is centered between the ears, not between the legs."

One function of the messages from the brain is to create *a state of psychosexual readiness* — a state of mind and body in which the messages reaching the spinal cord centers from the genitals can have their full effect. A 61-year-old Iowa wife has made this discovery for herself, and expresses her findings with grace and precision:

I think it was Shakespeare who said, "The readiness is all." And the modern term, "turned on," is exactly right. One has to be turned on *mentally* before any sort of physical stimulation can be effective.

We had asked our respondents how easily they become sexually aroused:

☐ Very easily
☐ Moderately easily
☐ With some difficulty
☐ With great difficulty
☐ Don't become aroused

This wife replies: "I could have checked any of the five squares in this question — *depending on how my mind is at the moment.*"

Asked about variant sexual activities — manual stimulation of the genitals, oral stimulation, stimulation of the anus, and so on — she answers: "If mentally I were turned on, my answers would make me look 'oversexed'; while if I started cold, most of these activities would be distasteful."

She continues:

I've often enjoyed sex more when I was already turned on by a TV movie, or a story, or whatever. Then our lovemaking was brief and I suspect [my husband] felt what a great success *he* was! Yet I could never explain . . . to him [the importance of being psychologically turned on in advance]. I have tried [to explain it to him] once or twice, but it didn't seem to make any difference the next time.

I can't stress enough how much the mental frame of mind has to do with whether the physical stimulation is successful. Of course, a bit of tenderness and attention during the day helps to prepare the way later — but *early* ardor can so easily cool by bedtime!

The methods our respondents — men and women alike — describe for turning themselves and one another on psychologicaly fall into three broad areas. One is the use of sexual fantasy. Another is the use of sexually explicit materials. The third is seeking (and finding) new sexual partners.

USE OF SEXUAL FANTASIES

Sexual fantasy is most commonly used for "getting into the mood" — that is, for sexual arousal. For some older women and men fantasy may also be a prerequisite for reaching orgasm. The 66-year-old Ohio widow quoted earlier makes this point: "For masturbation to end in orgasm, I think of a particular person and fantasize making love with that person — someone I love or have loved."

We asked respondents whether they have sexual fantasies when they masturbate and when they have sex with a partner.

More of our women and men fantasize when masturbating than when having sex with a partner:

	Women		Men	
Fantasies during masturbation	(N=750)		(N=1,285)	
Always	21%		33%	
Usually	23	74%	32	89%
Sometimes	30		24	
Never	26		11	
	100%		100%	

	Women		Men	
Fantasies during sex with partner	(N=1,175)		(N=1,755)	
Always	5%		4%	
Usually	9	52%	10	61%
Sometimes	38		47	
Never	48		39	
	100%		100%	

We also asked:

"How does this [use of sexual fantasies] compare with when you were 40?"

Nearly four-fifths of our sexually active respondents report no decline in fantasy use compared with age 40:

	Women	Men
	(N=1,121)	(N=1,830)
More fantasies now than around 40	9%	10%
About the same	68	70
Fewer now	22	20
	99%	100%

We requested:

"Please describe, on the Comment Pages at the end of the questionnaire, one of your recent sexual fantasies or dreams."

In all, 237 women and 390 men responded — some with only a sentence or two, others at substantial length. Many indicated the ways in which they use their fantasy for the enhancement of sexual response and enjoyment.

Some described their sexual dreams; some drew no distinction between fantasies and dreams; and some labeled as dreams what others might call fantasies. We are concerned here mostly (but not exclusively) with fantasies — that is, with sexual thoughts and scenes deliberately conjured up while awake. The ability to control and direct the action distinguishes fantasies from dreams.

Sexual fantasies as mood-establishers

The primary function of the sexual fantasy is to trigger appropriate messages from the sexual centers in the brain and thus to ready the spinal cord centers to respond to tactile messages. Fantasies in this way facilitate a sexually receptive mood.

All day long, a wife and husband may be busy with wholly nonsexual activities — business and family and social affairs and numerous other concerns. These concerns do not vanish on command merely because it is 10 P.M., or 11 P.M., or midnight. They may intrude and block sexual arousal if they are not swept out of the way. Sexual fantasies effectively play this mind-clearing role for some men and women.

Closely related to this function is the use of sexual fantasy as a focusing lens. Here the swinging pendulum, or other devices used by some hypnotists, provide the model. The hypnotic subject who focuses on the pendulum finds consciousness emptied of all distractions. A 52-year-old Cincinnati wife writes:

> I like to remember, especially during intercourse, previous experiences that were especially pleasurable — for instance, first times for new variations, or special and unusual places. [My husband and I have] been adventuresome together, and [I] have many memories that *help me concentrate and blot out various distractions.* [Emphasis added]

Sexual fantasies as rejuvenators

Sexual fantasies can also repair the damage done by time to one's self-image. Thus a never-married 57-year-old woman who lives alone and who is not currently having sex with anyone reports that in her fantasies, "[I am] young again, sexually attractive. [I] meet the perfect sexual partner and build an enduring love relationship." Readers may recall the 72-year-old husband who reports, "I'm gradually becoming impotent," but who adds that in his fantasies, "I'm young again — a straining, eager bull."

Fantasy can simultaneously rejuvenate and revivify one's image of an aging spouse or sexual partner. A 55-year-old wife in suburban New York City explains:

> I need to think "sex" thoughts to get into a mood where I can get aroused and complete the sex act, including orgasm. I think back to when we were first married, were young and more attractive physically.

This mutual rejuvenation process is admirably captured in a poem written by a 74-year-old wife who enclosed it with her questionnaire and authorized us to publish it:

FINDING THE FOUNTAIN

The slim young man I married
Has slowly gone to pot;
With wrinkled face and graying pate,
Slender he is not!
And when I meet a mirror,
I find a haggard crone;
I can't believe the face I see
Can really be my own!

But when we seek our bed each night,
The wrinkles melt away:
Our flesh is firm, our kisses warm,
Our ardent hearts are gay!
The Fountain of Eternal Youth
Is not so far to find:
Two things you need — a double bed,
A spouse who's true and kind!

Fantasy "reruns"

One type of sexual fantasy is particularly helpful in facilitating this rejuvenation process: "the rerun." An example is provided by a 54-year-old husband who writes from upstate New York: "In my early forties, I had my only extramarital affair, which lasted twenty-four hours. I experienced orgasm seven times. This has been the highlight of my life. Reliving this experience is my fantasy."

A 69-year-old husband still likes to rerun in fantasy "an experience with a girl when I was 37. She was fantastic in bed — a passionate, wildly manipulating, hot-blooded sylph."

An 85-year-old widow in Birmingham, Alabama, recalls similarly that fifteen years ago, at 70, "I had a sudden, violent love affair that lasted about three months. It remained in my fantasy for over ten years!"

Reruns are not always of nonmarital affairs, however. A substantial proportion of the reruns reported by both wives and husbands involve sexual encounters with their own spouses. Thus a 67-year-old husband writes: "It may sound unusual, but when I have [a fantasy during] sex with my wife, it includes her." A 66-

year-old Indiana husband, married for thirty-three years, says a recent sexual fantasy "concerned cunnilingus with my wife, causing her to become intensely aroused — more so than in reality."

A 54-year-old New Hampshire husband writes:

> My fantasies nearly all deal with getting a woman sexually aroused. Fictitious people are unsatisfactory for this. I find so few appealing women around that most fantasies deal with former girl friends — or my wife.

Even though many years have elapsed since a spouse's death, that spouse may still be the central figure in a rerun. One 65-year-old Pennsylvania woman whose husband died eight years ago writes that she fantasizes during masturbation. "[My] only fantasy at present is that my husband is with me. He liked the idea of masturbation."

A 54-year-old widow draws a distinction between her sexual fantasies and her sexual dreams:

> The fantasies usually relate to my late husband. We had an extremely active and exciting sexual relationship. The dreams, on the other hand, tend to involve someone I've met or known and never thought of in relation to sex. This always surprises me.

A 62-year-old Montana husband reports that his wife was the central figure in a recent sex dream.

> I had not had sexual intercourse or masturbated in several weeks. I dreamt that I was having one of [my] best sexual experiences with my wife — and on having mutual orgasm [in the dream], I awoke having a huge ejaculation.

A 66-year-old Maryland wife recalls:

> On one occasion I dreamed of having sexual intercourse with my husband. It was extremely exciting and realistic — better than we had been experiencing. I awoke very aroused.

The husband who fantasizes during intercourse with his wife that the woman in his arms is someone else is a familiar figure in folk humor. One of our women reports the opposite fantasy. Seventy-one years of age and widowed for many years, she now has sex with "an old friend." During these sexual encounters, she fantasizes that "my husband is making love to me. He was an ardent lover and we enjoyed our sex life together."

Readers may recall the fantasy of a 65-year-old Texas wife who had an extramarital affair and who now, twelve years later, reports: "My only fantasy for orgasm is 'my only love' when masturbating. Once it's triggered, I could have dozens."

A 75-year-old Connecticut widow has lived alone since her husband died eighteen years ago:

> My sexual fantasies since my husband's death have generally been with him as a partner, once or twice with another very close male friend. The fantasy frequently has to do with [my husband's] pain and my caring for him during his suffering. Such dreams wake me up and leave me wretchedly tense and longing. Generally they lead to masturbation, in which I often talk aloud to my partner.

A 69-year-old widow writes from Cambridge, Massachusetts:

> While masturbating I have sexual fantasies. They always involve my husband (that would come under the heading of remembering), or they involve [a] man I fell in love with and didn't have.

A 71-year-old widow who graduated from college and attended graduate school describes a different kind of rerun:

> In my youth, my work took me among rough-and-tumble, illiterate, *macho* types. When I fantasize, it's about them — being stripped while dancing in a speakeasy (remember?) in front of a mirror and an audience. (In the fantasy, of course, I look the way I did in speakeasy days.)

Fantasies as rehearsals

Just as fantasies can be reruns of past events, so they can be re-hearsals of coming events. The young woman or young man who has a very special date for next Saturday night may rehearse it repeatedly in fantasy during the intervening week — and the fantasy rehearsals may help the protagonist live through the actual event with more grace and less embarrassment.

It is interesting to note that the hundreds of sexual fantasies described by our respondents aged 50 or older include numerous reruns — but not a single clear example of the kind of rehearsal fantasy common in youth.

Fantasies that restructure reality

Some men and women who find their current sexual situation intolerable restructure that situation through fantasy to make sex enjoyable. A 55-year-old wife in Oakland, California, writes:

> My lack of interest in sex with my husband is of great concern to me. My husband became careless about personal cleanliness and attractiveness. He didn't care to be an interesting person. Not only women should pay attention to grooming and sex appeal.

She continues:

> Masturbation can be a help when your husband is unappealing and outside sex is felt to be immoral. I like to reassure myself that things are still "working."

While masturbating, she makes use of sexual fantasy. "My most recent fantasy was about my husband. He was able to turn me on and be the lover I need."

Another 55-year-old wife in western Massachusetts also described her husband in quite negative terms:

I am extremely frustrated in being married to a man who is a loner. . . . [He] is ultraconservative and I do not like being used. Sex was getting very boring and frustrating, to the point that I'd cry afterward because I was not satisfied or felt loved. Who needs that?

Asked about extramarital affairs, she replies: "Boy, is it tempting! I do not know how I would handle it if such an opportunity arose."

She adds, however: "My husband was the partner in my dream the last time. Sometimes it is a stranger — but rarely."

A 61-year-old Sacramento wife, married for thirty-one years, says that she and her husband have sex about once a week and that she almost always reaches orgasm. Despite this, she rates her enjoyment of sex with her husband as 6. She invariably engages in sexual fantasy during intercourse with her husband, and she says that her fantasies "always are of another couple altogether — never myself or my husband." She explains:

When I was being taught, as a child, how terrible sex is, they forgot to teach [that] it is acceptable after marriage. My fantasies range from teenage couples to prostitutes. Since I never engage in sex as myself, this probably accounts for my lack of interest.

Wish-fulfillment fantasies

Fantasy may be used to create a situation that a respondent finds sexually stimulating but that, as a practical matter, is not within reach in the real world.

A 56-year-old Gulf Coast husband, for example, says his favorite fantasy is "group sex — seeing other people make sex, being seen. This has occurred [in real life] only once, in a partner-swapping session. I like it much; my wife does not." Through fantasies about group sex, he achieves his sexual turn-on without putting pressure on his wife to participate in an activity she dislikes.

A 53-year-old Texas wife uses sexual fantasies in much the same way — to achieve what is beyond reach in real life. She and her husband "don't have sex with each other or anyone else.... This, of course, is frustrating.... I think I would have an extramarital affair if I had the opportunity — that is, if I were in love. But I might not, because I have two [teenagers at] home that I care about very much."

Lacking opportunities for an extramarital affair, she fantasizes one instead:

> I imagine I am a youngster being introduced to sex by an experienced man, or I am seduced by the count in *Rigoletto*, or the man I was in love with in my 20's makes love to me. (He didn't in real life.)

A 55-year-old wife in Richmond, Virginia, provides us with her wish-fulfillment fantasy and her own interpretation of it. She begins by explaining that her husband is having an affair with a woman who was *her* close friend for many years. This "is difficult for me to bear," she writes — but she sees nothing she can do about it. "Part of my belief system is that no person owns the other; so I feel I cannot demand [that] the relationship be ended."
She continues:

> My sexual fantasies have changed during the years. Now they always have a scene in which I am in a position of power over many men and women who are all there for the sole purpose of giving me pleasure. The scene is always Oriental and rather opulent, abounding in luxuries. I am a maharani or empress and all-powerful. (I have wondered if this fantasy is the result of a lifetime experience of being submissive to the will of men and being dependent financially and socially on them, living in a male-oriented society.)

One Maine wife who engages in wish-fulfillment fantasies tells us at some length just why she does. She is 64 years old and has been married for forty-one years. "The sexual side of [my] marriage was never very good," she writes, because of her husband's "partial impotence." They discontinued sex altogether "ten or fifteen" years ago. In other respects, however, her marriage is very satisfying. Asked if she masturbates, she replies:

Why not? I'd rather masturbate than jeopardize a good marriage by emotional involvement with someone other than my husband, and one's sexual needs don't necessarily disappear with age.

She uses sexual fantasies when she masturbates, and almost always reaches orgasm. She describes one fantasy in some detail:

I see myself (younger than I am) with a man who is strong and sure and tender. I see us dancing, driving, parking on the cliff to watch and hear the sea crashing on the rocks—always aware of each other, always reaching toward the ultimate, wondrous culmination, yet prolonging the anticipation. I feel his hands gently removing my dress, my underclothes, lingering on my body, caressing me as I caress him. I feel his body against mine and desire rises, rises, filling me, filling me, and I want that moment to last forever and ever. And I dream that this time, THIS time, there will be that perfect, earth-shaking realization of sexual love. An overwhelming joy in each other, then quiet and peace and sleep in each other's arms.

An 82-year-old widow writes:

Fantasy: While masturbating, it's fun to pretend that the relationship is with a loved one who lives far away. Murmuring sweet nothings, encouraging him to hold out a bit longer — and imagining I'm holding him close at the climax.

A 52-year-old husband writes from the Southwest:

I need an attractive female to stimulate (arouse) me. Physically, I am still as fit as I was thirty years ago, while my wife has deteriorated into a potbellied slob. Seeing her in clothes turns me off — let alone seeing her in the nude.

In this situation, he fantasizes a woman who is

young . . . , long hair, pleasant voice, obvious and firm breasts (not necessarily large), visible *linea alba* with firm belly and "Oriental" navel, shapely legs (no or minor hollow thighs), small feet. This dream creature indicates friendliness so there is no risk of rejection. We engage in tentative touching, leading to caresses, and slowly proceed to the ultimate union. Everything proceeds slowly — none of this "slam, bang, thank you ma'am" stuff. In fact, the dream allows time-reversal, so that especially pleasant scenes can be repeated several times before going on. . . .
A less frequent dream: I am "captured" by a bikini-clad maiden who proceeds to manipulate my body until I reach an agonizing ecstasy — but not in a painful or vicious manner.

In chapter 3, we recounted the life story of a 72-year-old never-married man who confesses, in the privacy of our Comment Pages, that he is still a virgin. His wish-fulfillment fantasy, however, is sophisticated: "A beautiful young woman giving me oral, manual, and regular sex; me French-kissing her, sucking her nipples, fondling her breasts and caressing her entire body."
A 54-year-old Ohio wife writes:

I sometimes fantasize about being made love to (as opposed to the all-purpose "having sex with") by a much younger man who is very beautiful but whom I will not name, even to you, dear CU, because I am old-fashioned.

A 60-year-old Arkansas widow writes that her "fantasies always involve strangers — sometimes women, older boys, and animals (dogs). I am always seduced, never the seducer; partner is very avid and passionate and so arouses me."

A 60-year-old Oklahoma widower says his fantasies concern "the person met at a party, the hitchhiker picked up on a long trip, the teenager wanting an adult to take her to an R-rated movie. . . . Such things don't happen to me except in fantasies. . . . Yet the excitement about it all has enough power to suggest yes, I'd like to try it — and know I never will!"

Heterosexual versus homosexual fantasies

As might be expected, women and men who consider themselves heterosexual tend to report heterosexual fantasies while those who consider themselves homosexual tend to report homosexual fantasies. There are exceptions, however. A 50-year-old Indiana wife who has never had a homosexual experience recalls: "I used to fantasize having relations with a woman because I thought a woman could better stimulate another woman — but since [then] I've lost all [lesbian] urges." Currently her fantasies involve "young men (25 or 26) having relations with me or my 'blowing' them."

A 53-year-old Toronto husband who occasionally has sex with men writes: "Sometimes I masturbate while having homosexual fantasies, sometimes with heterosexual fantasies — often with no fantasies."

A 53-year-old divorced man who considers himself a homosexual writes: "Fantasy: a young man and I are 69'ing — nude, out in the sun on a grassy knoll in a park near here; the day is very hot."

A 66-year-old husband writes: "My fantasy is the most common one: watching two girls making love."

"Ego-alien" fantasies

Women especially (but some men, too) report that they enjoy fantasizing experiences that would fill them with dread or disgust in real life. Such fantasies have been called "ego-alien"; they involve actions or situations quite foreign and unacceptable to the person who has them — but acceptable under the very special circumstances of sexual fantasy. An example is provided by a 66-year-old widow who recalls that her husband sometimes sought sex with her at inopportune moments.

> When it was hard to get in the mood on demand, I would fantasize that I was in a sex orgy as in times B.C., when girls were used publicly for entertainment or in pagan ceremonials. In real life, I would abhor seeing this or being involved. It's hard to understand.

A 60-year-old husband in northern California, married for ten years to a woman sixteen years younger, reports that his recurring sexual fantasy is "watching my wife suck several men's penises while I'm having intercourse with her." He promptly adds, however, that in real life, "I would NEVER go along with this." He has had no group-sex experience of any kind.

Readers may recall the 60-year-old adulterous husband who says, paradoxically, "I am against affairs during marriage, for they are sure to destroy the marriage" — but who adds: "My chief sexual fantasy is watching my wife have sex with another man, or her having sex with myself and another man simultaneously."

A 59-year-old wife in Colorado says that her fantasies are "generally masochistic [such as] kidnapping by white slavers who wish an older woman to have available for constant calls from clients." On other occasions, she fantasizes "sex with kings or current stars."

A 70-year-old San Diego widow starts to describe an ego-alien fantasy — and then stops. "I find I can't do this; sorry," she writes. "My waking (masturbation) fantasies tend to be sadomasochistic." She adds, however: "My *dreams* of sex are conventional and happy, involving my husband (now dead) in satisfying intercourse."

A 59-year-old wife who has been faithful to her husband throughout the thirty-three years of their marriage, and who rates both the happiness of her marriage and her enjoyment of sex with him as 2, describes an ego-alien fantasy: "having sex with the mailman or any other service man who is attractive — cheating on my husband."

A 54-year-old wife reports that her fantasy is "rape" and a 53-year-old wife reports similarly that her fantasy is "being raped." Neither provides any details. A 66-year-old wife writes:

> I sometimes have sexual fantasies when masturbating — but not while having sex with my husband. While having sex with my husband, it is *us*. Fantasies during masturbation: sometimes being raped, sometimes sex with a very virile black man.

Other studies of women's sexual fantasies have found rape fantasies to be rather common. This does not mean, of course, that women who fantasize rape would in fact enjoy being raped. On the contrary, rape can be regarded as the ultimate ego-alien fantasy — an intolerable outrage in real life, acceptable only under the special circumstances of private fantasy.

A woman sex therapist who served as a consultant to this study comments:

> Very few women fantasize about anything resembling a real rape. The fantasy rape is more like Robert Redford not taking no for an answer. The fantasy rape seldom involves an unattractive man, real threats of harm or death, or genuine physical pain.

One explanation sometimes given for fantasies of rape or bondage is that they eliminate *guilt* feelings. If a person is tied up and helpless or physically overpowered in the fantasy, there is no moral responsibility for what follows and it can therefore be enjoyed without guilt.

Fetishistic and transvestite fantasies

Back in the nineteenth century, authorities on human sexuality such as Krafft-Ebing and Freud described the phenomenon known as *fetishism*, in which sexual arousal is dependent on some small detail that others find wholly nonsexual. An example is the man — most fetishists are men — who cannot be sexually turned on or reach orgasm unless intercourse occurs on a rubber sheet, or unless the man holds in his hand a handkerchief with a lacy border, or unless his partner's hair is dressed in a particular manner. Some fetishists can experience arousal and orgasm by fantasizing the fetish even though it is not physically present.

A 60-year-old Midwestern husband reports that his fetishistic fantasy involves a pair of eyeglasses worn by a woman:

> [My] sexual partner may or may not be my wife. Usually, the [fantasy] begins innocently enough, but then becomes more intimate with each fondling [the] other's sex organs. Frequently it reaches sexual climax for me when female puts on spectacles (eyeglasses) and then we embrace tightly and I have an emission.

In reality, he adds, his wife never wears eyeglasses during sex.

A 62-year-old New England wife, married to a husband nine years younger, writes that she always has sexual fantasies during masturbation, and usually when having sex with her husband. She continues:

> My fantasies usually involve a scene where someone is being spanked. In my own childhood, my most common punishment was being spanked on my bare bottom. Ever since, I can usually arouse myself by reconstructing the whole scene — being sent to my room, being turned over mother's knee, having my pants taken down, and, finally, her hand or a hair brush on my bare botton while I screamed my loudest. This still excites me more than anything else! While masturbating, my best arousal comes from spanking my own bare bottom.

Transvestism, which is akin to fetishism in some respects, involves wearing the clothes of the opposite gender — or fantasizing that experience. A 59-year-old husband writes:

I have some tendency toward transvestism. . . . I don't think much can be done for . . . transvestites — and you may be startled to find out how many there are. I had always thought that my own feelings were unique until . . . others started to surface. They had a lot more courage than I did, to acknowledge their situation.

Since this respondent is still in the transvestite closet, he can experience his transvestism only in fantasy: "My dreams [fantasies?] sometimes take the form of my coming upon a pretty slip or nightgown and wearing it. Or perhaps even more."

Summary

Comparing the fantasies of our over-50 respondents with those of younger respondents described by others, we note only a few differences. Both older and younger people use fantasies for the *enrichment* of their sexual experience. Among our men and women, rehearsal fantasies are conspicuous by their absence, while rerun fantasies are quite common. We believe that sexual fantasy can be especially important for older people who fantasize because of its power to rejuvenate, to surmount rising thresholds of sexual response, and to compensate for those physiological changes due to aging reviewed in chapter 8.

USE OF SEXUALLY EXPLICIT MATERIALS

Just as many older women and men use sexual fantasies to surmount the rising sexual response thresholds they are experiencing, so some use pornography.

An example is the 60-year-old wife of an 80-year-old husband who had spinal surgery at age 72, leaving him "with paralysis and some permanently damaged autonomic nerves." She writes: "Pornography stimulates me to be more responsive to my husband, and we sometimes use it together during lovemaking."

A 56-year-old husband who lives on the Gulf Coast writes similarly:

> [My wife and I] have settled into a pattern where usually my
> wife reads in bed aloud pornographic material, while we
> stimulate each other's sex organs (clitoris, penis). Then I
> either bring her manually to orgasm or, if she feels she will
> not reach one after ten or fifteen minutes, she lets me insert
> my penis.

In both of these examples, and in others, pornography is used
directly to trigger sexual arousal. There is also an *indirect* use, in
which pornography serves as a sort of reservoir from which fantasies can be drawn on a later occasion. A 55-year-old wife, for example, writes that her sexual fantasies are "the same as always:
picturing intercourse between two people I have recently seen on
TV, or read about in a novel, or [seen in] pictures in a sex book."

A 70-year-old Rhode Island widow describes her indirect use
of pornography:

> Most of my sexual fantasies consist of recalling the explicit
> pictures in the current or old girlie magazines. I envision
> over-sexed girls or women and imagine their exploits. Nude
> male pictures do not turn me on.

The above quotation illustrates another point of some interest.
Quite a few women with no lesbian desires or leanings are nevertheless turned on by pictures of nude women. They react to these
pictures, however, quite differently from the usual male reaction.
The male viewer may fantasize that he is holding the woman in
his arms or making love to her. Some women viewers, in contrast,
are likely to identify with the woman in the picture and fantasize
that they *are* that woman. An 83-year-old widow makes this point,
quoted earlier:

> I read *Playboy* and look at pictures for identifying with
> women (I am lusty), and other erotic magazines for fanta-
> sies. . . . I do not like *really* pornographic magazines. The
> women look like pieces of meat.

Some men also "identify with." A 76-year-old widower writes: "When reading *Penthouse* magazine, I sometimes imagine myself one of the characters in the story."

Women and men who are able to create satisfying fantasies without pornography may feel no need for it. A 72-year-old St. Louis wife writes: "I think that people who feel they need porno stuff are pathetic. If they just used their imagination they could think up fantasies better than any porno movie that they have to pay money for!"

She has been engaging in sexual fantasies for more than seventy years:

> Nobody ever taught me to masturbate; I did it in my crib, with fantasies about a big choo-choo train and a red fox running across the road. I would feel my genitals and at first got no orgasm; but when I did, I saw the red fox running across in front of the train. As I got into that train oftener, I saw the red fox oftener.

In marked contrast to such experienced fantasizers is the 66-year-old wife who writes: "I can honestly say that I have *never* had sexual fantasies." Another wife, aged 59, asks in bewilderment, "What *is* a sexual fantasy?"

Many women and men who use pornographic materials appear to fall between these extremes; they can fantasize on their own — but find pornography helpful for fantasy enrichment.

Dr. Helen Singer Kaplan has discussed the usefulness of both sexual fantasies and pornography in the treatment of sexually dysfunctional women patients:

> If the patient has sexual fantasies and daydreams she is encouraged to immerse herself in these images while she stimulates herself. If she is bereft of erotic fantasies, she is advised to purchase erotic literature and read it as a *probe*, *i.e.*, to see what sort of scene or situation or picture or fantasy will stimulate her.*

---

*Kaplan, *The Illustrated Manual of Sex Therapy* (New York: Quadrangle/The New York Times Book Co., 1975), p. 78.

We suspect that some of our respondents draw on pornography for their subsequent fantasies without realizing it. Consider, for example, the 66-year-old widow, quoted earlier, who wrote that she would "fantasize I was in a sex orgy as in times B.C., when girls were used publicly for entertainment or in pagan ceremonials."

A possible explanation of this fantasy may come to mind among readers who remember the risqué Hollywood films of the early 1920s — before the Hays Office clamped down a nationwide film censorship. In those days, leading producers (Cecil B. De Mille among them) turned out a whole series of highly popular films featuring "sex orgies in times B.C." when thinly clad young women were "used publicly for entertainment or in pagan ceremonials." This respondent was a child when those films were being shown. Perhaps she has forgotten she saw them — but she seems not to have forgotten their content.

A women sex therapist who served as a consultant for this study comments: "De Mille may have provided the scenario — but the fantasy persists in younger women, too; it's really a mild rape or masochistic fantasy. De Mille's movies and others of that ilk may have been popular because they brought to life what was already a secret fantasy to many women!"

Another fantasy that may have been drawn from a prior exposure to pornography is reported by a 66-year-old wife in Nebraska. While having intercourse with her husband, she tells us, she fantasizes "me dancing in filmy clothing, in a darkened arena where the audience is made up of nude young men who are desirous of me."

We asked our respondents about "reading sexually explicit material" and "viewing 'hard core' pornographic films or photos." Have they tried it since age 50? If so, did they like it? If they have not tried it, would they like to? More than 3,000 respondents answered these questions. Their answers make it clear that there is a substantial interest in pornography among our women and men. Here are the data for use of sexual explicit material since age 50:

Reading sexually explicit material	*Women*	*Men*
Among all our women and men, how many have tried it?	(N=1,844) 37%	(N=2,402) 56%
Of those who have tried it, how many liked it?	(N=685) 81%	(N=1,348) 91%
Of those who have not tried it, how many would like to try?	(N=538) 9%	(N=554) 12%

Viewing hard-core pornographic films or photos

Among all our women and men, how many have tried it?	(N=1,844) 18%	(N=2,402) 42%
Of those who have tried it, how many liked it?	(N=330) 58%	(N=1,017) 89%
Of those who have not tried it, how many would like to try?	(N=878) 10%	(N=844) 21%

While more men than women use pornography and enjoy it, this does not necessarily mean that men are more sexually aroused by pornography than are women. Quite a few women who don't enjoy pornography are sexually aroused by the experience. A 54-year-old husband in the Southwest reports that this is the case with his wife:

> Interestingly, my wife abhors pornographic material in any form but will submit to viewing various things in *Playboy*, for example — and watching lurid movies. Though she claims not to like the movies, she is nevertheless "turned on" — sometimes extensively — by seeing them. The special ingredient for her is the suggestion of a story line, good-looking younger people, and watching men who have larger-than-average penis size.

This respondent's wife confirms that she has read sexually explicit material and viewed hard-core pornographic films or pictures; and she confirms that she does not like them.

One reason fewer women than men like pornography, of course, is that most pornography is so male-oriented as to be boring or disgusting to many women. The 83-year-old widow who says she enjoys *Playboy* adds: "I went to only one pornographic film but found it so degrading to women I never wanted to go to another."

Some men feel that way, too. Thus a 56-year-old Gulf Coast husband writes:

> I think that . . . in the last twenty years or so . . . the level of
> sexually stimulating material has gone from bad to better
> and, lately, to very poor. . . . Vulgar pornography is of no use
> to adults. . . . There is a great need for "good" pornography
> that is stimulating to both sexes.

SEEKING (AND FINDING) NEW PARTNERS

King Louis XIV of France was reputed to use aphrodisiacs and to enjoy a new partner each night. When he consulted his physician, complaining of a decline in sexual vigor, his physician is said to have instructed him to stop taking aphrodisiacs. Later, the king repeated his complaint, saying that he had noticed no improvement since discontinuing aphrodisiacs. The physician is alleged to have replied: "Sire, you have not discontinued. Surely you know that a fresh woman each night is the most potent of aphrodisiacs."

Quite a few of our respondents — women and men alike — know, or believe, that a new partner can be an effective method for heightening sexual arousal. They have sought new partners in a variety of contexts, discussed in earlier chapters:

- Some wives and husbands have turned to adultery.
- Some have divorced their spouses and remarried.
- Some have divorced their spouses and launched nonmarital sexual relationships with new partners.
- Some widows, widowers, and never-married women and men have launched new sexual relationships.

• Some respondents have found new partners through group-sex and swinging experiences.

• Some have found new partners in homosexual relationships.

• Finally, some of our married and unmarried men make use of prostitutes.

USE OF PROSTITUTES

For millennia, many men who want sex with a minimum of commitment have turned to sex for a fee. This practice is much less popular today, however, than in Victorian times. Then, despite the well-known ravages of the sexually transmitted diseases, prostitution was tolerated — in part because it was deemed less dangerous to the (male) body and soul than masturbation.

In 1918, Congress at the request of General John J. Pershing passed a law authorizing the military to declare any town or city harboring prostitutes "off limits" for military personnel. This meant that if a community failed to suppress its "red-light district," the entire community risked losing the patronage of free-spending "doughboys." Moreover, the new military regulations were not enforced by local "vice squads," so often corrupt, but by the Army's military police and the Navy's shore patrols. Only our oldest men — those over 75 or so — can remember the pre-1919 "red-light districts."

Kinsey makes it clear that this and other efforts to eradicate prostitution failed. The same proportion of men continued to have one or more encounters with prostitutes after the curb as before. *But the number of such contacts per man fell drastically.* Prostitution became a much less important part of male sexual behavior after 1918. "Moreover," Kinsey wrote in 1948:

prostitution does not now occupy the thinking of males as it did in past generations. Males of the older generation visited houses of prostitution, not only in search of intercourse, but on sight-seeing trips and in social groups as well. They were more often involved in the non-sexual activities that occurred in the established houses, such as drinking, gambling, etc.

Kinsey also clearly explains what men did after 1918 instead of resorting to prostitutes as frequently as their predecessors had. "The drives against prostitution," he found, "have succeeded in diverting a third to a half of the intercourse males used to have with prostitutes to pre-marital activities with other girls."* In short, the closing of the red-light districts after 1918 was one factor in increasing premarital intercourse among "respectable" women — thus giving rise to the "sexual laxity" of the "flappers" in the speakeasy days — the "Roaring Twenties."

Kinsey found that about 7 percent of American males in his sample had one or more experiences with prostitutes by the age of 15, 49 percent by age 21, and 69 percent by age 45. He also found that among married men having extramarital sex at age 55, 22 percent of that sex was with prostitutes.

Despite the far greater *visibility* of prostitution in many American cities today than at any time since 1918, our data indicate that prostitution now plays an exceedingly small role in the lives of our male respondents.

We asked:

"Have you ever employed the services of a female prostitute?"

While 34 percent of our men report using a female prostitute prior to age 50, only 7 percent have done so since.

Only 60 of our men report even one encounter with a prostitute during the past year:

	Men (*N=2,402*)
One encounter with prostitute	25 men
Two	11
Three to five	10
Six to eight	6
Nine or more	8

---

*Alfred C. Kinsey and others, *Sexual Behavior in the Human Male* (Philadelphia: W.B. Saunders Company, 1949); see especially pages 410–413 and 595–609.

Nor is the use of homosexual prostitutes common. Of our eighty-six men who report any homosexual activities since 50, seventeen report the use of a male prostitute since 50. Of the seventeen, eight report only one encounter and three report two. Four report more than two encounters, and two don't say how many.

A 70-year-old husband comments on the use of female prostitutes: "With so much free sex being offered, what's the point of looking for whores?"

Our 81-year-old Minnesota widower spells this out in greater detail:

> The other day . . . in a laundromat with a number of women present . . . I was "bitching" about having so much laundry — so many dirty clothes. . . . I stated I was going to stop wearing clothes, just go "bare-assed" when in my apartment. Quick was a retort: "What is your apartment number and when are you at home?". . . . Gad, in this day and age I do not know how prostitutes make it. There are so many women today ready, willing, and able; I do not think prostitutes have the field of a half-century or so ago. Oh! I guess in large transient cities they have a place — serve a good purpose! After all, a man (or woman) traveling may feel the urge and necessity and just not have the time (or opportunity) to promote a [noncommercial] sex act."

A 54-year-old husband in Mississippi says of prostitutes: "Don't need them. Good way to wind up in hell."

A 71-year-old husband in northern Virginia expresses a somewhat different view:

> I have never had a desire to use a prostitute. However, I can understand how some men would do so in later years due to disagreeable attitudes and actions by their partners — such as a domineering attitude, jealousy, "sloppiness" in housekeeping or personal appearance, and lack of reciprocal affection.

A 65-year-old husband in suburban New York City writes:

An expert at a trade or profession may not be the best
teacher; but [because of their] years of experience, one
should be able to learn "how to" from them. A prostitute is
an expert in sexual intercourse; and when an older man is
unable to find a suitable sex mate, he should look to an expert to give him the desired satisfaction.

A never-married respondent reports frequent use of a call-girl
service. He explains:

These "prostitutes" are actually very pretty girls in their
twenties as a rule. They are clean, bright, pleasant, not on
narcotics, and provide a pleasant sexual experience which I
do not regret. I obtain them through a "service" and no one
is harmed. I obtain their use occasionally when there is lack
of a regular partner — and for the sake of variety. . . . I have
never had an unpleasant experience with any of these girls.
Further, and this I would emphasize: under the ideal com-
mercial arrangement, I can have satisfying sex and an agreeable partner whenever I want it. It actually saves energy; I do
not have to drink and go through a routine; the purpose is
known and I am quite satisfied with the use of these nice call
girls.

A 52-year-old husband reports a very different reaction:

Several months ago, I hired an "escort service" woman.
When she removed those clothes and I saw those sagging
breasts and wrinkled belly, I was immediately turned off.
She [said she] was only 31 — but apparently well worn.

A 69-year-old husband writes:

I am now having occasional sexual relations with three
young women (unmarried working women). I believe they
are also having occasional relations with other men but I do
not think they can be classed as prostitutes. I do, however,

contribute money to them; I call it "contributing to their welfare."

The oldest respondent to report the use of a prostitute during the past year is an 80-year-old New Jersey widower whose wife died when he was 68. Five years later, he launched a relationship, which still continues, with a woman five years younger. When they are together, they have sex from four to six times a week — but they are together only rarely, for she lives in a foreign country.

He does not masturbate, but he does resort to prostitutes on occasion — twenty times since 50, and twice during the past year. "I see nothing wrong about an older man resorting to the use of a prostitute," he writes. "When I do, it is to relieve me of 'pressure'!"

We did not ask our women respondents whether they have employed the services of a male prostitute. Back in 1978, when our questionnaire was being drafted, there were few reports of male prostitutes serving a female clientele. Since then, a few more accounts have been published* — though there is still no evidence that prostitutes are resorted to by more than a tiny minority of women. A bit more common, perhaps, is the use by women of a "gigolo" or "kept man" — a man financially maintained by a woman on a continuing basis, at least in part for the sexual services he renders. None of our women volunteered information on this subject. We did not ask either our women or our men respondents whether, since age 50, they have accepted payment from others for sexual services, and no information was volunteered on our Comment Pages, with one possible exception — the 50-year-old divorcée who says that her 82-year-old lover is contributing to her support and that she thinks he should contribute more generously.

---

*In 1979, for example, it was reported that Honolulu, Hawaii, "has become noted among vacationing older women for the availability of paid sexual partners." Myrna J. Lewis, ACSW, "Sex and Aging," in *Aging: Research and Perspectives*, Columbia Journalism Monograph No. 3 (September 1979), p. 28.

Several of our women say they sometimes fantasize serving as a prostitute — a fantasy also reported in other studies.

SUMMARY

All or substantially all of our men and women are faced with rising sexual response thresholds and with other physiological changes due to health impairments and aging. Some have accepted these changes as a part of the natural life cycle and have lapsed into sexual inactivity. This chapter, however, has been concerned with the substantial majority of respondents who make use of effective countermeasures.

Some women and men have turned to physiological approaches — manual and oral stimulation of the breasts and genitals, anal stimulation, use of a vibrator, use of a vaginal lubricant, "stuffing" of the limp or only partially erect penis into the vagina, use of various coital positions, engaging in sex in the morning, or just fondling and cuddling. Others have turned to psychological approaches — use of sexually explicit or pornographic materials, use of fantasy, searching for (and perhaps finding) a new partner. Quite a few, of course — including some in their eighties — resort to both physiological and psychological means to maintain and in some cases enhance sexual enjoyment. The broad range of these approaches repeatedly astonished us as we read one questionnaire return after another — 4,246 of them in all.

⇘ 10 ⇙

Love, Sex, and Aging:
A Summary

THE 1,844 WOMEN AND 2,402 MEN AGED 50 OR OVER WHO PARTICI-
pated in this Consumers Union study have provided us with a
panorama of life experiences and of sexual likes, dislikes, satisfactions, frustrations, yearnings, and memories.

In a study of this kind, statistical data may consign respondents to one group or another; this grouping is valuable mainly as
the necessary access to generalizations. Members of such a group
may be alike in one or several respects, but they also invariably
differ in many other respects. From our statistical data, and
equally important, from our respondents' comments and life
stories, a central truth emerges again and again: Contrary to the
stereotype, older people are not alike, nor are they asexual; they
differ widely in many characteristics, and their sexuality is mani-
fest in the high proportion of those who are sexually active, and in
the quality, quantity, variety, and enjoyability of their sexual activities.

What have we learned from our 4,246 respondents?

They are very much the marrying kind: All but three percent
have been married at least once, and close to three-quarters of
them are married now. These 3,140 wives and husbands are over-
whelmingly happy with their marriage: 87 percent are happily
married. Their marriages are remarkably durable: 80 percent of

403

our wives and almost three-quarters of our husbands are married to their first and only spouse. Nearly three-quarters of our wives and two-thirds of our husbands have been married for thirty years or more. Five percent have celebrated their golden wedding anniversary, and some are still as sexually turned on to one another as lovers in a romantic novel.

But other respondents who have remained married through the decades are not happily married, and some report their marriage sexually unrewarding from the very beginning. Still others have secured divorces.

We reviewed fifteen *nonsexual* factors in relation to our happily and unhappily married respondents. We found that the wives and husbands most likely to be happily married after age 50 are those who maintain "excellent" or "very good" communications with their spouse. The relationship of the remaining nonsexual factors with marital happiness varied from small to negligible to none — and not always in accordance with the conventional wisdom. Family income, for example, seems to have only a modest and inconsistent effect on marital happiness. Wives and husbands with high incomes are no more likely to be happily married than those with low incomes. Happy marriages are reported slightly more often by respondents with an "empty nest" — that is, without dependent children at home — than by those who still have children living at home.

Among the interesting byproducts of our review of nonsexual factors, a remarkable finding was revealed concerning attitudes toward retirement, before and after the fact. Most employed respondents, married and unmarried alike, are troubled by the prospect of retirement; but most retired respondents are quite pleased with their retirement.

Our review of ten *sexual* factors associated with marital happiness found that respondents most likely to be happily married after 50 are those who enjoy having sex with their spouse. Among other factors almost as important were satisfaction with frequency of marital sex and comfort in discussing sex with one's spouse. The vast majority of our husbands, both happily and unhappily married, consider the sexual side of their marriage to be important, and this is true for our happily married wives as well. Among our unhappily married wives, however, most consider the sexual side of their marriage to be of little importance. This is the most powerful predictor of marital unhappiness for wives in our study.

While lifelong marital fidelity is the prevailing pattern among our wives and husbands, 8 percent of our wives and 23 percent of our husbands report one or more adulterous relationships or encounters since age 50. We don't know how many others engaged in adultery and then were divorced; our data are for those who stayed married despite adultery. Most of the adultery reported is "cheating" — outside sex without the spouse's knowledge. But some wives and husbands report adultery with the spouse's knowledge, and perhaps with his or her consent; a few engage in "swinging" — adultery as a mutual enterprise engaged in by wife and husband together. Here, too, the panorama is broad.

We have noted that our 925 unmarried respondents live in a society in which after age 50 unmarried women outnumber unmarried men by 2.7 to 1; when we consider the numbers of unattached heterosexual women and men in this age group, the ratio looks close to 5 to 1. This gender imbalance affects the lives of the unmarried in many important ways. More of our unmarried men than women, for example, have found close friends of the opposite gender. More men report ongoing sexual partners of the opposite gender. More men are living with a sexual partner of the opposite gender, and more of them report one or more casual sexual partners during the past year.

Despite the gender imbalance, however, a substantial minority of our unmarried women have also found sexual partners of the opposite gender. Most of the men with whom they are involved are either married to someone else or are much older. A surprising proportion of our women with men partners, moreover, have men much younger than they are. Some unmarried women discuss entering into a sexual relationship with another woman as a solution to the dearth-of-unmarried-men problem; but only a very few have taken that course.

Many unmarried women, like unmarried men and some wives and husbands, remain sexually active through masturbation; and

some unmarried women with sexual partners — like unmarried
men with sexual partners and like some wives and husbands —
engage in masturbation in addition to sex with a partner, as an
added form of sexual enjoyment. Unmarried women and men
whose only form of sexual activity is masturbation are more likely
to report high enjoyment of life than the sexually inactive; but
those who have a sexual partner are even more likely to report
high life enjoyment. A smaller proportion of our unmarried respondents than of our wives and husbands report high enjoyment
of life.

The overwhelming majority of our respondents are primarily
heterosexual. Quite a few, however, report pre-adolescent or adolescent sexual encounters with others of their gender (with little or
no harm reported); and quite a few essentially heterosexual
women and men report one or more homosexual partners or encounters after 50. These respondents seem to view such homosexual contacts as an additional, rather than an alternative, form of
sexual activity.

In this as in prior human sexuality surveys, more men than
women report homosexual experiences; but — and this is an un-
precedented finding — more of our women than men report that
they have been sexually attracted to someone of their gender. We
have suggested some possible reasons why fewer women than
men act upon their feelings of same-gender sexual attraction.

Almost all of our respondents were raised within the con-
straints of what many of them refer to as their Victorian upbringing. We explored our respondents' attitudes toward five Victorian
sexual taboos — masturbation, sex without marriage, sex without
love, pornography, and homosexuality. We found that some respondents still cling firmly to Victorian views on these five topics,
but substantial majorities have abandoned the Victorian position
on most or all of them. In opinions as well as behavior, older people are not all alike.

We have found that impaired health has an adverse impact,
but only a modest one, on sexual activity, sexual frequency, and
sexual enjoyment. Both women and men continue to engage in
sex, and to enjoy sex, despite health barriers, some of which to

others might seem insuperable. Substantial proportions of respondents who have had a heart attack remain sexually active and continue to enjoy sex. The same is true of respondents who are taking anti-hypertensive medication, those with diabetes, and those who have had a hysterectomy, ovariectomy, mastectomy, or prostate surgery.

We have explored a highly controversial topic: estrogen replacement therapy for postmenopausal women. We stress the fact that many postmenopausal women do not need estrogen because their body continues to produce enough of it. We consider four reasons why postmenopausal women who need estrogen may wish to take it: to prevent or minimize the hot flash syndrome; adverse vaginal changes, including vaginal dryness and vaginal atrophy; urinary tract problems; and to forestall bone changes and possible bone fractures due to osteoporosis. We discuss the risks — including the risk of endometrial cancer — associated with estrogen replacement therapy, and describe possible ways in which postmenopausal women taking estrogen can minimize those risks.

We have traced the impact of aging on sexuality among our women and men in their fifties, sixties, and thereafter. Decade by decade, respondents report declines in many aspects of sexual function: in sexual desire, ease of sexual arousal, and enjoyment of sex; in the proportions of respondents having sex with a partner, in the frequency of sex with a partner, and in the frequency of orgasm during sex with a partner; in the proportions of respondents who masturbate, in the frequency of their masturbation and frequency of orgasm during masturbation; and in other respects. We have presented our reasons for believing that these changes are much more frequently due to aging *per se* than to declining health or other factors.

We have also noted, however, that despite these progressive declines, large proportions of our respondents still report being sexually active and enjoying a wide variety of sexual activities. Indeed, this is true for a number of women and men in their eighties, including some who report continued sex with a partner and orgasm during sex with a partner.

Finally, we have described how the majority of our women and men have managed to surmount the rising barriers to sexual fulfillment posed by advancing age and by health impairments, and to maintain and in some cases enhance sexual enjoyment in their later years. The physiological and psychological methods for surmounting these barriers employed by our respondents are numerous and varied; describing and explaining them may well be the greatest single contribution our respondents have made to the well-being of other older women and men, and to the concerns of younger women and men as they approach their older years.

Both our statistical data and the written comments of our respondents provide an impressive testimonial to the capacity to enjoy life, often under the most adverse circumstances. We salute the women and men aged 50 to 93 who invested so much of their time and psychic energy in telling us how things are with them, and we again thank them for their contributions. We feel very sure that readers of this report will thank them with equal fervor.

Appendix
The Questionnaire

CONSUMER REPORTS BOOKS / CONSUMERS UNION
Mount Vernon, New York 10550

STUDY on LOVE, SEX, and AGING

Dear Friend,

We thank you for helping us with our study of love, intimate relationships, and human sexuality after the age of 50. Attached is a copy of the questionnaire as announced in the November 1977 issue (page 621) of *Consumer Reports* magazine. Before you fill out the questionnaire, we would like you to know what this study covers and why we think it is important.

Numerous studies, by government agencies and others, have been conducted among older people and those approaching the later years. Traditionally, such studies have focused on health, income, housing, transportation, and similar issues. This Consumers Union study, in contrast, seeks to approach each respondent as an individual whose needs and wants go far beyond basic material things to include friendship and companionship, intimate relationships, love, and sexual enjoyment and fulfillment.

In these respects, older people may well harbor as many differences as they do similarities. For some, love may have been a youthful one-time experience; others may continue to fall in love or to be in love through their 60s, 70s, and beyond. For some, sex may be merely something they enjoyed—or failed to enjoy—years ago; for others, sex may remain an important aspect of their lives. Our questionnaires seek to bring to light these and countless other differences and similarities to be found among the personal needs, wants, and interests of people in their middle and later years.

Two questionnaires have been prepared—one for women, the other for men. The two questionnaires are essentially alike, varying only in some details. Each questionnaire covers six topics:

A. Background information (age, education, employment status, etc.)
B. Your health (including health problems, medications)
C. Your opinions (about a variety of issues)
D. Friendship (non-sexual relationships)
E. Love (special relationships: falling in love, being in love)
F. Sexuality (covering a wide range of intimate feelings and experiences)

At the end of each questionnaire, you will find "Comment Pages" on which you may comment more fully about any of the topics in the questionnaire. (If you need more space, please use additional pages.) Be sure to number each of your comments with the number of the question to which the comment refers. Your using a pen (or typewriter) would be appreciated.

Some respondents will no doubt find some of the questions irrelevant or objectionable. Others may set a high value on precisely the same questions. In designing the questionnaires, we have sought to include questions likely to prove important for a wide range of respondents. By putting together the responses of many different people, we expect to get both a broad and a detailed view of how older women and men really feel about love, sex, and aging.

Because of the intimate nature of some of the questions, we ask that you fill out this questionnaire in privacy. Please do not show your responses to others. This is an anonymous survey; when your questionnaire is completed, do not sign your name to it. Because your responses cannot be identified with you in any way, you may feel free to answer even the most sensitive of questions with complete assurance that your confidences will be respected.

This letter is perforated so that you may remove it. Please mail us the completed questionnaire—without the letter—in the enclosed postage-paid envelope.

Again, our thanks for your interest and help. We hope that you will return the completed questionnaire very soon. We also hope that filling it out may prove beneficial to you in your current and future thinking about love, sex, and aging.

Sincerely,

Edward M. Brecher

Edward M. Brecher
and the
Editors of Consumer Reports Books

P.S. The results of this survey plus additional research are scheduled to be included in a Consumer Reports Book. Publication will be announced in the pages of *Consumer Reports* magazine.

CONSUMER REPORTS BOOKS / CONSUMERS UNION

Mount Vernon, New York 10550

STUDY on LOVE, SEX, and AGING

This questionnaire is for **WOMEN**

A. BACKGROUND INFORMATION

A1. How old were you on your last birthday? _____

A2. Do you live in a
Private house .... ☐
Apartment, co-op, or condominium .... ☐
Nursing home .... ☐
Home for the aging, retirement hotel......... ☐
Mobile home .... ☐
Other _____

A3. Do you live in a retirement community?
Yes .... ☐
No .... ☐

A4. How long have you been living in your present neighborhood?
Number of years _____

A5. What is the highest level of education you completed?
Grade school or less .... ☐
Some high school .... ☐
Completed high school .... ☐
Some college .... ☐
Completed 4-year college .... ☐
Some graduate school .... ☐
Received graduate degree .... ☐

A6. Who lives in your household with you? (Check *all* that apply)
Live alone .... ☐
Spouse or partner .... ☐
Adult children .... ☐
Dependent children .... ☐
Parent(s) or spouse's parent(s) .... ☐
Friend(s) .... ☐
Other _____

A7a. Since you were 50, have you ever been employed?
Yes .... ☐
No .... ☐

A7b. Current employment status
Employed full-time .... ☐
Employed part-time .... ☐
Not employed but seeking work .... ☐
Not employed and not seeking work .... ☐

A8a. Are you now or have you ever been retired?
Yes .... ☐
No .... ☐
(If NO, skip to Question A10.)

A8b. If YES, was retirement
Mandatory .... ☐
Voluntary .... ☐

A9. How do you feel about retirement?
Positive feelings .... ☐
Mixed feelings .... ☐
Negative feelings .... ☐

A10. If you've never retired, how do you feel about the prospect of retirement?
Positive feelings .... ☐
Mixed feelings .... ☐
Negative feelings .... ☐
Question does not apply to me................ ☐

A11. Please discuss your feelings about retirement in greater detail on the "Comment Pages" at the end of the questionnaire.

A12. What was your personal income (including spouse's, if any) for the past year?
Under $5,000 .... ☐
$5,000 to $9,999 .... ☐
$10,000 to $14,999 .... ☐
$15,000 to $19,999 .... ☐
$20,000 to $24,999 .... ☐
$25,000 to $34,999 .... ☐
$35,000 to $49,999 .... ☐
$50,000 and over .... ☐

A13. How many people live on this income? _____

A14. Does anyone else (besides spouse, if any) share or pay all of your household expenses?
Yes, all expenses .... ☐
Yes, some expenses .... ☐
No .... ☐

A15. Would you describe yourself as
Very religious .... ☐
Moderately religious .... ☐
Slightly religious .... ☐
Not at all religious .... ☐

A16. Please fill in your Zip Code _____

Please feel free to answer any of our questions in greater detail—especially questions with encircled numbers (such as A11, above)—on the **"Comment Pages"** at the end of the questionnaire.

B. YOUR HEALTH

B1. How would you rate your overall health at the present time?
- Excellent ☐
- Very good ☐
- Good ☐
- Fair ☐
- Poor ☐

B2. Compared with others your age, would you say your health is
- Better than average ☐
- About average ☐
- Worse than average ☐

B3. Do you have hypertension (high blood pressure)?
- Yes ☐
- No ☐

B4. Have you ever had a heart attack?
- Yes ☐
- No ☐

B5. Do you have diabetes?
- Yes ☐
- No ☐

B6. Do you regularly take any of the following prescribed medications? (Check *all* that apply)
- Anti-hypertension drug ☐
- Anti-coagulant ☐
- Insulin ☐
- Tranquilizer or sedative ☐
- Stimulant or anti-depressant ☐
- Other _____

B7. Have you had a mastectomy (removal of breast)?
- Yes ☐
- No ☐

B8. Have you had a hysterectomy (removal of uterus)?
- Yes ☐
- No ☐

B9. Have both your ovaries been removed?
- Yes ☐
- No ☐

B10. At what age did you have your last menstrual period? _____
- Check here if still menstruating ☐

B11. Since then have you experienced any of the following? (Check all that apply)
- Vaginal bleeding ☐
- Vaginal dryness ☐
- Loss of vaginal muscle tone ☐
- Marked changes in clitoris ☐
- Marked changes in breasts ☐
- Marked increase in interest in sex ☐
- Marked decrease in interest in sex ☐
- Other _____

B12. Overall how would you characterize your experience with menopause?
- Experienced little or no difficulty ☐
- Experienced some difficulty ☐
- Experienced great difficulty ☐

B13. If menopause affected your sexual interest, responsiveness or activities in particular ways, please describe in the "Comment Pages" at the end of the questionnaire.

B14a. Have you ever taken estrogen (female hormone) for menopausal or post-menopausal symptoms?
- Yes ☐
- No ☐
- (If NO, skip to Question B19)

B14b. If YES, at what age did you start? _____

B15a. Did you ever stop taking estrogen?
- Yes ☐
- No ☐
- (If NO, skip to Question B18)

B15b. If yes, why did you stop? _____

B16a. Did you resume taking estrogen?
- Yes ☐
- No ☐
- (If NO, skip to Question B18)

B16b. If yes, why did you resume? _____

B17. Are you currently taking estrogen?
- Yes ☐
- No ☐

B18. In what form was your most recent prescription for estrogen?
- Cream ☐
- Injection ☐
- Pill ☐
- Suppository ☐

B19. Please discuss any views you may have about post-menopausal use of estrogen on the "Comment Pages" the end of the questionnaire.

C.   YOUR OPINIONS

C1. Please indicate your level of agreement with each of the statements listed below by circling the number 1, 2, 3, 4, or 5 next to each statement.

	Strongly agree	Moderately agree	Neutral	Moderately disagree	Strongly disagree
Older people shouldn't try to appear younger than they are	1	2	3	4	5
I think it's a mistake for an older man to marry a much younger woman	1	2	3	4	5
It's okay for older couples who are not married to have sexual relations	1	2	3	4	5
Older people aren't portrayed fairly on television	1	2	3	4	5
Most people find me a likable person	1	2	3	4	5
Laws against homosexual and lesbian acts should be enforced	1	2	3	4	5
There should be courses in sex education for older people	1	2	3	4	5
In general, children don't like their widowed mother to become involved with a man	1	2	3	4	5
Young people tend to be uncomfortable with older people	1	2	3	4	5
Boys and girls need to be reassured that there's nothing wrong with masturbation	1	2	3	4	5
I think I'm as attractive as most people my age	1	2	3	4	5
In stores or restaurants older people get poorer service	1	2	3	4	5
Society thinks of older people as non-sexual	1	2	3	4	5
I think it's a mistake for an older woman to marry a much younger man	1	2	3	4	5
Our society places too much emphasis on sex	1	2	3	4	5
Older people should worry less about "what people might think"	1	2	3	4	5
Homosexual and lesbian relations between older people are nobody else's business	1	2	3	4	5
Masturbation is not proper for older people	1	2	3	4	5
There should be more sex education in public school	1	2	3	4	5
I feel much less attractive than when I was younger	1	2	3	4	5
Communities should have the right to ban all pornographic materials	1	2	3	4	5
Sex without love is better than no sex at all	1	2	3	4	5

C2. Please discuss any of the above statements which particularly interest you on the "Comment Pages" at the end of the questionnaire.

C3. Please characterize your overall enjoyment of life at the present time. Your feelings may match the phrase at the left-hand side, or the phrase at the right-hand side, or they may fall somewhere in between. Check the box that best expresses your feelings.

Life is very enjoyable for me ☐ 89-1 ☐ -2 ☐ -3 ☐ -4 ☐ -5 ☐ -6 ☐ -7 Life is not at all enjoyable for me

C4. Compared with when you were around 40, how would you characterize your present enjoyment of life?
- Much better now .... ☐
- Somewhat better now .... ☐
- About the same .... ☐
- Somewhat worse now .... ☐
- Much worse now .... ☐

D.   FRIENDSHIP

We would like you to think about the people with whom you feel especially close, to whom you can confide your innermost feelings but with whom you do *not* have a sexual relationship.

D1. Do you have any such close friends?
- Yes .... ☐
- No .... ☐
- (If NO, skip to Question D4)

D2. Are these close friends
- All female .... ☐
- All male .... ☐
- Some female and some male .... ☐

D3. Are any of these close friends

	Yes	No
Older than you by 10 years or more	☐	☐
Younger than you by 10 years or more	☐	☐

D4. Compared with when you were around 40, how many friends do you have?
- More now .... ☐
- About the same .... ☐
- Fewer now .... ☐

D5. **Would you like more opportunities to meet**

	Yes	No
A woman who might become a close friend	☐	☐
A man who might become a close friend	☐	☐

D6. **Compared with when you were around 40, how easy is it these days to make new friends?**
- Easier now ☐
- About the same ☐
- Easier then ☐

D7. **Which, if any, of the following now interfere with your making new friends?** (Check all that apply)
- Lack of privacy ☐
- Inadequate transportation ☐
- Health ☐
- Not enough social activities ☐
- Not enough money ☐
- Not enough time ☐
- Shyness ☐
- Other _____

D8. **How often do you find yourself feeling lonely?**
- Almost always ☐
- Often ☐
- Sometimes ☐
- Hardly ever ☐

D9. Please discuss, on the "Comment Pages" at the end of the questionnaire, any other aspects of friendship, close or otherwise, during the later years, which you consider important.

E. LOVE

E1a. **Sometimes love begins gradually and grows slowly, but sometimes it begins with a sudden and very vivid "falling-in-love" experience. Have you had such a falling-in-love experience since the age of 50?**
- Yes ☐
- No ☐

E1b. **If YES, at what age or ages?** _____

E2a. **Now we would like to ask about the continuing state of being in love rather than the initial falling-in-love experience. Since the age of 50, have you ever been in love?**
- Yes ☐
- No ☐

E2b. **If YES, are you currently in love with someone?**
- Yes, with my spouse ☐
- Yes, with someone else ☐
- No ☐
(If YES, skip to Question E5)

E3. **If NO, would you like to be in love?**
- Yes ☐
- No ☐

E4. **Would you like to have a sudden and very vivid "falling-in-love" experience?**
- Yes ☐
- No ☐

E5. **Do you feel love is experienced differently in the later years?**
- Yes ☐
- No ☐

E6. Please describe, on the "Comment Pages" at the end of the questionnaire, your feelings about love in the later years and about how it may differ from love in the earlier years.

F. SEXUALITY

F1a. **Have you ever been married?**
- Yes ☐
- No ☐

F1b. **If YES, how many times? (Include current marriage, if any)**
Number of times _____

F2. **What is your present marital status?**
- Married ☐
  (If married, skip to Question F9)
- Single ☐
- Widowed ☐
- Divorced or separated ☐

F3. **Do you have ongoing sexual relationships with someone to whom you are not married?**
- Yes ☐
- No ☐
  (If NO, skip to Question F6)

F4. **Are you currently living with that person?**
- Yes ☐
- No ☐

F5. **Is that person**
- Male ☐
  (If male, skip to Question F8)
- Female ☐
  (If female, skip to Question F9)

F6. **If you do not have an ongoing sexual relationship, are you living with someone with whom you once had a sexual relationship?**
- Yes, with a male ☐
  (If YES, skip to Question F9)
- Yes, with a female ☐
  (If YES, skip to Question F9)
- No ☐

F7a. **If NO, have you had any casual sexual partners in the past year?**
- Yes ☐
- No ☐
  (If NO, skip to Question F36)

F7b. **With how many persons in all did you have sex during the past year?**
Number of persons _____
(Skip to Question F36)

F8. **If you are having an ongoing sexual relationship with a male to whom you are not married, what are the reasons for not getting married?** (Check all that apply)

Because we haven't gotten around to it yet but plan to . . . . ☐
Because we prefer things the way they are . . . . ☐
Because we don't want to lose economic benefits (social security, alimony, etc.) . . . . ☐
Because my partner doesn't want to be responsible for my support or medical expenses . . . . ☐

Because I don't want to be responsible for my partner's support or medical expenses . . . . ☐
Neither of us wants to give up a separate home . . . . ☐
Because my partner is married to someone else . . . . ☐
Because my partner wants to get married but I don't . . . . ☐

I want to get married but my partner doesn't . . . . ☐
Because my children or my partner's children object . . . . ☐
Other reasons _____

F9. **How old is your husband or partner?** _____

F10. **How many years has the marriage or relationship lasted?**

Number of years _____

F11. **How would you rate your husband's/partner's overall health at the present time?**

Excellent . . . . ☐
Very good . . . . ☐
Good . . . . ☐
Fair . . . . ☐
Poor . . . . ☐

F12. **Check the box that best represents how happy your marriage or relationship is.**

Very happy ☐ ☐ ☐ ☐ ☐ ☐ ☐ -7 Very unhappy

F13. **Check which, if any, of the following are presently problems in your relationship with your husband/partner.**

Financial problems . . . . ☐
Job problems . . . . ☐
Where you live . . . . ☐
Religion . . . . ☐
Conflicts with children . . . . ☐
How to spend leisure time . . . . ☐
Health . . . . ☐
Sex . . . . ☐
Problems with husband's/partner's family . . . . . . ☐
Jealousy . . . . ☐
Other _____

F14. **In general, how would you characterize communications between you and your husband/partner?**

Excellent . . . . ☐
Very good . . . . ☐
Good . . . . ☐
Fair . . . . ☐
Poor . . . . ☐

F15. **How important is the sexual side of your relationship to you and to your husband/partner?**

	Self	Husband/Partner
Very important	☐ 43-1	☐
Moderately important	☐ -2	☐
Of little importance	☐ -3	☐
Don't know	☐ -4	☐

F16. **How comfortable are you discussing sexual matters with your husband/partner?**

Very comfortable . . . . ☐
Comfortable . . . . ☐
Uncomfortable . . . . ☐
Very uncomfortable . . . . ☐

F17. **Do you currently engage in sexual intercourse with your husband/partner?**

Yes . . . . ☐
(If YES. skip to Question F20)
No . . . . ☐

F18. **If NO, do you currently engage in other types of sexual activities with your husband/partner?**

Yes . . . . ☐
(If YES. skip to Question F20)
No . . . . ☐

F19a. **If NO, whose decision was it to stop sexual activities?**

My decision . . . . ☐
My husband's/partner's decision . . . . ☐
Mutual decision . . . . ☐
No decision, it just happened . . . . ☐

F19b. **How many years ago did you stop sexual activities with your husband/partner?**
Number of years _____

F19c. **Why did you stop sexual activities with your husband/partner?** (Check *all* that apply)

My illness . . . . ☐
Husband's/partner's illness . . . . ☐
My physical changes . . . . ☐
Husband's/partner's physical changes . . . . ☐
I lost interest . . . . ☐
Husband/partner lost interest . . . . ☐
No privacy . . . . ☐
Other _____

F19d. **Add any other thoughts you have about this subject on the "Comment Pages" at the end of this questionnaire.**

If you are NOT having sex with your husband/partner, skip to Question F31a.

F20. **Who usually initiates the activities leading to sex?**
I always do .... ☐
I usually do .... ☐
My husband/partner and I about equally often ...☐
My husband/partner usually does .... ☐
My husband/partner always does .... ☐

F21. **Are you satisfied with this arrangement?**
Yes .... ☐
No, I would like to initiate sexual activities more
frequently............................... ☐
No, I would like my husband/partner to initiate
sexual activities more frequently .... ☐

F22. **How do you feel about the variety of sexual activities in your relationship?**
I like it as it is .... ☐
I would like more variety .... ☐
I would like less variety .... ☐

F23. **At what time of day do you most commonly have sex with your husband/partner?**
Morning .... ☐
Afternoon .... ☐
Early evening .... ☐
After 10 P.M. .... ☐
Varies .... ☐

F24. **At what time of day is your husband/partner most sexually arousable?**
Morning .... ☐
Afternoon .... ☐
Early evening .... ☐
After 10 P.M. .... ☐
Varies .... ☐
Don't know............................. ☐

F25. **Some older men may experience changes in sexual functioning as they age. Following is a list of some of the changes that may occur. Check each of these changes that has occurred in your partner (if male).   For each change that has occurred, check if you find it a serious problem in your relationship.**

	Check here if this change has occurred	Check here if it is a serious problem
It takes him longer to get an erection	☐	☐
When fully erect his penis is not as stiff as before	☐	☐
Nowadays he more frequently loses his erection during sex	☐	☐
It takes more stimulation of his penis to reach orgasm now	☐	☐
He more often fails to reach orgasm nowadays	☐	☐
His "refractory period"—the time it takes to be able to have another erection after orgasm—is longer now	☐	☐

F26. **About how often do you have sex with your husband/partner?**
Once a day or more .... ☐
4-6 times a week .... ☐
2 or 3 times a week .... ☐
About once a week .... ☐
A few times a month .... ☐
Once a month or less .... ☐

F27. **Are you satisfied with the frequency of sex?**
Yes, it's about right .... ☐
No, it's too frequent .... ☐
No, it's not frequent enough .... ☐

F28. **How often do you and your husband/partner experience orgasm when you engage in sexual activities?**

	Self	Husband/ Partner
Every time	☐	☐
Almost every time —more than 90 percent of the time	☐	☐
Usually—about 75 percent of the time	☐	☐
About half of the time	☐	☐
Seldom—about 25 percent of the time	☐	☐
Never	☐	☐
Don't know	☐	☐

F29. **When you do reach orgasm, how often do you have multiple orgasms?**
Every time .... ☐
Almost every time—more than 90 percent
of the time............................. ☐
Usually—about 75 percent of the time .... ☐
About half of the time .... ☐
Seldom—about 25 percent of the time .... ☐
Never .... ☐
Don't know .... ☐

F30. Check the box that best represents how enjoyable for you sex with your husband/partner is at the present time.

Very enjoyable ☐ ☐ ☐ ☐ ☐ ☐ ☐ Not at all enjoyable

F31a. Since you were 50, have you ever engaged in sexual activities with anyone else outside of your marriage or relationship?
Yes ....☐
No ....☐
(If NO, skip to Question F34)

F31b. If YES, with how many partners?
Number of partners _____

F32. Have any of these activities occurred in the past year?
Yes ....☐
No ....☐

F33. Is your husband/partner aware of this outside sexual activity?
Yes ....☐
No ....☐
Don't know ....☐

F34. Has your husband/partner had any sexual activities outside your relationship since your husband/partner was 50?
Yes ....☐
No ....☐
Don't know ....☐

F35. Please discuss, on the "Comment Pages" at the end of the questionnaire, any further comments you have on sex outside of your marriage or relationship.

F36. About how often do you have sex? (Include all partners if more than one)
Once a day or more ....☐
4 to 6 times a week ....☐
2 or 3 times a week ....☐
About once a week ....☐
A few times a month ....☐
Once a month or less ....☐
Not currently having sex ....☐

F37. Compared with when you were around 40, how frequently do you have sex?
More frequently now ....☐
About the same ....☐
Less frequently now ....☐

F38. How adequate is the vaginal lubrication you produce during sexual arousal?
Too much lubrication ....☐
About the right amount ....☐
Not enough lubrication ....☐

F39. Compared with when you were around 40, is vaginal lubrication
Greater now ....☐
About the same ....☐
Less now ....☐

F40. Compared with when you were about 40, how frequently do you experience orgasm during sexual relations?
More frequently now ....☐
About the same ....☐
Less frequently now ....☐

F41. Compared with when you were about 40, how frequently do you have multiple orgasms when you have sexual relations?
More frequently now ....☐
About the same ....☐
Less frequently now ....☐

F42. How would you describe your present interest in sex?
Strong ....☐
Moderate ....☐
Weak ....☐
Absent ....☐

F43. Compared with when you were around 40, how would you describe your present interest in sex?
Stronger now ....☐
About the same ....☐
Weaker now ....☐

F44. **Check the box that best represents your present enjoyment of sex.**

Very enjoyable   ☐   ☐   ☐   ☐   ☐   ☐   ☐   Not at all enjoyable

F45. **Compared with when you were around 40, how would you describe your present enjoyment of sex?**

More enjoyable now .... ☐
About the same .... ☐
Less enjoyable now .... ☐

F46. **How easily do you become sexually aroused at the present time?**

Very easily .... ☐
Moderately easily .... ☐
With some difficulty .... ☐
With great difficulty .... ☐
Don't become aroused .... ☐

F47. **Compared with when you were around 40, how easily do you become sexually aroused?**

More easily now ....☐
About the same ....☐
Less easily now ....☐

F48. **Some women become uncomfortable or restless if they go without a release of sexual tension for too long a period. For about how long can you comfortably go without a sexual release?** _____

F49. **Please indicate, by checking the appropriate box, which of the following sexual activities you have engaged in since the age of 50, and—whether you have tried them or not—what you think of them.**

	Have you done this since 50?		If you have done this, did you like it?		If you have not done this, would you like to try it?	
	Yes	No	Yes	No	Yes	No
Being undressed by your partner	☐	☐	☐	☐	☐	☐
Undressing your partner	☐	☐	☐	☐	☐	☐
Your partner stimulating your breasts or nipples	☐	☐	☐	☐	☐	☐
Your stimulating your partner's breasts or nipples	☐	☐	☐	☐	☐	☐
Having your partner stimulate your genitals with mouth or tongue	☐	☐	☐	☐	☐	☐
Stimulating your partner's genitals with mouth or tongue	☐	☐	☐	☐	☐	☐
Seeing your partner naked	☐	☐	☐	☐	☐	☐
Being seen by your partner when you are naked	☐	☐	☐	☐	☐	☐
Using a vibrator or massager	☐	☐	☐	☐	☐	☐
Viewing 'hard core' pornographic films or photos	☐	☐	☐	☐	☐	☐
Reading sexually explicit material	☐	☐	☐	☐	☐	☐
Having your anus stimulated during sex	☐	☐	☐	☐	☐	☐
Stimulating your clitoris with your fingers during intercourse	☐	☐	☐	☐	☐	☐
Engaging in rough sex..........................	☐	☐	☐	☐	☐	☐
Having sex with someone you don't know very well ...	☐	☐	☐	☐	☐	☐
Being watched when you have sex	☐	☐	☐	☐	☐	☐
Watching people have sex	☐	☐	☐	☐	☐	☐
Having group sex..............................	☐	☐	☐	☐	☐	☐
Having your partner manually stimulate your genitals .	☐	☐	☐	☐	☐	☐
Manually stimulating your partner's genitals	☐	☐	☐	☐	☐	☐

F50. **Please discuss your feelings about any of the above on the "Comment Pages" at the end of the questionnaire.**

F51. Since you were 50, have you discussed your sexual needs, desires, or problems with any of the following?

	Discussed?		Was it helpful?	
	Yes	No	Yes	No
Physician	☐	☐	☐	☐
Psychiatrist	☐	☐	☐	☐
Psychologist	☐	☐	☐	☐
Marriage counselor	☐	☐	☐	☐
Sex Therapist	☐	☐	☐	☐
Other_____				

F52. In the last year, about how often have you masturbated?
Once a day or more .... ☐
4 to 6 times a week .... ☐
2 or 3 times a week .... ☐
About once a week .... ☐
A few times a month .... ☐
Once a month or less .... ☐
Not currently masturbating .... ☐

F53. If you masturbate, for what reasons or under what circumstances do you do so? (Check all that apply)
It makes me feel independent or self-sufficient .. ☐
Because I enjoy it .... ☐
Absence of acceptable partner .... ☐
Loneliness .... ☐
Sex with partner not fully satisfactory .... ☐
My partner likes to watch .... ☐
It's an additional source of sexual satisfaction ... ☐
It releases tension .... ☐
Other _____

F54. Compared with when you were around 40, how frequently do you masturbate?
More frequently now .... ☐
About the same .... ☐
Less frequently now .... ☐
If you do not currently masturbate, skip to Question F57.

F55. How often do you experience orgasm when you masturbate nowadays?
Every time .... ☐
Almost every time—more than 90 percent
  of the time .... ☐
Usually—about 75 percent of the time .... ☐
About half of the time .... ☐
Seldom—about 25 percent of the time .... ☐
Never .... ☐

F56. Do you have sexual fantasies while you masturbate?
Always .... ☐
Usually .... ☐
Sometimes .... ☐
Never .... ☐

(F57.) Please discuss, on the "Comment Pages" at the end of the questionnaire, your feelings about masturbation during the later years.

F58. Do you have sexual fantasies when engaging in sex with a partner?
Always .... ☐
Usually .... ☐
Sometimes .... ☐
Never .... ☐

F59. How does this compare with when you were 40?
More sexual fantasies now .... ☐
About the same .... ☐
Fewer sexual fantasies now .... ☐

F60. Do you sometimes dream about sex?
Yes .... ☐
No .... ☐

F61. Do you sometimes wake up feeling sexually aroused?
Yes .... ☐
No .... ☐

F62a. Do you sometimes have an orgasm when asleep or while waking up?
Yes .... ☐
No .... ☐

F62b. If YES, about how many times in the past year?
Number of times _____

(F63) Please describe, on the "Comment Pages" at the end of the questionnaire, one of your recent sexual fantasies or dreams.

F64. Have you ever felt sexually attracted to another woman?
	Yes	No
Before you were 50	☐	☐
Since you were 50	☐	☐

F65a. Have you ever had a sexual relationship with another woman?
Yes .... ☐
No .... ☐
(If NO, skip to Question F74)

F65b. If YES, with how many women have you had a sexual relationship?
Before you were 50 _____
Since you were 50 _____

F66. If you have had a sexual relationship with a woman much older than you
Your age when the relationship began _____
Her age when the relationship began _____

F67. **If you have had a sexual relationship with a woman much younger than you**
Your age when the relationship began _____
Her age when the relationship began _____

F68. **How long did your most enduring sexual relationship with another woman last?** _____

F69. **Do you consider yourself a lesbian?**
Yes ....□
No ....□
(If NO, skip to Question F71a)

F70a. **Have you publicly identified yourself as a lesbian?**
Yes ....□
No ....□
(If NO, skip to Question F71a)

F70b. **If YES, do you regret it?**
Yes ....□
No ....□

F71a. **Do you visit lesbian bars, clubs or social centers, or other gathering places of the lesbian community?**
Yes ....□
No ....□
(If NO, skip to Question F72)

F71b. **If YES, do you think older women are less welcome in such places than younger women?**
Yes ....□
No ....□

F72. **Looking back over your sexual experiences with other women, do you feel these relationships have been rewarding?**
Yes, very much so ....□
Yes, somewhat ....□
No ....□

F73. **Do you think your sexual relationships with other women have been a handicap in achieving your life goals?**
Yes ....□
No ....□

(F74.) **Please discuss, on the "Comment Pages" at the end of the questionnaire, your views on the effects of aging on lesbian and bisexual women, and on the lesbian and bisexual ways of life during the later years.**

Please answer Questions F75 through F79 on the "Comment Pages," which follow.

F75. Some older people regret some of the sexual things they did in their younger days. Some regret not having done certain sexual things. If you had your life to live over, what would you change or do differently with respect to love and sexual relationships?

F76. What do you think younger people should know about love and sexual relationships after the age of 50?

F77. Most people agree that we have been living through a "sexual revolution" in recent years—with much greater freedom to discuss sex; more sex in books, magazines, films, and television; greater tolerance of sex outside marriage and of homosexual relationships; and so on. What parts of this "sexual revolution" do you approve of? What parts do you disapprove of?

F78. What topics do you think should be covered in a Consumers Union study of love, sex, and aging that are not covered in this questionnaire?

F79. We would like to express to you our deepest appreciation for the time and thought you have devoted to this questionnaire. We hope that your participation has been a rewarding experience for you. Please know that your anonymous answers, when combined with those of many others, will provide the first comprehensive view of human intimacy and sexuality among men and women in their later years. We believe that this study, when published in book form, will be of help to older people—and to younger people as well. In conclusion, please use the "Comment Pages" that follow to add any feelings or experiences you haven't had a chance to express in this questionnaire.

CONSUMER REPORTS BOOKS / CONSUMERS UNION

Mount Vernon, New York 10550

STUDY on LOVE, SEX, and AGING

This questionnaire is for MEN

A. BACKGROUND INFORMATION

A1. **How old were you on your last birthday?** _____

A2. **Do you live in a**
Private house .... ☐
Apartment, co-op, or condominium .... ☐
Nursing home .... ☐
Home for the aging, retirement hotel.......... ☐
Mobile home .... ☐
Other_____

A3. **Do you live in a retirement community?**
Yes .... ☐
No .... ☐

A4. **How long have you been living in your present neighborhood?**
Number of years _____

A5. **What is the highest level of education you completed?**
Grade school or less .... ☐
Some high school .... ☐
Completed high school .... ☐
Some college .... ☐
Completed 4-year college .... ☐
Some graduate school .... ☐
Received graduate degree .... ☐

A6. **Who lives in your household with you?** (Check *all* that apply)
Live alone .... ☐
Spouse or partner .... ☐
Adult children .... ☐
Dependent children .... ☐
Parent(s) or spouse's parent(s) .... ☐
Friend(s) .... ☐
Other _____

A7a. **Since you were 50, have you ever been employed?**
Yes .... ☐
No .... ☐

A7b. **Current employment status**
Employed full-time .... ☐
Employed part-time .... ☐
Not employed but seeking work .... ☐
Not employed and not seeking work .... ☐

A8a. **Are you now or have you ever been retired?**
Yes .... ☐
No .... ☐
(If NO, skip to Question A10.)

A8b. **If YES, was retirement**
Mandatory .... ☐
Voluntary .... ☐

A9. **How do you feel about retirement?**
Positive feelings .... ☐
Mixed feelings .... ☐
Negative feelings .... ☐

A10. **If you've never retired, how do you feel about the prospect of retirement?**
Positive feelings .... ☐
Mixed feelings .... ☐
Negative feelings .... ☐
Question does not apply to me.............. ☐

(A11) **Please discuss your feelings about retirement in greater detail on the "Comment Pages" at the end of the questionnaire.**

Please feel free to answer any of our questions in greater detail—especially questions with encircled numbers (such as (A11), above)—on the "Comment Pages" at the end of the questionnaire.

A12. **What was your personal income (including spouse's, if any) for the past year?**
Under $5,000 ☐
$5,000 to $9,999 ☐
$10,000 to $14,999 ☐
$15,000 to $19,999 ☐
$20,000 to $24,999 ☐
$25,000 to $34,999 ☐
$35,000 to $49,999 ☐
$50,000 and over ☐

A13. **How many people live on this income?** _____

A14. **Does anyone else (besides spouse, if any) share or pay all of your household expenses?**
Yes, all expenses ☐
Yes, some expenses ☐
No ☐

A15. **Would you describe yourself as**
Very religious ☐
Moderately religious ☐
Slightly religious ☐
Not at all religious ☐

A16. **Please fill in your Zip Code** _____

B. YOUR HEALTH

B1. **How would you rate your overall health at the present time?**
Excellent ☐
Very good ☐
Good ☐
Fair ☐
Poor ☐

B2. **Compared with others your age, would you say your health is**
Better than average ☐
About average ☐
Worse than average ☐

B3. **Do you have hypertension (high blood pressure)?**
Yes ☐
No ☐

B4. **Have you ever had a heart attack?**
Yes ☐
No ☐

B5. **Do you have diabetes?**
Yes ☐
No ☐

B6. **Do you regularly take any of the following prescribed medications?** (Check *all* that apply)
Anti-hypertension drug ☐
Anti-coagulant ☐
Insulin ☐
Tranquilizer or sedative ☐
Stimulant or anti-depressant ☐
Other _____

B7a. **Do you have prostate trouble?**
Yes ☐
No ☐
(If NO, skip to Question B8)

B7b. **If YES, does it affect your sexual functioning?**
Yes ☐
No ☐

B7c. **Please describe effects, if any, on the "Comment Pages," at the end of this questionnaire.**

B8. **Have you had surgery of the prostate?**
Yes ☐
No ☐

B9a. **Have you ever taken male hormones—testosterone or one of the related substances known as androgens or anabolic agents?**
Yes ☐
No ☐
(If NO, skip to Question B11)

B9b. **If YES, at what age did you start taking male hormones** _____

B10. **Are you currently taking testosterone or a related substance?**
Yes ☐
No ☐

B11. **Please discuss any views you may have about male use of hormones on the "Comment Pages," at the end of the questionnaire.**

C. YOUR OPINIONS

C1. **Please indicate your level of agreement with each of the statements listed below by circling the number 1, 2, 3, 4, or 5 next to each statement.**

	Strongly agree	Moderately agree	Neutral	Moderately disagree	Strongly disagree
Older people shouldn't try to appear younger than they are	1	2	3	4	5
I think it's a mistake for an older man to marry a much younger woman	1	2	3	4	5
It's okay for older couples who are not married to have sexual relations	1	2	3	4	5
Older people aren't portrayed fairly on television	1	2	3	4	5
Most people find me a likable person	1	2	3	4	5
Laws against homosexual and lesbian acts should be enforced	1	2	3	4	5
There should be courses in sex education for older people	1	2	3	4	5
In general, children don't like their widowed father to become involved with a woman	1	2	3	4	5
Young people tend to be uncomfortable with older people	1	2	3	4	5
Boys and girls need to be reassured that there's nothing wrong with masturbation	1	2	3	4	5
I think I'm as attractive as most people my age	1	2	3	4	5
In stores or restaurants older people get poorer service	1	2	3	4	5
Society thinks of older people as non-sexual	1	2	3	4	5
I think it's a mistake for an older woman to marry a much younger man	1	2	3	4	5
Our society places too much emphasis on sex	1	2	3	4	5
Older people should worry less about "what people might think"	1	2	3	4	5
Homosexual and lesbian relations between older people are nobody else's business	1	2	3	4	5
Masturbation is not proper for older people	1	2	3	4	5
There should be more sex education in public school	1	2	3	4	5
I feel much less attractive than when I was younger	1	2	3	4	5
Communities should have the right to ban all pornographic materials	1	2	3	4	5
Sex without love is better than no sex at all	1	2	3	4	5

C2. **Please discuss any of the above statements which particularly interest you on the "Comment Pages" at the end of the questionnaire.**

C3. **Please characterize your overall enjoyment of life at the present time. Your feelings may match the phrase at the left-hand side, or the phrase at the right-hand side, or they may fall somewhere in between. Check the box that best expresses your feelings.**

Life is very enjoyable for me ☐ ☐ ☐ ☐ ☐ ☐ ☐ Life is not at all enjoyable for me

C4. **Compared with when you were around 40, how would you characterize your present enjoyment of life?**
Much better now .... ☐
Somewhat better now .... ☐
About the same .... ☐
Somewhat worse now .... ☐
Much worse now .... ☐

D. FRIENDSHIP

We would like you to think about the people with whom you feel especially close, to whom you can confide your innermost feelings but with whom you do *not* have a sexual relationship.

D1. **Do you have any such close friends?**
Yes .... ☐
No .... ☐
(If NO, skip to Question D4)

D2. **Are these close friends**
All male .... ☐
All female .... ☐
Some male and some female .... ☐

D3. **Are any of these close friends**

	Yes	No
Older than you by 10 years or more	☐	☐
Younger than you by 10 years or more	☐	☐

D4. **Compared with when you were around 40, how many close friends do you have?**
More now .... ☐
About the same .... ☐
Fewer now .... ☐

D5. Would you like more opportunities to meet

	Yes	No
A man who might become a close friend	☐	☐
A woman who might become a close friend	☐	☐

D6. Compared with when you were around 40, how easy is it these days to make new friends?
- Easier now ☐
- About the same ☐
- Easier then ☐

D7. Which, if any, of the following now interfere with your making new friends? (Check all that apply)
- Lack of privacy ☐
- Inadequate transportation ☐
- Health ☐
- Not enough social activities ☐
- Not enough money ☐
- Not enough time ☐
- Shyness ☐
- Other _____

D8. How often do you find yourself feeling lonely?
- Almost always ☐
- Often ☐
- Sometimes ☐
- Hardly ever ☐

(D9.) Please discuss, on the "Comment Pages" at the end of the questionnaire, any other aspects of friendship, close or otherwise, during the later years, which you consider important.

E.   LOVE

E1a. Sometimes love begins gradually and grows slowly, but sometimes it begins with a sudden and very vivid "falling-in-love" experience. Have you had such a falling-in-love experience since the age of 50?
- Yes ☐
- No ☐

E1b. If YES, at what age or ages? _____

E2a. Now we would like to ask about the continuing state of being in love rather than the initial falling-in-love experience. Since the age of 50, have you ever been in love?
- Yes ☐
- No ☐

E2b. If YES, are you currently in love with someone?
- Yes, with my spouse ☐
- Yes, with someone else ☐
- No ☐
- (If YES, skip to Question E5)

E3. If NO, would you like to be in love?
- Yes ☐
- No ☐

E4. Would you like to have a sudden and very vivid "falling-in-love" experience?
- Yes ☐
- No ☐

E5. Do you feel love is experienced differently in the later years?
- Yes ☐
- No ☐

(E6.) Please describe, on the "Comment Pages" at the end of the questionnaire, your feelings about love in the later years and about how it may differ from love in the earlier years.

F.   SEXUALITY

F1a. Have you ever been married?
- Yes ☐
- No ☐

F1b. If YES, how many times? (Include current marriage, if any)
Number of times _____

F2. What is your present marital status?
- Married ☐
  (If married, skip to Question F9)
- Single ☐
- Widower ☐
- Divorced or separated ☐

F3. Do you have ongoing sexual relationships with someone to whom you are not married?
- Yes ☐
- No ☐
- (If NO, skip to Question F6)

F4. Are you currently living with that person?
- Yes ☐
- No ☐

F5. Is that person
- Female ☐
  (If female, skip to Question F8)
- Male ☐
  (If male, skip to Question F9)

F6. If you do not have an ongoing sexual relationship, are you living with someone with whom you once had a sexual relationship?
- Yes, with a female ☐
  (If YES, skip to Question F9)
- Yes, with a male ☐
  (If YES, skip to Question F9)
- No ☐

F7a. If NO, have you had any casual sexual partners in the past year?
- Yes ☐
- No ☐
- (If NO, skip to Question F37)

F7b. With how many persons in all did you have sex during the past year?
Number of persons _____
(Skip to Question F37)

F8. **If you are having an ongoing sexual relationship with a female to whom you are not married, what are the reasons for not getting married?** (Check all that apply)

Because we haven't gotten around to it yet but plan to .... ☐
Because we prefer things the way they are .... ☐
Because we don't want to lose economic benefits (social security, alimony, etc.) .... ☐
Because my partner doesn't want to be responsible for my support or medical expenses .... ☐

Because I don't want to be responsible for my partner's support or medical expenses .... ☐
Neither of us wants to give up a separate home .... ☐
Because my partner is married to someone else .... ☐
Because my partner wants to get married but I don't .... ☐

I want to get married but my partner doesn't .... ☐
Because my children or my partner's children object .... ☐
Other reasons _____

F9. **How old is your wife/partner?** _____

F10. **How many years has the marriage or relationship lasted?**

Number of years _____

F11. **How would you rate your wife's/partner's overall heath at the present time?**

Excellent .... ☐
Very good .... ☐
Good .... ☐
Fair .... ☐
Poor .... ☐

F12. **Check the box that best represents how happy your marriage or relationship is.**

Very happy ☐ ☐ ☐ ☐ ☐ ☐ ☐ Very unhappy

F13. **Check which, if any, of the following are presently problems in your relationship with your wife/partner.**

Financial problems .... ☐
Job problems .... ☐
Where you live .... ☐
Religion .... ☐
Conflicts with children .... ☐
How to spend leisure time .... ☐
Health .... ☐
Sex .... ☐
Problems with wife's/partner's family .... ☐
Jealousy .... ☐
Other _____

F14. **In general, how would you characterize communications between you and your wife/partner?**

Excellent .... ☐
Very good .... ☐
Good .... ☐
Fair .... ☐
Poor .... ☐

F15. **How important is the sexual side of your relationship to you and to your wife/partner?**

	Self	Wife/Partner
Very important	☐	☐
Moderately important	☐	☐
Of little importance	☐	☐
Don't know	☐	☐

F16. **How comfortable are you discussing sexual matters with your wife/partner?**

Very comfortable .... ☐
Comfortable .... ☐
Uncomfortable .... ☐
Very uncomfortable .... ☐

F17. **Do you currently engage in sexual intercourse with your wife/partner?**

Yes .... ☐
(If YES, skip to Question F20)
No .... ☐

F18. **If NO, do you currently engage in other types of sexual activities with your wife/partner?**

Yes .... ☐
(If YES skip to Question F20)
No .... ☐

F19a. **If NO, whose decision was it to stop sexual activities?**

My decision .... ☐
My wife's/partner's decision .... ☐
Mutual decision .... ☐
No decision, it just happened .... ☐

F19b. **How many years ago did you stop sexual activities with your wife/partner?**

Number of years _____

F19c. **Why did you stop sexual activities with your wife/partner?** (Check *all* that apply)

My illness .... ☐
Wife's/partner's illness .... ☐
My physical changes .... ☐
Wife's/partner's physical changes .... ☐
I lost interest .... ☐
Wife/partner lost interest .... ☐
No privacy .... ☐
Other _____

(F19d.) **Add any other thoughts you have about this subject on the "Comment Pages" at the end of this questionnaire.**

If you are NOT having sex with your wife/partner, skip to Question F32a.

F20. **Who usually initiates the activities leading to sex?**
I always do ....□
I usually do ....□
My wife/partner and I about equally often ......□
My wife/partner usually does ....□
My wife/partner always does ....□

F21. **Are you satisfied with this arrangement?**
Yes ....□
No, I would like to initiate sexual activities more
frequently............................□
No, I would like my wife/partner to initiate sexual
activities more frequently ....□

F22. **How do you feel about the variety of sexual activities in your relationship?**
I like it as it is ....□
I would like more variety ....□
I would like less variety ....□

F23. **At what time of day do you most commonly have sex with your wife/partner?**
Morning ....□
Afternoon ....□
Early evening ....□
After 10 P.M. ....□
Varies ....□

F24. **At what time of day is your wife/partner most sexually arousable?**
Morning ....□
Afternoon ....□
Early evening ....□
After 10 P.M. ....□
Varies ....□
Don't know.............................□

F25a. **Has your wife/partner gone through menopause?**
Yes ....□
No ....□
(If NO, skip to Question F28)

F25b. **If YES, did menopause affect her sexual responsiveness?**
Yes, her responsiveness increased ....□
Yes, her responsiveness decreased ....□
No ....□

F26a. **Since menopause, has your wife's/partner's vaginal lubrication**
Increased ....□
Decreased ....□
Remained the same ....□
(If the same, skip to Question F27a)

F26b. **If vaginal lubrication has increased or decreased, is this change a problem in your relationship?**
Yes ....□
No ....□

F27a. **Since menopause, has your wife/partner experienced loss of vaginal muscle tone?**
Yes ....□
No ....□
Don't know ....□
(If NO, or DON'T KNOW, skip to Question F28)

F27b. **If YES, is this change in vaginal muscle tone a problem in your relationship?**
Yes ....□
No ....□

F28. **About how often do you have sex with your wife/partner?**

Once a day or more ....□
4-6 times a week ....□
2 or 3 times a week ....□
About once a week ....□
A few times a month ....□
Once a month or less ....□

F29. **Are you satisfied with the frequency of sex?**
Yes, it's about right ....□
No, it's too frequent ....□
No, it's not frequent enough ....□

F30. **How often do you and your wife/partner experience orgasm when you engage in sexual activities?**

	Self	Wife/ Partner
Every time	□	□
Almost every time —more than 90 percent of the time	□	□
Usually—about 75 percent of the time	□	□
About half of the time	□	□
Seldom—about 25 percent of the time	□	□
Never	□	□
Don't know	□	□

F31. **Check the box that best represents how enjoyable for you sex with your wife/partner is at the present time.**

Very enjoyable ☐ ☐ ☐ ☐ ☐ ☐ ☐ Not at all enjoyable

F32a. **Since you were 50, have you ever engaged in sexual activities with anyone else outside of your marriage or relationship?**

Yes .... ☐
No .... ☐
(If NO, skip to Question F35)

F32b. **If YES, with how many partners?**
Number of partners _____

F33. **Have any of these activities occurred in the past year?**
Yes .... ☐
No .... ☐

F34. **Is your wife/partner aware of this outside sexual activity?**

Yes .... ☐
No .... ☐
Don't know .... ☐

F35. **Has your wife/partner had any sexual activities outside your relationship since your wife/partner was 50?**
Yes .... ☐
No .... ☐
Don't know................................ ☐

(F36.) **Please discuss, on the "Comment Pages" at the end of the questionnaire, any further comments you have on sex outside of your marriage or relationship.**

F37. **About how often do you have sex? (Include all partners if more than one)**
Once a day or more .... ☐
4 to 6 times a week .... ☐
2 or 3 times a week .... ☐
About once a week .... ☐
A few times a month .... ☐
Once a month or less...................... ☐
Not currently having sex .... ☐

F38. **Compared with when you were around 40, how frequently do you have sex?**
More frequently now .... ☐
About the same .... ☐
Less frequently now .... ☐

F39. **Some older men may experience changes in sexual functioning as they age. Following is a list of some of the changes that may occur. Check each of these changes that has occurred with you. For each change that has occurred, check if you find it a serious problem.**

	Check here if this change has occurred	Check here if it is a serious problem
It takes me longer to get an erection	☐	☐
When fully erect my penis is not as stiff as before	☐	☐
I more frequently lose my erection during sex	☐	☐
It takes more stimulation of my penis to reach orgasm now	☐	☐
I more often fail to reach orgasm nowadays	☐	☐
My "refractory period"—the time it takes to be able to have another erection after orgasm—is longer now	☐	☐

(F40.) **Please discuss these or similar changes in the "Comment Pages," at the end of the questionnaire.**

F41. **Some men become uncomfortable or restless if they go without a release of sexual tension for too long a period. For about how long can you comfortably go without a sexual release?** _____

F42. **Compared with when you were about 40, how frequently do you experience orgasm during sexual relations?**
More frequently now .... ☐
About the same .... ☐
Less frequently now .... ☐

F43. **How would you describe your present interest in sex?**
Strong .... ☐
Moderate .... ☐
Weak .... ☐
Absent .... ☐

F44. **Compared with when you were around 40, how would you describe your present interest in sex?**
Stronger now .... ☐
About the same .... ☐
Weaker now .... ☐

F45. **Check the box that best represents your present enjoyment of sex.**

Very enjoyable ☐   ☐   ☐   ☐   ☐   ☐   ☐   Not at all enjoyable

F46. **Compared with when you were around 40, how would you describe your present enjoyment of sex?**
- More enjoyable now .... ☐
- About the same .... ☐
- Less enjoyable now .... ☐

F47. **How easily do you become sexually aroused at the present time?**
- Very easily .... ☐
- Moderately easily .... ☐
- With some difficulty .... ☐
- With great difficulty .... ☐
- Don't become aroused .... ☐

F48. **Compared with when you were around 40, how easily do you become sexually aroused?**
- More easily now .... ☐
- About the same .... ☐
- Less easily now .... ☐

F49. **Please indicate, by checking the appropriate box, which of the following sexual activities you have engaged in since the age of 50, and—whether you have tried them or not—what you think of them.**

	Have you done this since 50?		If you have done this, did you like it?		If you have not done this, would you like to try it?	
	Yes	No	Yes	No	Yes	No
Being undressed by your partner	☐	☐	☐	☐	☐	☐
Undressing your partner	☐	☐	☐	☐	☐	☐
Your partner stimulating your breasts or nipples	☐	☐	☐	☐	☐	☐
Your stimulating your partner's breasts or nipples	☐	☐	☐	☐	☐	☐
Having your partner stimulate your genitals with mouth or tongue	☐	☐	☐	☐	☐	☐
Stimulating your partner's genitals with mouth or tongue	☐	☐	☐	☐	☐	☐
Seeing your partner naked	☐	☐	☐	☐	☐	☐
Being seen by your partner when you are naked	☐	☐	☐	☐	☐	☐
Using a vibrator or massager	☐	☐	☐	☐	☐	☐
Viewing 'hard core' pornographic films or photos	☐	☐	☐	☐	☐	☐
Reading sexually explicit material	☐	☐	☐	☐	☐	☐
Having your anus stimulated during sex	☐	☐	☐	☐	☐	☐
Stimulating your partner's clitoris with your fingers during intercourse	☐	☐	☐	☐	☐	☐
Engaging in rough sex	☐	☐	☐	☐	☐	☐
Having sex with someone you don't know very well ...	☐	☐	☐	☐	☐	☐
Being watched when you have sex	☐	☐	☐	☐	☐	☐
Watching people have sex	☐	☐	☐	☐	☐	☐
Having group sex	☐	☐	☐	☐	☐	☐
Having your partner manually stimulate your genitals .	☐	☐	☐	☐	☐	☐
Manually stimulating your partner's genitals	☐	☐	☐	☐	☐	☐

F50. **Please discuss your feelings about any of the above on the "Comment Pages" at the end of the questionnaire.**

F51. Since you were 50, have you discussed your sexual needs, desires, or problems with any of the following?

	Discussed?		Was it helpful?	
	Yes	No	Yes	No
Physician	☐	☐	☐	☐
Psychiatrist	☐	☐	☐	☐
Psychologist	☐	☐	☐	☐
Marriage counselor	☐	☐	☐	☐
Sex therapist	☐	☐	☐	☐
Other_____				

F52. In the last year, about how often have you masturbated?
- Once a day or more ☐
- 4 to 6 times a week ☐
- 2 or 3 times a week ☐
- About once a week ☐
- A few times a month ☐
- Once a month or less ☐
- Not currently masturbating ☐

F53. If you masturbate, for what reasons or under what circumstances do you do so? (Check all that apply)
- It makes me feel independent or self-sufficient ☐
- Because I enjoy it ☐
- Absence of acceptable partner ☐
- Loneliness ☐
- Sex with partner not fully satisfactory ☐
- My partner likes to watch ☐
- It's an additional source of sexual satisfaction ☐
- It releases tension ☐
- Other _____

F54. Compared with when you were around 40, how frequently do you masturbate?
- More frequently now ☐
- About the same ☐
- Less frequently now ☐

If you do not currently masturbate, skip to Question F57.

F55. How often do you experience orgasm when you masturbate nowadays?
- Every time ☐
- Almost every time—more than 90 percent of the time ☐
- Usually—about 75 percent of the time ☐
- About half of the time ☐
- Seldom—about 25 percent of the time ☐
- Never ☐

F56. Do you have sexual fantasies while you masturbate?
- Always ☐
- Usually ☐
- Sometimes ☐
- Never ☐

(F57) Please discuss, on the "Comment Pages" at the end of the questionnaire, your feelings about masturbation during the later years.

F58. Do you have sexual fantasies when engaging in sex with a partner?
- Always ☐
- Usually ☐
- Sometimes ☐
- Never ☐

F59. How does this compare with when you were 40?
- More sexual fantasies now ☐
- About the same ☐
- Fewer sexual fantasies now ☐

F60. Do you sometimes dream about sex?
- Yes ☐
- No ☐

F61. Do you sometimes wake up feeling sexually aroused?
- Yes ☐
- No ☐

F62a. Do you sometimes have an orgasm when asleep or while waking up?
- Yes ☐
- No ☐

F62b. If YES, about how many times in the past year?
Number of times _____

(F63) Please describe, on the "Comment Pages" at the end of the questionnaire, one of your recent sexual fantasies or dreams.

F64. Have you ever felt sexually attracted to another man?

	Yes	No
Before you were 50	☐	☐
Since you were 50	☐	☐

F65a. Have you ever had a sexual relationship with another man?
- Yes ☐
- No ☐

(If NO, skip to Question F74)

F65b. If YES, with how many men have you had a sexual relationship?
Before you were 50 _____
Since you were 50 _____

F66. If you have had a sexual relationship with a man much older than you
Your age when the relationship began _____
His age when the relationship began _____

F67. **If you have had a sexual relationship with a man much younger than you**
Your age when the relationship began _____
His age when the relationship began _____

F68. **How long did your most enduring sexual relationship with another man last?** _____

F69. **Do you consider yourself a homosexual?**
Yes .... ☐
No .... ☐
(If NO, skip to Question F71a)

F70a. **Have you publicly identified yourself as a homosexual?**
Yes .... ☐
No .... ☐
(If NO, skip to Question F71a)

F70b. **If YES, do you regret it?**
Yes .... ☐
No .... ☐

F71a. **Do you visit "gay bars," homosexual clubs or social centers, or other gathering places of the gay community?**
Yes .... ☐
No .... ☐
(If NO, skip to Question F72)

F71b. **If YES, do you think older men are less welcome in such places than younger men?**
Yes .... ☐
No .... ☐

F72. **Looking back over your sexual experiences with other men, do you feel these relationships have been rewarding?**
Yes, very much so .... ☐
Yes, somewhat .... ☐
No .... ☐

F73. **Do you think your sexual relationships with other men have been a handicap in achieving your life goals?**
Yes .... ☐
No .... ☐

(F74) **Please discuss, on the "Comment Pages" at the end of the questionnaire, your views on the effects of aging on homosexual and bisexual men, and on the homosexual and bisexual ways of life during the later years.**

F75a. **Have you ever employed the services of a male prostitute?**

	Yes	No
Before you were 50	☐	☐
Since you were 50	☐	☐

F75b. **If YES, about how many times since age 50?**
Number of times _____ 99-

F76. **Have you ever employed the services of a female prostitute?**

	Yes	No
Before you were 50	☐	☐
Since you were 50	☐	☐

(If NO, skip to Question F78)

F77a. **If YES, about how many such experiences have you had since age 50?**
_____

F77b. **How many in the past year?** _____

(F78) **Please discuss, on the "Comment Pages" at the end of the questionnaire, the use of prostitutes by older men.**

Please answer Questions F79 through F83 on the "Comment Pages," which follow.

F79. Some older people regret some of the sexual things they did in their younger days. Some regret not having done certain sexual things. If you had your life to live over, what would you change or do differently with respect to love and sexual relationships?

F80. What do you think younger people should know about love and sexual relationships after the age of 50?

F81. Most people agree that we have been living through a "sexual revolution" in recent years—with much greater freedom to discuss sex; more sex in books, magazines, films, and television; greater tolerance of sex outside marriage and of homosexual relationships; and so on. What parts of this "sexual revolution" do you approve of? What parts do you disapprove of?

F82. What topics do you think should be covered in a Consumers Union study of love, sex, and aging that are not covered in this questionnaire?

F83. We would like to express to you our deepest appreciation for the time and thought you have devoted to this questionnaire. We hope that your participation has been a rewarding experience for you. Please know that your anonymous answers, when combined with those of many others, will provide the first comprehensive view of human intimacy and sexuality among men and women in their later years. We believe that this study, when published in book form, will be of help to older people—and to younger people as well. In conclusion, please use the "Comment Pages" that follow to add any feelings or experiences you haven't had a chance to express in this questionnaire.

Index